# THE GENESIS OF LANGUAGE

*A Psycholinguistic Approach*

# THE GENESIS OF LANGUAGE
## A Psycholinguistic Approach

*Proceedings of a conference on "Language Development in Children,"
sponsored by the National Institute of Child Health and Human
Development, National Institutes of Health*

Edited by Frank Smith and George A. Miller

**THE M.I.T. PRESS**
Massachusetts Institute of Technology
Cambridge, Massachusetts, and London, England

*Second Printing, May 1967*
*Third Printing, March 1968*
*First M.I.T. Press Paperback Printing, March, 1968*
*Second Paperback Printing, October 1969*

*SBN 262 69022 5 (paperback)*

*Library of Congress Catalog Card Number: 66–21358*
*Printed in the United States of America*

# PREFACE

This volume is the product of a conference entitled "Language Development in Children," sponsored by the Human Communication Program of the National Institute of Child Health and Human Development and held April 25 to 28, 1965, at Old Point Comfort, Virginia. The Conference was organized by Dr. Norman F. Gerrie, Director of the Program; Dr. James F. Kavanagh; and Dr. Francis J. Kendrick. The proceedings were arranged by the conference co-chairmen, Dr. Franklin S. Cooper and Dr. George A. Miller.

The National Institute of Child Health and Human Development was established in 1963 and is the youngest of the nine institutes within the National Institutes of Health, Public Health Service, Department of Health, Education, and Welfare. Its role is to stimulate, support, and develop research into broad areas of human development, concerning itself with both normal and relevant pathological processes and with the whole individual as well as with specific systems. The aim of this conference was to "direct attention to the stages in the acquisition of grammar and phonology by children and to whatever biological and clinical evidence we have concerning the child's innate capacities for this acquisition."

The conference participants were

RICHARD A. CHASE

Neurocommunications Laboratory
Department of Psychiatry
The Johns Hopkins University School of Medicine
Baltimore, Maryland.

FRANKLIN S. COOPER

Haskins Laboratory
New York, New York.

PETER B. DENES

Bell Telephone Laboratories
Murray Hill, New Jersey.

CHARLES A. FERGUSON

University of Washington
Seattle, Washington.

JERRY A. FODOR

Department of Psychology
Massachusetts Institute of Technology
Cambridge, Massachusetts.

DENIS FRY

Department of Phonetics
University College London
London, England.

HELEN H. GEE

National Institute of Child Health
    and Human Development
Bethesda, Maryland.

NORMAN F. GERRIE

National Institute of Child Health
    and Human Development
Bethesda, Maryland.

IRA J. HIRSH

Central Institute for the Deaf
St. Louis, Missouri.

ARTHUR S. HOUSE

Department of Audiology and
    Speech Pathology
Purdue University
Lafayette, Indiana.

JAMES J. JENKINS

Department of Psychology
University of Minnesota
Minneapolis, Minnesota

HANS KALMUS

Galton Laboratory
University College London
London, England.

JAMES F. KAVANAGH

National Institute of Child Health
    and Human Development
Bethesda, Maryland.

FRANCIS J. KENDRICK

National Institute of Child Health
    and Human Development
Bethesda, Maryland.

ERIC H. LENNEBERG

Department of Psychiatry
Children's Hospital Medical Center
Harvard Medical School
Cambridge, Massachusetts.

ALVIN M. LIBERMAN

Center for Advanced Study in the
    Behavioral Sciences
Stanford, California.

DAVID MC NEILL

Department of Psychology
University of Michigan
Ann Arbor, Michigan.

GEORGE A. MILLER

Center for Cognitive Studies
Harvard University
Cambridge, Massachusetts.

DAVID PREMACK

University of California
Santa Barbara, California.

DAN I. SLOBIN

Department of Psychology
University of California
Berkeley, California.

MILDRED C. TEMPLIN

Institute of Child Development
University of Minnesota
Minneapolis, Minnesota.

RUTH H. WEIR*

Department of Linguistics
Stanford University
Stanford, California.

Dr. Weir was unable to be present, but her paper, included in these proceedings, was presented and discussed. The presentation by Dr. Premack was prepared in association with his co-experimenter, Dr. Arthur Schwartz, of the University of Oregon.

At the time of the conference, Dr. McNeill was attached to the

* Dr. Weir died on November 13, 1965.

Center for Cognitive Studies, Harvard University; Dr. Lenneberg to the Children's Medical Center, Boston, Massachusetts; Dr. Premack to the University of Missouri; and Dr. Fodor and Dr. Jenkins to the Center for Advanced Study in the Behavioral Sciences, Stanford, California. Dr. Schwartz is at present a U.S.P.H.S. postdoctoral research fellow at the Massachusetts Institute of Technology.

Some of the ideas in Dr. Fodor's presentation will appear, in altered form, in Fodor, J. A., Jenkins, J. J., and Saporta, S., *An Introduction to Psycholinguistic Theory* (forthcoming, Prentice-Hall); and Dr. Fodor acknowledges the role of his co-authors in working these ideas out.

The figures in Dr. Fry's paper are taken from *The Deaf Child,* by Edith Whetnall and D. B. Fry, published by William Heinemann Medical Books Ltd., 23 Bedford Square, London W.C.1., whose permission to republish is gratefully acknowledged.

The United States Office of Education has supported Dr. Templin's research as Project No. 818, "The Identification of Kindergarten Children Least Likely to Show Spontaneous Improvement in Speech Sound Articulation," from January 1960 to June 1963, and as Project No. 2220, "Longitudinal Study through the Fourth Grade of Language Skills of Children with Varying Speech Sound Articulation in Kindergarten," from June 1, 1963, through December 31, 1966.

Dr. Lenneberg acknowledges assistance received through U.S.P.H.S. Career Development Grant K3-MH-21700-06. The material presented here constitutes excerpts from chapters of his forthcoming book with the tentative title *Biological Foundations of Language.* Several members of the conference had access to the more complete treatment of the original manuscript.

The preparation of Dr. Chase's paper was supported, in part, by Public Health Service Research Contract No. PH43-65-637 with the Human Communication Program of the National Institute of Child Health and Human Development, National Institutes of Health; N.I.H. General Research Support Grant to The Johns Hopkins University School of Medicine; and a gift from the Freda R. Caspersen Trust.

The pilot work upon which the Premack and Schwartz paper was based was supported by the Graduate Research Council of the University of Missouri and by the comparable office of the University of

California, Santa Barbara. Preparation of the report was aided by Grants N.S.F. GB 1379 and U.S.P.H.S. MH 05798.

The editors are particularly grateful to Professor Jenkins for revising his original summary statement in view of the many corrections, additions, and embellishments that the authors contributed after the conference was over. They acknowledge their debt to the authors for their cooperation in the face of considerable editorial badgering and to Mrs. Mavis Atamian for cheerful secretarial competence.

*Harvard Center for Cognitive Studies*   FRANK SMITH
*January 1966*   GEORGE A. MILLER

# CONTENTS

# THE GENESIS OF LANGUAGE
*A Psycholinguistic Approach*

*Frank Smith and George A. Miller*

# INTRODUCTION

Concern for the nature of human language is characteristic of twentieth-century thought. Our century has seen the emergence of descriptive linguistics as one of the most rigorous and best defined of the social sciences, and the general concern for language has also shaped the thinking of modern logicians, philosophers, psychologists. Anyone who, in the spirit of this century, tries to cope with the intricacies of human thought finds it necessary first to cope with the intricacies of the symbolic systems through which human thought makes itself manifest. Moreover, in parallel with this broad concern for language has run an amazing revolution in our technology of communication; the telegraph, telephone, phonograph, radio, television, and satellite have accustomed us to instantaneous communication from the most distant corners of the world. These two developments seem to have begun as independent manifestations of the same Zeitgeist, but with the emergence of digital computers as language-processing systems, the world of the academy and the world of technology have at last joined forces in their attack on the nature of language and communication. Each decade seems to bring some new advance, to open up some new possibilities.

It may seem pretentious to introduce the proceedings of a technical conference, where a handful of experts debated some of the more obscure points of their trade, in terms of these large generalizations about the spirit of twentieth-century thought. Nonetheless, participants in this conference felt themselves to be part of a much larger army of workers, contributing to the purification of ideas that rank among the great triumphs of the modern mind. This feeling of identification lent an excitement and often a tension to the experts' exchanges that would otherwise be difficult for an objective observer to comprehend.

What were the participants talking about? They were discussing the ungrammatical and often unintelligible, the sometimes cute but usually unimportant sounds that children make, a topic that might conceivably fascinate a devoted mother but that had been of little interest to scholars or scientists in any previous century. They were talking about the cries and other signals that animals produce, cries of some value perhaps to hunters or zoologists but almost wholly lacking in appeal to scholars of an earlier age. Animals and children have little to communicate, and great care is required to understand even that. On the surface, therefore, a practical man would be unlikely to discover much excuse for excitement about the subject matter of the conference.

It is only by placing that subject matter in the general context of our modern concern for language that the reason for excitement — indeed, the reason for the conference itself — becomes understandable. Infants and animals represent genetic approaches to language, and excitement stems from the fact that recent innovations in our conception of language might make it possible to formulate more sharply some venerable issues relating to the genesis of language.

The twentieth century cannot take credit for the observation that man is unique among all the animals in his possession of articulate speech; that piece of wisdom can be traced far back into the past. But the observation is hard to phrase clearly as long as we do not have clear criteria for distinguishing human language from other kinds of communication systems used by animals. One feels intuitively that there is something special about human language, but it is not something easy to characterize. With each advance in descriptive linguistics, therefore, it is necessary to re-examine this old problem in the new light.

Nor can the twentieth century claim to have been the first to notice that all men everywhere have language and that successive generations seem to acquire it without special training from parents or siblings. This, too, has been a familiar fact for many years — so familiar, indeed, that we have often forgotten how wonderful it is.

Language would be a rare achievement if parents had to give special lessons in phonology, morphology, or syntax, for few parents have the slightest notion what these skills consist of. That children can acquire language so readily can mean only that they have some innate pre-disposition for this kind of learning, and this in turn can mean only that evolution has prepared mankind in some very special way for this unique human accomplishment. Thus, consideration of the child's ontogenetic accomplishment leads us directly back to a consideration of man's phylogenetic accomplishment. Both topics — the signaling behaviors of animals and the development of human speech by children — stand to profit from the conceptual advances that have been taking place in the field of descriptive linguistics.

If the reader is willing to grant — at least until he has had an opportunity to examine the papers that follow — that any resolution of the evolutionary mysteries that have long surrounded man's gift of language is an exciting prospect, then perhaps he is also willing to grant that the assembled experts had an adequate reason for conferring with one another. At any rate, the experts thought they had good reason for a conference, so they attended it and contributed to it. We have collected their contributions and edited them for other workers interested in psychological and developmental aspects of language. And here they are. The goal is to characterize better the most uniquely human dimension of human nature.

But what are the innovations in descriptive linguistics that justify reopening these old debates once more? The modern science of linguistics has moved steadily forward toward accurate descriptions of existing languages and toward a deeper conception of what languages are in general. In this broad advance, however, one particular approach has been noteworthy, both for its power and rigor and for its attractiveness to workers in neighboring disciplines. This has been the approach of Chomsky (1957, 1965) and his collaborators, an approach that centers on the characterization of grammar. Earlier linguists tended to concentrate their descriptive efforts on phonology and morphology, and psychologists usually tried to begin their studies of language on semantic or pragmatic grounds. Chomsky, by providing a new, generative conception of grammar, showed how syntax could provide a common ground for fruitful collaboration between linguists and psychologists. Because Chomsky's ideas were so intricately interwoven into the intellectual background of several of the most vocal contributors to this conference, it is probably worth while to say just a word about them in this introduction.

Chomsky begins, as do most modern linguists and psychologists, with a fundamental distinction between *competence* and *performance*. A language user's competence is his knowledge of his language; his performance is the actual use he makes of that knowledge in concrete situations. It is to describe the language user's intrinsic competence that a grammar is developed. And if that grammar is perfectly explicit, in the sense that no intuitive processes of understanding are required of the reader, then it can be called a generative grammar. In Chomsky's (1965) words,

> A fully adequate grammar must assign to each of an infinite range of sentences a structural description indicating how this sentence is understood by the ideal speaker-hearer. This is the traditional problem of descriptive linguistics, and traditional grammars give a wealth of information concerning structural descriptions of sentences. However, valuable as they obviously are, traditional grammars are deficient in that they leave unexpressed many of the basic regularities of the language with which they are concerned. This fact is particularly clear on the level of syntax, where no traditional or structuralist grammar goes beyond classification of particular examples to the stage of formulation of generative rules on any significant scale.

By a "generative grammar" Chomsky means simply a system of rules that in some explicit and well-defined way assigns structural descriptions to sentences. Obviously, every native speaker of a language has mastered and internalized a generative grammar that constitutes his knowledge of his language. Nevertheless, a generative grammar is *not* a model for a user of the language, either a speaker or a listener. The construction of a performance model based on the generative competence of the language user is a further task for the theorist and one that linguists share with their colleagues in psychology. The term "generative grammar" does not mean that actual sentences are produced by the abstract generative system of rules; actually producing the sentences according to the rules is not a matter of generative competence but of productive performance.

For a detailed discussion of the kinds of rules and structural descriptions that Chomsky has advocated, the reader should refer directly to Chomsky's own writings. Some general characteristics of these rule systems are sufficiently important, however, to merit general notice here, however briefly.

First, it is important to understand that there is a difference between rules of *formation* and rules of *transformation*. And this distinction is closely related to a further distinction between the *surface* structure of a sentence and its *base*, or underlying, structure. Consider, for example, a passive sentence in English. It turns out to be parsimonious theoretically to consider that passive sentences are closely related to their corresponding active forms. At first thought, it would seem simplest to assume that the passive is derived by merely applying a transformation to the active, but on further reflection this turns out not to be a convenient way to characterize the relation between the two. In general, it is more satisfactory to assume that both the active and the passive sentence are surface structures, suitable for phonological representation, and that both are related by transformations to an underlying base structure (generated by the rules of formation). In the case of actives and passives, the base structures would presumably be identical except for an additional marker attached to the base structure underlying the passive sentence, a marker that indicated that the passive transformation should be applied to it in order to derive its surface structure.

This distinction between the deep structure and the surface structure proves to be quite useful when the question of semantic interpretation is considered. If the transformations always leave meaning unchanged, then semantic interpretations can be assigned to the base structures just as phonological representations can be assigned to the surface structures. Thus, transformational rules serve the crucial function of interrelating the two great domains of language, the domain of meaning and the domain of sound. It is for this reason that grammar plays such a central role in Chomsky's conception of language.

A grammar can be thought of as a scientific theory about the generative competence of speakers of some particular language. Chomsky's central concern, however, is less with particular grammars than it is with the general form that any grammar of a human language must assume — a concern to which he gives the name "linguistic theory." Linguistic theory is, if you will, the metatheory of grammar. It deals with the general form of particular theories, of particular grammars. Perhaps the most important thing to recognize about linguistic theory is that such a study can exist, that there actually is something common to all languages that leads linguists to formulate diverse grammars similarly and therefore provides subject matter for an extremely general study. It is this possibility that makes these theoretical developments directly relevant to the topics discussed in the present conference.

Given a number of grammars for natural languages, we can ask to what extent they embody similarities attributable to the general form of language as such, wherever it occurs. These similarities, insofar as they can be shown to hold for human languages everywhere, are known as *language universals*. In a sense, language universals are not part of language but are prelinguistic and psychological. They are exactly the features of any language that need not be described as part of its grammar because they are the same for all grammars. And for that very reason it is plausible to assume that the language universals, whatever they should prove to be, are part of every human being's innate linguistic competence and do not need to be learned by a child who is acquiring competence in some particular language. It is somewhat paradoxical to speak of language universals as constituting subject matter for psychology rather than for descriptive linguistics because it is perfectly obvious that language universals will be discovered and substantiated only as the result of the most careful and painstaking linguistic research. Nevertheless, the promise that such universals might be forthcoming cannot help but stimulate psychological speculation and color the view that psychologists will take of the development of language in children.

These, then, are some of the ideas from descriptive linguistics that have been filtering into psychological discussions of the genesis of language, both in evolutionary and developmental contexts. This conference served many purposes, as does any conference, but perhaps its most important function was to provide a confrontation of these ideas, and variants of these ideas, with the data that have been accumulating from recent studies of child and animal communication.

The formal presentations at the conference can be grouped roughly into three broad areas, which for convenience we can refer to as the development of competence, the development of performance, and the evolutionary matrix for language.

The first of these would include the papers by McNeill, by Fodor, and by Slobin, and also Slobin's discussion of McNeill's paper. McNeill interprets recent empirical studies of language acquisition in the light of current linguistic theory and argues that the innate equipment a child brings into the language-learning situation must include both formal and substantive linguistic universals — representations of basic grammatical relations and of hierarchical classificatory systems. In developing this theme, which became a central issue in the conference discussions, McNeill presents the case that early speech is not an abbreviated and distorted form of adult language but the product of a unique first grammar. He discusses the psycholinguistic distinction between competence and performance and the possible points of divergence between the child's comprehension and production of language. In the course of his argument he offers a reconsideration of the significance of practice, imitation, and expansion, and of the part played by the adult speech to which the child is exposed.

Slobin is receptive to this approach but underlines the need for further research in many of the areas delineated by McNeill, contributing evidence both from his own investigations and from his reviews of the Russian literature. He questions how much syntactic "preprogramming" ought to be attributed to the child and suggests more emphasis on the processes of the language-acquisition system and less on its content. He also raises the question of the relevance of semantic or conceptual features underlying grammatical categories.

Much of a protracted general discussion was taken up with a variety of confrontations related to McNeill's hypothesized universal hierarchy of grammatical categories. Many attempts were made to clarify, modify, defend, and undermine his position, and several alternative proposals were offered for the procedures by which a child comes to differentiate lexical items into the classifications assigned in adult grammar.

Fodor's contribution is concerned essentially with a strategic issue — the type of theory that might best offer a basis for the solution of the problem of syntax-learning. After considering the kind of information that a child must extract from his language environment and the kinds of prior information that he must bring into the language-learning situation, Fodor approaches the question of the priority and potential usefulness of various research goals. The important example he selects for detailed consideration is the induction of underlying structure from an input corpus.

The general discussion was largely an interrogation of Fodor regarding the relation of his position to that of McNeill, the operation of his inference rules, the systematic nature of a child's first sentences, the role of the mother's speech, an analogy with a linguist studying a new language, the relation between syntax and the facts of the world in general, and the extent to which children (and animals) could be said to "know rules."

Slobin's contribution on the acquisition of Russian as a native language deals with matters relating to both competence and performance and so bridges the first two groupings of papers. A rich vein of psycholinguistic data exists in the Russian literature, reflecting both the keen interest of Soviet investigators in the area and the opportunities that the highly inflected structure of the Russian language offers for novel and comparative analyses of language development. Partly because of the morphological productiveness of their language, Russian psychologists have been much more ready than many Americans to emphasize subtle, creative, nonimitative aspects of child speech. Slobin gives a brief review of the structure of Russian and surveys a number of studies of the acquisition of syntax, morphology, and word meaning. He includes some assessment of American theory in the light of Russian evidence.

The general discussion ranged over difficulties that appear to be experienced in teaching language to Russian children in large state nurseries, the early demonstration of particular inflectional competences in several domains simultaneously, the importance of semantic or logical correlates for syntactic operations, and the role of word order in the acquisition of inflected languages.

The next four papers — by Weir, Templin, Fry, and Hirsh — do not ignore theoretical issues, but they are more directly concerned with the development of performance and with deviations from normal performance in child language.

Weir's questions are broadly related to two stages in language development. The first is preverbal and is concerned with the acquisition of tonal contrast, which Weir argues is detectable and even discriminable among children at six months. The second discusses extension of the studies that she has made of the prespeech monologues of a child in his third year.

The general discussion focused on the perception of intonation and its relation to syntactic structure on the one hand and to the acoustic waveform on the other.

Children whose competence has developed far beyond the pivot and open classes are the subjects of an extensive project conducted by

Templin at the University of Minnesota's Institute of Child Development. The large-sample study, already in its sixth year, began with the aim of developing a method for detecting at kindergarten level children who would require speech therapy by second grade and has expanded into cross-sectional and longitudinal investigations comprehending many aspects of language performance. Although large amounts of data remain to be analyzed, a number of trends have been tentatively isolated relating articulatory skills to other aspects of language performance.

Points of clarification raised in the discussion included the proportion of children with articulation difficulties and the possibility of inherited or socially motivated sex differences. There was lengthy and wide-ranging consideration of possible explanations for difficulties with particular phonemes.

Fry, in the first part of his presentation, outlines the normal development of a child's phonological system from the earliest reactions to sound to the establishment of a complete phonemic repertory by the age of five to seven years. He discusses the joint role of auditory and kinesthetic feedback in the development of this system and the relative importance of imitation and social reinforcement. The second part of his paper concerns the critical effects of impoverished auditory feedback and restricted exposure to speech on the speech development of children with severe hearing loss and describes a surprisingly effective technique for reducing these effects in some cases.

Hirsh's discussion focuses on deaf children who did not have the advantage of the "new look" in deaf education during their earliest years or whose loss is so severe that they cannot benefit from it. The quality of speech of these children is compared with that of normally hearing children of the same age.

The general discussion contributed a definition of the "old look" in the education of deaf children and substantiation from other sources of Hirsh's analysis of the type of speech it produces There was a reference to a study of the utilization of visual information by the deaf.

The third and final group of papers is concerned less with the specific processes of human language than with the general processes of communication and their biological foundation. Lenneberg and Chase consider the evolution of language, with Lenneberg concentrating on the biological development of language-related processes and Chase concerning himself more with functional aspects of human, infrahuman, and biological communication systems.

The progressive development of language acquisition through a sequence of maturationally determined "milestones" is the thesis of Lenneberg's paper. He argues that language development is independent of general motor development and that it does not occur because language is useful or because the child has a "need" to learn. After proposing that the critical periods in language-learning are related to the lateralization of cerebral function, Lenneberg surveys evidence he has gathered on the comparative ontogenetic histories of apes and men to support his arguments.

Chase argues that the origin of language lies in the compelling needs for the transfer between biological systems of information essential for their preservation, growth, and development and asserts that it should not be expected that linear progression should be observed in the form of communication functions through the course of evolution.

In the general discussion, both Fodor and Lenneberg took issue with the role Chase attributes to need. A hypothesized relation between brain structure and language (Geschwind's "naming model" of the inferior parietal lobule) was also criticized. There was agreement that attempts to define a genetic substrate for language would probably prove unrewarding for the time being.

Like Chase, Kalmus draws an analogy between language and biological communication systems. He focuses first on ways in which the prelinguistic infant is able to communicate and then discusses the vocal transfer of information between animals. He criticizes the inappropriate use of terminology and concepts from genetics in the study of behavior and concludes with a consideration of the rate of evolutionary change and development, particularly with reference to language.

His view that the evolution of language must have been very rapid became one major focus of discussion; there was also an outline by Fodor of a possible approach to the syntactic analysis of noncommunicative behavior.

Premack, a psychologist, outlines a project he is undertaking with a linguist, Schwartz, to see if communication can be established with chimpanzees after appropriate training — both for the subjects and the experimenters. Without being overly optimistic, Premack is endeavoring to rectify what he considers essential inadequacies of previous attempts to teach chimpanzees to talk, namely, the requirement that they learn and vocalize human language without regard to either their physical or intellectual proclivities. More than prepared for his own experiment to fail, he hopes to demonstrate that chimpanzee has a limited language competence *per se,* not merely that it cannot accommodate to the type of performance humans find the most compatible.

The presentation provoked serious discussion by focusing attention on specific problems of language acquisition by humans. Denes, in his formal comments, points particularly to problems arising from discrepancies between articulatory and acoustic events and between acoustic sequences and their perception, stressing problems of segmentation of the acoustic signal and of imitation and babbling.

The general discussion elaborated on these points by Denes, and several participants were dubious about the techniques Premack proposes to employ. Discrepancies in the optimal rates of production and processing were foreseen. There was interest in the question of who would have the most trouble in learning to use the system, chimpanzee or experimenter.

By way of summary, Jenkins gives an overview that is both a statement of his personal opinions and an effort to highlight some of the more significant ideas presented at the conference. It is doubtful that any conference participant would agree wholly with Jenkins in terms of either his emphases or his interpretations, but his evaluation is at least a valuable frame of reference in terms of which others can define their own positions. It is perhaps indicative of his own approach that Jenkins concentrates upon topics specifically related to human verbal behavior, bypassing contributions dealing with the biological and evolutionary foundations of language and communication.

Finally, Slobin has contributed an appendix containing abstracts of significant recent Soviet studies of child language, together with a topical index to these abstracts.

Ferdinand de Saussure, the father of modern structural linguistics, once remarked that there is an important difference between a symphony and any particular performance of that symphony; the mistakes that musicians make in playing the symphony do not affect what the symphony actually is. Saussure, of course, was thinking of his distinction between language and speech, a distinction Chomsky refers to as that between competence and performance. The distinction is a generally useful one, however, and can be applied to many things other than languages and symphonies.

Take conferences, for example. After studying the records taken at a conference such as this, one gets a clear impression that something was being said but that a good many mistakes occurred in the saying of it. The editors' job, of course, is to try to reconstruct the symphony that the participants were performing. Sometimes this was easy to do, sometimes it was not. The participants themselves were not always certain what they had intended to say and so were encouraged to revise and clarify as much as they were willing.

Authors were given an opportunity to revise their circulated papers to include as much as they wished from the transcript of their conference remarks. This gave them an opportunity to read into the record any second thoughts they might have had as a consequence of points raised in discussion and thus to forestall, or even make irrelevant, particularly apposite criticisms. The same applied to the preparation of the formal comments. The remainder of the transcript, therefore, together with asides or interpolations left over from the formal sections, became the basis for the "general discussion"; it was to this material that the bulk of the editorial effort was applied.

Much of the discussion was reorganized for considerations of conciseness and continuity, large parts were eliminated, and almost all of the remainder was rewritten. In part, the reorganization was required because the sequence of papers as presented here differs slightly from the order at the conference. This applies particularly to the paper by Fodor, which originally constituted a more general summary of his conference impressions and was presented as the penultimate item on the final day. In its revised and expanded form this paper was considered more appropriate immediately following the discussion of McNeill's presentation, which was given on the first day. Further reorganization of the discussion resulted from the decision to arrange it as far as possible in terms of "topics," a constraint not applied to the discussants. This was a technique that the editors hoped might better display the trends of thought that the formal contributions provoked.

The editing of the discussion removed at the first pass many repetitions made for emphasis, by happenstance, or — as occurred not infrequently — to restate a disputed position in terms more amenable to demolition. Also suppressed were all questions of information and clarification. Either an author responded to these, in the discussion or in his revision, so that they became redundant, or else they were ignored, with the result that they became fruitless.

There is a fundamental injustice that is unavoidable when conference proceedings are dealt with in this manner. Reasonably relevant discussion points survive the final stages of editing, but the most telling contributions, by their very effectiveness, remove the grounds for their perpetuation in print because they persuade the author to amend his original position. For this reason alone we stress that the printed discussion should in no way be taken to represent either the quality or quantity of individual contributions to the actual conference proceedings.

A price must be paid for the transfer from conference to book. Spontaneity goes, and with it much individuality. Livelier moments are submerged with the dull, and a little asperity takes down with it a good deal of warmth and cordiality. However, the discussion that remains will, we hope, provide at least a flavor of the broad and often provocative reaction to the formal papers that now form a disproportionately large part of this record.

## REFERENCES

CHOMSKY, N. *Syntactic Structures*. The Hague: Mouton & Co., 1957.
———— *Aspects of the Theory of Syntax*. Cambridge, Mass.: M.I.T. Press, 1965.

David McNeill

# DEVELOPMENTAL PSYCHOLINGUISTICS

Major developments have recently been taking place in the scientific study of language. The present paper is concerned with two of them: the formulation of linguistic theory and empirical studies of language acquisition. Linguistic theory and studies of language acquisition have existed side by side, occasionally influencing each other, but in the main the two bodies of work have evolved separately. The intention of this paper is to examine their intersection in an effort to interpret empirical studies in the light of linguistic theory. The aim is to develop a theory of language acquisition that will be consistent with linguistic theory and will cover the facts of acquisition as they are now known.

The fundamental problem to which we address ourselves is the simple fact that language acquisition occurs in a surprisingly short time. Grammatical speech does not begin before one-and-one-half years of age; yet, as far as we can tell, the basic process is complete by three-and-one-half years. Thus a basis for the rich and intricate competence of adult grammar must emerge in the short span of twenty-four months. To appreciate this achievement, we need only compare the child with himself in other departments of cognitive growth as outlined, say, in the work of Piaget. Add to rapid acquisition the further fact that what is acquired is knowledge of abstract linguistic structure, and the problem of accounting for language development can be seen to pose unusual difficulties for our collection of explanatory devices. The implications of the very rapid growth of grammatical competence will become apparent in the following pages.

The past half-dozen years have seen a great change in the study of child language. Formerly, attention was concentrated on surveys of vocabulary, frequency counts of various grammatical classes, and case histories of the gradual elimination of errors in speaking. The basic assumption appears to have been that child language was adult language filtered through a great deal of cognitive noise and impoverished of vocabulary. The scholar supposed that he knew the child's grammar in advance and that it was reasonable to use categories of adult grammar to describe child language. The change from this point of view has been simple but fundamental and mainly methodological. Recent studies look upon a young child as a fluent speaker of an exotic language. The psycholinguist's problem, therefore, is analogous to the problem faced by a field linguist. Both the student of Urdu, say, and the student of child language want to characterize a speaker's grammar, and neither supposes he will profit much in imposing the grammar of well-formed English onto the corpus.

Most of the recent studies have been observational and longitudinal. Typically, a small sample of children is visited, roughly at monthly intervals, during the period of rapid linguistic growth. Usually everything is tape recorded in order to obtain a complete record of all speech to and from the child. With the evidence of these records the psycholinguist tries to write a grammar that accounts for what the child was overheard saying; this grammar is the principal object of interest, and changes in successive grammars are a way of picturing growth. For a good account of the technique of writing such grammars, see Brown and Fraser (1964). So far, the bulk of this new work has come from three sources: Brown and his colleagues at Harvard (Brown and Bellugi, 1964; Brown and Fraser, 1964; Brown, Fraser, and Bellugi, 1964); Ervin and Miller at the University of California at Berkeley (Ervin, 1964; Miller and Ervin, 1964); and Braine at Walter Reed Army Hospital (Braine, 1963).

Before describing their work, however, something must be said on the relation between linguistic competence and linguistic performance. These differ profoundly, although the distinction between them is often overlooked. Our concern in the study of language acquisition is with the development of competence; only after we have understood this to some degree can we hope to understand performance. First, consider the general distinction. Competence is an abstraction away from performance; it represents the knowledge a native speaker of a language must have in order to understand any of the infinitely many grammatical sentences of his language; it represents a native speaker's linguistic intuitions — his realization that *the man hit the ball* is grammatical but *the man virtued the ball* is not. Performance is the expression of competence in talking or listening to speech. One is competent to deal with an infinite number of grammatical sentences; but one's performance may be distracted in various ways. Performance operates under constraints of memory, which is finite, and time, which must be kept up with. Such limitations are irrelevant to competence. We know that one's competence can include grammatical constructions too long or complicated to be remembered, as evidenced by the fact that one can understand longer written than spoken sentences. And we know that competence includes sentences spoken too fast to be grasped, as evidenced by the fact that repetition of a sentence can lead to comprehension.

The same distinction between competence and performance must be honored in the case of child language. We want to account for the emergence of linguistic competence itself, something we shall not accomplish by confusing competence with performance. In addition, however, we are interested in eventually accounting for a child's linguistic performance, and this, too, requires that we rigorously maintain the performance-competence distinction. It is possible to describe performance without explaining it, but if we wish to explain performance, we must show how it derives from competence; that is, how the regularities in a child's grammatical knowledge produce regularities in his overt linguistic behavior. Nothing short of this will suffice.

There are, of course, serious difficulties that face any effort to discover the linguistic competence of children. The basic trouble is a severe constraint on the kinds of available data. A linguist devising a grammar for adult English has access to many sources of information. In particular, he can consult his own grammatical intuitions and obtain reports from other adults about theirs. In this way, a linguist can easily discover that *Adam was naughty* and *Adam was hit,* for example, have quite different structures. The situation for the grammarian of child language is far less convenient. We would also like to obtain grammatical judgments from children, as these would tap their linguistic intuitions if such exist; but usually this is impossible, for a reason that can be seen in the following dialogue (Brown and Bellugi, 1964):

> Interviewer: Now Adam, listen to what I say. Tell me which is
> better . . . some water or a water.
>
> Adam:       Pop go weasel.

The two-year-old child is recalcitrant, and we cannot expect to obtain grammatical judgments from him. Lacking such judgments, however, we must write grammars on a child's observed speech. This makes grammar-writing for children difficult though not impossible. As we shall see shortly, a good deal has been learned about the process of language acquisition through even these limited means.

## EARLY SPEECH

Sometime between eighteen and twenty-four months, most children begin to form simple two- and three-word sentences. Because our evidence is limited to what a child says, this is the earliest point at which we can study grammar. Before that time, roughly from the first birthday, children utter single words, but they produce none of the patterned speech from which a grammatical account is written.

What are the characteristics of these first sentences? They are greatly cut down, as the following examples show (taken from Brown's records):

> two boot
> a gas here
> hear tractor
> see truck Mommy
> there go one
> put truck window
> Adam make tower

Brown and Fraser (1963) called this kind of speech "telegraphic." The name is apt because one feature of these sentences is that they are reduced in almost the same way that adults reduce sentences for telegraphic transmission. In both cases, articles, prepositions, and auxiliary verbs are likely to be omitted. In these examples, we find an article missing from *hear tractor*, an article and preposition missing from *put truck window*, and an auxiliary verb missing from *Adam make tower*. However, the child also eliminates some things an adult would consider essential in his telegram. An inflection is missing from the verb in *there go one;* similarly an inflection, this time *-ing*, is missing in *Adam make tower;* and the plural inflection is not on the noun in *two boot*. There is one further difference, represented here by just one example, although it is quite common in child speech. A child combines things that an adult would not, as in *a gas here*. In sum, telegraphic speech generally leaves out articles, prepositions, auxiliary verbs, and inflections on verbs and nouns, whereas it adds ungrammatical word combinations. Except for ungrammatical combinations, all these features of telegraphic speech can be related to the fact that the missing words are unstressed in adult speech. Articles, prepositions, auxiliaries, and inflections are all phonetically obscure; their discrimination in the flow of adult speech presumably is more difficult for a child, and so they do not appear in his own (Brown and Fraser, 1964).

It is tempting to carry the telegraphic analogy farther. Perhaps children abbreviate for the same reasons adults do, to save on costs. An adult will eliminate words that do not contribute enough to the intelligibility of the message to justify the price in currency; similarly, a child may eliminate words that cannot be justified in terms of their cognitive cost. It is known that children of two have very limited memory spans; two digits is the standard performance on mental tests at this age. Thus it is conceivable that children, like adult telegram writers, try to preserve the informational content of their messages while economizing on length.

However, the telegraphic analogy becomes misleading if we take it so far as to conclude that children are actually abbreviating well-formed sentences. A limitation on memory probably constrains the length of children's sentences, but it does not work simply by eliminating words from sentences that otherwise would be fully grammatical. Rather, the child possesses a simple grammar, the output of which is telegraphic speech. If we found a two-year-old with an adult-sized memory, we would expect him to say such things as "Hear tractor go window not see Mommy," and not the well-formed equivalent, "I hear a tractor going by the window, but I can't see it, Mommy."

Telegraphic speech, therefore, is a generic term for the type of speech one hears from young children. It is a result, not a process, and it reflects more than limited memory. In order to account for it, we must look more closely at children's early grammars.

## The First Grammars

Brown, Ervin, and Braine have all collected records of the speech of two-year-old children. Braine's transcriptions are probably from a slightly earlier point in development than Brown's or Ervin's; none of Braine's subjects had been heard to produce any word combinations at all before he began to follow them, whereas Brown's and Ervin's subjects were already at the stage of two-, three-, and even four-word utterances by the time the studies began. Unfortunately, Braine did not make tape recordings of his subjects, but relied instead on parental diaries. It is difficult to say what differences there are between a diary sample and a tape-recorded one, but in most essential respects Braine's results are duplicated by Brown and Ervin.

In each of these studies the earliest word combinations were not random. A very large proportion of the children's utterances conformed to a small number of simple patterns; because they are patterned, these early utterances can be appropriately dignified by calling them "sentences."

In this section attention will be restricted to two-word sentences. They seem to be composed by selecting words from primitive grammatical classes in a fixed order. One common arrangement consists of the juxtaposition of what Braine has called "pivot" and "open" classes. Sentences of this type have been observed in every study, but terminology differs: Brown uses "modifier" instead of "pivot," and Ervin uses "operator." We shall adopt Braine's terminology for reasons of default. Brown's "modifier" refers to a special grammatical relation that does not always accompany a pivot-open construction, and Ervin's "operator" results in symbolic ambiguity with "open class" when we try to abbreviate. In adopting his terminology, however, we do not subscribe to Braine's theoretical interpretation of the P-O distinction (Braine, 1963).

The pivot class characteristically has few members compared with the open class, and each pivot word is used more frequently than individual open-class words. Moreover, the pivot class is relatively slow to take in new members. In all these characteristics, as Braine (1963) has pointed out, pivot words resemble function words rather than content words in adult speech. However, if we recall that adult function words are generally absent from early child speech, the analogy is

*Explain in class*

somewhat startling: it means that the statistical imbalance of the P-O distinction cannot be *imitated* from adults. If the imbalance were an imitation, all pivot words should be function words. But, as we shall see shortly, the pivot class can contain words from adult content classes (adjectives, verbs, etc.). We shall argue later that a P-O distinction could not be inferred from adult speech either, but thoughts on this subject are best postponed until we are prepared to discuss the role of linguistic universals in acquisition.

The statistical imbalance of the P-O distinction is difficult to explain. Braine's theory is specifically built around this imbalance, but it cannot account for numerous other facts of early child language, particularly the subsequent development of the pivot class. Braine believes that pivots are words for which the child has learned a fixed sentential position and that the statistical imbalance results from the fact that at first the position of only a few words is known. Thus any P-O sentence would use a few pivots with high frequency and many open-class words with low frequency. But basing the pivot class only on word position would lead to a haphazard assortment of words as members, and that is precisely what the pivot class is not.

Apart from the P-O construction, early two-word sentences can involve the juxtaposition of open-class words. Sometimes this is done with words from a single open class, at other times with words from different classes. It never happens, however, that two-word sentences are made up only of pivots. We shall take as an example the P-O construction, even though the O-O construction is more frequent in the records of some children's speech (Brown's, for example), because it nicely reveals one basic phenomenon of language acquisition — the emergence of grammatical classes. We will return to the O-O construction when we discuss children's early grammatical rules.

Consider Table 1, which summarizes some of the speech of one child in each of the three studies. On the left, in each column, are the pivot classes, and next to them are the corresponding open classes. A sentence is formed by selecting one word from the list on the left and following it by a word from the list on the right. Most children have more than one pivot class, which might appear in either first or second position. The position of any particular pivot and open class, however, is fixed. Table 1 reproduces only first-position pivots because these seem to be more common.

It is important to recognize the basis for classifying words together

*TABLE 1  Pivot and Open Classes from Three Studies of Child Language*

| Braine | | Brown | | Ervin | |
|---|---|---|---|---|---|
| allgone<br>byebye<br>big<br>more<br>pretty<br>my<br>see<br>night-<br>night<br>hi | boy<br>sock<br>boat<br>fan<br>milk<br>plane<br>shoe<br>vitamins<br>hot<br>Mommy<br>Daddy<br>.<br>. | my<br>that<br>two<br>a<br>the<br>big<br>green<br>poor<br>wet<br>dirty<br>fresh<br>pretty | Adam<br>Becky<br>boot<br>coat<br>coffee<br>knee<br>man<br>Mommy<br>nut<br>sock<br>stool<br>tinker-<br>toy<br>.<br>. | this<br>that | arm<br>baby<br>dolly's<br>pretty<br>yellow<br>come<br>doed<br>.<br>. |
| | | | | the<br>a | other<br>baby<br>dolly's<br>pretty<br>yellow<br>. |
| | | | | here<br>there | arm<br>baby<br>dolly's<br>pretty<br>yellow<br>.<br>. |

into a single class. The evidence is always distributional: two words are considered to be in the same grammatical class if their privileges of occurrence are the same. If the privileges of occurrence differ importantly, words must be classified differently. Look, for example, at Ervin's list in Table 1. *This* and *that* are classified together because they each occur with *arm, baby, dolly's,* etc. *The* and *a* also appear with some of these words, but *this* and *that* are not classified with *the* and *a* because the two pairs have some unique distributional possibilities. *The* and *a* appear with *other*, whereas *this* and *that* do not; and *this* and *that* appear with *come, doed,* etc., but *a* and *the* do not. The distributions overlap, but they are not identical.

Inevitably, the distributional procedure becomes vague in application. Once a child's vocabulary is of any size at all, individual open-class words are so rarely repeated that mechanically looking for shared privileges of occurrences leads to no classes at all. Thus Braine sometimes classifies words together as pivots when they have no open-class words in common. He feels justified in doing this because he can find no "systematic" differences in their distributions. *Byebye, more,* and *allgone,* for example, do not overlap at all in Braine's records if one measures overlap in terms of individual words. But if one measures overlap categorically, the three pivots have nearly identical distributions. *Byebye* is followed by *celery, allgone* is followed by *lettuce,* and *more* is followed by *melon;* similarly with another dimension, *more* is followed by *taxi,* and *byebye* is followed by *plane.* The grammarian necessarily imposes his knowledge of English onto the child's corpus if he wants to use the material at all. An advantage of this procedure over the earlier one of simply using the grammar of adult English is that the search for distributional similarities and dissimilarities will constrain the distortion of the grammarian's own grammar. It is clear, however, that distributional classification cannot eliminate such distortion entirely.

Table 1 merely summarizes speech, but we are taking it also as a description of children's competence. We suppose they really had organized their vocabularies into classes, roughly in the way indicated in the table. And since the children's sentences had the form of pivot word followed by open-class word, we also suppose their competence included the rule:

(1) $$S \rightarrow (P) + O.$$

This rule includes the possibility of not choosing the pivot because open-class words, but not pivot-class words, can stand alone in children's speech. That is to say, Rule (1) allows for both two-word and single-word utterances.

In every record, sentences three and four words long also appeared. In the case of Brown's subject, these sentences had a hierarchical structure, and probably the longer sentences in Braine's and Ervin's records were similarly produced. (Hierarchical aspects of children's grammar will be discussed later in a section devoted to grammatical rules.) The presence of hierarchical constructions does not affect our conclusions about the grammatical classes in the child's repertoire.

There is some support for the assumption that the P-O distinction and Rule (1) reflect children's competence at this early stage. For one thing, the chief alternative hypothesis — that the children had independently memorized each of the strings in the table — seems implausible in view of the quantity of the material. For the child in Braine's sample, for example, it would mean the memorization of at least 102 combinations — that being the size of his corpus — and surely this is an underestimate because these 102 sentences are only the ones that happened to turn up in Braine's sample. Another reason for crediting children with Rule (1) is the presence of combinations of P and O that are very unlikely to be imitations or reductions of adult sentences. Take, for example, the set of sentences with *allgone* as a pivot word in Braine's list. It includes *allgone shoe, allgone vitamins, allgone egg, allgone lettuce,* etc. None of these could be an imitation because each is an inversion of the appropriate adult model. Compare *allgone shoe* to *the shoe is allgone.* Ervin's subject produced sentences such as *that doed, there pretty,* and Brown's subject, making use of hierarchical constructions, produced *big a truck* and *a that horsie.* It is unlikely that children hear this kind of fractured English from their parents.

Sentences that cannot be accounted for as reductions of adult sentences provide the best evidence that children know productive rules. The point of these examples is that they are cut from the same pattern as many others in children's speech that are not fractured English. It would be completely *ad hoc* to distinguish the ones that are fractured from the ones that are not. Instead, it is more parsimonious to assume that children generate all these sentences according to rules and that the rules and word categories we can infer from their speech reflect some kind of primitive competence.

The same conclusion is suggested by a striking phenomenon reported by Weir in *Language in the Crib* (1962). The title is not fanciful. She collected the presleep monologues of her two-and-a-half-year-old son and subjected them to linguistic analysis. The striking phenomenon is that the boy practiced rules similar to (1). In the following series, for example, the boy repeatedly substituted expressions in the frame *go:*

> go for glasses
> go for them

> go to the top
> go throw
> go for blouse
> pants
> go for shoes

The verb is the pivot word, so the rule is of the form $S \rightarrow P + O$, and we can see the child trying one open-class expression after another, exercising the rule. Weir's child was older and had a considerably more elaborate grammar than the children in Braine's, Brown's, or Ervin's studies, and we find him sometimes carrying on more than one substitution at once, as in the first two lines. The fact that not all the substitutions are single open-class words again reflects a hierarchical development.

What can be said of the early competence of children? Let us first take up the problem of grammatical classes. Later we shall discuss the problem of children's rules for generating sentences.

The pivot and open classes are typically heterogeneous from the point of view of adult grammar. The pivot class in Braine's grammar, for example, contains adjectives (*big, more, pretty,* and possibly *all-gone*), verbs (*see,* and possibly *byebye* and *nightnight*), a pronoun (*my*), and a greeting (*hi*). Braine's criteria for placing words into the same class may have been too relaxed, so his list might overestimate the variety of adult grammatical classes likely to end up in a child's pivot class; but there is no question of the general fact of heterogeneity. It appears just as impressively in Brown's records for the pivot class of his subject and in the open class of Ervin's subject. Brown's subject had two kinds of pronouns (*my, that*), articles (*a, the*), and adjectives (*big, green,* etc.) in his pivot class. Ervin's subject had nouns (*arm, baby,* etc.) and adjectives (*pretty, yellow,* etc.) in every open class, and in addition there were verbs (*come, doed,* etc.) in one class and a determiner (*other*) in a second. No child in any of these studies revealed both pivot and open classes that agree exactly with classes in the adult grammar. Sometimes the pivot class may correspond to an adult category, as apparently was the case with Ervin's subject, or a child may have an open class that agrees fairly well with an adult class, as Brown's and Braine's subjects apparently did. But even here there is diversity on a reduced scale: Brown's subject did not honor the adult distinction between mass and count nouns, producing sentences such as *a gas* and *some milks;* and Braine's subject had one adjective, *hot*, in an open class that otherwise contained only nouns in adult grammar. One suspects that diversity is initially the rule for both the pivot and open classes, but it does not always appear in these studies because the two classes can develop at somewhat different rates. What we find in the case of Ervin's subject, therefore, probably is the outcome of faster development of pivot classes than open classes, whereas in the case of Brown's or Braine's subject we have the opposite, open classes developing faster than pivot classes. We do not have sufficient information to judge whether or not this suspicion is correct, for no one has kept the extremely detailed records that would be required, but it seems plausible. As we shall see next, the development of grammatical classes takes the form of differentiation, or subdivision, of a child's primitive grammatical classes. Thus the relative homogeneity of the pivot classes in Ervin's grammar and the open classes in Brown's and Braine's grammars could conceivably be the outcome of differentiation that went on before the studies began.

## *Differentiation of the Pivot Class*

Differentiation has been described by Brown and Bellugi (1964). Insofar as one can tell, this direction of development is followed by all children. Among Brown and Bellugi's subjects, open classes were relatively well differentiated at the time the children were first observed, so our usable information concerns the history of the pivot class. Moreover, information from different children in the Brown and Bellugi study cannot be combined because the particular words in the pivot class differ somewhat from child to child. Instead, we shall present the developmental history of one child, the same one whose initial P-O distinction is reproduced in Table 1. Essentially the same conclusions are reached from an examination of the records of other children in Brown's project.

We have information from three points in this child's development, the times at which grammars were written from the child's speech. The corpus at the first point was reproduced in part in Table 1. The second point is two-and-one-half months later, and the third point is two-and-one-half months later than that; the entire span covers five months. As we shall see, the process of differentiation is not complete by the time the third point is reached, but it is far advanced.

The child's progress during these five months can be summarized by the diagram in Figure 1. On the left is the actual history of the pivot class after the child was first observed. On the right are the rules of sentence formation with which the grammarian was compelled to credit the child in order to account for his sentences.

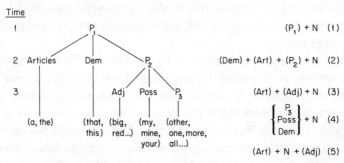

FIG. 1. Differentiation of the pivot class. Abbreviations are as follows: N = noun, that is, one of the open classes for this child; Art = articles; Dem = demonstrative pronouns; Adj = adjectives; Poss = possessive pronouns; $P_1$, $P_2$, and $P_3$ = pivot class at Times 1, 2, and 3, respectively.

The diagram on the left of Figure 1 is not a phrase marker. However, the fact that it is drawn as a tree structure may have some significance, which will be discussed later.

For the moment, Figure 1 can be taken as a chronology of the child's development. As was noted before, at Time 1 the pivot class consisted of *my, that, two, a, the, big, green,* etc. These words were classed together because they had identical privileges of occurrence in the child's sentences. By Time 2, articles and demonstrative pronouns had unique privileges of occurrence. The child produced sentences such as *that a my car,* in which the article, *a,* had a definite position before the pivot word, *my.* He avoided sentences such as *that my a car,* in which *my* and *a* are not distinguished with respect to sentence position. Similar evidence exists for the demonstrative pronouns. The child produced sentences such as *that a horsie* and avoided *a that horsie.* Demonstrative pronouns thus could appear before articles and pivot words. Both these new contingencies, the positions of demonstrative pronouns and articles, are represented in Rule (2).

By Time 2, the original pivot class had been reduced in membership through subdivision; the child had come to treat articles and demonstrative pronouns as unique classes. As before, we assume this reflects the child's competence and take the change in privileges of occurrence to indicate that *a* and *the,* on the one hand, and *this* and *that,* on the other, do indeed belong to separate grammatical classes for the child. However, there remains a residual pivot class, containing *my, two, more,* and the adjectives, to which *other* and *'nother* have been added. It is important to note that this class, too, has definite privileges of occurrence, and we suppose that it also represents a part of the child's competence at Time 2. It is still heterogeneous from the point of view of adult grammar.

There is further subdivision of $P_2$ by Time 3. The adjectives now have unique privileges of occurrence in that they can appear after nouns, as in *toy big* or *penguin big heavy,* as well as before nouns. Pivot words are restricted to positions before nouns, so we do not find the child saying *toy 'nother,* for example. Also, we credit the child with a separate class of possessive pronouns because he no longer produced sentences such as *a my cup,* which were possible at Time 2.

In five months' time, therefore, five grammatical classes have emerged from one primeval pivot class: articles, adjectives, demonstrative pronouns, possessive pronouns, and a pivot class that contains *other, 'nother, one, all,* and *more.* In each case, new classes appeared through subdivision of one of the pivot classes $P_1$ or $P_2$, and so we can say that the process of development here was differentiation of the pivot class. There is no evidence of independent discovery of the adult grammatical classes; they are merely removed from the pivot class like a banana peel.

## UNIVERSALS IN LANGUAGE ACQUISITION

The preceding characterization raises a fundamental problem. In order for differentiation to yield the grammatical classes of adult English, the original pivot (and, presumably, the open) class must be *generically* related to the adult classes. By a generic relation, we mean that the competence of the child on which the pivot class is based must ignore, but potentially admit, all the relevant distinctions of the adult grammar. In terms of actual content, such a relation clearly exists, as the facts of differentiation show. Every adjective in the vocabulary of Brown's subject at Time 1, for example, was within the pivot class, even though adjectives were not yet distinguished as a class. But in order for a generic relation to exist, we must assume that a child honors in advance some of the distinctions on which adult classes are based.

This implication seems to have gone unnoticed, so we shall take time to discuss it.

Consider first some difficulties with formulations that do not make this assumption. Braine's theory, for example, implies that the pivot class is merely a random selection of words. But clearly this is not the case. A random selection would make differentiation impossible because a child's pivot class would be as likely to include words from one adult grammatical class as another. Moreover, since the original pivot class appears to be part of a child's competence — and so has some psychological unity for him — we would have to conclude that a randomly constituted pivot class would actually be misleading. The best thing a child could do under these circumstances would be to forget the P-O distinction as a bad start and begin afresh. (For other criticisms of Braine's theory, see Bever, Fodor, and Weksel, 1965*a*, 1965*b*; see also Braine's reply, 1965).

Nor, to take another theory, could a child infer adult classes from parental speech without knowing in advance the range of possible distinctions. Parental speech offers useful guidance at this point *only* if this condition is met. An ability to infer something about language is the capacity to generalize a distinction once its relevance is noticed. We cannot conceive of it being a capacity to invent the distinctions themselves. A vast number of distinctions is possible in parental speech — only a few of which are important in English — and if a child had to invent rather than notice them, his chances of progressing to English would be microscopically small. For a complete discussion on this point, see Katz (1966).

Nor, to take a third view, can strictly distributional evidence from parental speech yield a generic classification of adult grammatical categories, even assuming that a child manages to solve the problem of inference just noted. The set of grammatical categories that follows from distributional evidence would presumably be the full adult set, not a generic set; it begs the question to claim that a child observes only those distributional facts that support a generic classification. It is circular to assert, for example, that Brown's subject formed a pivot class of articles, demonstrative pronouns, adjectives, etc., by sorting words according to whether or not they precede nouns, for we still do not know how the child came to use this basis of classification, and that is the question in which we are interested.

The role of distributional evidence seems to have been greatly overrated in speculations on language acquisition. Not only is it impossible for distributional evidence to yield generic grammatical classes for a child, it seems impossible for it to yield a P-O distinction of any kind. The line of development that would follow from distributional evidence would be differentiation of the class of *all* words in a child's vocabulary, not differentiation of the pivot or open class. Each step of differentiation would consist of precipitating just one adult grammatical category from the total vocabulary. (There is no way to conceive of a child removing two or more adult classes as an undifferentiated set unless we again beg the question of what criteria the child uses.) Of course it would be possible to say that the pivot class for Brown's subject *was* the original undifferentiated set of all words in the child's vocabulary. His open class, then, could be regarded as the outcome of the first subdivision of the total vocabulary; articles and demonstrative pronouns could be regarded as the second and third subdivisions; and so on. This would be differentiation of a single heterogeneous category, and it could rest on distributional evidence alone. In effect, the pivot class would not be a grammatical class at all under this interpretation but merely a collection of words out of which adult classes arise, and the P-O distinction would cease to exist. However, it is clear that Brown's subject did possess a genuine pivot class and that he did not derive adult grammatical classes through differentiation of his total vocabulary. If the pivot class at any given time really were a residual of the total stock of words, all members of the pivot class would be able to stand alone as single-word utterances. The original undifferentiated vocabulary of children, before there is any grammatical patterning, consists precisely of single-word utterances. But one characteristic of pivot words (for all children who have been studied) is that they rarely stand alone as single-word utterances; they almost always occur in combination with an open-class word. The composition of Rule (1), which has the pivot as an option, reflects this restriction on the occurrence of pivots. We must conclude, therefore, that the P-O distinction is somehow imposed by a child on his vocabulary; it does not arise from the distributional evidence that a child obtains from parental speech; and it does appear to involve a generic classification of adult grammatical categories. In order to account for the P-O distinction, stronger explanations will have to be considered than a child's use of distributional evidence. Some possibilities along these lines will be discussed later.

But let us first be certain that the concept of generic classification is clearly understood. An analogy might help. Suppose we give an adult the problem of discovering into which of two subclasses we have divided the class of English adjectives. He does not know the principle of our subclassification, but he does know what adjectives are. His position, therefore, is comparable with a child's. The class of adjectives corresponds to the child's pivot class, and the unknown principle corresponds to some adult distinction — say the one between demonstrative pronouns and articles. Like a child, our adult subject must discover how to differentiate his class of adjectives into the subcategories we have in mind. Now suppose that we divide the class of adjectives arbitrarily. We might take them in order from a dictionary, placing all even-numbered adjectives in one class, all odd-numbered adjectives in the other. Under these circumstances the class of adjectives — the adult's competence — would not be a generic classification of the two subcategories. Our subject knows no relation among adjectives that will allow him to differentiate the class. Probably the only strategy for discovering the two subclasses is to test and memorize each word individually, an exceedingly time-consuming procedure and one that is not differentiation. Noting distinctions in our speech — if, for example, we always use even-numbered adjectives after *be* and odd-numbered adjectives before nouns — certainly will not help this adult, for he will have no basis for recognizing the regularity. Each adjective will be a thing unto itself.

In contrast, suppose we subdivide the class of adjectives on some other principle. For example, we might place all adjectives beginning with the letters *A* through *L* into one class and adjectives beginning *M* through *Z* into another. Now there is a basis for segregating the two classes, for what our adult subject knows about the original class of adjectives encompasses the two subclasses. Our adult subject knows the initial letter of each adjective, which is relevant to the subclassification, and once he has discovered this principle, he can split the class of adjectives immediately.

The difference between these two situations is determined by whether or not our subject's original competence includes information relevant to the subdivision of the adjective class. When it does, he can then note the relevance in samples of our speech and adopt the distinction himself.

The suggestion is that the initial competence of children — the pivot and open classes — is similarly relevant to the distinctions honored in adult grammar. In this sense, children's early competence includes a generic classification of adult grammatical classes. The task now is to describe what this relevance is. In so doing, perhaps we shall be able to characterize more fully the nature of children's early competence. Notice, incidentally, that the problem raised here cannot be solved by assuming that the P-O distinction is not the original distinction children make in language acquisition, for that would merely push the difficulty back to an earlier point in the child's career.

Let us take an excursion into an aspect of transformational grammar that has to do with the problem of semigrammaticality. One interpretation of the P-O distinction and the differentiation of grammatical classes will emerge. The transformational grammar described by Chomsky and others is intended to reflect accurately a native speaker's intuitions about well-formed sentences. However, it is clear that our intuitions are not limited to well-formed sentences. We also can make sense of such semigrammatical sentences as Dylan Thomas's *a grief ago,* Veblen's *perform leisure,* or Chomsky's *colorless green ideas sleep furiously.* Not only can we make sense of them, but we also know that those sentences do less violence to our grammatical intuitions than *a the ago,* or *perform compel,* or *furiously sleep ideas green colorless.* The ability to judge relative grammaticality seems to be quite general, as the reader can verify by testing himself against the following set of sentences:

| | | |
|---|---|---|
| John plays golf | golf plays John | golf plays aggressive |
| John loves company | misery loves company | abundant loves company |
| sincerity frightens John | John frightens sincerity | John sincerity frightens |
| what did you do to the book, bite it? | what did you do to the book, understand it? | what did you do to the book, justice it? |

Chomsky (1961, 1964), from whom all these examples are taken, has discussed semigrammaticality in terms of supplementing generative grammar with a hierarchy of categories. A generative grammar of well-formed sentences can account for only the sentences of the left-most column above; the others fall beyond its scope. If one's competence included the grammar of well-formed sentences and nothing else, the central and right-most sentences would both be uninterpretable and would seem equally ungrammatical. They would be uninterpretable because neither *golf plays John* nor *golf plays aggressive* can be assigned a structural description, and they would be equally ungrammatical because the grammar is capable of registering only the binary decision — well formed or not. However, *golf plays John* is certainly meaningful; indeed it is an effectively devastating description of John precisely because it is grammatically deviant. *Golf plays John* causes us to impose an interpretation by noting the analogy to the well-formed *John plays golf*. We see that both are noun-verb-noun sentences, but *golf plays John* violates restrictions on what categories can be the subject and object of *play*. *Golf plays aggressive,* in contrast, is not even a noun-verb-noun sentence. Thus the two deviant sentences differ in the magnitude of the violence they do to the category restrictions of the grammar. *Golf plays John* honors the distinction between nouns and other parts of speech but does away with a distinction within the noun class, whereas *golf plays aggressive* obliterates a major distinction between two grammatical classes. Chomsky has maintained that the degree of grammaticalness of a sentence depends on the category restrictions that it preserves.

Imagine that we have before us a complete transformational grammar of English. We would find that the rules are expressed in terms of very narrow categories of words (actually, of morphemes or lexical items) that embody such distinctions as animate and inanimate nouns or pure transitive and mixed transitive-intransitive verbs, etc. This is the lowest level of Chomsky's hierarchy of categories; it represents all the distinctions that are necessary to a grammar of well-formed sentences. Suppose that above this level is another that categorizes the same words more broadly. And above this level, suppose yet another that classifies the same words still more broadly, and so on until at the top there is just one class containing all the words of English. That is, every level is an exhaustive classification of the lexicon, and moreover each successively lower level is a refinement of the level just above. The system of levels can be abstractly pictured by the tree graph in Figure 2. Every "C" is a category of words. Superscripts represent the level at which a particular category resides, and subscripts indicate the particular category we have in mind. Level m is the most

differentiated. This abstract diagram skips many levels and many categories; it merely presents a hierarchical arrangement of the sort Chomsky describes in accounting for semigrammatical sentences. There are,
of course, many different ways that the lower-level categories might
be combined. (See Miller and Chomsky, 1963, for an illustrative example.)

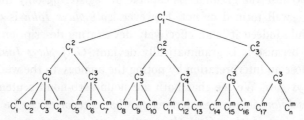

FIG. 2. An abstract hierarchy of syntactic categories.

Such a hierarchy provides a representation of every string of words,
whether or not well formed. The well-formed *John plays golf*, for example, is represented on all levels of the hierarchy. It honors the most
delicate distinctions of Level m as well as the broader ones of the levels
above. The rules of the grammar, therefore, can produce sentences of
the form of *John plays golf* throughout the hierarchy. On the other
hand, the semigrammatical sentence *golf plays John* can be represented
no farther down in the hierarchy than some intermediate level, say
where the categories are undifferentiated noun, verb, and some others.
For the sake of an example, suppose that these distinctions are drawn
at Level 2 in our diagram and $C_1^2$ is the class of verbs, $C_2^2$ is the class
of nouns, and $C_3^2$ includes everything else. Then *golf plays John* will
have a representation on Level 2 in common with one of the sentences
generated by the grammar, viz., noun-verb-noun. (So, of course, does
*John plays golf*.)

In this way, Chomsky can account for our ability to impose interpretations on semigrammatical sentences and to judge which of two
semigrammatical sentences is more remote from well-formed English.
We can impose an interpretation on *golf plays John* because it has
the same representation on Level 2 as *John plays golf*. We can judge
the degree of grammaticalness by noting the lowest level at which a

sentence receives a representation. Thus, *golf plays aggressive* is less grammatical by this reckoning than *golf plays John*.

The knowledge represented by the hierarchy of categories seems to be an essential part of our linguistic competence. It may also be an essential part of language acquisition. Perhaps the original P-O distinction of child grammar is one of the distinctions drawn near the top of Chomsky's hierarchy. Moreover, in a child's subsequent development, the differentiation of P and O may consist of moving down the hierarchy to more narrowly defined categories. It is in this sense that we can regard a child's original grammatical categories as a generic classification of the categories of adult grammar. The ever more refined classification of words represented in Chomsky's hierarchy, therefore, suggests a blueprint for the first stages of language acquisition. The tree diagram for the development of Brown's subject in Figure 1 may be more than a chronology; it may be the same hierarchy that underlies adults' interpretation of semigrammatical sentences. On this view, the successful differentiation of children's P and O classes is an automatic result of a basic congruence of children's and adult's competence.

There are two possible explanations for any such congruence. One is that the adult's hierarchy was learned in infancy, for if everyone acquires language by the process of differentiation exemplified by Brown's subject, the various levels of Chomsky's hierarchy could reflect adults' retention of the early stages of their own language acquisition. We can be certain that this explanation is false. For one thing, it fails to account for the similar intuitions of different adults about the relative grammaticality of sentences. For another thing, it implies that foreign speakers of English — persons who learned the language when they were already linguistically mature — should have intuitions about semigrammatical English sentences that are quite different from those of native speakers. Foreign speakers acquire English from textbooks, so their early stages of acquisition are fundamentally different from native speakers'. However, as will be seen later, native and foreign speakers of English are not consistently different in their judgments of relative grammaticality.

An alternative explanation is that the set of distinctions drawn from Chomsky's hierarchy of categories represents linguistic universals that are part of the child's innate endowment. The role of a universal hierarchy of categories would be to direct the child's discovery of the classes of English. It is as if he were equipped with a set of "templates" against which he can compare the speech he happens to hear from his parents. This speech is a haphazard sample (at least initially), not at all contrived to instruct a child in basic grammatical structure. Indeed, ordinarily a child's parents will be completely unaware of basic grammatical structure. However, parental speech will inevitably conform to some of the linguistic universals registered on the child's templates. We can imagine, then, that a child classifies the random specimens of adult speech he encounters according to universal categories that the speech exemplifies. Since these distinctions are at the top of a hierarchy that has the grammatical classes of English at its bottom, the child is prepared to discover the appropriate set of distinctions.

The case is the same as with the adult in our analogy: a child has knowledge of the set of distinctions that define the classes of English (or any other language), and his problem is to discover the ones that are relevant. Obviously, a child's knowledge of universal categories will not lead him to completely well-formed English. Learning of a different character must also take place, and something will be said about this phase of acquisition (p. 53). But in the main, we can agree with Brown and Bellugi (1964) when they write: "The very intricate simultaneous differentiation and integration that constitutes the evolution of the noun phrase is more reminiscent of the biological development of an embryo than it is of the acquisition of a conditioned reflex."

One superficial difficulty with the present line of thinking should be commented on. It looks embarrassing to the hypothesis of a universal hierarchy of categories that children differ on the particular distinctions they draw. For example, Brown's and Ervin's subjects both have adjectives in their simple sentences, yet one uses them as pivot words, the other as open-class words. Probably such disagreements are typical. However, in themselves, they are neutral with respect to the hypothesis that children begin their linguistic careers with linguistic universals. We have spoken of the hierarchy of categories as if it could be arranged in only one way. This is not necessarily the case. There are numerous arrangements, and a number of different distinctions can provide possible starting points. A decision as to whether the particular distinctions adopted first by children correspond to universal distinctions in a hierarchy of adult categories must wait until we have a more sophisticated idea of what distinctions are universal; this is a linguistic problem currently under active investigation. However, the linguistic findings are not yet in a form that allows us to compare children's sequences of development to adults' hierarchy of categories on the level of detail that is really needed.

Since that is the case, we must be content for the present with the following imprecise test of the hypothesis. The aim of the experiment to be described was to discover whether or not adults can judge which of two sentences from a child was produced later in development. None of the sentences was well formed, and the subjects had to determine the proximity of the child's sentences to adult grammar. The task, therefore, was exactly the same as deciding the relative degrees of grammaticalness of *a grief ago* and *a the ago*. If adults can make these judgments about children's sentences correctly, we would conclude that they know the hierarchy of categories through which the child had moved; there is no other basis for an adult to succeed in the experiment. (Several of the children's sentences deviate from the word order of well-formed English; however, as far as the experimental materials are concerned, converting early sentences to the well-formed order does not, on the average, require more changes than converting late sentences.) This result would not prove that knowledge of the child's hierarchy is the same as knowledge of the hierarchy that Chomsky discussed. The fact is, nonetheless, that the sentences children produce later in their careers usually strike adults as obviously more grammatical than earlier sentences, which if it does not prove, at least suggests, that the two hierarchies may be the same. This intuition grips adults so forcibly, in fact, that sometimes it is difficult to convince colleagues that the experiment is really a test of anything at all. Such doubts are welcomed, of course, because they support the hypothesis that a child's early grammatical categories are a generic specification of adult grammatical categories.

The experiment was conducted with ten native speakers of English and five speakers of English-as-a-second-language. All the foreign speakers learned English as adolescents, so it can be safely assumed that they did not pass through a phase of differentiation in acquiring English; all became fluent speakers of the language. The native languages were Hindi (three subjects), Japanese (one subject), and Spanish (one subject). Every adult subject judged the relative proximity to well-formed English of fifteen pairs of sentences taken from the grammar of Brown's subject. Every pair involved a contrast with the child's grammar at Time 1, when he had only the P-O distinction: four pairs compared Time 2 and Time 1, and eleven pairs compared Time 3 and Time 1. No sentences were well formed by adult standards. Length was constant within each pair, so that was not a cue. Some of the sentences used did not actually occur but were mechanically generated from the child's grammar; this is not unfair, as we are interested in the categories of the grammar and not in the particular sentences the child was overheard producing. Some examples are given in Table 2. All the sentences involved a hierarchical construction.

TABLE 2    *A Child's Sentences at Two Stages of Development*

| Time 1 | Time 2 |
|--------|--------|
| dats your a car | dats a your car |
| a dats cheese | dats a cheese |

| Time 1 | Time 3 |
|--------|--------|
| fast the car | the car fast |
| dis hammer other one | dis other one hammer |
| big Eve toy | Eve toy big |

Subjects were asked to indicate the member of each pair that came later in the child's career on the basis of how close the sentences were to adult English. There is no question that adults can make these judgments accurately. For native speakers over-all success was 81 per cent, whereas chance is 50 per cent. Foreign speakers did nearly as well, correctly ordering pairs 78 per cent of the time. No consistent differences appeared between native and foreign speakers in the sentences that were successfully ordered, except that foreign speakers generally did better than native speakers on pairs involving first-person possessive pronouns.

The hypothesis that the first stages of linguistic development are guided by a universal hierarchy of categories can be considered in relation to an abstract characterization of language acquisition that has been outlined by Chomsky (1961, 1965) and Katz (1966). They discuss the form of a Language Acquisition Device (LAD) or System (LAS). LAD receives primary linguistic data — essentially a corpus of speech from fluent speakers within hearing range — as input and has grammatical competence as output. It can be represented schematically as follows:

Primary Linguistic Data → | LAD | → G

The contents of the box — the properties of LAD — will explain the linguistic intuitions of adults because it determines the properties of G, or grammatical competence. The internal structure of LAD is given by the linguistic universals, one of which, according to the present argument, is the competence that underlies adult judgments of semigrammatical sentences.

Linguistic universals may be classified into two types, formal and substantive (Chomsky, 1965). The hierarchy of categories would be an example of a substantive universal. It constitutes, as it were, a part of the basic set of concepts that LAD uses to devise the particular grammatical rules of English. The form that these rules take, in turn, is prescribed by the formal universals that are also part of LAD's internal structure. Equipped with both formal and substantive universals, LAD operates something like a scientist constructing a theory. LAD observes a certain amount of empirical data, the primary linguistic data, and formulates hypotheses that will account for them from its knowledge of the formal and substantive universals. Further observation may lead to changes in LAD's hypotheses, but all new hypotheses will also be phrased in terms of the formal and substantive universals. Thus, the universals guide and limit acquisition. In the case of real children, the original P-O distinction would then reflect an initial hypothesis to account for the examples of English that the child has heard. With time, a child modifies this hypothesis, presumably to accord better with new observations, and so separates articles, adjectives, demonstrative pronouns, and the like. In a sense, of course, the observations that give rise to these distinctions are not new — they are always present in adult speech.

The advantage to a child of having universals such as the hierarchy of categories is that he can progress toward the grammatical classes of adult English step-by-step. He does not have to notice, hypothesize, and test all distinctions at once. A simple dichotomy or trichotomy will serve at first. The rest of the distinctions are taken up in an order determined by the hierarchical arrangement of categories. If the same hierarchy underlies both adult grammar and a child's development, the child would be able to progress rapidly and surely to full linguistic competence.

## EARLY GRAMMATICAL RULES

Some rules that appear to be part of children's early grammatical competence have already been mentioned. In the case of Brown's subject, there were five rules (Figure 1). Rules (2) through (5) were derived from Rule (1) by the process of differentiation of the pivot class. All these rules are basically P-O constructions, and there is some question whether we should think of five different rules or just one basic rule operating with different grammatical classes at different times; Brown and Bellugi (1964) favor the latter interpretation. In any case, the P-O construction is not the only rule present in children's early grammars. Children also have sentences of an open-open type, some of which are covered by Rule (6) in Brown's grammar (in which some open-class words were nouns):

$$(6) \qquad\qquad\qquad S \rightarrow N + N$$

Rule (6) generates such sentences as *Adam car, mommy soup, Urler suitcase,* etc., and it was highly productive. Indeed, Brown's early records contain many more sentences produced by Rule (6) than by Rule (1). Sentences from Rule (6) usually strike adults as telegraphic versions of the possessive: *Urler suitcase* probably corresponds to *Urler's suitcase* in the adult grammar.

Rule (6), even though it is not a pivot-open construction, is identical to Rules (1) through (5) in one respect; all are sequential and lack any sort of hierarchical structure. In this they differ from Rules (7) and (8), which are both hierarchical and generate such sentences as *that my coat* and *want my coat.* Rules (7) and (8) can be written as follows:

$$(7) \qquad\qquad\qquad S \rightarrow (P) + NP$$

$$NP \rightarrow \left\{ \begin{array}{c} (P) + N \\ N + N \end{array} \right\}$$

$$(8) \qquad\qquad\qquad S \rightarrow Pred\ P$$

$$Pred\ P \rightarrow (V) + NP$$

$$NP \rightarrow \left\{ \begin{array}{c} (P) + N \\ N + N \end{array} \right\}$$

The difference between Rules (1) through (6) and Rules (7) and (8) can readily be seen by comparing their phrase markers, which are drawn in Figure 3. The markers generated by Rules (1) and (6) represent the sequential type. (The alternate choice of P or N in Rules (7) and (8) is indicated in the usual way by braces.) Notice that the only difference between the sequential and hierarchical phrase markers — aside from the appearance of V in Rule (8) — is the presence of NP or Pred P. And notice, also, that the material dominated by NP is the right-hand sides of Rules (1) and (6) combined and that the material dominated by Pred P contains this same NP. We might suspect that Rules (1) through (6), the sequential set, and Rules (7) and (8), the hierarchical set, are related in some way.

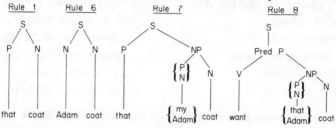

Fig. 3. Phrase markers generated by early grammatical rules.

At Time 1, Rule (7) was not used frequently. Most sentences came from Rules (1), (6), and (8). The option of choosing P in Rule (8) was rarely taken. Thus most sentences were two words long and consisted of either a pivot word followed by a noun, or a noun followed by a noun, or a verb followed by a noun. There were also some sentences in which a noun was followed by a verb, such as *Bambi go* and *Adam change diaper*. They do not fit any of the rules individually but seem instead to be a combination of two rules, probably (7) and (8); more will be said about this. Most three-word sentences at this age followed Rule (8), using the (N + N) alternative of NP. By Time 2, the frequency of three-word sentences had increased, and Rule (7) had come to play a more important role. No new patterns seem to have crept into the child's grammar at Time 2, all the changes being in the relative frequency with which sentences were generated by these various rules. Time 3 continues the same story: further frequency changes, but no new rules.

Thus the development of grammatical rules is quite different from the development of grammatical classes. During the same five-month period that saw great changes in the system of grammatical categories, the basic set of grammatical rules remained more or less constant (disregarding frequency changes, which probably depend on practice, interests, memory span, etc., that is, on various performance factors). This constancy may indicate another aspect of the child's fundamental linguistic capacity, but before that can be discussed, we must try to establish the psychological reality of hierarchical rules.

Brown and Bellugi (1964) present several kinds of evidence for the psychological reality of the NP constituent in the speech of children. For one thing, the NP and the single N have identical privileges of occurrence, as in the following sentences:

| Positions for Single N | Positions for NP |
|---|---|
| that (flower) | that (a blue flower) |
| where (ball) go? | where (the puzzle) go? |
| Adam write (penguin) | doggie eat (the breakfast) |
| (horsie) stop | (a horsie) crying |
| put (hat) on | put (the red hat) on |

These demonstrate that the syntactic position of the NP is the same as its head word, the N. The NP is "endocentric," as linguists say. The endocentricity of the NP itself suggests that such constructions are psychological units for children. Pointing to the same conclusion is the fact that pauses, when they occur, usually bracket the NP. A child might say "Put . . . the red hat . . . on," but not likely "Put the red . . . hat on." Similar evidence has been described by Huttenlocher (1964). Finally, there is use of the pronoun *it*. As Brown and Bellugi point out, *it* is actually a pro-noun phrase, which stands for an NP, not a single N. To quote them,

> The unity of noun phrases in adult English is evidenced, in the first place, by the syntactic equivalence between such phrases and nouns alone. It is evidenced, in the second place, by the fact that the pronouns are able to substitute for total noun phrases. In our immediately preceding sentence the pronoun "It" stands for the rather involved construction from the first sentence of this paragraph: "The unity of noun phrases in adult English . . ." One does not replace "unity" with "it" and say "The it of noun phrases in adult English . . ."

Similarly, in the speech of Brown and Bellugi's subjects, *it* replaced noun phrases, suggesting that the NP is capable of replacement as a unit and so, psychologically, as a whole.

In the case of one child, the replacement itself did not occur for a time, but instead the child produced both *it* and the constituent it should have replaced. For example,

> Mommy get it ladder
> Mommy get it my ladder

In the first sentence, *it* and a single N come out together; in the second, *it* and an NP co-occur. Thus the child treats N and NP alike in making this quaint error, a fact that provides further evidence for the psychological unity of NP.

However, the psychological unity of the NP raises a vexing question about the status of our rules. It has already been mentioned that Rules (1) through (5) might be regarded as one rule operating with different grammatical categories. If, along with Brown and Bellugi, we decide to group them, we are left with four rules; Rule (1) in its various forms, and Rules (6), and (7), and (8). To decide this much is relatively easy because the grounds for keeping Rules (1) through (5) apart really have nothing to do with the form of the rules themselves. The hard decision is what to do with Rules (6), (7), and (8). It was pointed out that Rules (1) and (6) — the pivot-noun and noun-noun constructions — are both involved in Rules (7) and (8) as the NP. It seems that there are two alternative interpretations of this inter-digitation. One is to regard Rules (1) and (6) as basic and Rule (7) as a later development growing out of Rules (1) and (6), which would imply that a child does not have higher-order constituents in his early sentences. The fact that Rule (7) was not used frequently in Brown's earliest records supports this view.

However, now we must also suppose that Rule (8) is simplified to read merely $(S \rightarrow V + N)$, which runs afoul of the fact that the most common three-word sentence at Time 1 was VNN, a sentence type generated by Rule (8) *with* an NP (NP $\rightarrow$ N + N, one of the options). We are faced, therefore, with the inconsistency that NP is possible in Rule (8) but not Rule (7). If the NP is psychologically unitary for the child, he should treat it everywhere alike. Thus we are led to a second interpretation of the interdigitation of Rules (1), (6), (7), and (8): all the rules, (1) through (8), make use of NP. NP is psychologically unitary from the outset. But now we must account for the fact that sentences with single N occur more frequently than ones with a developed NP. One possibility here is that a child tends to restrict himself to using just one pivot position in each sentence. This makes Rules (1) and (6) into variants of Rule (7). Rule (1) comes out of Rule (7) when the child picks the P dominated by S or the P dominated by NP; whichever he chooses, the other would be suppressed. Rule (6) comes out of Rule (7) when the child elects the N under NP. The first pivot position would then be suppressed, and the second pivot position is already occupied by N. The advantage of this scheme is that it lets Rule (8) have its NP. It may also account for the fact that PNN and PPN sentences were infrequent at Time 1, while VNN sentences were the most numerous of all three-word utterances (two pivot positions are used in PNN or PPN as against one in VNN). It was the low frequency of PNN and PPN from Rule (7) that seemed to support the first view that we described. Therefore, we are inclined to accept the second interpretation and assume that the child generated all his sentences by either Rule (7) or (8).

These rules do not generate well-formed sentences according to adult grammar. The basic paradigm for adults is NP + Pred P, and neither Rule (7) nor Rule (8) results in this structure. However, Rules (7) and (8) are, roughly, the two halves of the basic adult pattern. With the exception of the initial pivot word, Rule (7) defines an NP, and Rule (8) produces the Pred P of adult grammar. Thus, although the rules of the child's grammar do not result in well-formed sentences, they do appear to generate major constituents of well-formed sentences. All the child lacks is the simultaneous application of both rules in the generation of a single sentence. This seems to have happened in about 15 per cent of the two-word sentences and in about 10 per cent of the three-word sentences recorded at Time 1. These are the percentages of NV (e.g., *Bambi go*), NNV (e.g., *Adam panda march*), and NVN (e.g., *Adam change diaper*) sentences. By this line of reasoning, we are led to conclude that the child's first grammatical productions are the NP's and Pred P's of adult grammar. Most often he produces them independently, though occasionally they are brought together to result in the skeleton of a well-formed sentence, and the child says NV, NNV, or NVN.

With time, of course, the frequency of NV, NNV, and NVN sentences increases. In part, this may result from the relaxation of some restrictions on performance. The child's growing memory span is a very good candidate here. But it is also possible that the basic NP + Pred P paradigm is not part of the child's earliest grammatical competence. He may still have to discover, after Rules (7) and (8) are within his repertoire, that in English they are to be used together. There is no way at present to decide this question.

Nonetheless, the facts now available are consistent with the view that the earliest grammatical constructions are at least noun and predicate phrases and, on occasion, possibly full sentences. The early appearance of the basic structures of adult grammar is a finding of considerable interest, since it gives some insight into what might be another aspect of the innate linguistic capacity of children.

If one tries to account for the origin of the NP or the Pred P in children's grammar, one immediately encounters a shroud of mystery. Expressions like "somehow" abound in the literature. The difficulty lies in describing a reasonable mechanism by which children might arrive at hierarchical structures. Imitation is obviously inappropriate because it cannot account for the emergence of a constituent with psychological unity, and that is what we are concerned with here. Appealing, as some do, to a child's "creative abilities" is too vague to be of much help. We want to explain these abilities if we can. Inference, or the formation of structures on the basis of analogy, is of little assistance either; there is nothing in overt speech to suggest a hierarchical arrangement of sentences, so it is difficult to see on what basis a child could draw an analogy. The only evidence available to a child is his parents' distribution of NP's or Pred P's in the same sentence positions as nouns or verbs. This *could* lead a child to imitate, but he would then be wedded to examples that his parents provided him, and the problem of productive and psychologically "real" hierarchical structures would not even be approached; we would still have no theory of what a child does to obtain these structures. Distributional evidence from parental speech can give a child nothing more than examples to imitate. The essential feature of hierarchical structures — that they are hierarchical — is abstract and completely unmarked in overt speech, yet children always discover these structures. In order to account for this feat, a principle fundamentally different from inference is required.

It has already been argued that knowledge of the hierarchy of categories directs children to discover the classes of adult grammar. The fact that all a child's early sentences seem to be produced by Rules (7) and (8) leads to a parallel hypothesis that the *basic grammatical relations* also are part of innate linguistic capacity.

The grammatical relations are the concepts "subject of a sentence — predicate of a sentence," "main verb of a predicate phrase — object of a predicate phrase," "modifier of a noun phrase — head noun of a noun phrase." Each relation is defined in terms of the deep structure of sentences, by which is meant that they exist in competence as configurations in underlying phrase markers. Thus the subject of a sentence is the NP immediately dominated by S; the predicate of a sentence is the Pred P immediately dominated by S; the object of a predicate phrase is the NP immediately dominated by Pred P; the main verb of a predicate phrase is the V immediately dominated by Pred P; the modifier of a noun phrase is the determiner immediately dominated by NP; the head noun of a noun phrase is the N immediately dominated by NP. By these definitions, each basic grammatical relation is uniquely specified by a configuration in the underlying phrase marker of a sentence. They account for the fact, for example, that native speakers of English can correctly distinguish subject from object in the pair of sentences *John is easy to please* and *John is eager to please,* which have identical surface structures but quite different base structures. The subject in both cases is the NP immediately dominated by S — an unspoken *someone* in the first sentence and *John* in the second, whereas the object is the NP immediately dominated by Pred P — *John* in the first case and an unspoken *someone* in the second (Katz and Postal, 1964).

Suppose that a child has these basic concepts as part of his biological endowment. Suppose that he knows, for example, what the relation is between main verb and object. Then we credit him with the realization that in order to have a noun, say *ball,* operated on by a verb, say *hit,* the two words must both be part of a single sentence constituent; and that if the noun and verb are not part of a single constituent, the meaning of the verb does not interact with the meaning of the noun. We can then see Rules (7) and (8) as inventions by the child that give the basic grammatical relations expression. They are the child's solution to the problem of exploiting the concepts of main verb, object of verb, etc. Rules (7) and (8), indeed, express the basic grammatical relations very economically. Rule (7) defines what a modifier and a head noun are, and Rule (8) defines main verb and object. Moreover, if we assume that children's competence includes using Rules (7) and (8) simultaneously, so as to generate NV, NNV, and NVN sentences, the two rules also define subject and predicate.

By assigning the basic grammatical relations a place in the child's innate linguistic endowment, we assume them to be universal. Greenberg (1963), in a survey of some thirty languages, has found these grammatical relations to hold in every case; there appears to be no language lacking such concepts. Thus a child who knew them could commence acquiring any natural language by striving to discover how each of these relations is expressed locally.

Brown's subject seems to have done this for English by Time 1. His sentences at this point show a perfect match with the patterns one would predict on the assumption that he was trying to express the grammatical relations. To appreciate the degree of constraint this places on a child's speech, consider the following arithmetic. As noted before, Brown's subject had three grammatical categories at Time 1: pivots, nouns, and verbs. There are $(3)^2 = 9$ different two-word sentences and $(3)^3 = 27$ different three-word sentences that can be constructed from these three classes. However, only four of the two-word sentences and eight of the three-word sentences are consistent with the basic grammatical relations; the remaining patterns are inadmissible from this point of view — and none of them occurs in the child's speech.

*TABLE 3   Sentence Patterns That Correspond to Basic Grammatical Relations*

| Child's Speech | | Corresponding Grammatical Relations |
|---|---|---|
| Pattern | Frequency | |
| P + N | 23 | modifier, head noun |
| N + N | 115 | modifier, head noun, subject, predicate |
| V + N | 162 | main verb, object |
| N + V | 49 | subject, predicate |
| Sum | 349 | |
| P + N + N | 3 | modifier, head noun |
| N + P + N | 1 | subject, predicate, modifier, head noun |
| V + P + N | 3 | main verb, object, modifier, head noun |
| V + N + N | 29 | main verb, object, modifier, head noun |
| P + N + V | 1 | subject, predicate, modifier, head noun |
| N + N + V | 1 | subject, predicate, modifier, head noun |
| N + V + N | 4 | main verb, object, subject, predicate |
| N + N + N | 7 | subject, predicate, modifier, head noun |
| Sum | 49 | |

In Table 3 are all the sentences that express the basic grammatical relations under Rules (7) and (8). Opposite each is the frequency of the pattern in the corpus of Brown's subject at Time 1. As the frequency distribution shows, sentences of every admissible type appeared in the child's corpus. This fact is not conclusive, of course, since we would expect most patterns to appear in a large sample of speech from a child who is trying out combinations at random. However, there is the additional fact that all the child's sentences had these patterns; there were no others. The entries in Table 3 include the child's whole corpus at Time 1. Thus the child seems to confine his efforts to sentences that express the grammatical relations, but within these limits he tries every possibility.

It might appear that a child's sentences would reveal the patterns in Table 3 almost as a matter of course, perhaps even through imitation, since each pattern is present in adult speech. The difficulty is that there are many other two- and three-word patterns in adult speech as well, none of which correspond to the basic grammatical relations. A verb-verb-noun sequence, for example, is contained in *come and eat your Pablum;* however, VVN is not consistent with the basic grammatical relations, and it does not appear in the speech of Brown's child. Such inadmissible patterns, although presented to a child in abundance, are either suppressed or ignored — presumably because a child looks for ways to exemplify the basic grammatical relations.

Throughout Table 3, it has been assumed that a child can apply Rules (7) and (8) together. Without this assumption we would lose NV, NNV, NVN sentences, as well as the relation of subject and predicate. Striking these sentence types from the record would reduce the size of the corpus, but it would not change the perfect agreement between the basic grammatical relations and the sentence types that the child produced. Another assumption that has been made is that pivot words never stand alone in a child's speech. This seems to have been true of every child studied. The assumption eliminates such patterns as PVN (e.g., *that bounce ball*) as admissible expressions of the basic grammatical relations. Finally, it has been assumed that verbs can be omitted from Pred P's, as in *Adam two boot,* which to most adults means *Adam has two boots.* This assumption accounts for NN, NPN, and NNN as patterns all corresponding to the subject-predicate relation.

We can now return to LAD and summarize what is known about the process of acquisition. We have said, following Katz (1966) and

Chomsky (1965), that the internal structure of LAD consists of the various linguistic universals, both substantive and formal. We pointed out that the hierarchy of categories is a substantive universal. So now are the basic grammatical relations. Undoubtedly, more universals than these two make up the internal structure of LAD; however, we can be most clear about the two that have been discussed, and attention will be restricted to them.

We can imagine LAD going about its assigned task roughly as follows. Two things are done simultaneously, both of which make possible the remarkable "induction of latent structure" that numerous psycholinguists have observed in children. LAD receives a certain amount of preliminary linguistic data which it scans for distinctions that match the distinctions drawn in the universal hierarchy of categories. Because LAD is exposed to a natural language, some of the universal distinctions are bound to be present. Thus, we can imagine that whenever LAD observes such a distinction in the preliminary linguistic data, it is incorporated into LAD's own version of the underlying grammar. The function of the preliminary data, therefore, is to give LAD a basis for selecting among various universal distinctions. The function of the universal hierarchy of categories is to organize the preliminary linguistic data. Moreover, because it is a hierarchy of categories, distinctions can be drawn successively, and LAD embarks upon its career by differentiating gross categories to obtain refined ones.

At the same time, LAD searches the preliminary linguistic data for sentence patterns that correspond to the basic grammatical relations. Presumably LAD recognizes them within limits set by the grammatical categories it has differentiated, so LAD's activity here is not independent of what it does with the universal hierarchy of categories. Each pattern in the preliminary linguistic data that corresponds to a basic grammatical relation will suggest one or another hierarchical structure to LAD. However, the basic grammatical relations leave open only a few possibilities, so LAD has a very good chance to hit on the locally appropriate structures soon after it begins to collect data. It is committed to the NP + Pred P format for sentences, and within this limit there are only two possible orders of constituents: (NP + Pred P) and (Pred P + NP). There are only two possibilities for Pred P: (V + NP) and (NP + V). Likewise, if LAD has only pivot and noun classes, there are just two variants of

NP: (P + N) and (N + P), plus a third, (N + N), where order is irrelevant. LAD must discover from the preliminary linguistic data the particular orders of constituents used in its local language. Distributional evidence of various sorts could be useful at this point, and a certain amount of hypothesis-testing will become necessary. That is, LAD's first choice may not predict later sentences. However, the only possible error, if this hypothesis is correct, is inversion — for example, using Pred P + NP for S when trying to learn English. This inversion is, in fact, a common pattern in early speech — cf., *allgone shoe* in Braine's subject. However, LAD does not have to discover from the preliminary linguistic data the fundamental fact that hierarchical structures exist; that is implied — indeed, required — by the definitions of the basic grammatical relations.

The role of the preliminary linguistic data in acquisition, therefore, is essentially directional. They help LAD to choose among a narrow set of possibilities defined by the linguistic universals. To quote Katz (1966, p. 278, fn. 28), ". . . the role of experience is primarily to provide the data against which predictions and thus hypotheses are judged. Experience serves not to provide the things to be copied by the mind, as on the empiricist's account, but to help eliminate false hypotheses about the rules of the language." LAD must be equipped with knowledge of just those specific aspects of linguistic competence that cannot be extracted from overt speech, namely, appropriate generic grammatical classes and hierarchical structures. (There are other requirements that have not been discussed; for a more extensive discussion, see Katz, 1966.) We might turn this assertion around and say that languages *have* deep features, unmarked in overt speech, precisely because children (like LAD) have the specific linguistic capacities that correspond to them. A language with different features would be unlearnable by LAD and, presumably, by children. The evolution of language so as to include particular universal features, therefore, is necessarily tied to the linguistic capacities of language learners.

It has already been argued that adults can interpret the speech of children because it is, in effect, at some intermediate level of grammaticality; the reasoning there had to do with the hierarchy of categories through which children move. We have in the basic grammatical relations another reason that adults find children's speech interpretable: all children's sentences are generated by simple rules — or their inversions — that also exist in adult grammar. Indeed, the basic grammatical relations and the hierarchy of categories, taken together, almost guarantee that everything children say can be understood by adults (problems of pronunciation aside, that being a different matter), even though the speech is very telegraphic. Every sentence will be constructed by rules something like (7) and (8) operating on classes generically related to classes of adult grammar. Children's sentences, in fact, are semigrammatical and exactly comparable to the examples from Chomsky that we saw above. This fact has important consequences for the reaction of adults to child speech: it makes possible "expansions" of child speech into completely well-formed English. Expansions often occur in child-parent dialogues, and they may be an important source of information by which children choose among the possibilities offered by the linguistic universals. Expansions have been discussed by Brown (1964); we return to them later when we take up the role of parental speech in acquisition.

Early speech of children, so much as we have seen of it, reflects a severely limited grammatical competence. They have a few grammatical classes, which are used in simple hierarchical rules, and the rules reflect the basic grammatical relations; there is little else. However, it is important to note that these aspects of children's competence — classes, rules, and relations — are all properties of the base structure of sentences. On the other hand, children's earliest speech does not reflect the operation of transformational rules; those seem to come into children's grammar only later. Full adult competence includes semantic interpretation of base structures to obtain meaning, transformations of base structures to obtain surface structures, and phonological interpretation of surface structures to obtain a representation of speech. Therefore, it is not too unreasonable to think of children "talking" base strings directly. We can conceive of their phonological rules as interpreting base structures rather than surface structure in the generation of sentences. Children, according to this view, begin their grammatical careers with the part of syntax that is necessary to semantic interpretation and only later attach the grammatical machinery that in mature grammar provides input to phonological interpretation. This hypothesis might, in part, account for the widespread impression that children's early speech is exclusively semantic, an assertion that overlooks the features of the base structure that are present in children's early competence but is correct in that the relation between sound and meaning is much more rigid and (in a way) immediate for children than it is for adults. The often noted identification of the sound of a word and its meaning, which seems to be most typical of children, might be another aspect of this condition.

An interpretation of Vygotsky's (1962) concept of inner speech is suggested by this view of early competence. If phonological rules apply to deep structure directly, it should be difficult to avoid saying whatever you think. The privacy of inner speech may be afforded by the existence of transformational rules; and until they are added to the grammar, inner speech would not occur. That situation is roughly what Vygotsky observed in young children. Perhaps, therefore, these children were pretransformational, not necessarily excessively social, as Vygotsky thought. Vygotsky said that inner speech is "speech almost without words," made up almost entirely of psychological predicates. The fact that inner speech is almost without words would follow naturally from the assumption that it consists of the untransformed base structure of sentences. In fact, inner speech should be completely without words because phonological interpretation is not applied directly to base structures for mature speakers. However, Vygotsky's claim that inner speech is largely reduced to predication is harder to account for; perhaps, like some early sentences from children, inner speech generally follows Rule (8).

One conclusion implicit in all the preceding paragraphs is sufficiently important to be made explicit. If children begin their productive linguistic careers with a competence limited to the base structure of sentences, it is difficult to see how it can be explained by any theory of language acquisition that restricts attention to what a child might obtain from the observable surface characteristics of parental speech. Such theories would have to predict the opposite course of development: first, surface structure; then, base structure. Most behaviorist theories have assumed this order, with notable lack of success; failure is inevitable when children produce only the base structure, and behaviorist theories produce only the surface structure of sentences. What is needed is either a child who commences acquisition with surface structure or a theory that focuses on base structure. Since it is easier to change theories than children, the latter course has been followed here.

A widely accepted generalization about languages is that there is a close connection between phonology and syntax, especially in the imposition of intonation contours. The existence of this connection has caused some psycholinguists to suggest that intonation — which is observable in speech — might be the vehicle on which children arrive at the rudiments of syntax. At first glance this is a plausible view. In its favor is the fact that children, even before the first birthday, imitate intonation contours in parental speech. There is also the fact that early grammatical speech is telegraphic in that it leaves out the unstressed elements of well-formed sentences, thus indicating that children are sensitive to intonation differences. However, this view can be questioned on logical grounds. Lieberman (1965) compared the ability of linguists to transcribe the intonation contours of real speech with their ability to transcribe physically identical contours of simulated speech that consisted of a single prolonged vowel sound. He found that linguists' transcriptions matched the actual physical contour only on the simulated speech. When the linguists transcribed real speech, the actual and the perceived intonation contours often differed strikingly, which suggests that structure is an important source of information about perceived intonation but not vice versa. A prelingual child listening to adult speech is in a position comparable to Lieberman's linguists transcribing a simulated vowel. He is not comparable to Lieberman's linguists transcribing real speech. Infants could note only the physical contour in parental speech, not the perceived contour that is correlated with grammatical structure. It is difficult, therefore, to see how intonation could guide a child to syntax; for no matter how strong the tendency is for children to imitate speech they receive from their parents, they will not imitate the appropriate feature unless important parts of the syntax have already been acquired.

## GROWTH OF TRANSFORMATIONS

If children's earliest syntactic competence comprises the base structure of sentences, then obviously the major portion of syntactic acquisition after this point will be taken up with the growth of transformations. We know little about this phase of development aside from the fact that transformations appear relatively late in a child's career. The late appearance of transformations, of course, is one reason that we know little about them. Most projects have not yet continued long enough to cover the period during which transformations develop. However, one study of two children has recently been completed by

Bellugi (1964). Her work — while limited to negation — is the only complete history of the development of transformations that is familiar to this writer, although scattered bits and pieces have been described by Ervin (1964), and Menyuk (1963, 1964) has published the results of several surveys.

To discover the exact point at which a child's grammar contains transformational rules is a difficult, obscure problem. In the case of negation, we are probably safe in assuming that the earliest sentences with negative import are not generated by transformational rules. Rather they seem more like base-structure sentences with an underlying negative morpheme that the child pronounces. Bellugi gives such examples as *no wipe finger, not fit, no singing song, no drop mitten.* These sentences probably were produced by simply prefixing *no* or *not* to Rule (8), hence, their close relation to base structure. However, they are superficially similar to some adult sentences of different structure, for example, *no, I don't want it.* Nonetheless, we can be fairly sure that a child's early negatives are not modeled on these adult negatives. The adult sentence has a terminal contour over *no* and interposes a juncture (pause) between *no* and the rest of the sentence; that is, the comma is spoken. The child's sentences, on the other hand, are produced without the contour or juncture, so we may assume that they have a different structure from *no, I don't want it.* If the child's sentences were comparable with the adults', we would expect *no, no wipe fingers, no, not fit,* etc.

We see here, in a child's untransformed negative sentences, an example of what appears to be a quite general phenomenon in the development of language. It is the appearance in child speech of forms analogous to adult forms but with very different structure. In some cases, as in the present one, we feel confident that the child's form is essentially the base structure on which the transformation will ultimately operate. Perhaps this is always the case, although we cannot invariably tell. But regardless of that, the analogy of form raises a difficult question; namely, why do transformations develop? In part, the task of this section will be to seek an answer to that question.

Bellugi divides the growth of the negative system into four periods. The essentials of the first period (roughly Time 1) are what we have just seen. The only other feature at this point is a rudimentary negative question (NQ), *why not?* Since *why* appears in no other context, the pairs of words, *why not,* probably are a single vocabulary item for the child. On the other hand, *why not* seems to be a construction. The *?* makes the difference. A rising intonation is the child's only form of query at this time, and he applies it to any declarative sentence, as in *that Urler suitcase?* Thus NQ, even at this early stage, can be broken into two parts: negation (*why not*) and query (*?*), in much the fashion of the adult's NQ transformation (Miller, 1962; Mehler, 1963). Again, however, a child's sentences have a form appropriate to the base structure of English grammar; the rising intonation, *?,* seems to result from direct application of phonological rules to a base structure that we can regard as containing a query morpheme Q. The NQ does not come from application of either a negative or a query transformation. Period 1, therefore, appears to be pretransformational.

Period 2, which comes some three to six months later, depending on the child, still contains no sign of transformations. There is, nonetheless, a considerable flowering of negative forms. Some typical sentences from Period 2 are

> I can't see you
> I don't sit on Cromer coffee
>
> why not cracker can't talk
> why not you looking right place
>
> don't leave me
> don't wake me up again
>
> that no fish school
> there no squirrels
>
> no Rusty hat
> no square . . . is clown

Some of these (*no Rusty hat, no square . . . is clown*) are identical to the negative declarative sentences of Period 1 (*no wipe finger*). The child continues to "print out" the base structure of a negative sentence. But now there is also a set of sentences with auxiliary verbs (*I don't see you, I don't sit on Cromer coffee,* etc.). In adult grammar these are all formed by transformations. It is doubtful, however, that that is the history of the child's sentences, for these auxiliaries appear only in negative form. He does not yet say *can* or *do* plus verb. It is more likely, therefore, that *can't* and *don't* are independent vocabulary items included in the child's speech by the same rules that produce *I*, or *see*, or *you*.

Negative questions also appear to follow the same principles as in Period 1 except that *why not* is now produced together with negative sentences, giving such examples as *why not cracker can't talk?* Again, there is no indication of a transformational rule. The child simply seems to have taken the NQ of Period 1 and joined it to the negative declarative of Period 2. The fact that he produces a double negative is good evidence that NQ is a construction. Double negatives are absent from the speech of the child's parents.

*That no fish school* seems to be a telegraphic version of a negative copular sentence. It is produced by Rules (7) and (8) together, supplemented by *no* (or *not,* in some cases), and again does not involve a transformation.

Finally, there are negative imperatives (*don't leave me*) which, as far as negation is concerned, are free of transformations. (The imperative itself, however, might be a transformation; it is difficult to account for the deletion of the subject, *you,* on other grounds. See Katz and Postal, 1964, and Katz, 1966, for a discussion of this point.)

In sum, the negative sentences of Period 2 still appear to result directly from the base structure. In this respect they are not different from the sentences of Period 1. In Period 2, however, the negative system is more complex than before. Compared to the simple NQ and *no* of Period 1, we now have negatives being used in five different and unrelated grammatical settings: they co-occur with Rule (7) and Rule (8); they appear in imperatives; they come up as separate vocabulary (*don't* and *can't*); and they occur as *why not* plus negative sentence to form the NQ. The situation is cumbersome and inelegant, two characteristics that might lead to the events of Period 3.

Period 3 is again three to six months later, depending on the child. It includes such sentences as the following:

> no, it isn't
> no, I don't have a book
>
> I can't see it
> I don't want cover on it
>
> that not a clown
> I am not a doctor

> I not crying
> that not turning
>
> why I didn't see something?
> why he don't know how to pretend?
>
> you don't want some supper
> I didn't see something
>
> don't touch the fish
> don't put the two wings on

If we characterize a child's negative system as before, we are confronted with even more diversity, cumbersomeness, and inelegance. Negation appears in full adult form — with terminal contour and juncture — in *no, it isn't*. It continues to appear in the form of *can't* and *don't,* as in *I can't see it.* However, now *can* also occurs as an auxiliary verb in the child's sentences (*I can do it*), so we have grounds for assuming that *-n't* is a negative element in its own right. Negation appears in copular sentences, sometimes with a form of the verb *be* (*I am not a doctor*), sometimes not (*that not a clown*). The verb *be* thus appears to be an option for the child. Also, there are telegraphic versions of *be*-auxiliary sentences that contain the negative (*I not crying*). In this case, however, *be* is never included, so the environment for negation differs in auxiliary and copular sentences. Negative questions are changed from Period 2; in fact, they are only an inversion away from the full adult form (*why I didn't see something?*), the formula *why not* now having disappeared. This (temporarily) eliminates double negatives from the child's speech. Negation is used for the first time with an indefinite determiner and pronoun: *you don't want some sugar, I didn't see something.* These are parallel to affirmative sentences with the same determiner and pronoun (*you want some supper, I see something*), and all these sentences probably are generated by the same rules that produce *I can see it* and *I can't see it.* Finally negative imperatives (*don't touch the fish*) continue unchanged and in adult form from Period 2.

In all, negatives appear in seven different environments. Considered superficially these require seven (or, taking determiners and pronouns as instances of the negative declarative, six) different rules. The child's mind appears to be a clutter of special cases.

However, there are reasons to believe that the child's sentence-gen-

erating rules are not as we have just described them. Sentences such as
*no wipe finger, no Rusty hat,* and *not fit* have disappeared altogether
by Period 3. We interpreted these sentences to be the result of the child
applying his phonological rules directly to the base structure. Assuming this interpretation to be correct, the fact that these sentences have
disappeared suggests that the child is now transforming the base structure and applying his phonological rules to the resulting surface structure. Thus a fundamental change may have taken place in the system
of negation by Period 3. For the first time the child may use transformational rules for negation and so produce sentences with both a
base and surface structure. It is significant then that we have in Period
3 the first evidence of an auxiliary transformation, as evidenced by
affirmative sentences with *can* (e.g., *I can see it*).

It is not at all clear what form a statement of these transformational
rules should take. A transformation to handle auxiliaries is clearly
necessary; five of the seven settings for the negative involve one or
another of them. A rule to reposition the negative element (which is
usually preposed in early speech, as in *no drop mitten,* as well as in the
base structure of negative sentences in the adult grammar) becomes
necessary once an auxiliary transformation is established. This rule is
involved in every negative sentence and accounts for the nonoccurrence
of such strings as *no I can see it,* pronounced without contour and
pause.

We could try to write explicit transformational rules for the child's
speech in Period 3, but the effort seems to require so many arbitrary
decisions that we shall forgo it. Nonetheless, we can consider an example of what these rules would be like. Assuming that the child has the
two transformations mentioned, auxiliary and negative-repositioning, we can give the following derivation of *you don't want some supper*
(Bellugi, 1965): first the phrase marker, which is shown in Figure 4.

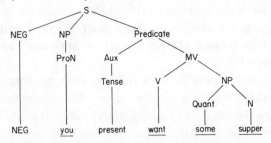

Fɪɢ. 4. Base structure of the sentence, *you don't want some supper.*

We have assumed that in Periods 1 and 2, phrase markers of the type in Figure 4 were directly interpreted by phonological rules. Since those sentences seemed to be generated by Rule (8) alone and also did not use *some,* we could delete both the determiner and the subject from this phrase marker and come out with *not want supper,* thus duplicating the child's performance in the first two periods.

In Period 3, however, the child can apply at least two transformations. Negative-repositioning carries

$$\text{NEG} - you - \text{present} - want - some - supper$$

into

$$you - \text{present} - \text{NEG} - want - some - supper$$

and the auxiliary rule introduces *do,* so that we have

$$you - do + \text{present} - \text{NEG} - want - some - supper.$$

This is the surface structure of the underlying phrase marker in Figure 4. It is interpreted by phonological rules, and we obtain the child's sentence *you don't want some supper.* (The + here signifies that the phonological rules cause *do* to incorporate "present"; it is a different operation than simple concatenation, represented here by a dash.)

Period 4 includes such sentences as:

> I can't push it back and forth
> I hope he won't bother you
>
> you don't like to be rolled into clay
> it's doesn't fall out
>
> that duck isn't a very good driver
> I am not a toy
>
> I can't do nothing with no string
> nobody won't recognize us
>
> why it won't go up?
> why I didn't live in Italy?
>
> don't cry
> don't do it on me
>
> did I didn't mean to?
> do she don't need that one?

observed by C. Chomsky, in phases of transition to incorporate a greater number of forms.

60                                         David McNeill

The reappearance of double negatives in these sentences is striking. They had occurred in Period 2, dropped out in Period 3, and came back again in Period 4. (We shall consider the cause of this oscillation in the next paragraph.) Otherwise, the child's speech of Period 4 continues the new developments of Period 3 — the disappearance of directly spoken base structures and the presence of some transformations. One new phenomenon is the appearance of auxiliaries at two places in question (*did I didn't mean to?*), which confirms the suggestion that NQ is formed in two steps by the child. He has one auxiliary for Q (*did I . . .*) and another for N (*. . . I didn't . . .*); he simply puts them together to get NQ.

The double negatives of Period 2 were the result of the way in which the child formed NQ: *why not* + negative declarative. In Period 3, *why not* was replaced by a simple *why* in the NQ, and with this change the double negative necessarily disappeared. The double negatives of Period 4 have a different basis. They all involve indefinite pronouns and determiners built around *no* (*nobody* and *nothing,* in the example above, as well as *never* and *not*). Thus we get such sentences as *nobody won't recognize us* and the truly monstrous *I can't do nothing with no string*. At the same time, *some* as a determiner and pronoun has dropped out. The double negatives of Period 4 are thus an automatic result of the child's changing system of rules.

No doubt the double and triple negatives of Period 4 are a way station in a child's progress to the complete negative system. Among adults, the various indefinite and indeterminate pronouns are so interrelated by transformational rules (Klima, 1964) that the indeterminant pronouns built on *some* (e.g., *something*) can be changed into indefinite pronouns built on *any* (e.g., *anything*), which in turn can be changed into indeterminate pronouns built on *no* (e.g., *nothing*). The order of derivation is relevant to the structure of the negative system over-all and so presumably reflects something about adult competence. One suggestive hypothesis about development is that the order of rules in a transformational grammar is at the same time the order of their acquisition by children. However, this does not seem to be true of the pronouns and determiners of the negation system. The first of these (*something*) appears in the child's speech only to be replaced by another (*nothing*), so possibly the *some* pronouns and the *no* pronouns are connected for the child in some way. It is difficult to guess what this connection is, but at least we can see that the child's route to adult competence is not the derivational part that adults follow. The derivational order for adults is *something → anything → nothing*, whereas the developmental order for children is *something → nothing → anything*. Moreover, since *something* disappears when *nothing* comes in, the child is not simply adding transformational rules in order; if he were doing that, *something* and *nothing* should both appear in his sentences at Period 4. In short, order of acquisition does not anticipate order of application. Rather, a child appears to build up his transformational competence by successive approximations, passing through several steps that are not yet English but are, nonetheless, transformational.

What causes a child to develop transformations? Since transformations do not affect the semantic content of sentences, their growth cannot be ascribed to some desire to express, say, the concept of negation. Moreover, in the case of that particular transformation, we found the child in possession of the appropriate semantic apparatus before he had any transformational rules at all. What, then, propels the child to devise sophisticated rules such as negative-repositioning or the auxiliary transformation?

The answer reflects a basic fact about language acquisition that goes beyond the transformations themselves. It is convenient, however, to introduce the argument first in terms of transformational rules and point out the implications for other departments of language acquisition later.

At Period 2, the child's negation system did not appear to involve transformational rules. Instead, negation was derived directly from the base structure in five independent grammatical settings. We characterized this system as cumbersome and inelegant. These adjectives would apply with even more force in Period 3 except that, by then, the child showed signs of using transformational rules. That is, and this is the point, the transformations achieved some economy of rules for the child. Rather than seven (or six) different rules for placing the negative, the child has only two — both transformations.

A child seems to operate like a professional grammarian who takes advantage of the fact that transformations are intrinsically more powerful than base-structure rules and so can express grammatical relations more economically. The pressure — or, if you prefer, the motivation — to devise transformation rules may come from the cognitive clutter that results from not having them. In Period 1, the child had to remember only two rules for the placement of the negative. In Period 2, he had to remember five. By Period 3, if it were not for the transformations, he would have had to remember six or seven. It is possible, then, that the load on the child's memory by Period 2 was so great that the two transformational rules we observe in Period 3 were precipitated. The pressure here to change must be considerable. The child needs to process sentences in short intervals of time; presumably it takes less time and a child tends to forget less when the placement of the negative is done by transformational rules rather than by independent base-structure rules.

This hypothesis, of course, is not complete. It provides a motive for the development of transformations that is purely aversive. We can suppose that a child wants to escape the mess into which his base-structure grammar places him, but escape to where? By now, this is a familiar problem. Once again we can appeal to linguistic universals to guide the child. This time we must evoke formal universals: some will specify the general form that base-structure rules, such as Rules (7) and (8), must take; others will describe in a general way the form of transformations. One part of the formal universals pertaining to transformations presumably would be a characterization of appropriate input, viz., a phrase marker from the base structure. Thus the clutter of special-purpose rules in Period 2 would present exactly the conditions a child would need to formulate transformational rules — providing that he knew roughly the format of transformations and the fact that they take base structure as input.

This basic schema — developing the simplest possible grammar, experiencing pressure from too many special cases, reducing the pressure by resorting to new grammatical devices that accord with the linguistic universals — can be applied to all the steps of language acquisition that we have discussed so far. In so doing, we can raise the problem of the motivation for language development.

## WHY DOES CHILD LANGUAGE CHANGE?

The earliest vocalizations of infants and the evolution of babbling during the first year of life are matters of maturation (Lenneberg, forthcoming), and the original impetus to language acquisition probably lies in this maturational process. However, our interests are now in the developments that take place after the child first begins to produce single-word utterances; we may take it for granted that the child is already moving in the direction of language by this time. The problem we shall consider is analogous to the one discussed with the transformations: the child always moves on to a new system, even though his original system appears to meet the purely functional purpose of expressing his needs, desires, and interests. From a strictly functional point of view, there would seem to be little reason for child language to change.

Let us assume that compiling a sentence dictionary would be one way to meet the requirement that linguistic competence include the ability to assign semantic interpretations to sentences. If we were to undertake this, we would try to construct a list of all the simple sentences of English and pair them with their interpretations. However, such a dictionary, while feasible in theory, would not be possible in practice. There are simply too many grammatical sentences that must be included. In this light, the semantic theory described by Katz and Fodor (1963) and Katz and Postal (1964) can be regarded as a substitute for the dictionary; it has the same effect as a sentence dictionary but not the same bulk (Miller, personal communication).

Children between the ages of twelve months and eighteen to twenty-four months produce only one-word utterances. Most often these are nouns in adult grammar, but verbs and adjectives appear in some numbers also. Many observers consider these single-word utterances to be "holophrastic," by which is meant that each word has a much broader and more diffuse meaning for a child than it does for adults (McCarthy, 1954). In effect, holophrastic words stand for sentences. The utterance "milk," for example, can mean for a one-year-old "I want some milk," "The milk is on the floor," "Don't give me any more milk; I want Pablum," etc. A range of meanings, at least, is the impression one gets from the range of circumstances in which a child produces these single-word utterances. If they are holophrastic, it is conceivable that these utterances indicate that the child is trying to construct a sentence dictionary in which each word corresponds to a sentence interpretation.

But if that is the case, why do children change? If each word expresses the meaning of a whole sentence, why abandon this simplicity for the contraptions of English syntax where the same content is expressed in a more complex manner? There might be two reasons. One is that the child is constantly adding words to his vocabulary, and soon the list becomes too long; it is the same difficulty that causes us to reject a sentence dictionary in semantic theory. It is true that a child's vocabulary increases from one or two words when he is a year old to approximately 200 words by the time he is two years old (Smith, 1926). However, this number is not yet so great as to force a child to abandon his lexicographic project; no matter what grammatical developments occur, he will still need a dictionary. Indeed, he will have to increase it further by a very large factor. So it cannot be the number of entries that motivates him to change his strategy. A second factor is probably more important. In the beginning, each entry, although it sounds like a word to adults, is a sentence for the child, which means that each entry actually has a great number of different interpretations, is highly ambiguous, and can only be "disambiguated" by knowledge of its context. If we measure memory load, not in terms of the number of entries but in terms of the number of interpretations, a child would have to remember if he persisted in his attempt to construct a holophrastic dictionary, then the size of the project would actually be much greater than it might seem and communication efficiency would be impaired by its intrinsic ambiguity. By resorting to a word dictionary supplemented by syntactic and semantic rules, a child not only reduces the number of interpretations he will eventually have to remember, but he also gains precision of expression by increasing the variety of his sentences and thus decreases the over-all ratio of interpretations per sentence.

According to this view, a driving force behind language development is the rapidly growing variety of semantic interpretations for which the child must find some means of differentiation and expression. (A similar idea has been under development by Gloria Cooper [personal communication].) A holophrastic dictionary fails both on grounds of size and ambiguity; a sentence dictionary fails on grounds of size; a word dictionary supplemented by syntactic and semantic rules provides the eventual solution. If we imagine a child beginning with a holophrastic dictionary, shifting to a sentence dictionary for greater precision, and finally shifting to a word dictionary to reduce the memory load as his vocabulary grows, then we would expect to find initially a very intimate relation between sound and meaning that would first give way to mediation by simple base structures of the syntax and ultimately to mediation by the whole complex structure of transformational grammar. This is, of course, exactly the sequence that has been described in the preceding pages.

To say that a need for precision and cognitive economy motivates the developmental sequence is not to explain how a child is able to meet these needs or why he chooses the particular manner of meeting them that he does. For this we can only appeal to the child's innate *faculté de langage*. Since all languages have this general structure and since all children seem able to acquire its local manifestation in their own communities, we assume that this ability is part of a child's natural endowment as a human being. This claim is much stronger than most empiricists would care to make, but nothing less seems adequate to account for the facts as they are known at the present time.

## THE ROLE OF PARENTAL SPEECH IN LANGUAGE ACQUISITION

We have said that parental speech serves the function of helping a child to choose among a narrow set of possibilities defined by the linguistic universals. The basic grammatical relations, for example, commit a child to an NP + Pred P format for sentences, but they leave the order of these constituents unspecified; it might be NP + Pred P or Pred P + NP, and a child must discover which it is from parental speech. The role of parental speech is essentially directional; it provides a child with some basis for choosing among the options offered by the linguistic universals. The purpose of this section is to discuss what is known about this process of choice.

There are many points in grammar at which we might study the role played by parental speech. We could, for example, look at a child's decision to use NP + Pred P rather than Pred P + NP; or we could examine the pairing of words with entries in the dictionary as a child develops his lexicon; or we could study a child's discovery of the significance of the distinction between mass and count nouns in English, etc. Indeed, parental speech will play the role of arbitrating choice at every point in acquisition, for it is probably true that linguistic universals never so determine competence that there are no alternatives open to a child. The basic grammatical relations — where evidence from parental speech must decide between just two possibilities — probably represents the maximum degree of constraint imposed by the universals. Elsewhere the degree of constraint appears to be less. One such case is the acquisition of noun and verb inflections in English. The importance of linguistic universals in a child's learning to use these inflections is probably not less than in the development of hierarchical rules, but the number of possibilities consistent with the universals is much larger. In the case of the plural inflection on nouns, for example, any number of phonemes situated anywhere on a word would be consistent with the universal requirements that phonemes must be constructed out of distinctive features and that the rules for adding plural inflections to sentences must correspond to the formal universals. Given these universals, there is still an enormous number of possibilities from which a child must choose, including the option of not marking plurality in the surface structure at all. Thus we might expect that the use a child makes of parental speech would be more obvious, since parental speech must perform a larger task in acquiring noun and verb inflections than in acquiring the NP + Pred P order for sentences. It is fortunate, therefore, that much of the recent work on language acquisition has focused on precisely this problem.

Two techniques have been commonly employed to study the development of noun and verb inflections. One is simply to note the occurrence of inflections in a child's speech. With such data we can inquire whether regular or irregular forms appear first, whether the order of appearance of inflections corresponds to the frequency with which they are used in speech, etc. The other technique is to introduce a child to nonsense nouns, verbs, and the like, to see if he can apply inflectional rules to "words" that are completely novel, ones for which there are no parental models. The advantage of the second technique is that it eliminates the possibility that a child will place an inflection appropriately merely by imitating parental speech. As always, we are interested in the productive use of linguistic forms, but so long as actual words are used to test a child's grasp of inflectional rules, correct performance through imitation is always a theoretical possibility. The fact that a child says *glasses* does not necessarily indicate that the rule for forming plural nouns is part of linguistic competence. There are other ways to assure ourselves that children have productive inflectional rules, the main one being the occurrence of systematic errors (e.g., *foots*), but the introduction of nonsense words is one of the easiest techniques to use.

Berko (1958), in a well-known paper, was the first to study children's inflectional rules by introducing the children to nonsense words. She presented four- and five-year-old children with monosyllables such as *wug,* saying "Here is a *wug;* now there are two of them; there are two ———— ," her voice trailing off, hoping to elicit from the child the plural, *wugs.* If that is what she got, the child would be credited with knowledge of the inflectional rule that governs the addition of plurals to nouns. To test for verb inflection, she might have said, "Here is a man who knows how to *wug;* today he is *wugging;* yesterday he ————," looking for the past tense, *wugged.* In general, Berko found that most four- and five-year-olds had mastered the inflectional rules of English, though her five-year-olds did better on most items than her four-year-olds, so some growth continues as late as age five.

Although Berko's results show that four- and five-year-old children have largely mastered the inflectional rules of English, her findings indicate nothing about how acquisition proceeds. For this, we must turn to studies where the development of individual children is followed over time. It is in the emergence of noun and verb inflections that we can see the role played by parental speech in acquisition.

## The Role of Overt Practice

The assumption that practice somehow plays a determinative role in language acquisition is, perhaps, the original psycholinguistic theory. It has figured in one or another psychological speculation since at least the 1920's (e.g., Allport, 1924), and the tradition continues unbroken, though not unmodified, up to the present time (e.g., Jenkins and Palermo, 1964). The basic assertion in all such theories is always that there exists a fundamental continuity between language acquisition and the forms of learning studied in the psychological laboratory. This view has been questioned on general grounds by Miller (1965). However, our concern is now more specific: does practice theory characterize what children do in order to find the locally appropriate expression of the linguistic universals? This question, it should be noted, already represents a considerable reduction in the customary scope of practice theory. Some authors seem to believe that all of language acquisition can be attributed to the gradual strengthening of responses. It is clear, however, that this sanguine view is condemned to frustration, for there are no responses to be strengthened in the base structure of language, and in any case, practice theory cannot explain how a child bridges the gap between elevated response strength and linguistic competence. But it is conceivable that practice is important within the restricted portion of language acquisition that has to do with the discovery of the locally appropriate expression of the linguistic universals. Perhaps a child is able to integrate into his innate linguistic competence just those surface features that have developed some degree of response strength. One hypothesis, therefore, is that response strength is a child's criterion for choosing among the possibilities offered by the linguistic universals.

Any version of practice theory, including the one just suggested, rests on two fundamental assumptions. One is actually the basic assertion of all such theories, the assumption that linguistic forms can be strengthened by practice. The other is that the forms that a child practices are novel in his grammar. The consequences of both assumptions are important. Suppose, for example, that practice does not strengthen a child's grip on linguistic forms; then the value of practice (as a criterion, or whatever) would be completely lost. Suppose, on the other hand, that practiced forms are not novel, that a child practices only forms that have arrived in his grammar from some source other than practice; then the effects of practice, however great they may be in strengthening responses, cannot cause a child's grammar to change. This second assumption — that practiced forms are novel to a child's grammar — is the familiar theory that acquisition proceeds through imitation. It is only through imitation that practice could influence the introduction of new forms into a child's grammar. Obviously, a child could not *acquire* a form by spontaneously practicing it; in that case the form has already been acquired. We can evaluate the hypothesis that a child enlarges his grammar by imitating adults by inquiring whether imitations contain features of adult grammar that are otherwise absent from a child's speech. Ervin (1964) has made this comparison for the imitations of five children. For each child, she compared the spontaneous imitations in her records to the grammars written from her subjects' unimitated free speech. She found that imitations and free speech were identical for every subject except one, and in this case imitations were grammatically more primitive. The children's imitations were not, as Ervin put it, "grammatically progressive." If a child was not producing the progressive inflection, for example, he would not imitate it: *Adam is running fast* might be imitated as *Adam run* or *run fast* but not as *Adam running* or *running fast*. In short, children assimilated the adult models to their current grammars; when there was no place for -*ing* in the grammar, -*ing* did not appear in imitation. But, of course, assimilating imitations to the current grammar means that imitation cannot change the grammar. The suffix -*ing* must enter a child's competence in some other way.

The signs are that sometimes a child's tendency to assimilate adult models into his current grammar is so strong that even when he makes a deliberate effort to copy adult speech, the effort may at first fail. One child, in the phase of producing double negatives while developing the negative transformation, had the following exchange with his mother:

Child:　Nobody don't like me.
Mother:　No, say "nobody like*s* me."
Child:　Nobody don't like me.

.
.
.

(eight repetitions of this dialogue)

.
.
.
.
.

Mother:　No, now listen carefully; say "*nobody likes me.*"
Child:　Oh! Nobody don't like*s* me.

The exchange is interesting because it demonstrates the relative impenetrability of the child's grammar to adult models, even under the instruction (given by the mother's "no") to change. The child behaves at first as if he did not perceive the difference between his mother's sentence and his own, though later, when the mother supplied great emphasis, the child recognized a distinction. With this much delay in introducing changes, spontaneous imitations are bound not to be grammatically progressive because they consist only of a single exchange. The fact that a change ultimately was made, however, illustrates that children can profit from adult models. We shall return to this possibility when we discuss parental expansions of child speech.

In any case, it seems clear that one assumption of practice theory is not supported by the facts of language acquisition. Let us now examine the second of these assumptions, the basic assertion that practice increases response strength. Since we know that practice does not lead to the incorporation of novel forms, changes in response strength could affect acquisition only in stabilizing grammatical features already acquired. Perhaps new forms, whatever the manner by which they enter the grammar, are at first unstable, and practice is essential for their solidification as smoothly running grammatical skills. The question in this case becomes one of inquiring whether forms that receive much practice are more stable than forms that receive little practice. Practice may be given through imitation or through spontaneous use.

Ervin (1964) again has appropriate observations. She was interested in the emergence of the past-tense inflection on verbs. In children's earliest speech, verbs are unmarked for tense. A child will say *Adam go,* regardless of whether the event referred to took place yesterday, or will take place tomorrow, or is taking place while the child speaks. Ervin searched through her records for the first occurrence of any verb marked for the past tense and found that these were always strong verbs, that is, ones that form the past tense irregularly. It is well known that children regularize the past tense of strong verbs: they say *comed, goed,* and *sitted* on analogy with such regular verbs as *looked, walked,* and *laughed,* a tendency that often persists into grade school. However, Ervin found that the initial past-tense inflections of strong verbs took the correct adult form. The first occurrence of the past tense were words such as *came, went, sat,* etc.; the regularizations come later in a child's career. The same order of events — past tense appearing first in correctly inflected strong verbs — appears also in Brown's records. There is nothing surprising in this fact when we take into consideration the high frequency with which the strong verbs occur in parental speech, and their early emergence probably indicates that they are learned as vocabulary items, picked up independently of the corresponding unmarked verbs. The strong verbs are frequent in child speech as well, and once a child possesses *came, went, sat,* etc., he finds many opportunities to use them — many more opportunities, in fact, than he finds to use the weak, regularly inflected, verbs. Consequently a child receives much more practice on individual strong verbs in the past tense than he does on individual weak verbs, with or without inflections. If practice offers stabilization of linguistic forms, the correctly inflected strong verbs ought to be fairly well anchored in a child's repertoire. Nevertheless, they are not. Indeed they turn out to be far less stable than the weak verbs that receive little practice. Ervin searched her records for the first occurrences of the regular past-tense inflection, -d, and discovered what at first seems to be a paradox: the first regular inflections appeared on the strong verbs. She observed the children in her sample saying *comed, goed, sitted*, etc. before she observed them saying *looked, walked, laughed*, etc., as if the children were able to generalize before there was anything to generalize from. The explanation of this apparent anomaly is that Ervin's samples of speech, being of small size in relation to a child's total output, failed to pick up any of the correctly inflected weak verbs that must have existed. Because the strong verbs are frequent and the weak verbs are infrequent, the regular past-tense inflection had a better chance of appearing in the speech records on the strong verbs; chance so worked out in Ervin's samples that the miraculous appeared to happen, and strong verbs registered the regular past-tense inflection before weak verbs did. But none of this robs Ervin's findings of their force; the very difference in frequency that favored the appearance of the strong verbs means that highly practiced forms, the strong verbs, were so unstable as to be swept away by a few occurrences of the regular past-tense inflection on weak verbs. Indeed the number of occurrences of these verbs was so small that they did not appear in Ervin's records.

What is the cause of this remarkable instability of the strong verbs? It seems to be that each strong verb, although frequent, is unique unto itself. In contrast, the weak verbs, although infrequent, all exemplify a pattern. Apparently patterns weigh more heavily with children than frequency of repetition does. In the case of the past-tense inflection, therefore, it seems that response strength is not the criterion by which a child chooses among the possibilities offered by the linguistic universals; rather, a child's criterion appears to rest on the occurrence of the same form in analogous constructions in parental speech. The appearance of /t/ and /d/ as suffixes on verbs in parental speech apparently suggests to a child a rule that converts the "past" morpheme of the underlying structure, which may be a possibility offered by the universals, into /t/ or /d/, a feature unique to English. A child's criterion for adopting features from parental speech, therefore, may be to accept only those parental features that can be produced by a rule, a criterion that only patterned features, such as the weak verbs, will meet. On this criterion, the amount of practice given to a feature is less relevant to language acquisition than the ability of a child to notice that a feature is part of a pattern. Insofar as verb inflections are representative, the paradigm for finding the locally appropriate expression of the universals is the concept-attainment experiment, not the rote-learning experiment. Other features of English should be examined from this same point of view; it may turn out that practice plays some role in acquisition, although on present evidence this role appears to be peripheral.

We have seen that imitation is not the means of introducing new forms into a child's grammar; now we see that whatever salutary effects on practice imitation might offer, practice may not be very important to language acquisition. The fact is, nonetheless, that children imitate adult speech a good deal. Roughly 10 per cent of all utterances recorded in Ervin's project were imitations (Ervin, 1964), and similar proportions of imitations have been found in Brown's records (Slobin, 1964). We can barely even speculate on why children imitate so much. Part of the mystery may be removed, however, if we note that the difficulty in explaining imitation is probably not unique to imitation. Aside from its potential for introducing novel forms, imitation does not seem to be different from the spontaneous verbal play that Weir observed in her son's bedtime soliloquies (Weir, 1962). It may be unimportant that parental speech happens to initiate the play that we call imitation; by seeking some special function for imitation, we may have allowed children to deceive us.

That a child is actually at play when he imitates is the compelling suggestion of the following fugue by one of Brown's subjects (mentioned by Slobin, 1964):

Adult: That's the tattooed man.
Child: Tooman. Tattoo man. Find too tattoo man. Tattoo
       man. Who dat? Tattoo. Too man go, mommy? Too
       man. Tattoo man go? Who dat? Read dat. Tractor
       dere. Tattoo man.

This example, while exceptional for its virtuosity, is typical of many imitations and suggests that imitation as well as bedtime soliloquies are examples of children's tendency to play with the skills at their disposal. If that is the case, they should be afforded no more (or no less) significance in language acquisition than children's play with blocks, crayons, etc. has in motor development.

Hockett and Ascher (1964) have suggested that verbal play may have served a crucial function in the origin of language by introducing the property of displacement, the capacity to talk about things not present (cf. Hockett, 1959). It is conceivable that the play of Weir's child and the play of children imitating serves a similar function. Part of the fun, in fact, might be saying things that bear no relation to the situation in which a child finds himself, a necessary condition for future talk about scientific hypotheses, theological dogma, shopping lists, and so forth.

## Expansions

We have said that the speech of adults from which a child discovers the locally appropriate manifestation of the linguistic universals is a completely random, haphazard sample, in no way contrived to instruct a child on grammar. Although this statement is true of adult speech in general, there is one respect in which parental speech is not random. Quite often adults repeat the speech of small children and, in so doing, change the children's sentences into the nearest well-formed adult equivalent. Brown has called this phenomenon "expansion of child speech" (Brown, 1964). It is a kind of imitation in reverse, in which the parent echoes the child and, at the same time, supplies features that are missing from the child's sentence. About 30 per cent of the children's sentences in Brown's records were expanded, forming such exchanges as: Child: *Papa name Papa;* Adult: *Papa's name is Papa, uh-hum* (mentioned by Slobin, 1964). In this case, the adult filled out the child's sentence with the possessive inflection ($s$) and a form of the copular verb; other expansions might add missing articles, prepositions, etc. Some change word order: Child: *table hit head;* Adult: *no, the head hit the table.* Adults probably perform these expansions in order to check their understanding of what children say (thus making the assumption that children can comprehend more grammatical features than they can produce [Slobin, 1964], a possibility that is discussed later).

Aside from the motivation of parents to expand child speech, however, expansions can be considered from the point of view of influencing the course of language acquisition. It is possible that they play an important role in a child's discovery of the local manifestations of the linguistic universals. Children, we have said, produce semigrammatical speech. They generate speech by simple base-structure rules that operate on generic grammatical classes defined in terms of a universal hierarchy of categories. Since these rules — or their inversions — are part of adult competence, it is possible for adults to impose interpretations on child speech by a process that is exactly the same as the imposition of an interpretation on *a grief ago* or *golf plays John*. A child's sentence will have a representation at some level of the universal hierarchy of categories in common with the set of well-formed sentences that can be generated by the base-structure rules. Presumably an adult's expansion of a child's sentence is one of the well-formed sentences in this set. Moreover there is good reason to believe that the particular sentence that an adult uses as an expansion will be the one member of the set that best exemplifies distinctions that a child has not yet marked in his grammar. Suppose, for example, that a child produces the telegraphic *Adam cry*. It has a representation at some (fairly high) level in the hierarchy of categories in common with a set of well-formed sentences that includes *Adam is crying, Adam cried, Adam will cry, Adam's crying* . . . , and probably more. Each of the well-formed sentences honors the distinctions preserved in *Adam cry*, and the rules for generating the child's sentence are all involved in the generation of the well-formed sentences. In addition, however, the well-formed sentences embody distinctions that are not honored by *Adam cry*, and most of them involve transformation rules that are not included in the child's grammar. The situation is propitious for demonstrating to the child a locally appropriate manifestation of one or more of the linguistic universals.

Suppose that context indicates to the parent that Adam is talking about an event that took place yesterday. The only appropriate expansion, then, would be *Adam cried*, and so the child would be presented with an example of how the category "past" is expressed in English, viz., by the suffix *-d*. Expansions, in short, may present suitable conditions for children to discover the local expression of linguistic universals and do so in a way that imitation and practice do not.

Not every expansion, of course, will be appropriate. A parent must judge from extralinguistic considerations which member from the set of well-formed sentences should be the expansion, and sometimes this judgment will be wrong. Adam might have meant that he is about to cry. However, it is doubtful that inappropriate expansions occur frequently, and in any case the child must be able to discover the locally appropriate form of the universals from sources other than expansions so he can check his information from one source against the other.

The role of parental expansions, therefore, would be to facilitate a child's acquisition by presenting models tailor-made to exemplify the parts of competence not completely determined by the universals. It may be, as Brown (1964) has written, that "by expanding the child's words into the nearest sentence appropriate to the circumstances a mother may teach a child to conceive of those circumstances as they are conceived in our community and to code them as we code them."

There is scattered evidence that expansions are effective instructional devices. In the case of the child described earlier, who changed from *nobody don't like me* to *nobody don't likes me,* the mother's repeated expansions eventually had some effect, though only after considerable travail. There are indications elsewhere that expansions can have more immediate influence on a child's speech. Slobin (1964) has examined children's imitations of expansions and found — in contrast to imitations of spontaneous adult speech — that roughly half of imitated expansions are grammatically progressive. Since the effects of expansion must be immediate in order to influence imitation, it is evident that expansions are not always first absorbed into a child's grammar, as adults' free sentences appear to be. Expansions might indeed provide, as Brown speculated, a situation in which a child can discover the means appropriate in his community of encoding such circumstances as "action in the past" — i.e., a situation in which he can find the local manifestation of a linguistic universal.

Because expansions are a means of facilitating a child's discovery of local features, one would suppose that children whose parents expand a great deal would show more rapid acquisition of language than children whose parents expand little. A difference in the amount of parental expansion, in turn, might depend on the amount of interest parents have in understanding what their children say. We mentioned before that parents' motivation to expand is probably to verify their understanding of child speech, so we might expect that the tendency to expand is greatest among those parents with a conviction that children do have something to say, parents who believe that the behavior of children is worthy of attention, parents who are, in short, subscribers to middle-class values and middle-class child-rearing practices. As a matter of fact, the expansion rate of 30 per cent in Brown's records came from academic parents. In contrast to these parents are the parents of another child in Brown's project, whose background is more proletarian. They expand their child's speech far less often, and the child's rate of development is strikingly slower than the development of the middle-class children. We can speculate, therefore, that the lower-class child is retarded at least in part because he must work out the appropriate English manifestation of the linguistic universals on his own. He must discover such features as noun and verb inflections from the haphazard stream of speech, not at all contrived to instruct on grammar, that happens to issue willy-nilly from his parents. Such children may not be deficient in their innate linguistic competence. A project that examines this assumption is now underway in which the speech of culturally deprived children is systematically expanded (Cazden, 1965).

## COMPREHENSION VERSUS PRODUCTION OF SPEECH

It is common in discussions of child language to distinguish active and passive linguistic skills. The distinction is sometimes drawn in terms of a child's development of vocabulary, sometimes in terms of his command of syntax, and most often in terms of both. The gist of the distinction is that comprehension of features of language (passive control) occurs earlier in development than does production of the same features (active control). The emphasis here is on the word "same"; the hypothesis is trivially true if all that is meant is that some features are comprehended before any features are produced. But if every feature is first under passive control, and only later under active control, a significant claim is being made about the course of language acquisition. Much ink has been spilled on this distinction, and the issue continues very much alive today. It is all the more remarkable, therefore, that almost no one has tried systematically to study it. Aside from numerous anecdotal accounts (e.g., Jespersen, 1925; Kahane, Kahane, and Saporta, 1958), there is only one experimental study that is known to this writer (Fraser, Bellugi, and Brown, 1963).

Before describing their work, however, we must say a few words on the theoretical significance of the distinction between comprehension and production. Discussions of the topic are often made difficult because of a confusion of this distinction with the distinction between competence and performance. Competence and performance on the one hand and comprehension and production on the other are different although related distinctions, and it is important to see what both the differences and the relations are. Competence is the knowledge of linguistic rules, categories, etc., that accounts for a native speaker's intuitions about his language. Performance is the expression of competence in talking and listening. In these terms, production and comprehension of speech are both categories of linguistic performance; both involve the expression of competence, the one in producing or encoding speech, the other in receiving or decoding speech. The claim that passive control precedes active control in development, therefore, can be rendered to mean that comprehending speech somehow involves fewer distorting and obstructing factors in the passage from competence to performance than producing speech does. Accordingly, an explanation of the comprehension-production difference will come from a performance model that states, among other things, what the "parameters" of conversion are for production and comprehension and how they differ. In this framework, a distinction between active and passive *grammars,* which some have wanted to draw, is not necessary; a grammar is a statement of competence, whereas comprehension and production are parts of a theory of performance, and we can assume that there is but one grammar that feeds into both kinds of performance.

The experiment of Fraser, Bellugi, and Brown (1963) compared children's production and comprehension of grammatical contrasts. We can regard the experiment as a study of the relative difficulty of converting syntactic competence into the two kinds of performance. They devised an ingenious test built around pairs of sentences that contrasted on single grammatical features. Associated with each pair of sentences was a pair of contrasting pictures, the contrast in this case hinging on the referential distinction that corresponds to the grammatical contrast. One pair of sentences, for example, was *the sheep is jumping* versus *the sheep are jumping,* which had associated with it two drawings, one of a single sheep jumping over a fence while a second sheep looked on and the other showing two sheep jumping over a fence. The two sentences differed only in whether the auxiliary verb *be* was singular or plural; the two pictures differed only in whether one or two sheep performed the action. This set of pictures and sentences, therefore, provided a test of a child's control over the plural-singular distinction on auxiliary verbs. Fraser *et al.* were able to find contrasting pictures for ten grammatical contrasts: for example, singular-plural marked by inflections (*the boy draws* versus *the boys draw*);

present progressive-past tense (*the paint is spilling* versus *the paint spilled,* which involves more than a minimal contrast); subject-object in the passive voice (*the car is bumped by the train* versus *the train is bumped by the car*), and so forth.

In order to test comprehension, a child was asked to point to the picture that corresponded to one of these contrasting sentences; he was scored right or wrong according to which picture he indicated. The test of production was roughly the mirror image of the test of comprehension. The experimenter pointed to one of the contrasting pictures and requested a child to say the corresponding sentence; he was scored right or wrong depending on whether or not his response included the appropriate grammatical feature. In addition to tests of comprehension and production, other children were asked to imitate contrasting sentences. In this case, a child saw no pictures and merely heard the sentences. His response was the same as in the production test, but it was not necessary for him to relate grammatical and referential contrasts.

The results of these tests can be simply stated: in the case of every grammatical contrast, comprehension exceeded production, often by a large margin; moreover, imitation exceeded comprehension on every contrast except one, again often by a large margin. The results of the experiment, therefore, strongly support the assumption that passive control appears earlier in development than active control. The superiority of comprehension over production might tell us, as Fraser *et al.* suggest, that one difference between the two kinds of performance is that production places a greater load on a child's memory. Production and comprehension both operate under various constraints, among which, as we have said, is the need to remain within the limits of memory span. It is conceivable that there is more than one such span, resulting from production and comprehension having to pass through different systems, with the system for comprehension having a greater capacity. This would cause a child to forget features in production that he remembers in comprehension, as apparently occurred in the test of Fraser *et al.*

The fact that imitation exceeded comprehension probably means that there is a third span, larger yet, associated with a child's phonological performance. As Fraser *et al.* commented in their study, imitation appeared to be a perceptual-motor skill not operating through the meaning system. Thus the results of their experiment lead us to conclude that there are at least three memory spans of different capacities involved in linguistic performance: one for phonological production which appears to be largest; one for grammatical comprehension, which appears to be next largest; and one for grammatical production, which appears to be smallest. (These three spans suggest three others, none of which is distinguishable in the experiment of Fraser *et al.*: phonological comprehension, semantic comprehension, and semantic production.) Whether a child will perform accurately in a given task will depend on the length of the sentence on which he is required to operate in relation to the size of the appropriate memory span. The principle would be: if a sentence is shorter than a given span, the corresponding performance can occur; if a sentence is longer than the memory span, the corresponding performance cannot occur with complete accuracy. The performance in every case is preservation of a given grammatical feature, such as plural marking on the auxiliary verb. We can imagine, therefore, four different relations among imitation, comprehension, and production, all depending on the length of the required sentence. (1) If sentences are short in relation to the grammatical production span, imitation, comprehension, and production should be equivalent because underlying competence — phonological or grammatical — can be expressed in every task. (2) If sentences are long in relation to the grammatical production span but short in relation to the grammatical comprehension span, comprehension and imitation should be equivalent, and both should be superior to production. Presumably, many of the sentences used by Fraser *et al.* fell into this category. (3) If sentences are long in relation to both the grammatical comprehension and production span but short in relation to the phonological production span, imitation should be superior to both comprehension and production, which in turn should be equivalent. Such sentences can be imitated, but they are not understood or spontaneously produced. Presumably, some of the sentences used by Fraser *et al.* fell into this third category, hence causing an over-all superiority for imitation. (4) Finally, if sentences are long in relation to the phonological production span, all three types of performance — imitation, comprehension, and production — should again be equivalent because underlying competence is not likely to be expressed in any task. These four relations are illustrated in Figure 5.

One advantage of this scheme is that it accounts for the apparent contradiction between the finding of Fraser *et al.* that imitation was more accurate than production and the finding of Ervin (1964) that imitation was not grammatically progressive. As Slobin (1964) has pointed out, the two studies differed in exactly the respects illustrated in Figure 5. Ervin's subjects were very young (two years) and so had small memory spans, and they spontaneously imitated adult sentences, which on the average are longer than the test items used by Fraser *et al.* Thus it is likely that many of the sentences in Ervin's study were characterized by relation (4) in Figure 5, a condition where imitation, comprehension, and production are equivalent. In order to imitate sentences longer than the phonological span, subjects would either have

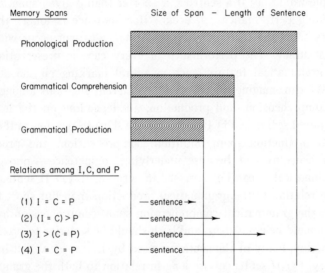

FIG. 5. The relations among Imitation (I), Comprehension (C), and Production (P) depend on sentence length and size of memory span. Numbers refer to the relations mentioned in the text.

to recode them grammatically or parrot as much of the sentence as remained in the phonological span. In neither case would the crucial grammatical features that mark imitations as "progressive" be likely to be preserved. Since there was no particular reason for Ervin's subjects to strive for accuracy, it is probable, as Slobin noted, that they recoded the adult sentences before repeating them back. On the other hand, the subjects of Fraser *et al.* were older (three years) and were given short sentences (average of four morphemes; maximum of eight morphemes) to work with. Most of the sentences in Fraser *et al.*, therefore, were probably characterized by relations (2) and (3), where imitation exceeds production. This analysis, of course, does not affect

Ervin's conclusion that imitations are not the means of entry for new features into a child's grammar.

A great deal more work is necessary on the difference between production and comprehension, for it occupies an important position in studies of language acquisition. The study of comprehension is, first of all, methodologically important. There is no reason to assume that production and comprehension differ only on size of memory span. Indeed, every aspect of a linguistic performance model is a point of potential difference between comprehension and production; it is conceivable that these various factors constrain the two kinds of performance in nonparallel ways — it is theoretically possible that some even constrain comprehension more than production — and there may be qualitative differences as well as quantitative ones. Without a reasonably clear vision of the form of a performance model, therefore, we cannot tell what differences there are between production and comprehension; yet all that we know about language acquisition is based on children's production of speech. It is possible that the inferences we draw about children's competence will be different when based on comprehension.

There is a second, more basic reason to study children's comprehension. If, as Ervin's findings indicate, children gain little from overt practice, a child's own production of speech will not be critically involved in the process of acquisition. On the other hand, children appear to profit from examples of well-formed sentences that are presented (through expansions or otherwise) by parental speech, which means that a child's additions to competence are made through his comprehension. Study of the competence-comprehension cycle, therefore, may turn out to be a study of the principal avenue over which a child acquires the local form of the linguistic universals, and the problem of how children comprehend language may be inseparable from the problem of how they acquire it.

The technical difficulties of studies of comprehension are formidable. One must try to devise nonlinguistic techniques that will register a child's comprehension; the technique must be usable with very young children if we want to catch acquisition at its most active time; and the techniques must be sensitive to a wide range of grammatical features. Perhaps the last requirement is the most difficult. Fraser *et al.* used correctness of pointing as a test of comprehension, which works well enough when the grammatical contrast has a picturable correlate. But how does one get a child to point to the correlate of a basic grammatical relation or a differentiated pivot class? For that matter, is it correct even to speak of the correlates of such fundamental linguistic features? The answer is not obvious. Probably, therefore, the most difficult part of the study of comprehension will arise in the development of useful nonlinguistic responses. On the other hand, there is one signal advantage in the study of comprehension that is totally lacking in all studies of production. As one of the linguists participating in the Fourth Conference on Intellective Processes (Brown and Bellugi, 1964, p. 42) pointed out, we always know in a comprehension task what the input is — it is the sentence being understood. In production this is not the case; the input is completely obscure. We have no conception of what input from (to?) competence leads to the generation of a sentence. What input leads to *want milk Mommy* or *where doggie?* Perhaps future research will find ways to exploit this advantage while solving the problem of obtaining sensitive indicators of comprehension.

## REFERENCES

ALLPORT, F. H. *Social Psychology*. Cambridge, Mass.: Houghton Mifflin, 1924.

BELLUGI, U. The emergence of inflections and negation systems in the speech of two children. Paper presented at *New England Psychol. Assn.*, 1964.

———The development of interrogative structures in children's speech. In *The Development of Language Functions*, K. Riegel (Ed.), Univ. of Michigan Lang. Developm. Program, Rep. No. 8, 1965.

——— and BROWN, R. *The Acquisition of Language. Monogr. Soc. Res. Child Develpm.*, 1964, *29*, 1.

BERKO, J. The child's learning of English morphology. *Word*, 1958, *14*, 150–177.

BEVER, T., FODOR, J. A., and WEKSEL, W. On the acquisition of syntax: a critique of "contextual generalization." *Psychol. Rev.*, 1965, *72*, 6, 467–482 (a). Is linguistics empirical? *Psychol. Rev.*, 1965, *72*, 6, 493–500 (b).

BRAINE, M. The ontogeny of English phrase structure: the first phase. *Language*, 1963, *39*, 1–13.

——— On the basis of phrase structure: a reply to Bever, Fodor, and Weksel. *Psychol. Rev.*, 1965, *72*, 6, 483–492.

BROWN, R. The acquisition of language. In *Disorders of Communication*, D. McK. Riach and E. A. Weinstein (Eds.), *Res. Publ. Ass. nerv. ment. Dis.*, 1964, *42*, 56–61.

——— and BELLUGI, U. Three processes in the child's acquisition of syntax. *Harvard Educ. Rev.*, 1964, *34*, 133–151.

———and FRASER, C. The acquisition of syntax. In *Verbal Behavior and Learning*, C. N. Cofer and B. S. Musgrave (Eds.), New York: McGraw-Hill, 1963.

——— The acquisition of syntax. In *The Acquisition of Language*, U. Bellugi and R. Brown (Eds.), *Monogr. Soc. Res. Child Develpm.*, 1964, *29*, 1, 43–79.

———— and BELLUGI, U. Explorations in grammar evaluation. In *The Acquisition of Language*, U. Bellugi and R. Brown (Eds.), *Monogr. Soc. Res. Child. Develpm.*, 1964, *29*, 1, 79–92.

CAZDEN, C. *Environmental Assistance to the Child's Acquisition of Grammar.* Doctoral thesis, School of Education, Harvard University, 1965.

CHOMSKY, N. Some methodological remarks on generative grammar. *Word*, 1961, *17*, 219–239.

———— Degrees of grammaticalness. In *The Structure of Language*, J. A. Fodor and J. J. Katz (Eds.), Englewood Cliffs, N.J.: Prentice-Hall, 1964.

———— *Aspects of the Theory of Language.* Cambridge, Mass.: M.I.T. Press, 1965.

ERVIN, S. Imitation and structural change in children's language. In *New Directions in the Study of Language*, E. Lenneberg (Ed.), Cambridge, Mass.: M.I.T. Press, 1964.

FRASER, C., BELLUGI, U., and BROWN, R. Control of grammar in imitation, comprehension, and production. *J. verb. Learn. verb. Behav.*, 1963, *2*, 121–135.

GREENBERG, J. H. Some universals of grammar with particular reference to the order of meaningful elements. In *Universals of Language*, J. H. Greenberg (Ed.), Cambridge, Mass.: M.I.T. Press, 1963; 2nd ed., 1966.

HOCKETT, C. F. Animal "languages" as human languages. In *The Evolution of Man's Capacity for Culture*, J. N. Spuhler (Ed.), Detroit: Wayne State University Press, 1959.

———— and ASCHER, R. The human revolution. *Current Anthro.*, 1964, *5*, 135–147.

HUTTENLOCHER, J. Children's language: word-phrase relationship. *Science*, 1964, *143*, 264–265.

JENKINS, J. J., and PALERMO, D. S. Mediation processes and the acquisition of linguistic structure. In *The Acquisition of Language*, U. Bellugi and R. Brown (Eds.), *Monogr. Soc. Res. Child Develpm.*, 1964, *29*, 1, 141–169.

JESPERSEN, O. *Language, Its Nature, Development, and Origin.* New York: Holt, Rinehart & Winston, 1925.

KAHANE, H., KAHANE, R., and SAPORTA, S. *Development of Verbal Categories in Child Language.* Bloomington, Ind., Indiana Univ. Res. Ctr. Anthro. Folklore Ling., 1958.

KATZ, J. J. *The Philosophy of Language.* New York: Harper, 1966.

———— and FODOR, J. A. The structure of a semantic theory. *Language*, 1963, *39*, 170–210.

———— and POSTAL, P. M. *An Integrated Theory of Linguistic Descriptions.* Cambridge, Mass.: M.I.T. Press, 1964.

KLIMA, E. S. Negation in English. In *The Structure of Language*, J. A. Fodor and J. J. Katz (Eds.), Englewood Cliffs, N.J.: Prentice-Hall, 1964.

LENNEBERG, E. *The Biological Bases of Language.* New York: Wiley, 1967.

LIEBERMAN, P. On the acoustic basis of the perception of intonation by linguists. *Word*, 1965, *21*, 1, 40–54.

MC CARTHY, D. Language development in children. In *Manual of Child Psychology*, L. Carmichael (Ed.), New York: Wiley, 1954.

MEHLER, J. Some effects of grammatical transformations on the recall of English sentences. *J. verb. Learn. verb. Behav.*, 1963, *2*, 346–351.

MENYUK, P. A preliminary evaluation of grammatical capacity in children. *J. verb. Learn. verb. Behav.*, 1963, *2*, 429–439.

—— Alternation of rules in children's grammar. *J. verb. Learn. verb. Behav.*, 1964, *3*, 480–488.

MILLER, G. A. Some psychological studies of grammar. *Amer. Psychol.*, 1962, *17*, 748–762.

—— Some preliminaries to psycholinguistics. *Amer. Psychol.*, 1965, *20*, 15–20.

—— and CHOMSKY, N. Finitary models of language users. In *Handbook of Mathematical Psychology*, R. D. Luce, R. Bush, and E. Galanter (Eds.), Vol. II, Ch. 13, pp. 419–492, New York: Wiley, 1963.

MILLER, W., and ERVIN, S. The development of grammar in child language. In *The Acquisition of Language*, U. Bellugi and R. Brown (Eds.), *Monogr. Soc. Res. Child Develpm.*, 1964, *29*, 1, 9–34.

SLOBIN, D. I. Imitation and the acquisition of syntax. Paper presented at *Second Research Planning Conference of Project Literacy*, 1964.

SMITH, M. E. An investigation of the development of the sentence and the extent of vocabulary in young children. *Univ. of Iowa Studies in Child Welfare*, 1926, *3*, No. 5.

VYGOTSKY, L. *Thought and Language* (translated by E. Haufmann and G. Vakar). Cambridge, Mass.: M.I.T. Press, 1962.

WEIR, R. *Language in the Crib*. The Hague: Mouton & Co., 1962.

## Dan I. Slobin

## COMMENTS ON "DEVELOPMENTAL PSYCHOLINGUISTICS"

*A discussion of McNeill's presentation*

McNeill has written a splendid and very useful paper. I am highly impressed with his clear and lucid handling of a wide range of topics, with his completely up-to-date contact with the field and its literature, and with his many insightful and often bold theoretical propositions. As far as I know, he is the first to use the term "developmental psycholinguistics," and his paper certainly shows that this is a valuable and viable subfield of psycholinguistics. Actually this is more than a subfield: the questions framed by McNeill constitute, to me, the core of the psycholinguistic quest. Let me state at once that I agree completely with his characterization of the basic question of developmental psycholinguistics as he has put it on the first page of his paper: "The aim is to develop a theory of language acquisition that will be consistent with linguistic theory and will cover the facts of acquisition as they are now known. The fundamental problem . . . is the simple fact that language acquisition occurs in a surprisingly short time." Taking this approach, I think one must look upon the child as engaged in an active, productive endeavor, supported by a biological *Anlage* for such an endeavor.

In this light I think it is very useful that McNeill points out that telegraphic speech is a result, not a process — a result that is in need of explanation. I think the use of the word "telegraphic" as descriptive of child speech has caused some confusion. Clearly the child is not simply speaking shortened adult sentences. He is, to a great extent, pro-

85

ducing his own types of sentences. This is a profound point underlying the entire presentation.

I also applaud McNeill's insightful discussion of the role of practice. Clearly, stimulus-response (S-R) theories are going to be of no help to us in our present endeavor — as he implies throughout. The role of practice in specific situations is still, however, very much an open question. Imitations and expansions, for example, seem to provide useful practice opportunities, though we have very little specific knowledge of their use. I have examined the longitudinal data on two of Brown's child subjects, and it is evident that adults very frequently expand child speech — in fact, the two mothers expanded 30 per cent of their children's utterances (while the children imitated adult utterances only about 10 per cent of the time). For both of these children, about 15 per cent of their imitations are repetitions of expansions or responses to expansion questions; and — what is most interesting — about 50 per cent of the time these imitations of expansions are themselves partial expansions of the child's original utterance. That is to say, the child's second utterance, like the parental expansion, is longer or more complex than his first utterance. Here is a situation where practice may perhaps carry the child forward in his grammatical development. These utterances, if not beyond the child's spontaneous capacities, seem at least to stretch those capacities to their maximal length or complexity.

If this sort of practice is held to play a role in grammatical development, however, we will want to know what happens to children whose speech is not frequently expanded. We do not really know yet what is important in child-parent dialogue for the development of grammar — is it simply the total amount of verbal interchange, or is it a matter of expansions versus other kinds of dialogue? And if imitations of expansions play the role that McNeill and I think they may, we will want to know more about the nature of imitations. When and what does a child choose to imitate? What are the relations, more precisely, between productive use of a linguistic form, comprehension of that form, and the child's imitation of the form at various stages in development? Again drawing from Brown's data, it appears that as the child gains mastery of the language the amount of time he spends imitating greatly decreases. We will want to know why this should occur. It may be that there is a sort of critical age for expansions — an age when the child is most helped by an expanded model of his own utterance to imitate (and is most prone to imitate it). These are all intriguing and research-able questions raised by McNeill's discussion.

McNeill does an excellent job also of pointing out other areas where more research is needed. We are going to need more longitudinal studies to answer many of the questions he poses — and they must be studies of different sorts of children: children of different social-class back-grounds and, especially, children learning different native languages. It will be necessary to study the acquisition of languages quite differ-ent from English if we are going to get any hold on the question of what is universal and what is language-specific in child speech develop-ment. In all study of child language much more attention should be paid to comprehension — I am especially happy that McNeill em-phasizes this point. We have little knowledge of the ways in which comprehension of linguistic forms influences the course of their acqui-sition and use. And McNeill is perfectly correct in emphasizing at the same time that "the technical difficulties of studies of comprehension are formidable." I hope that we will overcome these difficulties, for this is one of the few sources of information about the underlying lin-guistic competence of young children.

The main problem raised by McNeill's paper is the proposal of a significant innate component in language acquisition — the LAD or LAS of Chomsky, Katz, *et al.* Let me say at the outset that I am very sympathetic to this approach. I don't think we will be able to build a viable developmental psycholinguistics without postulating this sort of component. The problem that troubles me is how to determine just what sorts of things should be considered as "preprogrammed." To what extent is a human child "wired up" with linguistic competence — and with specifically linguistic competence? I believe that McNeill — if I understand him correctly — has preprogrammed more than I would; but this is a knotty question indeed. It seems, from my reading of the paper, that a child is held to be born with the entire set of lin-guistic universals and that he somehow uses this set as a grid through which he filters the particular language he happens to hear around him. The reason that human languages utilize such strikingly universal grammatical relations and formal devices is, therefore, due to the fact that these universal characteristics are themselves part of the innate structure of man. Thus it seems to me that McNeill takes a "content approach" to LAD, while I would favor a "process approach." It seems to me that the child is born not with a set of linguistic categories but with some sort of process mechanism — a set of procedures and inference rules, if you will — that he uses to process linguistic data. These mechanisms are such that, applying them to the input data, the child ends up with something which is a member of the class of human languages. The linguistic universals, then, are the *result* of an innate cognitive competence rather than the content of such a competence. The universals may thus be a derivative consequence of, say, the application of certain inference rules rather than constitute the actual initial information in terms of which the child processes linguistic input. This, I take it, is the approach of Fodor's paper in this volume (p. 105).

This discussion may be, however, primarily a terminological dispute. It is obvious that the child does not begin speaking at birth and that, when he does begin to speak, he speaks the language of his environment. It seems also clear that experience with the linguistic input alone is insufficient to support the task of grammar construction. How much of the necessary information can come from the speech the child hears, and what sort of information must the child bring with him in addition? I do not have much difficulty in accepting McNeill's proposal that grammatical relations and formal universals are "built in." But I do have trouble when it comes to some of the substantive universals that he discusses. Even if it is granted, as he proposes on p. 35, that the top of a generic hierarchy may be given, I do not find it necessary to postulate that the child know in advance all of the distinctions at the lower levels in order to deal with the more general classes at the top, or that he need be born with knowledge of all possible subcategories. For one thing, the child may not always pick his generic category correctly. Some of Ervin and Miller's subjects, for example, had adjectives in both the pivot and open classes. However, if the child does pick his generic category correctly, he cannot help but imply the various subdivisions at the same time. For example, if a generic noun category is developed, it is by its *semantic* nature subdividable into animate-inanimate or masculine-feminine-neuter or count-mass, etc. It seems to me that the child, to begin with, must know only the criteria of setting up the generic class — for example, the criteria for nounness — and not all of the other criteria of noun subcategories as they are embodied in various languages.

What I am trying to say is that it seems to me that McNeill's model lacks an account of the semantic features underlying grammatical categories[1] — and such features are learnable. If, for example, you look at the nouns used by very young children, you find that they are much more consistently names of "things" than are adult nouns. Indeed, as McNeill has pointed out, the child has to notice rather than invent classes. But his noticing is not necessarily based only on criteria available to him at birth. For example, human languages distinguish animate from inanimate because of objective facts of referents; may not the child come to notice this distinction as a result of experience with these same objective facts? According to McNeill's model, the child searches the "local language" for embodiments of a subset of the substantive universals he carries about with him. McNeill's example is compelling: the child wishes to say something about a past event (presumably a substantive universal); he uses an unmarked form; his mother's expansion provides him with the "local" inflection. But let us take a Russian child who wants to tell his mother that he saw a fireman. He says the equivalent of "see fireman," and his mother expands — but she provides not only the tense marker but a marker on the noun as well, to indicate that it is an animate accusative as opposed to an inanimate accusative. I would rather think of the child as learning this category through feedback than to have him waiting for confirmation of dozens of such categories from his mother's expansions. It seems to me more reasonable to suppose that it is language that plays a role in drawing the child's attention to the possibility of dividing nouns on the basis of animation; or verbs on the basis of duration, or determinacy, or validity; or pronouns on the basis of social status, and the like.

Perhaps all that is needed is an ability to learn certain types of semantic or conceptual categories, the knowledge that learnable semantic criteria can be the basis for grammatical categories, and, along with this substantive knowledge, the formal knowledge that such categories can be expressed by such morphological devices as affixing, sound alternation, and so on. The child's "preprogramming" for substantive universals is probably not for specific categories like past, animate, plural, and the like, but consists rather of the ability to learn categories of a certain as-yet-unspecified type.

[1] As I point out in my discussion of the acquisition of Russian as a native language (this volume, pp. 129–148), discussion of semantic and conceptual correlates of grammatical categories provides a much-needed explanation of the fact that all categories are not developed at once and that they vary greatly in speed, order, and time of onset in development.

McNeill's thought experiment, in which adults learn to classify adjectives into those beginning with letters from the first or second half of the alphabet, avoids this point of semantic criteria. This adjective category is an "empty" one, much like grammatical gender, which as I discuss elsewhere in this volume is one of the latest grammatical categories to be learned by Russian children — probably because of its arbitrary, nonsemantic nature. On the other hand, grammatical categories like number and tense, which have clearer semantic correlates, are learned much earlier. Similarly, using McNeill's example, the subdivision of the pivot class into demonstratives and possessive pronouns and adjectives is not just an elaboration of grammatical categories — these categories are meaningfully different. McNeill's paper does not seem to speak to the question of why ontogenetic change in language performance is gradual; why it is that some grammatical categories are late to emerge. One reason could be — at least with regard to the substantive categories — that, if the distinctions are semantic, they require varying amounts of experience to be learned. Another explanation could be that the child comes equipped with a set of hypotheses or inference rules that vary in their saliency and simplicity and that the child begins by trying out the more salient or simpler hypotheses.

The concept-formation ability underlying the substantive universals need not be linked only with linguistic performance. There are probably certain sorts of classifications a child can learn easily — whether expressed syntactically, lexically, or in nonlinguistic behavior. An understanding of innate cognitive competence will require a characterization of such classifications. Although language acquisition is very rapid, acquisition of the category and relational structures of other, as-yet-unstudied domains may be just as rapid. For example, a child may quickly learn to distinguish between such cultural categories as, say, colineal and ablineal kin, either because the distinction is made lexically (as in English — e.g., "uncle" versus "cousin") or syntactically (if, for example, a language had separate pronominal and verbal address forms for ablineal and colineal relatives) or because the two kin groups receive different behaviors in his culture. I do not see why grammatical linguistic marking of learnable categories should be afforded special status. I would imagine that McNeill's substantive universals reflect a more general innate cognitive competence for classifying and organizing experience on the basis of such abstract criteria as symmetry, transitivity, and the like. It remains to be seen whether categories like status and solidarity or past action or intention or plurality — in short, the whole collection of substantive universals — are acquired more rapidly in those cases where they are grammatically expressed in the child's experience, rather than lexically or in terms of some other behavior.

As a final comment, it should be noted that McNeill's model of successive fractionation of categories, explained by substantive universals, is not at all like the picture presented for the application of formal universals. The "banana peel" analogy works quite well for the division of the pivot class; "cognitive clutter" is a much better description of the development of the negative. Here the child develops negation systems of unwieldy complexity — systems that are presumably too complicated to deal with and must be abandoned or seriously modified. In order to explain the sequence of such syntactic attempts, one must postulate some sort of simplicity motivation, as McNeill does on p. 61. It may also be, as Fodor seems to suggest elsewhere in this volume, that the child is also built to develop certain transformational principles when simple principles break down. These proposals of ordered hypothesis-testing and the application of a simplicity metric need much more elaboration.

In conclusion, it is certainly necessary to postulate a language-acquisition device with much innate knowledge, but it is a serious and difficult question to decide just when to appeal to such a device as explanatory and when to hold off such an appeal and seek for other sorts of explanation. I applaud David McNeill for grappling with this question.

# GENERAL DISCUSSION

## McNeill and Slobin presentations

McNeill's arguments prompted extensive discussion, both during his presentation and after, much of it fragmentary and overlapping. The novelty of many of his proposals precluded any quick and tidy grasp of their implications, although his general theme was one that was frequently adverted to throughout the conference. A number of points of clarification have been attended to in McNeill's revision of his paper, which now includes emendations or elaborations prompted by the conference discussion; as a consequence several of the more fruitful exchanges became redundant and have been omitted here. Some critical issues broached by various conference participants are similarly represented in the Slobin discussion and elsewhere, and these will not be reiterated either. However, this attempt by the editors to impose order and economy on what was a lively and often multiply directed debate should not be taken as indicating that any issues have been resolved.

1. A large part of the discussion was taken up with how the progressive differentiation of word classes into the eventual adult grammar could occur, centering on McNeill's hypothesis that the child was innately equipped with a universal hierarchy of grammatical categories. A good deal of water was splashed around at this well, but not many buckets were brought to it. McNeill persisted that grammatical classes arose from a child's first and most primitive grammatical organization by a process of successive differentiation based on substantive linguistic universals. The model was one of hypothesis-testing

— a child did not invent any distinction on the basis of evidence in parental speech, but he did use this speech to evaluate distinctions that he tried to impose.

One of the difficulties McNeill had to face was that words destined to belong to the same adult syntactic class sometimes appeared to occur in different primitive classes. In part this difficulty arises from the way the grammar for a child's utterances is formulated, as brought out in the following exchange:

> SLOBIN: One of Braine's children has the statement *want do*, which Braine classifies as pivot + open. But the same child also uses *do* as a pivot in utterances like *baby do, daddy do*, and so on.
>
> MC NEILL: That's obviously the outcome of Braine's decision to classify *do* as both a pivot and open word.
>
> FODOR: It is required by the fact that you can't have two pivots in the same sentence. You can't have both *want* and *do* as pivot.
>
> MC NEILL: Braine could have called *do* an open-class word throughout.
>
> FODOR: Then he would have many more instances of two open-class words in the same sentence, which is something to be minimized.
>
> MC NEILL: Braine, I know, wanted to minimize it.
>
> FODOR: That was my impression.
>
> MC NEILL: In fact, open + open is the more common pattern in the case of Roger Brown's records.

Some discussion followed as to whether a word like *do*, which appeared to require assignment to both pivot and open classes, should be regarded as a single lexical element. It was suggested that it might better be considered as two distinct morphemes, one with a pivot role and one an open, that happened to share the same phonological form. This failed to capture the imagination of the main protagonists. Fodor felt that McNeill's view made it hard to understand how a child could ever alter a word classification once it appeared in his repertoire. For McNeill, argued Fodor, progress consisted of the assignment of items in the corpus to increasingly smaller subclasses, and no mechanisms were provided for revising assignments. The Braine data suggested that radical revisions could occur after the early splits. Doubt about whether shifts in classification could occur was one of the factors that kept this particular point unresolved.

Several participants who sympathized with McNeill's general rationale for a substantial innate component in language found difficulty in accepting the notion that this would have to include substantive universals rather than simply formal or relational structures. Slobin's objections have been summed up in his discussion, and Fodor's alternative formulation is outlined in his own paper, which follows. The summary of the discussion of Fodor's presentation also touches upon the frequent attempts to make a manageable distinction between Fodor's arguments and McNeill's and upon the problems associated with the classificatory procedures that Fodor suggests.

During the McNeill discussion, Fodor introduced his counterargument that a child requires inference procedures that need only be defined formally, not substantively. Even if a child were innately equipped with the kind of hierarchical structure McNeill suggested, he would still require some technique for analyzing the items in his language in terms of that structure. The information that his language includes for example "nouns," "verbs," and "adjectives," together with their various subclasses, would be of no use if the child had no way to determine which items in his corpus belonged to each of the classes. The alternative possibility was that a child is equipped with analytic procedures which, when applied to his data, automatically produce candidate grammars that satisfy the relevant formal and substantive universals, that is, which exhibit a hierarchical arrangement of lexical items into classes. Fodor also argued that there was good reason for keeping a child's first class-differentiation cuts flexible. Phrase structure provides a segmentation that indicates to what units transformations apply. Whatever motivation a child might have for supposing that his language came in segments, phrase structure — as far as the formalism was concerned — was a device for articulating the underlying structure of transformational forms. This fact alone would imply that a child would require the possibility of revising his classification of language units as more transformations were learned. It could be assumed that a child would want to maximize the joint simplicity of the segmentation and the transformational analysis. He would require a segmentation that was optimal for stating the forms of the transformations and would refrain from making irreversible segmental judgments until he had learned enough about transformational structure to know what the best groupings were.

Premack wanted to translate McNeill's hierarchy into an "ordered staging of hypotheses." He suggested that a child might be equipped with a set of general hypotheses that would be brought to bear in wide areas of discrimination problems in an ordered sequence. For language-learning, he would assume that the initial differentiation would be morphological on the basis of a positional hypothesis rather than semantic. It might be assumed that both the set of the hypotheses and the order in which they were brought in were not tied specifically to language but were part of a general behavior mechanism such that, given any kind of material to which these hypotheses might be relevant, they would be brought to bear in a particular order. The emergence of discrimination of color and form might be examples of where the same system of ordered hypotheses applied. Premack thought the idea of an ordered staging of hypotheses easier to get into the head (without specifying whether he was referring to a child's or a psychologist's) than McNeill's suggested hierarchy. When McNeill objected that he did not see any difference, Premack said that his view was process and McNeill's product. McNeill also commented that it would probably be much more difficult — a kind of higher-order question — to try to establish a relation between the ability to acquire language and other more general cognitive capacities. He thought the logically prior question was to establish what was to be explained in terms of the more general capacities. He would not quarrel with Premack that a child's disposition to learn language was necessarily or uniquely linguistic, but language was the obvious domain in which the structure might be revealed.

Miller commented that it was not necessary to assume that (*a*) a tree describing the chronological differentiation of syntactic categories in development and (*b*) a tree describing the adult organization of those same categories would have to be identical, even though exactly the same criteria of classification might be involved in both cases. Suppose, for example, that content versus function words is the most fundamental syntactic classification in adult speech, and suppose further that pivot versus open does *not* correspond to function versus content for some particular child; then at some later stage of development, when that child acquired the function-content distinction, some pivot words could go into the function class and some into the content class, and some open words could also go into both. In short, two morphemes could start, one in the pivot and one in the open, and yet they could end up having a superordinate classification in common. This could look as if a reclassification had occurred — that the child had made a "mistake" — whereas in fact he had not. This might be thought of as a weaker version of McNeill's hypothesis. McNeill acknowledged that this scheme might offer the required amount of flexibility to account for cross-classification, but he still wanted to claim that hierarchy of categories had to be universal, not simply a differentiation process.

Cooper suggested that the question of whether a child got his first basic classificatory split correct was a factual one that could be settled by direct observation. McNeill replied that there were several tests, none of which had been made so far. One was interlinguistic and not as simple and straightforward as might first appear because of interchild differences. McNeill was then challenged as to whether the fact of interchild differences was damaging to his own notion of substantive universals. He thought not. A hierarchy of classes was bound to be complex, and he saw no reason why there should not be a number of universal options, only some of which would be inappropriate for any particular language. The fact that class membership might differ among children would demonstrate that there were several different routes at each point in differentiation. A child might change course, but not invent a unique one. It would be possible to make a revision every time a hypothesis was tested against adult speech.

After considering Slobin's critique, McNeill proposed that some of the difficulty with his concept of a generic grammatical relation had arisen because in the passage on p. 28, ". . . we must assume that a child honors in advance the distinctions on which adult classes are based," he originally used the word "knows" rather than "honors." This, he thought, had misled Slobin when he remarked ". . . if the child does pick his generic category correctly, he cannot help but imply the various subdivisions at the same time" (p. 88). In this passage, Slobin had in fact provided a succinct statement of the notion of a generic grammatical classification. No suggestion had been intended that a child had to have at his active disposal the full range of possible grammatical distinctions when he established a pivot class (just as in the alphabet analogy, p. 31, the adult need not have in mind all possible alphabetical combinations of adjectives in order to have a generic classification of the particular combination employed in the example). Indeed, it was the ability of children to form a generic pivot class without drawing subordinate grammatical distinctions that raised the interesting problem at this point; the question that had to be answered was how children formed such generic categories. McNeill's proposal was that they followed a universal hierarchy of categories.

However, McNeill continued, a potentially serious difficulty was raised for just this suggestion by the observation of Slobin (p. 88) that the early grammars of some of Ervin and Miller's subjects showed adjectives in both the pivot and open classes. Such cross-classification was completely inexplicable in terms of a universal hierarchy of categories except as a "mistake" on the child's part. It was not yet clear how general this phenomenon was. If cross-classification was an infrequent phenomenon in language development, it might be best to account for it in terms of some as-yet-unknown aberration of the hierarchy of categories. If, however, cross-classification should prove to be common, it might be necessary to think of children as organizing sets of syntactic features much in the manner discussed by Chomsky (1965) rather than as progressing through a hierarchy of categories.

2. The suggestion was several times made that the child might be making transformations at a very early stage, for example, in using the same two or three word combinations to express different intents, like questions and statements. It was implied that the use of transformation might be related to the apparent ability to handle words that had the same phonemic form but appeared in different classes. Miller said that because an adult would need to make transformations to interpret a child's intent did not mean that the child used transformations in generating the utterance. McNeill argued that multiple-classification, if accepted, merely postponed the problem of describing grammar. Sooner or later the child would come to classify lexical items exactly according to adult speech. The fact that some words or combinations were ambiguous did not contribute to the evolution of grammatical classes. If the same word was used as a noun and as a verb, some distinction was evidently being made on a grammatical basis.

3. McNeill hoped that studies of the development of noun and verb inflections (p. 70) might reveal something about the way a child chose among the rival hypotheses that he formulated. He noted the difficulty facing an assumption of traditional learning-theoretic approaches to language — that overt practice led to a strengthening of linguistic forms — from the evidence of Ervin that there was a sudden discontinuity in the correct use of strong verb forms like *came, went,* and *sat* with the appearance of unpracticed (and unimitated) forms like *comed, goed,* and *sitted.* The child was clearly generalizing to strong verbs an inflection rule appropriate to less commonly occurring weak verbs. Premack proposed that this was a reclassification phenom-

enon. Although an adult would call *came, went,* and *sat* verbs, a child might not classify them in this way until later. The new forms would be members of a different class which underwent a transformation that the original forms did not. McNeill pointed out that the two forms were not independent vocabulary; the old forms disappeared and did not coexist with the new. Premack said he was offering an *ad hoc* mechanism for reclassification. If the grounds for the child to reclassify were sufficiently strong, they could compete with and overcome a response disposition based upon some other strengthening mechanism. McNeill insisted that no strengthening mechanism could be involved. To assert that the emergence of regular past-tense inflection was evidence of a strengthening mechanism was to use the term in a totally arbitrary sense. A much simpler explanation was consistent with the fact of little practice on weak verbs and a lot of practice on strong. With strong verbs each past-tense inflection was a case unto itself; no pattern was revealed. Each correct inflection of a weak verb, however, represented a pattern; it could be formulated by a rule that the child picked up. He did not see where any notion of strengthening applied. Premack replied that the rule was what he had been calling classification, and it was to classification that strengthening applied. The next portion of the discussion is most appropriately summed up in a remark that the hapless stenotypist inserted into the conference transcript, "Whereupon a number of simultaneous conversations broke out."

McNeill's contribution was to reiterate his interpretation that practice was not the criterion by which a child adopted linguistic forms; instead, he followed a rule. Reclassification must have preceded the occurrence of the aberrant forms because the only basis a child could have for generalizing the regular inflection to the strong verbs was that they had already been classified as "verb + past." Reclassification must in fact have preceded the overt evidence of past-tense inflection on the weak verbs themselves. Slobin suggested another example of the way in which a child was probably looking for a regular past-tense form before he actually got it. If he wanted to use *bite* in the past and had never used the verb in that form, he would almost certainly say *I bited*. There were a number of indications that the child was trying to find some kind of regularity that he could use productively to get at the past tense of strong verbs. Slobin saw no question of reclassification here; the child had past tenses and was trying to find a means of producing them all in the same way. Replying to a question from Fodor, McNeill said that a child going from the correct to an incorrectly inflected form of *go* might produce either *goed* or *wented*. Fodor thought this would make a difference; the assumption that *went* was in fact coded as "verb + past" would be compatible with the child producing *goed* but not *wented*. McNeill disagreed and said there could be a more complicated rule. Ferguson pointed out that double markings did in fact occur; in plurals, for example, the child might say *wugses* in response to Berko's *wug*.

Ferguson also remarked that a similar phenomenon had been detected with the French language, where there were many common irregular verbs. As soon as French children started learning the conjugations of just a few verbs that were more regular, they began expanding the use of these regularities to the strong verbs. Kalmus observed that this also happened with German.

4. Cooper had been struck that a child's open class tended to contain items of direct experience and wondered whether the child might be dividing his use of sounds into those that represented things, in a broad context, and those that were somehow necessary but did not relate directly to experience. McNeill said a child might very well be doing this, but he could not see how subsequent grammatical evolvement would develop from this. Such an approach would not in itself seem to be sufficient to generate a theory of grammatical development.

Pursuing Cooper's lead, Chase thought a child's interest in naming might speak to totally different psychological functions from the evolution of adult linguistic competence, for example, the differentiation of the organism from the rest of the physical environment. One obstacle, he thought, had been the effort to look at the development of language exclusively in its vertical dimension — the closer and closer approximation of the child's verbal behavior to that of the adult. Another approach would be to study language development horizontally, looking at the specific systems of information exchange pertinent to the problems of a child at each stage of his development. Some of the needs of a young child, such as differentiation of and from the environment by naming, might be unique to a particular stage of development and inexplicable in terms of adult competence. Fodor responded that there was no objection to studying naming instead of grammar except that nobody knew what a name was. Normally, what a psychologist meant by naming was effectively using nouns. The fact that there were names for people and objects and actions did not help describe the semantic system of language and provide a model of how it worked. The notion of reference was completely misunderstood if it was thought that language consisted simply of nouns, pronouns, and connectives. Such a model could not explain anything because this was not the way language worked. Chase persisted under attack that a different kind of field study would be made if the position were accepted that language competence at different stages of development might speak to special problems at each stage. Instead of recording the speech of a child and cataloguing it by formal principles, the language behavior would be studied in the context in which it was produced. In the analyses of child speech that had been presented, he had been interested in the questions of to whom the child had been addressing himself and what were the particular patterns of linguistic performance generated by the contingencies of his environment. Chase did not think that abstracting form would allow any kind of reasonable reconstruction by any principle whatever. However successful or unsuccessful systems for studying animal communication had been, they always had a keen respect for the environment and for the contextual features of informational exchange. Chase pursued his argument further in his own presentation, which begins on p. 253.

5. While agreeing that it was probably necessary to postulate a language-acquisition device with a large innate component, Slobin had expressed concern about just when appeal should be made to an innate device for explanatory purposes. It was a little too easy to throw a lot of problems into a basket labeled "built in." Miller tried to clear up some anxieties by pointing out that not even Leibnitz would have said that an innate idea was in any sense known prior to the time that experience had caused it to appear in the organism. It would be much more accurate to say the innate components were simply potentialities that would develop if the environment presented the occasion for them to do so; they were the things that an organism would learn easily, quickly, and immediately; the way it would structure its experience in order to profit from it. To suggest that the child might know the difference between colineal and ablineal kin as an innate idea (Slobin, p. 90) was to make fun of the whole notion of innate ideas.

Fodor saw a fine point here. Although the behavior or response

capacity correlated with innate ideas might be assumed to be a disposition in the sense that it was realized just in case certain experiences
occurred, nevertheless the underlying information in terms of which
the experience was used to develop the particular behavior was presumed to be innate. The information was presumed to be "wired in"
in a very strong sense — perhaps not in the same sense that a child
at birth knew the difference between red and green but at least in as
strong a sense as that. In this respect Fodor was sympathetic, at least
transiently, to Slobin's point. It was not necessary to suppose that a
child knew the difference between colineal and ablineal relations as
long as he was able to assimilate rapidly the difference between symmetrical and nonsymmetrical relations; that was the kind of information or propensity bias Fodor thought should be assumed to be innate.

Lenneberg thought he saw a way of avoiding the label of "lazy
thinking" often attached to postulations of innate components of
behavior. These could be made empirical questions, and in animal
studies there were operations that could decide their validity. He saw
no reason why similar techniques could not be developed for the
study of language. For example, there was nothing to indicate that a
child went through a hypothesis-testing-and-discarding process with the
naming of objects, although there was clearly some kind of coincidence
between what was presented and what was learned. This was different
from saying that a child was innately equipped with the notions of
table or chair. Nevertheless his perceptual processing seemed to coincide
very closely with what was reflected in language. Lenneberg thought
that within limits very good guesses might be made about the first
demonstrations of what might be thought of as innate; this would be
a first step, and further research could be done.

6. A passing comment by McNeill that the grammar of a four-year-
old child appeared to be just trivially different from that of an adult
roused some opposition. Hirsh, for example, referred to the observed
increased use of subordinate clauses and other elaborated forms as
the child progressed through elementary school and asked whether
this linguistic development was "trivial." McNeill said that very large
changes in performance obviously occurred, but that children followed
up to the age of three years had just about everything that should be
included in a grammar of competence. Slobin said the same appeared
to be true of Russian children, although the process might take a

little longer; by four or five years, however, the basic grammar had been acquired.

7. Following the Weir presentation, as part of a discussion of the relation between syntactic structure and intonation, McNeill's reference (p. 53) to Philip Lieberman's study on the way linguists assigned intonation contours to speech was expanded and commented upon. The summary of this discussion begins on p. 169.

Jerry A. Fodor

# HOW TO LEARN TO TALK:
# SOME SIMPLE WAYS

I should like to say something about what kind of problem the problem of syntax-learning is and something about the kind of theory that might offer a basis for the solution of the problem. I wish to emphasize at the outset, however, that these remarks are very tentative and that, even if they should prove correct, they could not possibly prove exhaustive. To characterize the form of a theory of syntax-learning is to do considerably less than to provide such a theory, and the more we learn about language the harder language-learning looks.

There are, nevertheless, some points that are presumably not in dispute. One is that speaking a language requires information about the structural relations within and among the sentences of that language. The speaker's possession of such information is assumed, even on the most primitive associationistic views of verbal behavior, for according to such views the speaker's ability to produce coherent utterances depends upon his exploitation of knowledge about transition probabilities between elements of his language.

A second point that cannot be seriously questioned is that some, at least, of the speaker's information about his language must be learned. It is a platitude that no one is born talking, and it seems self-evident that a period of learning is a precondition of fluency, whatever maturational processes may also be involved. No child talks without having been exposed to the utterances of fluent speakers, and the language and dialect he eventually speaks are precisely the language and dialect to which he is exposed. It should be noticed, however, that to say that the child must learn his language is not to say that the child must be conditioned to speak his language. What kinds of learning mechanisms may be supposed to be involved in mastering the syntax of a first language is the question to which this paper is addressed.

A third point that ought to be treated as self-evident (though it often is not) is that the child must bring to the language-learning situation some amount of intrinsic structure. This structure may take the form of general learning principles or it may take the form of relatively detailed and language-specific information about the kind of grammatical system that underlies natural languages. But what cannot be denied is that any organism that extrapolates from its experience does so on the basis of principles that are not themselves supplied by its experience.

It will be noticed that in talking about the child's contribution to language-learning, I referred to "intrinsic" rather than to "innate" structure. This is because it is at least conceivable that the learning principles in terms of which the child organizes his linguistic experience are themselves learned; for example, that the child is born with a very general capacity to learn learning principles and that it is such learned principles that the child brings to the problem of mastering his language. I do not, in fact, think that suggestion is true in any significant sense, but that is beside the point. What is important is that the task of characterizing the information the child brings to language-learning is, at least in principle, distinguishable from the question of whether the child's intrinsic information is innate. In this paper I shall be concerned solely with the former problem.

How, then, can we proceed in investigating the psychological processes involved in the assimilation of the syntax of a first language? Clearly there are three terms to the relation under consideration. In the first place, there is a body of *observations* that the child must be assumed to make, a body of data about his language provided by the child's exposure to the verbalizations of adults, siblings, and so on. Second, there are whatever *learning principles* the child employs to organize and extrapolate these observations. Third, there is the body of *linguistic information* provided by the application of the principles to the data, the body of knowledge about the structure of his language that the child-cum-fluent-speaker will employ in speaking and understanding the language.

What we say about any of these must condition what we say about each of the others. For example, the child's data plus his intrinsic structure must jointly determine the linguistic information at which he arrives. Hence it is a conclusive disproof of any theory about the child's intrinsic structure to demonstrate that a device having that structure could not learn the syntax of a language on the basis of the kinds of data that the child's verbal environment provides. Suppose, for example, that someone were to maintain that all that is required for language-learning is that the child should be able and inclined to imitate the utterances he hears. It would be a conclusive refutation of that suggestion to point out that a speaker's information about his language is sufficiently rich to permit him to produce or understand novel utterances *ad libitum*. For the fact that the child will learn to deal with utterances of a type not found in his data entails that something must be involved in language-learning other than the imitation of the utterances that are found there.

In short, a comparison of the child's data with a formulation of the linguistic information necessary to speak the language the child learns permits us to estimate the nature and complexity of the child's intrinsic structure. If the information in the child's data closely approximates the linguistic information he must master, we may assume that the role of intrinsic structure is relatively insignificant. Conversely, if the linguistic information at which the child arrives is only indirectly and abstractly related to the data provided by the child's exposure to adult speech, we shall have to suppose that the child's intrinsic structure is correspondingly complex. We have already seen that the two limiting theories can be dismissed with some confidence. On the one hand, it is inconceivable that the child's data contribute no linguistic information, for this would mean that all such information is intrinsic. On the other hand, it seems that the data cannot contribute all the relevant information, for this would be logically incompatible with the fact that the child eventually learns to deal with utterances of sentences he has not previously encountered. It appears that the theory we want must lie somewhere between the two.

To summarize: I propose to consider the child to be a "black box" that converts some body of data about a language into whatever syntactic information is required to speak the language. By comparing what is known about the input to this device with what is known about its output, something about its manner of operation and internal organization may perhaps be deduced.

## THE ANALYSIS OF LANGUAGE INPUT

What is known about these inputs and outputs? About certain features of the latter a good deal can be said as a result of recent work in linguistics. I shall return to this presently. For the moment, let us consider what kinds of data the child's encounters with fluent speakers may be assumed to provide.

In the first place, the child gets a *corpus*. That is, he gets a sample of the kinds of utterances fluent speakers of his language typically produce. It is conceivable that this sample is biased in certain respects in comparison to a purely random sample. Thus, it has been suggested that speakers addressing children often consciously simplify their utterances both in point of vocabulary choice and in point of syntactic structure; and it is quite certain that adult speakers often complicate the induction of the morphology the child must learn by indulging in baby talk. Research is now being carried out in an attempt to determine the precise character of the verbal environment of the child. Until the results of this research are known, however, it would be methodologically sound to assume that the child's increasing linguistic proficiency is not to be attributed to any significant extent to the special character of the utterances he hears. For if it is true that utterances specifically directed to children tend to be syntactically simple and that children now and then receive the benefit of language tuition in the form of corrections of their incorrect utterances, it is equally true that much of what children hear is overheard and that all normal children learn to speak, though the differences in the amount of special attention and conscious tuition children receive must vary enormously with variables like social class and birth order.

One point about the corpus should, however, be noticed. If it is anything like a randomly selected corpus of adult utterances, it must contain a very substantial number of false starts, slips, grammatical mistakes, and so forth. Most of these the adult speaker is capable of recognizing as distortions of his dialect, hence the attainment of this capacity is part of what the child must master in learning to speak that dialect. Thus the description of the child's task as that of extrapolating from the utterances in his corpus to the sentences of his language makes the task seem simpler than it is. The child's problem is rather to determine which proper subset of the utterances he hears constitute utterances of sentences and to extrapolate that subset. To put it slightly differently, we may think of the linguistic information at which the child arrives as constituting *inter alia* a theory of the regularities in its corpus, a theory about which such regularities are of systematic significance and which are "accidental." The optimal theory need not count every utterance in the corpus as regular because, as a matter of fact, much of what the child hears is almost certain to violate one or another of the grammatical rules that define the dialect from which the corpus is drawn.

The similarities between the child's problem and normal problems of scientific induction are thus very striking. Like the scientist, the child finds himself with a finite body of observations, some of which are almost certain to be unsystematic. His problem is to discover regularities in these data that, at very least, can be relied upon to hold however much additional data is added. Characteristically the extrapolation takes the form of the construction of a theory that simultaneously marks the systematic similarities among the data at various levels of abstraction, permits the rejection of some of the observational data as unsystematic, and automatically provides a general characterization of the possible future observations. In the case of the learning of language, this theory is precisely the linguistic information at which the child arrives by applying his intrinsic information to the analysis of the corpus. In particular, this linguistic information is at very least required to provide an abstract account of syntactic structure in terms of which systematically relevant features of the observed utterances can be marked, in terms of which some of the observations can be discarded as violating the formation rules of the dialect, and in terms of which the notion "possible sentence of the language" can be defined.

It must be noted that the child's linguistic environment provides him with more than a corpus of utterances. It also provides him with correlations that obtain among members of the corpus and between members of the corpus and various nonlinguistic events. On the one hand, most discourses clearly possess structure beyond the sentence level *Good morning. Isn't it a beautiful day?* but probably not *Good morning. Isn't it a beautiful evening?* On the other hand, many of the assertions the child hears must be true, many of the things he hears referred to must exist, many of the questions he hears asked must be answerable, and many of the commands he receives must be performable. Clearly the child could not learn to talk if adults talked at random.

That the child takes advantage of such correlations in learning the semantic system of his language can hardly be doubted. It is also quite conceivable that they may provide him with clues for the learning of one or another syntactic relation. To say that the syntax of a language can be *represented* independently of a representation of its semantics is by no means to claim that the systems are *learned* independently. The difficulty with relying upon "semantic" considerations in explaining language-learning is not, then, that such considerations are known to be irrelevant but simply that we do not know how to describe them in any very revealing way. Which of the indefinitely many correlations between features of language and features of "the world" are relevant to a systematic account of language-learning (or, for that matter, to a systematic account of meaning) is a currently unanswered question. What is perfectly clear, however, is that the story is enormously more complicated than has usually been realized by psycholinguists. If it be said that the learning-theoretic accounts of reference psychologists have proposed have only been intended as a first step, it must be replied that they are quite certainly a first step in the wrong direction (cf. Chomsky, 1959; Fodor, 1965).

Fortunately, the question of how the child exploits correlations between features of the utterances in his corpus and features of the nonlinguistic environment is probably irrelevant to the problem with which this paper is mainly concerned. The sort of syntactic information that provides the deepest problems for the theory of language-learning is precisely that which concerns the abstract formal structures underlying sentences rather than obviously and immediately meaningful units, such as morphemes and words. To understand this, let us turn from a discussion of the data that provide an input to the child's intrinsic language-learning principles to a discussion of the theory of his language that constitutes their output.

Consider the following linguistically trivial example. For each English active sentence with a certain sort of transitive verb (including *eat, bite, catch, . . .* etc. but excluding *cost, weigh, . . .* etc.), there exists a corresponding passive sentence with the same verb but with the subject and object interchanged. Hence, corresponding to *the dog eats the meat,* there is *the meat was eaten by the dog;* corresponding to *the wolf eats the serfs,* there is *the serfs were eaten by the wolf,* and so on.

It is obvious that the linguistic information at which the child will arrive is sufficient to specify both the indefinite set of actives and the indefinite set of corresponding passives. Nor does it seem plausible to suppose that, having learned that *eat* can take *dog* as subject and *meat* as object in the active, the child must then learn as an entirely independent fact that *eat* can take *dog* as object and *meat* as subject in the passive. On the contrary, an adult speaker, given a novel active, can supply the corresponding passive without further information. It thus seems undeniable that the information that allows the speaker to construct the one form is intimately related to the information that allows him to construct the other.

A reasonable first guess would be that the child learns rules for constructing actives and further rules for converting them into their corresponding passives. For example, having constructed *the dog eats the meat,* the child knows that to form the passive he must interchange the subject and object, attach *en by* to the main verb, and introduce the appropriate inflection of *be* in the auxiliary position. Indeed, most psychologists who have discussed transformations seem to have supposed that some such rule for converting actives into passives is a paradigm for the syntactic characterization of intersentential relations.

That this is a misunderstanding can be seen from the second example just mentioned. Corresponding to *the wolf ate the serfs,* we have *the serfs were eaten by the wolf* not *the serfs was eaten by the wolf.* But notice that it is this latter form that would be produced by a rule which derived the passive from its corresponding active. The difficulty is that in both the active and the passive the number of the verb agrees with the number of its subject. Hence we have the wrong agreement if we allow the passive to be derived from the active in cases where the subject and object differ in number.

From a linguistic point of view, the solution of this problem is simple enough. We hypothesize an underlying base structure in which all the components of the sentence are represented and appropriately marked (*subject, verb, object,* and so on) but in which the verb is not inflected for number. That is, we postulate a base form that is not a sentence, hence *a fortiori* neither an active nor a passive sentence. It is this underlying form to which the transformational operations are assumed to apply. In particular, the underlying form is converted into the active by *inter alia* supplying the appropriate number inflection for the verb and into the passive by first interchanging the subject and object and then applying the rule that inflects the verb for number. Since the rearrangement of subject and object occurs prior to inflection, the same rule that inflects the verb in the active can also be employed in the passive; namely, the number of the verb agrees with the number of its subject.

In short, we conclude that the linguistic information available to the speaker must include rules that permit him to construct nonsentential base structures from which such related sentence forms as actives and passives (and, of course, questions, imperatives, and so on) are derived. But while the postulation of such base structures provides no partic-ular problem for the linguist, it raises profound difficulties for any theory of language-learning. In particular the question immediately presents itself: how does the child learn what the correct base structure for a type of sentence is?

Notice that imitation and reinforcement, the two concepts with which American psychologists have traditionally approached problems about language-learning, are simply useless here. On the one hand, imitation can be relevant as a learning mechanism only where the environment of the organism provides it with a model of the behaviors it is required to learn. But, by definition, the base structures of a language are not themselves possible utterances in the language. On the contrary, the construction of a base structure is presumed to be no more than an intermediate step in the integration of verbal behavior, and it is therefore the verbal behavior, and not the base forms that are assumed to underlie it, that is available to the child as a possible model for imitation.

Similarly, differential reinforcement, insofar as it may be supposed to play some role in learning, must be contingent either upon the spontaneous occurrence of the desired behavior as part of the organism's operant repertoire or upon the occurrence of some related operant that can be "shaped" into an approximation of the behavior desired. Since, however, base forms are not uttered by children either in operant babbling or at any other stage of verbalization, the desired behavior is not available for selective reinforcement. Hence, in the case of the learning of the base structures of a language, the essential prerequisite for operant conditioning is not satisfied.

In short, a problem that is central to understanding the learning of syntax is that of arriving at a theory of how the child determines the appropriate base structures for the types of sentences that appear in his corpus. However, the peculiarly abstract relation between base structures and sentences unfits any of the usual learning mechanisms for explaining their assimilation.

## THE INDUCTION OF BASE STRUCTURES

The problem of characterizing a device that, given as input a sample of utterances drawn from a natural language, supplies as output a system of rules that correctly assigns base structures to the sentences of the language is considerably beyond the capacities of current psycholinguistic theory. There is, however, an intermediate problem that can and should be investigated.

Given any corpus of utterances, there are indefinitely many possible abstract descriptions it satisfies. Hence there are indefinitely many infinite sets of which the corpus may represent a finite subset and indefinitely many ways of extrapolating from the corpus to some logically possible language. Of these, all but a very small finite number may be presumed to be "phony" because all but a very small finite number of the possible extrapolations from a corpus exploit properties of utterances that are not of the type that enter into systematic linguistic descriptions. For example, such extrapolations might be defined over intensity of the utterances, or over the number of words they contain, or over the height of the person who speaks them, or with respect to the distance in statute miles between the speaker and the Tower of London. Clearly, whatever intrinsic structure the child brings to the language-learning situation must at least be sufficient to preclude the necessity of running through indefinitely many such absurd hypotheses, or the child would stand no chance whatever of arriving at a reasonable representation of the syntax of his language in any reasonably short period of time.

We may therefore think of the problem of characterizing the child's intrinsic information as dividing into two distinguishable stages. The first task is to provide a characterization of a device that is at least guaranteed only to attempt to describe its input in terms of the kinds of relations that are known to be relevant to systematic linguistic description. Such a device would not, in the normal case, be expected to arrive at a unique best description of the syntax of the language from which its corpus is derived or a unique best mapping of the corpus onto the set of sentences of that language. Hence a secondary research goal ought to be the characterization of a simplicity metric that, given the various candidate descriptions such a device would produce, would choose among them in terms of such considerations as their formal complexity, their coherence with putative linguistic universals, the ease with which they can be integrated with semantic descriptions, and so forth. The problem of characterizing this simplicity metric is clearly much harder than the problem of characterizing a device that produces only non-"phony" extrapolations of corpuses. Fortunately, however, it is also much less pressing. The currently urgent problem is to devise a reasonable account of the induction of underlying structure, a form of mental operation about which traditional learning mechanisms appear to have nothing whatever to say. We can afford to delay answering the question of how, given a number of competitive inductions all of which operate in terms of systematically significant linguistic relations, we might go about choosing the best one.

Moreover, it is not entirely unreasonable to suggest that these two phases of investigation correspond to the way that children work. It seems likely, on the basis of recent investigations of children's speech, that a child runs through a series of candidate syntaxes, all but the last of which are discarded because they fail to capture (or because they misdescribe) relevant regularities in his corpus. That is, the decision to revise or abandon such candidate syntaxes is presumably made on the basis of their empirical adequacy *vis-à-vis* the increasingly large corpus available to the child and their simplicity, both in respect of the number of rules they require the child to store and in respect of their coherence with nonsyntactic portions of the grammar.

I have nothing to say about the character of the simplicity metric. But I think it is possible to make a few comments about the character of the kind of quasi discovery procedure that I have suggested ought to be an immediate research goal. That is, I want to make a few proposals about the construction of a device that will at least ignore the indefinitely many, obviously incorrect, extrapolations of a corpus in favor of extrapolations that project only features of the type known to be linguistically relevant.

It is worth considering the possibility that the child may bring to the language-learning situation a set of rules that takes him from the recognition of specified formal relations within and among the strings in his data to specific putative characterizations of underlying structures for strings of those types. Such rules would implicitly define the space of hypotheses through which the child must search in order to arrive at the precisely correct syntactic analysis of his corpus. Presumably the rules would have to be so formulated as to assure (1) that the number of possible analyses assigned to a given corpus is fairly small; (2) that the correct analysis (or, at any event, a best analysis) is among these; (3) that the rules project no analysis that describes the corpus in terms of the sorts of phony properties already discussed, but that all the analyses exploit only relations of types that sometimes figure in adequate syntactic theories.

To see how this might work, consider the kinds of relations between base structures and terminal strings that obtain in the case of the English auxiliary construction. That construction permits an indefinite class of sentences, of which A and B are subsets, but excludes an indefinite class of strings, of which *C is a subset.

| A | B |
|---|---|
| John *is* eat*ing* lunch | John *has* eat*en* lunch |
| they *are* play*ing* ball | they *have* be*en* playing ball |
| John and Mary *are* see*ing* a ghost | John and Mary *have* se*en* a ghost |

.
.
.

etc.                                    etc.

*C

John *has* eat*ing* lunch
they *have* be*ing* playing ball
John and Mary *have* see*ing* a ghost

.
.
.

etc.

In short, when the auxiliary is developed as some inflection of *be*, the main verb takes *ing*, but when the auxiliary is developed as some inflection of *have*, the main verb takes *en*. This relation is expressed in the syntax by assuming (*a*) that "have + en" and "be + ing" are constituents in the base structure and (*b*) that the base structures of sentences in A and B have undergone a permutation transformation that effects the appropriate reordering, roughly:

$$(\text{have} + \text{en}) + (\text{be} + \text{ing}) + \text{verb} \Rightarrow \left\{ \begin{array}{l} (\text{have}) + \text{verb} + (\text{en}) \\ (\text{be}) + \text{verb} + (\text{ing}) \end{array} \right\}$$

We may reformulate this situation slightly more abstractly. The sentences in A and B all have the abstract description *IXJ*, where the form of the *J*th element depends upon the form of the *I*th element and where *X* represents some intervening string. To arrive at the proper syntactic analysis of strings that satisfy this description, the child must assume that (*IJ*) (*X*) represents the constituent analysis of the base structure and that their transformational history includes a transformation

$$(IJ) \ (X) \Rightarrow IXJ$$

What I wish to suggest as a working hypothesis is that precisely this information is included in (and typical of) the child's intrinsic structure. That is, that the child comes to the language-learning situation with the instruction that whenever he finds sets of terminals that satisfy the description *IXJ* under the conditions just mentioned, one of the preferred hypotheses about their syntactic analysis is that their base structure contains (*IJ*) and that their transformational history contains the operation just cited.

It is worth noticing that this rule also provides for the correct analysis of the class of sentences instanced by such examples as *John phoned Mary up; John phoned the girl he knew in Chicago up; a friend of mine looked over the car; a friend of mine looked the car over*. In these cases the interdependent items *IJ* are a verb with its related particle, and the *X* is a noun phrase (NP). The usual syntactic treatment of such cases is to assume that the underlying structure is (Verb + Particle) (NP) and that the terminal sequence is produced by the application of an (optional) transformation that permutes the particle with the NP.

There are three major points I want to make about the suggestion implicit in these examples. The first is that the child would clearly be unable to employ the sort of information I am supposing to be intrinsic unless he was able to recognize a relation of abstract conformity between elements and/or sequences of elements in his corpus. In the present cases, employing the relevant rule for inducing base structures requires his having available the morphological information that *has* and *have* on the one hand and *is* and *are* on the other are both representations of the same underlying elements, *have* in the former case and *be* in the latter. Analogously, he could not employ the relevant rule for analyzing constructions like *John phoned Mary up* unless he had available the syntactic information that *phone up, look over,* and so on all have the abstract representation "Verb Particle." Without such information, it would be impossible for the child to analyze the sentences in his corpus as *IXJ* and hence impossible for him to apply the sort of rule suggested above for arriving at their base structures.

It may be that the techniques of substitution and classification traditionally employed in attempts to formulate linguistic discovery procedure will prove useful here. It is, of course, notorious that such procedures do not arrive at unique correct grammars for arbitrary finite corpuses. But the present point is that they need not do so in order to aid the child in arriving at tentative hypotheses about conformity relations. I am proposing, rather, that the child may employ such relations as substitutability-in-frames to arrive at tentative classifications of elements and sequences of elements in his corpus and hence at tentative domains for the application of intrinsic rules for inducing base structures. Whether a given such classification is retained or discarded would be contingent upon the relative simplicity of the entire system of which it forms a part. Thus, if the child arrives at a taxonomy of a set of strings such that each string in the set has the representation *IXJ*, then if he has some independent reason for supposing that the base form for these strings is not *(IJ) (X)*, one of the options available to him is to abandon the original taxonomy. He might, for example, suppose that what appear to be recurrences of conforming *I* elements are in fact occurrences of syntactically unrelated homonyms.

In short, I am suggesting a process for the induction of base structures that includes the following phases: (1) provide tentative abstract representations of the derived structure of the corpus by employing techniques that would, presumably, depend in part upon the assumption that distributionally similar sequences often belong to the same class; (2) provide tentative base structures for each such representation by employing intrinsic rules like the one already mentioned; (3) select as the appropriate syntactic description the one that maximizes the joint simplicity of the description of the underlying and the derived structure. This procedure might be assumed to have a more or less cyclic character because the level at which it can be employed would depend upon the level at which the child is able to recognize relations of abstract conformity. It is, for example, conceivable (though by no means obvious) that the child must recognize that nouns have a common class membership before he can recognize that noun phrases do. If it is correct that the recognition of conformity for morphemes is prior to the recognition of conformity for phrases, then one would suppose the assignment of correct underlying structures to sentences exhibiting dependencies between morphemes ought to be ontogenetically prior to the assignment of the correct underlying structures to sentences exhibiting dependencies between phrases.

Once again, in suggesting that the recognition of conformity is ontologically prior to the induction of base structures and that distributional criteria may be of use in recognizing conformity, I am not attempting to resuscitate the notion of a discovery procedure based upon substitution and classification. On the contrary, the kinds of rules I am supposing would be intrinsic to a device capable of inducing base structures are consciously formulated with more than half an eye to the formal relations employed by transformational grammars. It is, however, unreasonable to deny *a priori* that in learning his language the child may take advantage of distributional regularities in his corpus. Such regularities would be good guides to the tentative analysis of the corpus into classes, and it is precisely such tentative analyses that are required if he is to employ rules that project putative descriptions of underlying structure.

The second point I want to make about this suggestion is that the assignment of underlying structures to classes of sentences arrived at by using rules like these would very often be wrong, for a number of reasons. In the first place, the corpus may be insufficiently rich at the time that the hypothesis about base structure is projected. There may, for example, be cases in which a given *I*th item is followed by one or a small class of *J*th items for reasons that have nothing whatever to do with syntax. To take an extreme case, a corpus that contains *the sea is blue today; my, but the sea is blue; isn't the sea blue today? sure is a blue sea* might tempt the injudicious child to the conclusion that (*sea blue*) is a constituent in the underlying representation of each of these sentences. It may be confidently assumed, however, that considerations of general syntactic simplicity, plus access to further data, would eventually preclude a treatment of *sea blue* that parallels the treatment of *phone up*.

Finally, there are more serious reasons why the child might arrive at the wrong analysis of the base structure by using the kinds of rules mentioned here. Suppose the child has a corpus that contains only or primarily sentences from C to the relative exclusion of sentences from D. The child might reasonably treat the sentences

| C | D |
|---|---|
| John swims | John swims and runs |
| John and Mary swim | John and Mary swim and run |
| Mary swims | Mary swims and runs |
| John runs | John swims, runs, and jumps |
| . | . |
| . | . |
| . | . |
| etc. | etc. |

in C as having the form *IXJ*, where the dependency between *I* and *J* is the dependency between the number of the NP and the number of the verb. That this analysis is incorrect would become apparent only insofar as he eventually attempts to make his treament of the sentences in C homogeneous with his treatment of the sentences in D. In short, despite the superficial similarity between the dependence of the verb on its subject and the dependence of a particle on its verb, these constructions must be treated quite differently. This is because, in the former case, the number of possible occurrences of dependent verbal elements in a sentence is unbounded. This precludes a derivational history in which the dependent element is generated together with the element it depends upon and is subsequently relocated by permutation. Hence, though one permutes (*call* + *up*)NP to get *call* NP *up,* one does *not* permute (*John* + *s*) *run* to get *John runs.* Rather, one gets this construction by the application of some addition transformation like

$$(\text{NP} + \text{number}) \; \text{Verb} \Rightarrow (\text{NP} + \text{number}) \; (\text{Verb} + \text{number})$$

This, then, is a rather clear case in which the acceptability of a putative analysis of a certain set of strings in the data is a function of the relative simplicity of the entire syntactic theory of the language the child eventually arrives at. What makes the analysis of strings in C as permuted forms of *IXJ* unacceptable is simply that it would require that, in the generation of the strings in C, we use a number agreement rule that differs from the number agreement rule employed in generating strings in D, and this proliferation of rules is in conflict with general principles of parsimony. (The example also suggests, by the way, that if parents do simplify the syntax of their speech when they address children, they may thereby make it harder for the child to learn the correct syntactic analysis of his language. Rules that hold for selected sets of simple sentences may have to be abandoned in the light of examples of sentences of more complicated types. The view that one makes language-learning easier by unsystematically limiting the child's access to data about his language is a decidedly peculiar one.)

I do not mind that using the sorts of rules I am supposing may be intrinsic will often lead the child to the wrong syntactic analysis. For, once again, I am not attempting to answer the extremely difficult question, "What sort of device would project a unique correct grammar on the basis of exposure to a corpus?" I am only attempting to formulate a strategy for answering the much easier question, "What sort of device would project candidate grammars that are reasonably sensitive to the contents of the corpus and that operate only with the sorts of relations that are known to figure in linguistic descriptions?" What the example just discussed shows is that if we want the device to handle dependencies in a reasonably sophisticated way, it will be required to take account of more subtle relations among terminals than the ones it needs to notice in projecting underlying structures for constructions of the form "Verb NP Particle." In particular, it will have to take account of the difference between a corpus in which the strings can be analyzed *IXJ* and a corpus in which the strings can be analyzed $IXJ_1, J_2, \ldots, J_n$ and employ correspondingly different inference rules for the induction of the underlying forms of these two types of sets.

The final point I should like to make about this proposal is that it is surely incorrect as stated. What seems to me reasonable as a research strategy is to attempt to analyze the kinds of relations well-confirmed syntaxes claim obtain between strings of specified formal character and their respective underlying structures, and to work on the assumption that the intrinsic structure of children includes representations of such relations. Clearly this view is capable in principle of accounting for the child's induction of syntactic analyses far more complicated than those he could arrive at solely by applying such restricted techniques as substitution and classification. It is thus a virtue of the proposal that it makes the induction of underlying structure appear a little less mysterious than it has sometimes seemed and thus takes the sting out of the objection that transformational grammars could not be psychologically revealing because they hypothesize relations too complicated for a child to learn.

Moreover, even the linguistically trivial examples already mentioned suggest that an appropriate formulation of the rules that map from features of the strings in the corpus to features of their underlying structure might permit the homogeneous (and hence parsimonious) treatment of a fairly wide variety of superficially heterogeneous structures. Thus, the rule I mentioned would account for both the child's ability to induce the underlying structure of "Verb Particle" constructions and his ability to handle certain agreements in the auxiliary. For, though constructions like *have eaten* are syntactically unrelated to constructions like *phone him up,* both such constructions bear the same abstract relation to their respective base forms, and I have assumed that the child's intrinsic information permits him to take account of that fact.

But if such examples reveal the virtues of the present proposal, they also reveal its difficulties. What one would need to make it interesting would be a more general characterization of the kinds of relations that obtain between base forms and derived forms than is now available. To make the proposal plausible one would need to show that a reasonably wide variety of such relations can be induced on the basis of a relatively small amount of intrinsic information of an abstract and general sort. The difference between the present proposal and the *ad hoc* suggestion that the child is born with a list of the solutions to all the language-learning problems he will encounter resides, after all, precisely in the generality and simplicity with which the presumed intrinsic information can be specified. At the present stage I am unable to do more than provide examples of the kinds of inference rules that might work for certain specific kinds of cases. I am sure the examples must be wrong as stated, and I do not know how to state them so that they are at once more powerful and more precise. But I suspect that that would be a good problem to think about when one is inclined to speculate on the role of intrinsic structure in first-language-learning.

## REFERENCES

CHOMSKY, N. A review of Skinner's *Verbal Behavior. Language*, 1959, *35*, 26.
FODOR, J. A. Could meaning be an $r_m$? *J. verb. Learn. and verb. Behav.*, 1965, *4*, 2.

# GENERAL DISCUSSION

## Fodor presentation

1. An insistent question concerned the difference, if any, between Fodor's proposal and that of McNeill. Several participants, including McNeill, felt that Fodor's position would reduce to McNeill's. Fodor acknowledged that the distinction might well be between two senses of parsimony. McNeill's child had a lot of structural information wired in, for example about the kinds of trees (patterns of hierarchical organization) relating grammatical classes, and Fodor's child was equipped with a set of inference rules permitting the generation of a variety of candidate grammars, all of which must share formal universals like the possession of a hierarchically organized component. This led McNeill to wonder whether Fodor was in fact attributing less foreknowledge to the child than he was; Fodor replied that his child was equipped with no structures at all, for example, no characterizations of the abstract form of particular trees. Rather, the child was assumed to possess rules for processing the information in his corpus such that the consequence of applying those rules was the generation of trees of the relevant shape. This might turn out to be the same proposal as McNeill's, but superficially it did not seem to be, for although Fodor's proposal did not imply less prestructure than McNeill's, it implied that the innate information was available in a rather different form from the one which McNeill proposed. Given the right set of inference rules, the problem of the formal facts of language might be resolved automatically.

2. Another persistent discussion topic centered on the fact that in

Fodor's scheme grammatical classes were being assigned to input elements on the basis of actual or hypothesized formal relations, while at the same time the formal relations were being inferred from the occurrence of classified elements. The conditions under which a particular rule was to be applied required classification of the input elements, but no classificatory criteria were proposed. Fodor said many questions were being dealt with at the same time, by more than one technique. For example, one general rule might be that if at any level of analysis a string of the form *IXJ* occurred, the relevant underlying structure should be postulated. At the same time, a substitution technique might be employed to obtain a rough characterization of the syntactic classes. The particular rule could be used over and over at various levels, at the morphological as well as the syntactic. If analysis were made of a structure that appeared to satisfy the left-hand side of the particular rule, but it turned out that the underlying structure the rule predicted was wrong, then the child would make some redistribution of classes. Some form of simplicity metric would assure an optimal product of the class category and relational rules.

In one response to a specific (and reiterated) inquiry regarding possible rules for the differentiation of an *IXJ* input, Fodor argued that two points were involved. On the one hand there was the question of how a child knew when a piece of the corpus satisfied some abstract description. To that the general answer might be: try assigning that description, and see if so doing simplifies the characterization of the structure of that part of the corpus in particular and of the language in general. Part of the reason he wanted to treat strings like *phone her up* as *IXJ* was that it permitted a uniform treatment of the relation of that locution to others in which the morphemes *phone* and *up* occurred. On the other hand Fodor saw difficulty from the point of view of McNeill's position. He did not see how such information as "there exist subclasses of nouns" could be of use to a child at any stage unless he had language-independent definitions of such notions as "noun" and "subclass." Such definitions would allow him, given enough corpus, to generate reasonable guesses about what the main nouns in some of the sentences were. Then and only then would the information that the items so specified arranged into hierarchically ordered classes be of some use to him.

Fodor restated what he considered to be the fundamental problem of learning syntax — the learning of underlying structure. This problem was egregious because no paradigm theory existed for dealing with the learning of responses for which the experience of the organism provided no model and which did not constitute part of the organism's gross behavioral output. The kinds of inference rules about which reasonable suggestions ought to be made included those where continuous elements in underlying strings were separated by intervening strings in output structures. An explanation of how the underlying structure *he has + en eat* became the observable *he has eaten* would go a long way toward saying how syntax might be learned. Fodor noted that he himself was keeping more than half an eye on the actual form of the eventual grammar, on the assumption that it was now known in general what kinds of structure a correct grammar would employ. His hypothesis was that the discovery device should contain rules of inference that determine a class of candidate grammars, which in turn employ precisely those logical operations required by universal linguistic theory.

Like the question of the precise distinction between the Fodor and McNeill positions, the discussion of this topic concluded without any feeling that the problem had been resolved, except possibly to the satisfaction of Fodor's intuition. Fodor himself stressed that all discussion of the validity of different hypotheses was merely "hand-waving" at a problem until somebody actually wrote a program that would test mechanisms for converting corpuses into representations of grammar. Until it was possible to see exactly what kinds of operations were capable of performing the various functions attributed to innate structures, such discussion would have little practical import.

3. Fodor could not accept a suggestion that children started their verbal life by uttering underlying structures, with the consequence that their speech was produced in odd orders, without affixes, and so forth. Obligatory morphological transformations applied right from the beginning. Even in two-word sentences, if a choice existed between underlying structure and a transformed structure, presumably one thing a child would get right was the morphological order. However, it might be a good analogy that a child uttered kernel sentences, that is, sentences with none but obligatory transformations.

Lenneberg thought that the underlying structure might be of a kernel type, but argued that what was produced had usually already undergone transformation of some kind. In order to achieve any degree of competence in dealing with strings of phonemes, a child required a highly structured system similar to that being discussed with respect to syntax. He agreed with a suggestion by Cooper that by the time a child could deal with one- or two-word sentences, the idea of hierarchical structure was a long way behind.

Fodor rejected a suggestion that any part of the mother's didactic set might establish a bias toward kernel structures in early speech, particularly if the kernel was defined as a simple declarative sentence and probably even if it included all obligatory transformations. He felt the best working assumption to be that the language environment of a child did not differ in any useful way from that of an adult. In this context, Ferguson was asked what the grammatical structure of baby talk (talk directed at babies) was like. He said that it tended to have a lot of the structures that might be expected in two-word sentences and in fact represented a crude attempt on the part of adults to imitate what they thought happened in language-learning.

4. On the general question of language acquisition, Ferguson thought that a useful attack might be to look at what was known must exist in adult grammar and try to imagine what was necessary in order to reach that point. Nevertheless, the most progress in recent years had been made not by taking that approach but by observing very carefully what seemed to happen at a particular age and by describing that on its own merits, without reference to what the adult grammar might be. In this respect he found it difficult to understand how the hierarchical structures proposed by McNeill related to observations of child speech at the two-word sentence level. The two-word sentence did however seem to have a very striking general feature applicable to observations of the learning of Russian and other languages as well as English. At a certain point there seemed to be only three sentence types — a single word (presumably of the content-word class), two of these content words in the same sentence, or a pivot word and an open-class content word (in either order). The first thing to be accounted for in a theory of language acquisition was how this elementary structure was achieved. The most it would require would be a simple relationship of predication, and this might also be found in nonverbal aspects of a child's behavior. It could be represented by a simple permutation of elements between which some kind of discontinuous dependency existed.

In response, Fodor tried to draw a distinction between "stages" and "biological way stations" in the child's acquisition of language. The only way to discover which was which would be to find out whether a structure demonstrated at a particular level offered a route to where the acquisition process was going to go. So far this had not been done, although McNeill had tried to show that there was a route from the pivot–open-class construction to adult grammar. McNeill felt it was not essential for his argument to show that the first sentences necessarily reflected a hierarchical structure. He posed the problem facing a child who had mastered something like a verb-noun or verb-pivot nonhierarchical structure when he heard a verb-pivot-noun construction. At this stage the child had to compose a new rule to account for the longer sequence, and it was known that his solution was a hierarchical one.

5. Fodor was asked whether a child's problem paralleled that of a field worker trying to write a grammar without the services of an informant who knew both the linguist's and the target language. He replied that the interesting part of his discovery procedure left off where the serious linguist would begin. The linguist would have access to an enormous consensus about how a grammar ought to be constructed. The logically difficult problem was how to get into the area of that consensus. The point perhaps was that the linguist and the child shared a considerable amount of prejudice about what kinds of grammars might be worth trying. All he would like to do at this stage was state what that prejudice was.

6. Fodor was also asked whether he expected his eventual system to remain in a "glass house of formal structure," stripped of any contact with reality. He thought it very likely that the way a syntactic system interacted with reality was through the underlying structure. In a sense, however, learning of syntax had to go the opposite way to the implication of the question; a child had to find some way of getting the underlying representation if he was to understand what was said to him. The obvious relation between lexical items and facts about the world was not a problem to be solved at the syntactic level; there the concern was with how the organization of sentences, especially their underlying structure, was learned.

7. Hirsh drew a parallel between current theory of grammar and the state of animal psychology at the end of the nineteenth century. The experimenter discovered a pattern in a complicated piece of behavior, and addressed himself to the problem of how the organism learned that pattern. It was asserted that the pattern that the theorist superimposed on his analysis of the organism's behavior was known

to the organism, and the problem became one of finding out how the organism acquired that pattern. Fodor said this fundamentally was his position with respect to children and language, and he would want to say the same thing — with certain caveats entered — for characteristically organized patterns of animal behavior. As an example, he would assert that a dog learned that the angle of incidence of a ball thrown against a wall equaled the angle of reflection. This knowledge could be tested. This was not the same thing as asserting — as had been suggested — that a falling rock knew the law of gravity. The difference was that counterfactual possibilities existed for the dog, which might have learned something else in an artificial environment. The neonate dog had a space of possible behaviors and faced an induction problem of what kind of universe it was in. Presumably it learned the rule that it lived in a universe where incident and reflected angles were equal.

*Dan I. Slobin*

# THE ACQUISITION OF RUSSIAN AS A NATIVE LANGUAGE

Developmental psycholinguistics has made great strides in recent years, bringing new and powerful analytical tools to bear upon the intriguing and puzzling question of how a child comes to master his native tongue. The overwhelming majority of this work, however, has dealt with the acquisition of English as a first language. Unfortunately, extensive data on child speech in non-Indo-European languages are not yet available; there is, however, a sizable Soviet body of literature that is worthy of the attention of American psycholinguists. Although Russian is also an Indo-European language, it is sufficiently different from English — most clearly in its highly inflectional grammatical structure — to serve as a useful contrast case to sharpen notions of universal aspects of language acquisition and linguistic competence.

Language behavior — and especially child language — has long been a central concern of Soviet psychologists (Slobin, forthcoming; Luria, 1959a). In a hundred-page review of Soviet psycholinguistics, covering the period 1918 to 1958, no less than forty-eight pages are devoted to child speech (Raevskiĭ, 1958). This abiding interest in language has both a theoretical and a practical basis in Soviet psychology. Soviet philosophical principles of dialectical materialism are tied together in the so-called "Leninist theory of reflection," which states that man perceives the universe by acting purposively upon it. In this way consciousness is introduced as a reflection of external material reality and comes to be the cornerstone of much of modern Soviet psychology.

Conscious understanding works through human language to free man from a rigid determinism of the material stimuli present in the immediate environment and makes it possible for him to direct his actions toward goals beyond the present situation. There is, accordingly, a large body of psychological research on pragmatic aspects of language behavior — on regulatory, planning, and directive functions of speech. This research is usually cast in physiological or quasi-physiological terms by referring to Pavlov's formulation of the "second signal system." In his words: "The word created a second system of signals of reality which is peculiarly ours, being the signal of signals. On the one hand, numerous speech stimuli have removed us from reality. . . . On the other, it is precisely speech which has made us human" (1927, p. 357). The underlying ontogenetic notion here is that the acquisition of language qualitatively changes the nature of the child's behavior in almost all spheres of activity. Quoting Pavlov again: "Of course a word is for man as much a real conditioned stimulus as are other stimuli common to men and animals, yet at the same time it is so all-comprehending that it allows no quantitative or qualitative comparisons with conditioned stimuli in animals" (1927, p. 401).

For Soviet psychological theory the unity of consciousness and activity is best seen in the development of language, both phylo- and ontogenetically. Frequent reference is made to the proposal of Marx and Engels that language developed as a result of human activity — namely, the need for cooperation in labor; accordingly, extensive research has been devoted to the development of language in the child as a result of social intercourse and practical needs for communication. The basic problem in this area was early formulated by Vygotsky as "the investigation of how a function, arising in communication and at first divided between two people, can re-structure all of the activity of the child and gradually change into the complicated mediated functional system which characterizes the structure of his mental processes" (Luria, in *Psikhologicheskaya nauka v SSSR*, 1959, p. 524). This point of view has stimulated much research on relations between language and thought, particularly directed toward the development and functions of so-called "inner speech" in children. The approach has its roots in the ideas of "the father of Russian physiology," Sechenov, who wrote in 1863: "When a child thinks he invariably talks at the same time. Thought in five-year-olds is mediated through words or whispers, surely through movements of tongue and lips, which is also very frequently (perhaps always, but in different degrees) true of the thinking of adults" (1863, p. 498).

The other chief impetus to Soviet developmental psycholinguistics has been the practical task of raising infants and very young children in state nurseries. Lyamina pointed out in 1958 that "insufficiencies of group upbringing have an especially unfavorable influence on the development of the speech of children" (p. 119). (Soviet psychology in general has a strong practical bent, and many leading psychology departments are to be found in pedagogical institutes. This principle of "the unity of theory and practice" is clearly stated in the current handbook of Soviet psychology: "The results of investigations are directed towards life, towards practice; in practice they find their application. Practice is the criterion of the truth of the results of scientific research" [*Psikhologicheskaya nauka v SSSR*, 1959, p. 6].)

For all of these reasons, there is at our disposal a body of research on children's learning and use of the Russian language. The present paper deals only with the ontogenetic development of the language itself and not with its use by children for pragmatic and social purposes. (For reviews of Soviet studies of language functions in childhood, see: Ivanov-Smolenskiĭ, 1956; Leontjew and Luria, 1958; Luria, 1957, 1959a, 1959b; Luria and Yudovich, 1956; Vygotsky, 1962.) Further, attention will be limited to aspects of grammar and semantics.[1]

In order to make the discussion intelligible to non-Russian-speakers, a few words about the grammatical structure of the language are in order. Russian has three genders and six cases; nouns, adjectives, and pronouns show gender, case, and number. Verbs are conjugated for person and number, and, in the past tense, also for gender of subject noun. Verbs are marked for tense (three tenses) and aspect (perfective-imperfective, and, for verbs of motion, also determinate-indeterminate). There are many participial forms. The morphology is highly productive, and freely used suffixes of many sorts abound (e.g., diminutive, augmentative, endearing, pejorative, agentive, and so on). Word order is much freer than in English.

Perhaps because the morphological system of Russian facilitates neologisms — which are a marked and delightful aspect of Russian child language — Soviet psychologists have not been attracted by mechanistic and imitation-based, passive models of language acquisi-

---

[1] Abstracts of Soviet studies of many different aspects of child language, in addition to those discussed here, can be found in the appendix.

tion. They see first-language-learning as a highly active, creative process, rivaling the productions of the poet and artist in subtlety and originality. To quote Gvozdev, whose careful work on child language forms the basis of much of the following presentation: "The keenness of the child's observations and the artistic clarity of many childish words are common knowledge; they are truly very close to the linguistic creativity of literary artists. We are therefore dealing here with authentic creativity, attesting to the linguistic endowment of children" (1949, Part 2, p. 187). And El'konin, one of the Soviet Union's leading developmental psychologists, says: "It is perfectly clear that [language acquisition] is not a mechanical process in which the child acquires each separate linguistic form by means of simple repetition" (1958).

## SYNTAX AND MORPHOLOGY

The most careful and intensive longitudinal study of a child's language development ever published anywhere is probably the monumental work of Aleksandr N. Gvozdev (1949, 1961), a Soviet linguist and teacher. He kept a diary of the speech of his son, Zhenya, almost daily for the first few years of the child's life and recorded his language extensively until the age of nine (1921 to 1929). The diary was recorded in a phonetic notation, either during the child's speech or shortly thereafter. Gvozdev's books are topically arranged, with continuing intensive and insightful analysis of the material. The following discussion is based primarily on the speech of Zhenya, supplemented with data from psycholinguistic experiments with preschool children.

Gvozdev characterizes his task in terms of discovering the child's developing linguistic competence: he is clearly interested in discovering the child's *generative* systems, although it appears that he rarely intervened to test his son's comprehension or production by systematic experimentation. He avoids the usual errors of diary studies by stressing contrastive analysis of forms in the corpus, usually setting up classes in terms of the child's system rather than in terms of adult Russian.

### Early Syntax

The beginning stages of syntactic development look very much like those of English-speaking children described by Braine (1963a), Brown and Fraser (1963), and Miller and Ervin (1964). There is clearly a small class of pivot words (P) and a large open class of words (O), which can be combined into three types of two-word sentences: P + O, O + P, and O + O (cf. McNeill, this volume). Gvozdev argues that these sentences are constructed, rather than imitated or memorized as units, because most of the single words appear as separate utterances and the two-word combinations differ from adult sentences in form.

Two-word sentences appear at about 1,8; at first there are only a few such sentences, but they become the usual utterance type by 1,9. By 1,10, they are replaced in frequency by longer sentences. As has been noted by other investigators, new pivots are often playfully practiced, the child uttering long series of pivot sentences, holding the pivot constant and substituting a variety of words from the open class (cf. Weir, 1962). In line with American findings, membership in both pivot and open classes is heterogeneous from the point of view of part-of-speech membership in the adult language.

The first three-word sentence is a simple negation, which involves placing a negative element at the beginning of a sentence. This is the same initial negation form found by Bellugi (1964), though the adult model in Russian often involves a double negative. For example, the adult form *nyet nikavó*[2] (not no-one — i.e., there is no one) is given by the child as *nyet kavó*. *Nyet, dam* is the child's equivalent of adult *nyet, ni dam* (no, not I-will-give). The same negative element, *nyet*, is used in all cases, even where the adult form would have only the single negative element *ni*: e.g., instead of *ni karmí* (don't feed), the child says *nyet kamlí*. Presumably, acoustic marking singles out *nyet*, rather than *ni* or *nye*, as the primordial negative element. (It should also be noted that *nyet* is the independent negative element in Russian, analogous to the English *no*.)

Another source of length is the addition of content words to short sentences. Gvozdev thinks that forms learned more recently appear later in sentences and gives the example of elaboration of one-word utterances to two-word subject-object sentences and, with the acquisition of new verbs, to subject-object-verb sentences, although subject-verb-object order is dominant in Russian. For example, at the first stage the child may say *Mama*; at the second, *Mama niska* (Mama book); and at the third, *Mama niska tsitats* (Mama book read). (The forms are all unmarked in the child's system, and Russian does not use articles.) This subject-object-verb order is at first the dominant order in the child's speech, being replaced by subject-verb-object at about 1,11. (It is of interest to note that, according to Greenberg [1963], it is apparently a linguistic universal that subject precede object in the dominant actor-action construction of a language, and that the two most common patterns are SVO and SOV.)

As other examples of his theory that new items are tacked on to the ends of sentences, Gvozdev points out that (1) personal conjugations of the verb are developed later than the infinitive and, in sentences, follow the infinitive, although usual Russian word order is the reverse (e.g., *spat' khachu* — to-sleep I-want, *Mama kupat' myasa padyot* — Mama to-buy meat will-go); (2) adjectives and possessive pronouns develop later than nouns and at first follow nouns in the child's sentences, again, usual Russian word order being the reverse (e.g., *kubik bal'shaya* — block big, *pyero tvayo* — pen your).

Yet, word order is quite inflexible at each of the early stages of syntactic development. One might have predicted that Russian children, being exposed to a great variety of word orders, would first learn the morphological markers for such classes as subject, object, and verb and combine them in any order. This is, however, hardly the case. Child grammar begins with unmarked forms — generally the noun in what corresponds to the nominative singular, the verb in its adult imperative or infinitive form, and so on. Morphology develops later than syntax, and word order is as inflexible for little Russian children as it is for Americans. The flexibility of adult Russian word order depends on the inflectional systems. Arguments have been advanced by Braine (1963*b*) and by Jenkins and Palermo (1964) that rely upon the ordinal sequences of words in adult language to account for the order of elements in child sentences and for the formation of word classes. Not only do the Soviet data cast doubt on these interpretations, but (as Bever, Fodor, and Weksel [1965] have pointed out) even in English, which does not make great use of inflection, order is not as important a feature of syntactic structure as might be imagined. It is certainly a much less important feature in Russian, thus lending further support to the critique developed by Bever *et al.* There must be something in LAD, the built-in "language acquisition device" discussed by McNeill (this volume), Chomsky, and others, that favors beginning language with ordered sequences of unmarked classes, regardless of the degree of correspondence of such a system with the input language.

It may well be that order is important in the base structure of Russian, thus supporting McNeill's proposal (this volume) that children "talk base strings directly." The most economical representation of an inflected language like Russian would order the language in the underlying representation. Inflections could then be added to the characteristic positions of parts of speech, and an additional rule or rules would then reorder this string. All of the world's languages make use of order in their grammatical structure, but not all languages have inflectional systems. It would be reasonable, then, for LAD to assume the language to be ordered, to adopt a given order as a first guess, and later learn that it can be changed. Again, this interpretation minimizes the contribution of the linguistic input, suggesting that it is more important in providing tests for hypotheses about the organization of language than it is in acting as an observation base for inferences.

The reliance upon ordering as a linguistic device may continue well after Russian children have mastered the language, if we can believe an experiment reported by El'kin (1957). He conditioned an eyeblink response to sentences as stimuli in subjects aged ten to fourteen. In children in the twelve- to fourteen-year-old range, reversing the word order in the stimulus sentence had no decremental effect on the conditioned-reflex activity. The reversed sentences were grammatical and synonymous with the original sentences, and apparently were treated as very similar or identical stimuli. This was not the case, however, for the younger children. Admittedly this experiment is difficult to interpret — perhaps, however, for children as old as ten or eleven the reversed sentences were somehow not quite the same stimuli as the original sentences.

## Later Syntax

Gvozdev's work has not yet been examined to determine what happens to syntactic patterns after this early level; his classification of sentence types is not always the most useful, and extensive effort would be required — and should be expended — to reorganize his data for other sorts of analysis (though a transformational grammar of Russian is, unfortunately, not yet available). He contends that by age three almost all of the complex and complex-subordinate sentence types of adult Russian are present, and that the child knows all of the generic grammatical categories (case, gender, tense, and so on) and has a good idea of their meanings. No new uses of grammatical cases enter after 3,9. By contrast, the learning of morphology and morphophonemics goes on for very much longer. It takes until seven or eight to sort out all of the proper conjugational and declensional suffixes and categories, stress and sound alternations, and the like. The Russian child does not fully master his morphology until he is several years older than the age at which the American child is believed to have essentially completed his primary grammatical learning. In this sense, then, it may be more difficult to learn to speak one language natively than another — though the basic learning is accomplished very rapidly. (This point cannot be properly evaluated, however, until we have more information about the grammar of English-speaking children between the ages of five and eight. Full mastery of the auxiliary system, the subjunctive, and quantifiers, for example, is quite late in American children. It is not yet possible to compare adequately the lateness of such accomplishments with the lateness of other sorts of accomplishments in Russian. The unanswered question is whether the speech of a Russian seven-year-old is heard as more deviant from adult speech than is the speech of an American seven-year-old.)

## *Morphology*

Morphological markers enter when sentences increase from two to three or four words in length. All words are unmarked in Zhenya's speech until about 1,10, and then, in the one month between 1,11 and 2,0, there is a sudden emergence of contrasting morphological elements in various grammatical categories. In this one month, previously unmarked nouns are marked for (1) number, (2) nominative, accusative, and genitive cases, and (3) diminutive; verbs are marked for (1) imperative, (2) infinitive, (3) past tense, and (4) present tense. Apparently once the principles of inflection and derivation are acquired — or at any rate the principle of suffixing — the principle is immediately applied over a wide range of types.

It is especially in the field of morphology, where Russian is so rich, that many striking examples can be found of principles that are often difficult to discern — or to discern in many embodiments — in studying English-speaking children. This matter of simultaneous emergence of a grammatical principle in several domains can be seen repeatedly in Russian children. Several more examples from this one boy follow:

1. Between the ages of 2,10 and 3,0, gender agreement appeared simultaneously in two domains — in regard to both adjective-noun agreement and noun–past-tense-of-verb agreement (the verb is inflected for gender in the past tense in Russian).

2. When a new grammatical case enters, it serves several functions at once. For example, between 2,0 and 2,2, the first datives were used; they were used to indicate both the indirect object of action and directed motion toward an individual. In these same two months the instrumental also emerged and was used immediately to indicate the instrument of action, mutuality of action, and goal of action (in consonance with these uses in adult Russian but lacking the required preposition in the latter two examples). One has the impression that the child understood these semantic distinctions before he began using the declensions — when his nouns were still unmarked — and that rapid acquisition and differentiation of the markers and their senses reflects this earlier knowledge.

3. Shortly after grammatical cases enter, the child begins to use a variety of prepositions with them. (Prepositions control case selection in Russian.) Between 2,4 and 2,6, Zhenya began to use eight different new prepositions, combining them with nouns in five different grammatical cases. Again, the principle is suddenly and widely applied to an entire domain — and to the correct domain.

(Note, by the way, that the Russian child has no apparent difficulty in discovering morpheme boundaries. From the very beginning of inflections one sees a free use of word stems combined with a huge variety of bound morphemes. The word stem is clearly a psychologically real unit.)

Overregularizations are rampant in the child's learning of Russian morphology — small wonder, with the great variety of inflectional categories and with the additional great variety of forms within each category, determined on the basis of both sound relations and grammatical relations. For example, not only must the child learn an instrumental case ending for each masculine, feminine, and neuter singular and plural noun and adjective, but within each of these subcategories there are several different phonologically conditioned suffixes. The child's solution is to seize upon one suffix at first — probably the most frequent and/or most clearly marked acoustically — and use it for every instance of that particular grammatical category. For example, Gvozdev's son Zhenya at first used the suffix -om for all singular noun instrumental endings, although this suffix is used only for masculine and neuter singular nouns. This suffix, however, has only one other function — a masculine and neuter prepositional case ending for adjectives. The corresponding dominant feminine singular noun instrumental ending (-oĭ), on the other hand, serves a variety of functions, being an adjectival suffix for four cases in the feminine and one in the masculine. Thus to begin with (though feminine nouns are more frequent in Russian child speech), Zhenya used the suffix of fewer meanings — -om — for all instances of the instrumental case. This clarifies Gvozdev's statement that grammatical categories are acquired earlier than morphological details. The child already possesses the category of instrumental case — and marks it accordingly — but it will take several years, perhaps, before he learns to mark correctly every instance of the instrumental in accordance with gender and morphophonemic principles.

This is the first question discussed here for which data from other Russian children are available. Zakharova (1958) did an experiment in which 200 children between the ages of three and seven were shown objects named in the nominative and were asked questions whose answers required placing the names (both familiar and unfamiliar) in another case form. She found that the youngest children did not attend to the gender of the noun, revealed by the nominative form, but used stereotyped case endings for each case in their repertoire, regardless of gender. Like Zhenya, they used the suffix -om as a universal instrumental, and -u as a universal accusative. These endings are of high frequency, clearly marked acoustically in adult speech and limited in the number of functions they perform.

As gender comes to be more important in classifying nouns, other additional endings for each case enter. They do not, however, peacefully coexist with the already established endings. When a child learns, for example, that -oĭ — the feminine noun singular instrumental ending — can also serve as a noun instrumental ending, he abandons the masculine and neuter instrumental -om, which he has been using, and for a while uses -oĭ as a universal instrumental. Only later does -om re-enter to assume its place in standard Russian. Practice clearly does not ensure the survival of a form in child speech, regardless of whether or not that form corresponds to adult usage (and, presumably, regardless of whether or not its usage by the child is "reinforced" by adults). (This is very similar to the development of the past tense in English, in which irregular strong forms, like *did,* are at first used correctly, only to be driven out later by overgeneralizations from the regular weak forms, giving rise to transitory though persistent forms like *doed.*)

The phenomenon of one suffix driving out another is also visible in other domains. Popova (1958), for example, investigated gender agreement between nouns and verbs in the past tense in a cross-sectional study of fifty-five children ranging in age from 1,10 to 3,6. She used only masculine and feminine nouns, telling the children stories in the present tense and asking questions about the stories in the past-tense plural form, which does not distinguish as to gender. (It can be seen that the structure of Russian is well suited to the design of psycholinguistic experiments!) Masculine nouns and the corresponding past-tense forms end in consonants; that is, the masculine is marked by a zero ending, the feminine is marked with *-a.* The younger children overgeneralized the feminine verb ending, often using it as the past-tense form for actions predicated of nouns of both genders. In older children, the masculine zero ending predominated as a verb ending; and in yet older children the two forms both appeared, though used consistently only by the oldest subjects. Although this study samples a number of ages synchronically, it is reasonable to assume that an ontogenetic series is also revealed. In a fashion similar to the successive overgeneralizations of case endings, it would seem that when the masculine (zero) ending of the past tense emerges in a child's speech, it tends to drive out entirely the earlier feminine (*-a*) ending, which re-enters only later in a period of mixed usage.

Zakharova offers the following explanations for the finding that the initial gender suffix to be overgeneralized is the feminine: (1) this is a strongly and consistently marked gender (*-a,* as opposed to a variety of consonants in the masculine; again, the most consistent form is chosen first); (2) Russian-speaking little children tend to use open, prolonged syllables, even in uttering masculine nouns (e.g., saying *tigra* instead of *tigr*); and (3) diary materials show that 70 per cent of the words of children of this age end in *-a.*

It is not only in the domain of choosing a universal suffix to perform a given grammatical function that the Russian child attempts to apply a single principle to all words in a system. In studying number in nouns, one discovers not only that the child applies the same phonological rules to make the plural for all types of nouns, but that it seems as if he also feels that every noun must have both forms — singular and plural. Thus he pluralizes mass nouns (*bumagi*), counts mass nouns (*odna sakhara*), and invents singulars for plural nouns that have no singular forms in Russian (e.g., *lyut* as the singular of *lyudi*).

With time, gross categories (such as a single noun class pluralized in the same fashion for all members) are subdivided. As McNeill suggests, "children's early competence includes a generic classification of adult grammatical classes" (this volume, p. 32), and the child moves down a hierarchy of grammatical categories to arrive at the more narrowly defined categories playing a role in his particular native language. There are a number of examples in Gvozdev's data of such subdivisions of initially gross categories:

1. At first all nouns are pluralized; later the noun class is divided into mass and count nouns that behave differently in the plural.
2. Animate and inanimate nouns have different accusative forms in Russian. Subdivision of the noun class into these two categories, in regard to the accusative, is quite late in Russian children.
3. A general modifier class is successively subdivided into classes of possessive pronouns, adjectives, and so on (analogous to the differentiation described by Brown and Bellugi [1964]).
4. At first only the feminine past tense of verbs is used, then only the masculine; following a period of mixed usage, all three genders emerge as separate entities.
5. Copular predicates in Russian are expressed by the instrumental case, but Russian children use a nominative copular predicate universally, not subdividing the predicate until age six or later.

In most of these cases it is of interest to note once again that full mastery of the morphological system comes relatively late in Russian-speaking children. The distinction between mass and count nouns is not stabilized until age eight; the distinction between animate and inanimate nouns in the accusative is mastered only at four; gender agreement between nouns and verbs in the past comes at three, although agreement of number and person comes a year earlier; and the subdivision of the predicate is not mastered until about age six. Other evidence of late morphological learning comes from the experiment of Zakharova. She found that declension of masculine and feminine nouns ending in palatalized consonants was not mastered until six or seven. This is a particularly difficult distinction because the gender of each such noun must be rote memorized and the declensional patterns deviate from the standard in some respects.

Perhaps "Anglocentrically," the multitudinous diversity of Russian morphological classes and devices has been proposed as one explanation of the protracted period of language acquisition in Russian children. This argument, however, does not speak to the question of the order and rate of acquisition of particular morphological classes. Soviet psycholinguists interpret this order in terms of the relative semantic or conceptual difficulty of various classification criteria. One line of evidence in this argument is the observation that lexical items referring to certain semantic categories appear at the same time as those categories become morphologically marked. For example, at 1,10 one finds the first use of the word *mnogo* (much, many) at the same time as the singular-plural distinction in noun markings. The words *right away* and *soon* enter at the same time as the future tense.

An attempt is made to set up the following order of acquisition of morphological classes in reference to their meanings:

1. Those classes whose reference is clearly concrete emerge first. The first morphological distinction is number, at 1,10, followed shortly by diminutive suffixing of nouns. The imperative, with its immediate, expressive character, also appears very early.

   In reference to common prepositions within the preposition class, Feofanov points out that "Initially, their use is confined to relations with a concrete meaning understood by the child from visual perception (space relations, relations involving mutuality . . .) ; then it extends to relations without such visual support (relations of purpose, time relations, and space relations used figuratively)" (1958, p. 124).

2. Classes based on relational semantic criteria — cases, tenses, and persons of the verb — emerge later than those with concrete reference.

3. The conditional is very late, not being used until 2,10, though its grammatical structure is exceedingly simple. Conditional subordinate clauses are also later, emerging at about 2,8. In both

cases it seems to be the semantic and not the grammatical aspect that is difficult for the child.

4. Noun endings indicating abstract categories of quality and action continue to be added until as late as seven. The only noun suffixes learned before three are those of clearly concrete or emotive reference — diminutive and augmentative, endearing and pejorative.

5. Finally, grammatical gender is responsible for what is perhaps the most difficult and drawn-out linguistic learning of the Russian-speaking child, although it is almost always unequivocally marked phonetically. This is a category almost entirely lacking in semantic correlates, and apparently such correlates are an important aid in learning form-class distinctions. As pointed out, at first the child uses the feminine past-tense ending for almost all nouns regardless of their gender markings — even if he knows they are semantically masculine (e.g., *papa*). Later the child will use the masculine past tense for many nouns that are semantically feminine. The verb inflection is simply not treated as having semantic content. In a like manner, as pointed out, the child will first use one stereotyped case ending for all nouns in that case, regardless of their gender (even if he can correctly identify gender-class membership on the basis of pronoun substitution and adjective agreement).

The semantic and conceptual aspects of grammatical classes thus clearly play an important role in determining the order of their development and subdivision.

An experiment performed by Bogoyavlenskiĭ (1957) reveals the ability of Russian children to understand and produce various morphological features and also shows that conscious metalinguistic attention is extremely difficult to achieve at early ages. Children of five and six were tested for their understanding of various noun suffixes (augmentative, diminutive, and agentive). The suffixes were appended to words not familiar to the children (an animal called a *lar,* a sweet kvas drink called *lafit,* and the fabric *kashemir*). The words were used to name pictured referents. The children were then asked to explain the meanings of these words with suffixes attached. If this task was difficult for the children, the words, with the various suffixes, were then embedded in stories. All of the children could correctly identify the relative sizes of the referents on the basis of the augmentative and diminutive suffixes, but the agentive suffix was more difficult for them to interpret. Bogoyavlenskiĭ points out that the former do not change the "basic lexical meaning" of a word, while the latter (agentive) does change this meaning, and he speculates that morphological principles of "word change" (e.g., diminutive) are achieved at an earlier age than those of "word formation" (e.g., agentive).

When a child's performance was correct in this experiment, he still could not be brought to explain the formal differences between the words. For example, the experimenter would ask: "You were right about the difference between the animals — one is little and the other is big; now pay attention to the words themselves as I say them: *lar — larenok;* what's the difference between them?" It was found that "Regardless of the repeated oral presentation of these words, not one of the children (who had no difficulty in determining the semantic difference between these words) could give any sort of answer in this case. The children gave confused and embarrassed smiles or simply remained silent, making no attempt to analyze the sounds of the words" (Bogoyavlenskiĭ, 1957, p. 263).

In another experiment, Bogoyavlenskiĭ asked children to supply diminutive suffixes to words that do not generally receive such suffixes, or at least not in the experience of the child (e.g., giraffe, acorn, oak, lion, ostrich, wolf, nail). All of the children successfully provided diminutive, and only diminutive, suffixes of many sorts. Their productions were generally correct, though all of them of course do not occur in the Russian language (since at least eight different suffixes were used by the children with these nouns). The only clearly incorrect usage from the standpoint of standard, adult Russian was the application of suffixes used only to diminish animate objects to inanimate objects as well. The children were generally correct in choosing suffixes following phonological rules of agreement with the final sound of the root word.

## WORD MEANING

A fairly large body of Soviet pedagogical-developmental research deals with the problem of teaching very young children to understand and use individual words. The impetus for this work is the problem of collective child-rearing, as noted earlier. Soviet investigators have a great advantage in investigating a child's original learning of word meanings in that a large number of very young children are available for research in the state nurseries.

In this research, action is generally seen as a principal component of the learning of word meanings. Kol'tsova (Razran, 1961), for example, presented a doll 1500 times to each of ten twenty-month-old children in the course of several months. None of them knew the word *doll*. For five of the children, the presentation was accompanied by a limited number of sentences, which treated the doll simply as an object (*here is the doll, give me the doll,* etc.). The other five children heard thirty different sentences, bringing the word *doll* into meaningful connections with a number of other words (*rock the doll, feed the doll,* etc.). Finally the children were presented with an array of dolls and other toys and asked to *pick a doll*. The children in the first group picked a variety of toys, including the experimental doll, while the children of the second group selected only dolls. Kol'tsova explains that it is by dealing with objects in a variety of different ways that children pass from diffuse to more specific word meanings. The theory here is apparently similar to Osgood's response theory of meaning.

Lyamina (1960) studied thirty-two children longitudinally, from the ages 1,2 to 2,6, attempting to teach them new word meanings. She found it extremely difficult to work with children under 1,6 — as one might well imagine — but did succeed in teaching children older than 1,6 to point to objects whose names they had learned and to hand named objects to the experimenter. She found it easiest to teach a child the name of an object if it is the one new object among a collection of familiar ones. Under such conditions, in Soviet terms the new object calls forth an orienting response that facilitates word learning. In another paper (1958), Lyamina reports that contrary to previous opinion and report (such as that of Kol'tsova), her subjects (ages 1,8 to 2,1) were not better at naming familiar, everyday objects than they were at naming objects whose names were taught in an experimental setting without the opportunity to manipulate them; apparently the important variable was the child's attention to the new object. As a matter of fact, Lyamina proposes that motor and verbal responses may often be in competition for children of this age: (1) it is more difficult to name objects while playing with them, (2) the output of speech is said to be diminished while the child is learning to walk and while he is walking, and (3) the form of speech is said to be more primitive while the child is walking. She proposes further that there is a rapid spurt in language development once various motor acts are coordinated with each other and with speaking.

Mallitskaya (1960) attempted to work with children even younger than those of Lyamina. Her subjects were ten children between the ages of 0,9 and 1,6. Pictures were attached to four sides of a cube. The experimenter would point to a picture and repeat its name two or three times (e.g., *vot lisa* — this is a fox) and would then turn the cube, removing the designated picture from view, and tell the child to find that picture. It took several weeks to train the children to sit calmly and attend to the experiment, and even longer to train them to perform as required. Once this training was completed, however, the children became very adept at the task, and by eleven to twelve months of age could generally learn a new word after two or three repetitions and could easily differentiate and find eight different pictures on two cubes. After this stage the child was presented with three pictures, one of which was new to him. Mallitskaya states that the new picture evoked a strong orienting response, which weakened as soon as the picture was named, and that the children were generally able to learn such names after one presentation. She concludes that "even at the age of twelve to thirteen months (word-image) connections can be formed under some conditions after a single reinforcement. The most important condition for developing these connections is the presence of an intense orienting reaction to the named image, as is the case when a new image is placed among other images whose names the child already knows" (1960, p. 126).

Sokhin (1959), in a cross-sectional study, found that the comprehension of some prepositions by two-year-olds is very much tied to action: while a child could correctly perform the action of *put the block under the table*, he could not *put the block under the ring* when the ring was lying on the table. Sokhin argues that *under*, in the second case, requires two actions — lifting up the ring and placing the block under it — whereas *under* in the first case requires only one. This notion is supported by the fact that some children held the block under the table beneath the point where the ring was lying rather than pick up the ring and place the block under it on the surface of the table. In this very insightful study of the understanding of prepositions by children of various ages, Sokhin points out that the meaning of a word changes with age. In this case, for example, although two-year-olds have a general idea of the spatial relations denoted by the preposition *under,* they have yet to separate this notion from specific actions; it is not yet a general concept of spatial relations, though the children seem to understand it correctly when dealing with a variety of everyday situations.

These are but a few examples of an approach to developmental psycholinguistics almost unknown in the West — painstaking, longitudinal and cross-sectional, experimental investigation of very early stages of language development, using large numbers of children. One can only hope that such studies will continue, with greater methodological finesse and with more detailed publication in both Russian and English.

## REFERENCES

BELLUGI, URSULA. The emergence of inflections and negation systems in the speech of two children. Paper presented to New England Psychol. Assoc., 1964.

BEVER, T., FODOR, J. A., and WEKSEL, W. On the acquisition of syntax: A critique of "contextual generalization." *Psychol. Rev.,* 1965, *72,* 6, 467–482.

BOGOYAVLENSKIĬ, D. N. *Psikhologiya usvoeniya orfografii (Psychology of learning orthography).* Moscow: Akad. Pedag. Nauk RSFSR, 1957.

BRAINE, M. D. S. The ontogeny of English phrase structure: The first phase. *Language,* 1963a, *39,* 1–13.

——— On learning the grammatical order of words. *Psychol. Rev.,* 1963b, *70,* 323–348.

BROWN, R., and BELLUGI, URSULA. Three processes in the child's acquisition of syntax. *Harvard Educ. Rev.,* 1964, *34,* 133–151.

——— and FRASER, C. The acquisition of syntax. In *Verbal Behavior and Learning,* C. N. Cofer and Barbara S. Musgrave (Eds.), New York: McGraw-Hill, 1963. (Also in *The Acquisition of Language,* Ursula Bellugi and R. Brown (Eds.), *Monogr. Soc. Res. Child Develpm.,* 1964, *29,* 1, 43–79.)

EL'KIN, D. G. Ob uslovnykh refleksakh na slozhnye slovesnye razdrazhiteli u shkol'nikov (On conditioned reflexes to complex verbal stimuli in children of school age). In *Materialy soveshchaniya po psikhologii.* Moscow: Akad. Pedag. Nauk RSFSR, 1957, pp. 371–379.

EL'KONIN, D. B. *Razvitie rechi v doshkol'nom vozraste (The development of speech in preschool age).* Moscow: Akad. Pedag. Nauk RSFSR, 1958.

FEOFANOV, M. P. Ob upotreblenii predlogóv v detskoĭ rechi (On the use of prepositions in child speech). *Voprosy Psikhol.,* 1958, No. 3, 118–124.

GREENBERG, J. H. *Universals of Language.* Cambridge, Mass.: M.I.T. Press, 1963; 2nd ed., 1966.

GVOZDEV, A. N. *Formirovanie u rebenka grammaticheskogo stroya russkogo yazyka*

(*Formation in the child of the grammatical structure of the Russian language*), Parts I and II. Moscow: Akad. Pedag. Nauk RSFSR, 1949.

—— *Voprosy izucheniya detskoĭ rechi* (*Questions of the study of child speech*). Moscow: Akad. Pedag. Nauk RSFSR, 1961.

IVANOV-SMOLENSKIĬ, A. G. Puti razvitiya eksperimental'nogo issledovaniya raboty vzaimodeĭstviya pervoĭ i vtoroĭ signal'nykh sistem (Developmental paths of experimental research into the work and interaction of the first and second signal systems). *Trudy Inst. Vyssh. Nervn. Deyat., Seriya Patofiziologicheskaya,* Vol. II, 1956.

(Translation in *Works Inst. High. Nerv. Act., Pathophysiological Series,* Vol. II. Washington, D. C.: Natl. Sci. Found., 1960, pp. 1–31.)

JENKINS, J. J., and PALERMO, D. S. Mediation processes and the acquisition of linguistic structure. In *The Acquisition of Language,* Ursula Bellugi and R. Brown (Eds.), *Monogr. Soc. Res. Child Develpm.,* 1964, *29,* 1, 141–169.

LEONTJEW, A. N., and LURIA, A. R. Die psychologischen Anschauungen L. S. Wygotskis. *Z. für Psychol.,* 1958, *162,* 3–4, 165–205.

LURIA, A. R. The role of language in the formation of temporary connections. In *Psychology in the Soviet Union,* B. Simon (Ed.), Stanford: Stanford University Press, 1957, pp. 115–129.

—— Razvitie rechi v formirovanie psikhicheskikh protsessov (Speech development in the formation of mental processes). In *Psikhologicheskaya nauka v SSSR,* Vol. I. Moscow: Akad. Pedag. Nauk RSFSR, 1959a, 516–577.

(Translated in *Psychological Science in the USSR,* Vol. I. Washington, D. C.: U.S. Joint Publication Res. Serv. No. 11466, 1961, pp. 704–787.)

—— The directive function of speech; I: Its development in early childhood; II: Its dissolution in pathological states of the brain. *Word,* 1959b, *15,* 115–129, 341–352.

—— *The Role of Speech in the Regulation of Normal and Abnormal Behavior.* Oxford: Pergamon, 1961.

—— and YUDOVICH, F. YA. *Rech' i razvitie psikhicheskikh protsessov u rebenka.* Moscow: Akad. Pedag. Nauk RSFSR, 1956.

(Translation: *Speech and the Development of Mental Processes in the Child.* London: Staples Press, 1959.)

LYAMINA, G. M. K voprosu o mekhanizme ovladeniya proiznosheniem slov u deteĭ vtorogo i tret'ego goda zhizni (On the mechanism of mastery of pronunciation of words by children in the second and third years of life). *Voprosy Psikhol.,* 1958, No. 6, 119–130.

—— Razvitie ponimaniya rechi u deteĭ vtorogo goda zhizni (Development of speech comprehension in children in the second year of life). *Voprosy Psikhol.,* 1960, No. 3, 106–121.

MALLITSKAYA, M. K. K metodike ispol'zovaniya kartinok dlya razvitiya ponimaniya rechi u deteĭ v kontse pervogo i na vtorom godu zhizni (A method for using pictures to develop speech comprehension in children at the end of the first and in the second year of life). *Voprosy Psikhol.,* 1960, No. 3, 122–126.

MILLER, W., and ERVIN, SUSAN. The development of grammar in child language. In *The Acquisition of Language,* Ursula Bellugi and R. Brown (Eds.), *Monogr. Soc. Res. Child Develpm.*, 1964, *29*, 1, 9–34.

PAVLOV, I. P. *Conditioned Reflexes: An Investigation of the Physiological Activity of the Cerebral Cortex.* London: Oxford University Press, 1927.

POPOVA, M. I. Grammaticheskie elementy yazyka v rechi deteĭ preddoshkol'nogo vozrasta (Grammatical elements of language in the speech of pre-preschool children). *Voprosy Psikhol.*, 1958, No. 3, 106–117.

*Psikhologicheskaya nauka v SSSR,* Vol. I. Moscow: Akad. Pedag. Nauk RSFSR, 1959.

   (Translation: *Psychological Science in the USSR,* Vol. I. Washington, D. C.: U.S. Joint Publications Res. Serv. No. 11466, 1961.)

RAEVSKIĬ, A. N. *Psikhologiya rechi v sovetskoĭ psikhologicheskoĭ nauke za 40 let (The psychology of speech in Soviet psychological science for 40 years).* Kiev: Kiev University Press, 1958.

RAZRAN, G. The observable unconscious and the inferable conscious in current Soviet psychophysiology: Interoceptive conditioning, semantic conditioning, and the orienting reflex. *Psychol. Rev.*, 1961, *68*, 81–147.

SECHENOV, I. M. Refleksy golovnogo mozga (Reflexes of the brain). *Meditsinskiĭ Vestnik,* 1863, *3*, 461–464, 493–512; also available in M.I.T. Press paperback.

SLOBIN, D. I. Soviet psycholinguistics. In *Present-day Russian Psychology,* N. O'Connor (Ed.), Oxford: Pergamon (forthcoming).

SOKHIN, F. A. O formirovanii yazykovykh obobshcheniĭ v protsesse rechevogo razvitiya (On the formation of linguistic generalizations in the process of speech development). *Voprosy Psikhol.*, 1959, No. 5, 112–123.

VYGOTSKY, L. S. *Thought and Language.* New York: M.I.T. Press and Wiley, 1962.

WEIR, RUTH. *Language in the Crib.* The Hague: Mouton & Co., 1962.

ZAKHAROVA, A. V. Usvoenie doshkol'nikami padezhnykh form (Mastery by pre-schoolers of forms of grammatical case). *Doklady Akad. Pedag. Nauk RSFSR,* 1958, No. 3, 81–84.

# GENERAL DISCUSSION
## Slobin presentation

1. There was interest in Slobin's comment that difficulties had been experienced in the large Russian state nurseries, for example in getting children to pronounce certain sounds well. Children were raised in these nurseries from about six months, and all kinds of experiments were being tried to establish what the optimal conditions for first-language-learning might be. Slobin said that few details were available about particular problems, but Lyamina (1958) had pointed out that "insufficiencies of group upbringing have an especially unfavorable influence on the development of the speech of children." There was evidence that phonological development was much better for children who went home in the evening, even though the ratio of well-trained upbringers in the schools was about one to three and they spent a great deal of time with the children. Two possibly significant factors were suggested in the discussion — the Russian emphasis on the importance of the peer group, which might mean that the children were exposed to more child speech than they would be at home, and the concentration on formal training devices, trying to see how children could learn the name of an object quickly or improve pronunciation quickly. These might be critical in the areas in which difficulty had been experienced.

2. Several participants were impressed by the demonstrations of early and simultaneous mastery of case constructions in several domains because a child would require access to a very large memory of word endings that he had not previously used in order to employ a single

new inflection. Slobin pointed out, however, that there was generally considerable overregulation, with a single ending being used consistently for the various instances of a particular case. Unfortunately there appeared to be no studies of comprehension of the various inflectional forms before a child began to use the case. The same ending tended to be used by all children, and its selection appeared to be determined by the clarity of its acoustic marking and limited number of alternative functions rather than by the frequency of its occurrence in the speech environment or of the child's own practice with it. Ferguson thought that a linguist familiar with Russian might make a reasonable job of predicting which endings the children would tend to use — a prospect which prompted the observation that this could produce a methodological revolution and eliminate the child altogether. Slobin underlined the relevance of these findings to the discussion of the child's segmentation of speech. It was clear that the children had no trouble in distinguishing morphemic boundaries and in differentiating entire collections of suffixes for application to word stems.

3. The importance of semantic criteria in the development of syntactic operations received attention; for example, the delayed appearance of the conditional, which in Russian had a particularly simple grammatical construction. Slobin had pointed out that the only derivational noun endings learned before three years of age were those of clearly concrete or emotive meaning — diminutive and augmentative, endearing and pejorative; the learning of a number of suffixes related to abstract qualities and quantities took much more time. The use of gender was probably the most protracted and difficult; it was usually unequivocally marked phonetically but was a category almost completely lacking in semantic correlates. Several participants felt that the delay should be attributed to difficulty in discriminating in what kind of situation a particular category was appropriate rather than to the late emergence of the fundamental concept. McNeill, for example, proposed that a correlation between order of acquisition and apparent semantic difficulty did not require that semantic criteria were involved in the acquisition of the syntactic rule. Hirsh thought that in second-language-learning the kinds of morphological changes that could be taught and justified logically tended to be the ones that were learned most easily. Ferguson, however, believed that what came early in the first-language-learning of Russian would not necessarily come early in the learning of Russian by an American adult. A related

example was in Arabic; Arabs found it very difficult to learn case endings in their classical language, although American students found them among the easiest things to learn. Slobin pointed out that Russian endings that were apparently arbitrary, such as the use of the instrumental for a predicate, were learned very late even though heard consistently. Such rules were also very difficult for American students to learn.

4. The role of word order in the acquisition of language prompted some debate after Slobin's observation that a built-in language acquisition device would appear to favor beginning language with ordered sequences of unmarked classes, regardless of the correspondence of such a system to the input language. Some Russian sentences said backward meant the same thing (and were grammatical), yet in one generalization study, until a child was about twelve years old the reversal of word order in stimulus sentences had a decremental result. Younger children just did not respond to reversed sentences. Fodor proposed that case rules were acquired first by assigning positions to parts of speech and then by marking inflection on the basis of position. The underlying order would allow the inflection transformations to operate, and there would be a rule that any distribution was permitted after inflection had taken place. Hypotheses about the underlying representation of sentences could not be disconfirmed simply by the data that sentences as produced were not ordered. All this was consistent with the model that the input language was not used as a source of inference but rather as a testing ground for various hypotheses about the organization of language. Logically, it was the most economical way to learn inflections. Ferguson thought that the random ordering that it was assumed a child heard was overemphasized. Counts of normal Russian would demonstrate that some orders were more frequent than others, and he suspected that adults would distort their normal word order or limit their range of variation when speaking to children. Slobin added that Russian children used some word orders that occurred less frequently in adult speech.

The question was asked whether a highly inflected language was more redundant in its structure than one like English. Slobin thought Russian was not especially redundant when word order was considered because without inflection the speaker would be lost. Fodor said information could be transmitted either by order or by inflection, and there was no reasonable way of measuring the information gain by doing it one way rather than the other. There was an apparent economy in trading morphemes of order for morphemes of inflection; the former did not take up type space, and thus the same message could be encoded in fewer units. If this constituted a definition of redundancy, then more information could be transmitted where order was the criterion. In terms of the number of morphological elements, however, both systems would be equally redundant. Ferguson said that the traditional point of view, for example, of people who liked Latin was that if inflection was freely employed, word order could be used for other purposes, for connotation and emphasis, and so forth. Languages varied considerably in this respect; both Arabic and Old Norse had highly inflected systems, but word order was quite rigid in the former and free in the latter.

*Ruth H. Weir*

## SOME QUESTIONS ON THE CHILD'S LEARNING OF PHONOLOGY

The word "questions" in the title of this paper was chosen deliberately. I have no definite answers to problems I am about to raise, but I do believe that they are important enough to warrant discussion.

I have chosen my questions from two different chronological areas in the phonological development of the child. The first problem is within the time of acquisition of the first phonological contrast, and the second relates to my previous work, published in *Language in The Crib* (1962), dealing with children between the ages of two and five.

### ACQUISITION OF PHONOLOGICAL CONTRAST

In listening to recordings of young children there seems to be little difficulty in segmenting utterances into sentencelike chunks, regardless of the intelligibility of the utterance to an adult listener. On the basis of this evidence I have hypothesized that pitch or intonation patterns may be the signals perceived and that these are learned early, perhaps independently of the segmental phonemes. This has brought me to look once again at the literature dealing with the acquisition of early phonological contrasts.

There seems to be a good deal of theoretical disagreement between linguists and psychologists on the relation of an infant's babbling to his acquisition of the sound pattern of his mother tongue. Psychologists have generally held that language is gradually shaped out of the multitude of sounds the infant makes in babbling, and there are a number of theories that make this assumption. Mowrer (1950), for example, believes that early language acquisition proceeds in the following way: the sounds made by the parents come to have secondary reinforcing properties through their association with the primary reinforcements that they dispense to the child (e.g., feeding). When a child babbles, even when the parents are not present, any sound he happens to make that resembles those sounds frequently spoken by the parents will be selectively reinforced, and the probabilities of this recurrence will increase. In this way he will gradually select a repertoire of sounds that resemble those of the language in which he is being reared; the sounds thus learned will form basic blocks for word and sentence construction.

In this account, however, a number of important questions remain unanswered for a linguist. What is meant by "frequently spoken"? What is the acquisition order? Are we dealing with phones or articulatory exercises or with the phonemes as functional units of a language? Brown (1958) has suggested the term "babbling drift" in describing the gradual transition from babbling to language. He cites Irwin and Chen (1948), but here again the linguist is met with frustration in determining exactly what Irwin and Chen mean by "phonemes." Their units do not seem to correspond to the usual linguistic notion of functional units of a given language.

Jakobson (1941), in his classic article, and Jakobson and Halle (1956) make a sharp division between babbling and language, even suggesting a period of silence between the two. They then go on to demonstrate that the order of acquisition of vowel and consonant phonemes proceeds according to linguistic universals, regardless of the multitude of sounds produced in the infant's babbling or of the phonemic structure of the language the infant is about to learn. Without dwelling on details, which are readily available, let me just point out that Jakobson stresses the fact that he is concerned with phonemic acquisition, the functional use of sounds by the infant, a phenomenon that is usually placed after the child is nine months of age or older. Jakobson makes no mention of the learning of intonation patterns in his theory of order of acquisition; however, in the reverse of language-learning he comments that sentence intonation is preserved with aphasic patients after many linguistic contrasts have been lost.

Bolinger (1964) leaves little doubt about intonation as a universal;

the question raised in his article is primarily how wide or narrow an interpretation should be placed on the universality of intonation. Bolinger also carefully distinguishes between phonemic tone of tone languages on the one hand and intonation patterns on the other. In our further discussion we will not draw this careful distinction because our interest is concerned with the acquisition of pitch patterns in general, be they tones or intonations. I am sure, however, that ultimately phonemic tones and intonation patterns must be considered separately. As most of the literature I have been able to consult does not deal with tone languages, I will refer to intonation more often than to tone, although it is the latter to which our own research brings some new evidence.

Since generalizations of infant learning of phonology have been based on separate studies that were later compared, Eleanor Maccoby of Stanford University and I decided to examine the relations of babbling to language acquisition more directly by studying infants being reared in different linguistic environments. For a pilot study we sought families in which languages were spoken that differed considerably in the inventory of their phonemic systems. We were, of course, also constrained to work with those languages spoken by at least a small number of families living in the San Francisco Bay area. We elected to work with three languages: Chinese (Mandarin), Arabic (Syrian), and American English. We took some recordings of the vocalizations of four infants between six and eight months of age, growing up in households where one of these languages was spoken almost exclusively. We found that it was technically possible to use voice-key recorders in the infants' bedrooms and to get recordings of acceptable phonetic quality. We have by no means solved transcription and classification problems, but usually we were able to identify the Chinese infant by distinct pitch patterns. We were unable readily to distinguish the two Arabic babies from the American one.

With this encouragement we decided to study systematically fifteen infants from three different linguistic backgrounds (five from each language) over a period of about a year. The infants are about five or six months old initially, and we take a twenty-four-hour monthly sample recording of their speech production until they reach about eighteen months. In addition to five American-English-speaking families, we have been able to find five practically monolingual Chinese (Cantonese) families and five families where Russian is spoken almost exclusively. This study was begun only a few months ago, and thus far we have been able to collect and listen to only one or two recording sessions of three Chinese, one Russian, and one English infant.

Based on this scant evidence, I will dare to make a few general statements. One Chinese infant, recorded first at five-and-one-half and then at six-and-one-half months, shows in the second recording a very different pattern from the Russian and American infants. The utterances produced by the Chinese baby are usually monosyllabic and only vocalic, with much tonal variation over individual vowels. A neutral single vowel with various pitches is also typical of another six-month-old Chinese infant, as well as of a still different seven-month-old one. The Russian and American babies, at six and seven months, show little pitch variation over individual syllables; they usually have a CV (consonant-vowel) syllable, often reduplicated or repeated at intervals several times, with stress patterns occurring occasionally and intonation patterns usually over a number of syllables. If these general initial impressions can be substantiated, with the additional evidence of ease of segmentation mentioned earlier, we must ask ourselves how or when pitch and intonation patterns are acquired.

In studying the literature on learning tone languages, I have been able to find only Chao's (1951) observations on "Cantian," the language spoken by his young granddaughter Canta. "The tones of Cantian are much more regular and stable [than consonant or vowel phonemes], though distinctly different from standard Mandarin in several respects. Canta acquired tones very early, as most Chinese children do. Isolated tones of stressed syllables are practically the same as in standard Mandarin" (p. 32). In a personal communication, Chao amplified his statement of "different from standard Mandarin" as referring mainly to tone sandhi and to some irregularities, and he reiterated his observation of early functional use of tones.

My search for observations on the learning of intonation has been somewhat more fruitful, although most writers on child language pay little attention to it. A notable exception is Lewis (1951, 1963) who deplores the lack of work on the child's acquisition of intonation patterns and who makes a convincing case for early learning of these patterns. He distinguishes between expressive and representational intonations, showing affect closely linked to the former, even dominating over the situation, and representational intonation developing rather early from it. Lewis (1951) gives the following chronological account:

1. At an early stage (before the infant is about nine months old), the child shows discrimination, in a broad way, among different patterns of expression in intonation.
2. When the total pattern — the phonetic form together with intonational form — is made effective by training, at first the intonational rather than the phonetic form dominates the child's response.
3. Then the phonetic pattern becomes the dominant feature in evoking the specific response; but while the function of the intonational pattern may be considerably subordinated, it certainly does not vanish (pp. 115–116).

There are some other investigators who have observed early intonation patterns, e.g., Champneys (1881), Meumann (1903), Tappolet (1907), Jespersen (1922), Stern (1928), C. Bühler (1931), Shirley (1933), Delacroix (1934), Grégoire (1937), Leopold (1947, 1949), and Kainz (1962). Kaczmarek (1953), in establishing periods of the child's language-learning process, considers the intonation period as the first of the true language periods, following the stages of crying, cooing, and babbling. He claims that the child's response to intonation occurs as early as the fifth month, and he has tested his hypothesis by presenting a child growing up in a Polish speech community with non-Polish segmental sequences with Polish intonations. The child's response was the same, regardless of the segmental phonemes. Some Czech linguists have looked at the learning of intonation as well, e.g., Čáda (1906), Oberpfalcer (1932), and more recently and thoroughly Ohnesorg (1948, 1959). He, like Lewis, points to the originally affective quality of intonation, but Ohnesorg goes further in showing some overarticulation of intonation on the part of the adult speaking to the child. Therefore, he reasons, the child's intonation patterns at times are almost caricatures of the adult patterns. Also, because most utterances addressed to a child are questions, it is often the rising intonation pattern requiring a "yes" or "no" answer that is most frequently used with children; it often remains structurally ambiguous until other patterns are learned as well. I find this last observation of Ohnesorg's particularly interesting because it would resolve the apparent contradiction I have encountered in my own work: the apparent early use of intonation patterns on the one hand and my own inability to find systematically contrasting patterns with a two-and-a-half-year-old child on the other. This would also bring me back to Bolinger's question — to what extent are intonations universal?

What is obviously needed is more first-hand research on phonemic acquisition by the child, but even more important I believe that we also have to show the learning of phonology and the learning of syntax as more closely interrelated than we have thus far. Perhaps these two learning processes are much more concurrent than we had assumed them to be, and the learning of intonation patterns by the child may offer some relevant clues here.

## FUNCTIONS OF CHILD LANGUAGE

The second part of my paper deals with some observations and questions raised in some of my earlier work as published in *Language in The Crib*. That study dealt with presleep monologues of a two-and-a-half-year-old child. One of its shortcomings was lack of a systematic record of the child's language outside the presleep period. I have tried to remedy that omission in my present work, studying our two younger children, David and Michael, who are now roughly four-and-a-half and three years old, respectively. Between January 1963 and about January 1965, once or twice a week, sometimes every other week, I recorded samples of the children's conversations with or without an adult present, at different times of the day, in various locations inside or immediately outside our house. In addition I have also taped presleep monologues whenever they occurred, although they were much less frequent, almost rare, in comparison with the output of our first-born child. As to the reason for the paucity of soliloquies, I am inclined to blame a certain loss of privacy. Although each of our three children has his own room, present-day building techniques do not provide for much soundproofing, and frequently I recorded a dialogue with the brother next door rather than the monologue of one of the children. (From the point of view of quality of recording, however, the barrier of the wall was sufficient to make transcription of the child in the other room almost impossible.) The physical ease of across-wall communication was probably not the only or the crucial factor to account for the dialogue; Anthony has his imaginary or toy interlocutors in his monologues which really had in many instances the form of a dialogue; therefore, having a sibling of not too different age nearby may just have simplified David's problem of finding an addressee without having to resort to an imaginary one.

The recordings during the day were made by "wiring" one of the children with a small Vega lapel-type microphone that has a separate receiver connected in turn with a tape recorder. This wireless microphone enabled the child to move around freely indoors, in our garden, and a barely adequate signal was even received from the neighbor's house when the children visited there. The variety of locales as well as the different times of day for recordings seemed important to me because presleep soliloquies are by their nature confined to the same place and roughly the same time. The question I had raised earlier in this connection was the effect of the constancy of surroundings on the content of what was said. It seems to me now that the child's physical environment is less important than I had originally thought.

I am still transcribing those hours and hours of recordings, but I have also tried to analyze some of the transcriptions made, selecting different points in time over the past two years. In the first sample I have looked at, David was about 2,4 and Michael was one year old. As David wore the microphone at the time and Michael was not too social as yet, most of the content was David's output. In comparing our three children, David is overtly the least "verbal" and least aggressive one, the most creative and also the most dependent one. In terms of his phonology, at 2,4 he had by no means mastered what his older brother had or his younger brother would be able to do at a comparable age. He was also quite uncommunicative in social situations when he wore the microphone. However, when he did talk, the structure of his utterances was quite similar to that of his or Anthony's monologues, only shorter. For example, David in a social situation:

(1) myself
(2) me
(3) Mom
(4) hi, Mommy
(5) dat's Mikey

where the /m/ is obviously of great interest to him. (Here, as well as later, I will be using standard orthography as much as possible and resort to phonetics only when absolutely necessary.) Here is David in a monologue:[1]

(1) you comin?
(2) where you comin, Domar?
(3) I comin Domar (2×)
(4) now callin Domar (2×)
(5) Daddy do
(6) like you (4×)
(7) light you
(8) lighter (3×)
(9) like you
(10) [kʰɛdú] (2×)
(11) [kʰəbú] ("Cobbers" is our dog's name.)
(12) dere go?
(13) car?
(14) like car?
(15) like block
(16) [kʰəlɔ́k˺]
(17) Domar
(18) duck
(19) [dada]
(20) [tata]

The resemblance of this "paragraph" to Anthony's monologues is quite apparent, here particularly in regard to play with sound.

The next sampling I took was some two or three months later. Michael, 1,3, was heard a little more frequently, usually with a CVCV pattern, often reduplicated or semireduplicated. The CVC pattern was rare, except for [bəm]. David continued with his sound play in his monologues:

(1) I go dis way
(2) way bay
(3) baby go dis bib
(4) all bib
(5) bib
(6) dere

---

[1] Monologues will seem much more common in this discussion than I have previously indicated, and the reason is twofold: I have concentrated on the analysis of monologues at this point, and I have also classified as monologues some across-wall communications where the interlocutor remained mostly passive.

He also had substitution drills:

(1) coat
(2) 'ts coat
(3) where Mommy's coat?
(4) Mommy's home sick (2×)
(5) where's Mommy home sick?
(6) where's Mikey sick?
(7) Mikey sick

Again, like Anthony, David also practiced his sounds; he did not merely play with them. The following exchange took place during the day:

David:    [dɛts oɪnts]
Anthony:  No, Dave, that's orange (pronounces carefully, in order
          to correct).
David:    No, dat's geen.
Anthony:  That's orange.
David:    No, [ɔlɪnts].

The same evening David conscientiously practiced the following forms: [ɔːnč], [əɪndz], [əɪ̯dz], [ənts], all attempts at getting the form *orange*.

In social situations, David had also become more articulate than he had been a couple of months previously. Frequently he echoed part of the previously heard adult talk or Anthony's utterance: e.g., after having heard *that was long ago,* he responded with [dɛz lɔŋægɔ]; to *he loves you* his answer was [ləfu]. After Anthony said *he's washing the bike,* David did away with redundancies in answering *he wash bike.* He also acquired the habit, and still retains it, of echoing part of what he has just heard in a whisper. I am sure that there is a pattern to what he chooses to echo, but I am not yet certain what it is. At other times, however, instead of a fragmentary echo, he would improvise on an adult sentence and work the linguistic as well as situational problem through, so to speak. For example, after his father said to Anthony *he needs a haircut, hm, Anthony?* (referring to Michael), David joined the conversation:

(1) he needs a haircut
(2) no one needs haircut
(3) haircut

    (4)  no one
    (5)  haircut today

I also noticed that repetition of a sentence, perhaps with some expansion, as David's

    (1)  I cose dat up
    (2)  I wan to cose dat
    (3)  I close dat
    (4)  me did!
    (5)  did

was not at all atypical of some adult patterns in speaking to the child, e.g., my saying *open the door, open the door please, Dave;* or *do you have your fancy spoon? your fancy spoon?* I do believe that if we look carefully at how and what we say to children, we should not be surprised to find so-called characteristics of children's language in our own speech.

The third sampling was taken when David was about three years old and Michael 1,9. Shortly after David's third birthday, his over-all, including his linguistic, development suddenly took some giant leaps forward. A number of consonant clusters became part of his language; [r] became an allophone of /r/ together with [l], and even occasional pre- and posttonic syllables made their appearance. Michael was working on his velar phonemes, substituting them frequently for alveolars. Interestingly enough, he also used the personal pronoun *I* consistently rather than his own name in referring to himself, a characteristic feature of his linguistic development. By that time the microphone had also become a trusted friend for David, so that one morning alone in his room he entered into a conversation with it: *micophone, I go to school.* Following is a sample of David's monologue at that time, a little more sophisticated than some four or five months previously:

    (1)  who?
    (2)  Dave
    (3)  [hánt$^h$ɪ]  (Humpty)
    (4)  here's de place
    (5)  bad boy, bad boy Dave (2×)
    (6)  Dave is not a bad boy
    (7)  Mike is a bad boy
    (8)  Dave is OK, but Mike is not

(9) [kʰɪbr]

(10) [kʰɔ́bl̩]

(11) cable car and apple

(12) apple, Mike, not cereal

(13) but apples

(14) but nose

(15) how bout de nose

(16) how bout?

(17) I can

(18) but dinner

(19) Daddy go here

(20) Daddy come dere

(21) Daddy go [bæpʰu]

(22) bite it

(23) [pʰǽpʰú ai supʰó.s]

(24) [supʰɔ́.s]

(25) Cobbes is a [pʰuːs] (3×, decreasing volume, sleepy)

He also practiced the newly acquired [r]:

(1) stoly

(2) stoly here

(3) want a stoly

(4) Dave, stoly

(5) story (2×)

(6) story's de hat

(7) story's de big hat

(8) story's a hat

This is a sample of his rhyming exercises:

(1) [lalɪpʰɪkiupʰai̯]

(2) the sky

(3) he went away cause high

(4) he did de sky

David and Michael would also converse occasionally, apart from referential exchanges, with David intentionally playing and Michael seriously learning sound sequences:

David:  My [tʰɪkʰɛdúː].

My [tʰɪkʰəbúː].

Michael:  My [tʰɪkʰədúː]. (3×)
David:    My [tʰɪkʰədúː]. Mine.
Michael:  My [tʰɪkʰədúː].
David:    My peek-a-boo, Mike (said with certainty and defini-
          tiveness).

At the fourth and last sampling I took, the ages of the children were
the following: Michael 2,4 to 2,6, David 3,7 to 3,9, and Anthony 5,4 to
5,6. Michael's connected speech had become quite intelligible by then,
and it was characterized by a good deal of echo response. He was learning the interdentals, and the voiced [ð] alternated with [d] in the
definite article and in demonstratives. David, although some fifteen
months older, was about at the same stage of development on interdentals, but his consonant clusters had become about standard by then
whereas Michael did not handle clusters too well as yet. The following
exchange is quite typical of that period.

Michael:  [rɛkʰət] top.
          Mine!
Anthony:  Mike says only top instead of stop.
Myself:   He can say stop, I'm sure, can't you Mikey?
Michael:  Stop.
David:    I can say stop! (2×)

Anthony had become particularly sensitive to Michael's mishandling
of the language. When corrected by Anthony on phonological grounds,
Michael usually tried to satisfy his mentor, as in the above example.
Another one, similar in nature, is the following:

Michael:  How bout a coom?
Myself:   You have a spoon.
Anthony:  Why does he say coom?
Myself:   I don't know.
Anthony:  Mikey, can you say spoon?
Michael:  Spoon.

However, when Michael had performed his own analysis on some
words to make them conform to his morpheme inventory, he did not
accept Anthony's corrections and persisted in his new formations. For
example, he would insist on *Bayshort* for *Bayshore* (the name of a
local freeway), *locomotor* for *locomotive*, etc. David's language had
also come under Anthony's scrutiny, particularly the omission of pre-
tonic syllables:

David:     I don't have a raser, Antony. I don't have dis.

Anthony:  David, you need an *e*raser (overstressing the omitted syllable).

Presleep monologues were exceedingly rare at that time. I recorded one of Anthony's which he recited laughingly as if to acknowledge its nonsense:

(1) tee (many times)
(2) toe
(3) tow truck
(4) the tow truck has a toe

Michael carried on monologues in social situations, as David did at a roughly comparable age; e.g.,

(1) turn off de water
(2) I turn de water
(3) I turn [ð] is water
(4) I turn off de water
(5) here Mommy now
(6) de bottle

Or with David's intervention:

Michael:   (1) dat sharp?
           (2) no dat sharp
           (3) no more sharp
           (4) my sharp
           (5) my shop
           (6) no more shop
           (7) beep beep
           (8) dat mine?
David:     (9) no, over dere
          (10) dose go
Michael:  (11) shopping? (2×)
          (12) I wan to have room
          (13) I wan some
          (14) room
          (15) a room (2×)
          (16) a broom (2×)

Also, when playing by himself, Michael would frequently talk to himself. Here is a sample soliloquy while he was outside in our driveway;

although no one was physically present, he used me as his interlocutor:

    (1) paper bag
    (2) here goes (throws newspaper)
    (3) that's higher
    (4) you see it higher
    (5) why
    (6) he go have a whine
    (7) have a have a on it
    (8) I have a nine
    (9) Mommy, see we playin
    (10) I don have a mine
    (11) pick up (2×)
    (12) pick up book
    (13) I'm a paper boy
    (14) Mommy, a paper boy
    (15) I pick up paper, Mommy
    (16) Mommy, I get paper
    (17) boy
    (18) I get paper boy, Mommy
    (19) I do
    (20) I give paper to you
    (21) that's a paper boy
    (22) [au̯x] side
    (23) dop
    (24) dop it here
    (25) at's my luch?
    (26) it's in de mail
    (27) beep, beep, beep
    (28) don eat lunch
    (29) like Athony? (2×)
    (30) come (2×)
    (31) go!
    (32) look what! (2×)
    (33) loquat (2×)
    (34) see look?

The rare presleep monologues that Michael did have are based on practice or play with sounds:

    (1) fumbelina (2×)
    (2) tumbelina

(3) lumbelina
(4) Thumbelina (2×)

Or

(1) [m::]
(2) my motocyke
(3) [m::]
(4) I make motocyke
(5) dis a black box
(6) I [bɔbɔ]
(7) [bɔbɔ]
(8) [m::]otocyke
(9) man
(10) I kiss my door man
(11) my Daddy
(12) door man
(13) I turn on dis
(14) not be de door
(15) I wan to turn dis, Dave

In concluding this part of my paper, I do not want to dwell any further on the similarities of these recordings with the previous ones I have made, but I would like to point out some differences in my observations with those of Flavell (1964, 1965) who is studying the private speech of children of late preschool and early school age. With the younger child, as I have been able to observe, need for social and communicative contact is not the primary cause of private speech, an observation Flavell makes. Also, in older children, the highly verbal, talkative individual tends to have a high operant level of private speech, according to Flavell. The case of David would contradict this assumption, but of course we are dealing with a child much younger than the children in Flavell's group. Needless to say, I consider my observations as detailed here only preliminary as they are based on a small fraction of the corpus on hand.

## REFERENCES

BOLINGER, D. L. Intonation as a Universal. In *Proc. 9th International Congress of Linguists*, Cambridge, Mass., 1962, Utrecht: Het Spectrum, 1964, 833–848.

BROWN, ROGER. *Words and Things*. Glencoe, Ill.: Free Press, 1958.

BÜHLER, C. *Kindheit und Jugend.* 3rd ed., Leipzig, 1931.

ČÁDA, FRANTIŠEK. *Studium řeči dětské. I,* 1906; *II,* 1908; Prague.

CHAMPNEYS, F. E. Notes on an infant. *Mind,* 1881, *6,* 104–107.

CHAO, Y. R. The Cantian idiolect. *Semitic and Oriental Studies Presented to William Popper, Univ. of Calif. Publications in Semitic Philology,* 1951, *II,* 27–44.

DELACROIX, H. *L'enfant et le Langage.* Paris: F. Alcan, 1934.

FLAVELL, J. B. Private Speech. Paper read at Am. Spell. and Hear. Assoc. Mtgs., Nov. 1964.

—— The Function of Private Speech in Children's Thinking. Paper read at Soc. Res. Child Developm. Mtgs., March 1965.

GRÉGOIRE, A. *L'apprentissage du Langage. I,* 1937; *II,* 1947; Gembloux: J. Duculot.

IRWIN, O. C. and CHEN, H. P. Infant speech: vowel and consonant frequency. *J. Hearing and Speech Disorders,* 1948. *13.* 123–125.

JAKOBSON, R. Kindersprache, Aphasie und allgemeine Lautgesetze. *Selected Writings I,* The Hague: Mouton & Co., 1962, pp. 328–401 (original date of pub. 1941).

—— and HALLE, M. *Fundamentals of Language.* The Hague: Mouton & Co., 1956.

JESPERSEN, O. *Language, Its Nature, Development and Origin.* London: Allen and Unwin Ltd., 1922; reprinted 1964.

KACZMAREK, L. *Ksztaltowanie sie mowy dziecka.* Poznan, 1953.

KAINZ, F. *Psychologie der Sprache I.* 3rd ed., Stuttgart: Enke, 1962.

LEOPOLD, W. F. *Speech Development of a Bilingual Child. II,* 1947; *III,* 1949; Northwestern University, Evanston.

LEWIS, M. M. *Infant Speech.* New York: Humanities Press, 1951.

—— *Language, Thought and Personality in Infancy and Childhood.* New York, 1963.

MEUMANN, E. *Die Sprache des Kindes.* Abhandlungen herausgegeben von der Geselischaft für deutsche Sprache in Zürich, Zürich: Zürcher & Furrer, 1903, *8.*

MOWRER, O. H. On the psychology of talking birds. In *Learning Theory and Personality Dynamics,* O. H. Mowrer, New York: Ronald Press; 1950, pp. 688–726.

OBERPFALCER, F. *Jazykozpyt,* Prague, 1932.

OHNESORG, K. D. *Fonetická studie o dětské řeči.* Prague, 1948.

—— *Druhá fonetická studie ordétské řeči.* Brno, 1959.

SHIRLEY, M. M. *The First Two Years: A Study of 25 Babies. Vol. II., Intellectual Development.* Inst. Child Welfare Monogr. Series No. 7, University of Minnesota, 1933.

STERN, C., and STERN, W. *Die Kindersprache.* 4th ed., Leipzig: Barth, 1928.

TAPPOLET, E. *Die Sprache des Kindes.* Basel, 1907.

WEIR, RUTH H. *Language in the Crib.* The Hague: Mouton & Co., 1962.

## GENERAL DISCUSSION
### Weir presentation

1. In the absence of Weir to speak to her paper, discussion was limited mainly to comments on the first of her questions, whether babbling was shaped into tonal or intonation systems. Fodor thought the evidence demonstrated that early babbling was taking a particular shape, but this did not necessitate that it was being shaped. Jenkins said it showed that the child did not learn an intonation system by approximating it in later years.

Hirsh referred to a study by Tervoort, a phonetician and teacher of the deaf in the Netherlands, who reported that his Dutch college students could distinguish the babbling, from six months onward, of Dutch from non-Dutch children but could not distinguish among the non-Dutch. The languages involved were all nontonal. Tervoort later performed the same experiment with similar recordings in the United States and found that his American students could distinguish between the American and non-American samples but not among the non-American.

2. More information was requested concerning the study by Philip Lieberman, referred to by McNeill (p. 53), on the manner in which linguists assigned intonation contours to speech signals. Lieberman (1965) asked two experienced linguists to assign a system of four pitch levels and three terminal junctures (the commonly used Trager-Smith system) to a set of short sentences recorded by untrained readers in a variety of "emotional modes," such as "bored," "fearful," "happy." The results were reasonably consistent for each linguist and between the two but not consistent with the actual fundamental frequency pat-

terns of the sentences presented. The linguists tended to assign a commonly encountered intonation contour that they "heard" regardless of the actual variations in the frequency patterns presented. Lieberman then used an electronic vocal simulator to extract the pitch and amplitude patterns from each of the original sentences and impose them on a neutral [a]. In transcribing the intonation patterns of these signals, each linguist changed 50 per cent of the pitch levels and junctures previously assigned, in the direction of greater objective accuracy. "The linguists' ears were remarkably good as long as they did not hear the message," Lieberman commented. He concluded that although pitch levels and terminals were supposed to provide acoustic cues about where sentence phrases began or ended, in fact the linguists inferred their notation from the words of the sentences and their knowledge of the language.

House stressed that this was not a question of tonal differences. Lieberman was arguing that intonation as it was usually understood by linguists was more than variation in the fundamental frequency of speech. They were able to assign consistent intonation contours to complex, fully articulated speech signals but lost this ability when only the frequency variation was present.

A. Liberman (the conference participant) proposed that certain aspects of stress and intonation represented a kind of intermediate case in which some of the information was in the acoustic signal but that appeal had to be made to syntax to fill in the rest. For segmental phonemes, all the information could in principle be in the acoustic signal. Lieberman's study presented no essential contradiction to the conclusions of Weir. There could be sufficient information in the acoustic signal for a child to pick it up and babble it without syntax, and this would be recognized as intonation typical of American-English. Miller said that in discussion of other experimental data he had heard Lieberman argue that the major segmentation of the sentence was acquired from intonation. This was circular if it was also believed that intonation was derived from the syntactic structure of the sentence.

Fodor thought there was no paradox; it was not true that segmentation was invariably obtained from intonation. It had been shown that ambiguous sentences were assigned different segmentations depending on their linguistic environment, despite the fact that exactly the same physical signal was being dealt with (Garrett, Bever, and Fodor, 1966). If the syntactic segmentation was specified by contextual disambiguation, the listener would quite happily put the pause in a position where no energy drop occurred. On the other hand, Bolinger and Gerstman (1957) had taken structures like *light housekeeper* and *lighthouse keeper* and shown that the interpretation could be changed by the insertion of a pause into the tape. The pause marked the difference between the bracketings ((*light*) (*housekeeper*)) versus ((*lighthouse*) (*keeper*)), and the acoustic signals were otherwise identical. The sentences were heard as they ought to be, with the segmentation being assigned in accordance with the pause. There was clearly a two-way relationship — if the segmentation was known, the "pause" was appropriately placed, and if the pause was heard, segmentation followed. There was probably loose correlation between such aspects of speech as pause, segmentation, intonation, and syntactic structure such that any of them could be used as a cue to the others.

Ferguson observed that there were varieties of English where the basic syntax had to be assumed to be the same as that of standard English, but where the intonation and junction system was totally different. The English spoken in India was an example. He also suggested there would normally be a difference in stress between sentences with identical surface structure but different deep structure, such as *they are drinking companions* and *they are drinking glasses*, two examples that had earlier been given by Miller.

Miller proposed an experiment on this. He and Chomsky had already conducted one experiment using the ambiguous sentence *flying planes can be dangerous*. Both interpretations — that flying planes was dangerous and that flying planes were dangerous — were put into a context that made it perfectly clear what was intended. Recordings were made of ten people reading the sentence aloud in one context and ten reading it in the other; at the end, the sentence was pointed to and the readers asked, "Did that mean flying planes is dangerous or that flying planes are dangerous?" They were all puzzled by the question. None had perceived the sentence as ambiguous and, when asked what the sentence meant, they all gave the interpretation consistent with the context. The sentence was then clipped out of the different tapes, the extracts put into random order and presented to a class of students debating exactly that point, who tried to assign to each extract the meaning the reader had in mind. There was absolutely no discrimination. Miller was therefore reasonably convinced that there was no natural way in which a difference at the deep level could be represented by pauses, special intonation, or any other contrastive verbal device. He had previously assumed that it would be quite simple to give a distinguishing intonation to differences at a surface level. This was, of course, close to whether it was believed that syntax and intonation were related or whether intonation was a nonsegmental phoneme that could be combined with any particular sentence. The experiment he had described was now going to be conducted with sentences in which the disambiguation was in the surface structure (e.g., *they are flying planes*), and his conjecture was that the jury would again not be able to tell the difference.

Ferguson could not see why it should be assumed that intonation differences would go along with either deep or surface structure exclusively. But he thought that in most normal speech performances a surface distinction between interpretations of an ambiguous sentence would be made. This, said Miller, was what he now wanted to test.

## REFERENCES

BOLINGER, D. L., and GERSTMAN, L. J. Disjuncture as a cue to constructs. *Word*, 1957, *13*, 246–255.

GARRETT, M., BEVER, T., and FODOR, J. A. The active use of grammar in speech perception. *Perception and Psychophysics*, 1966, *1*, 1, 30–32.

LIEBERMAN, P. On the acoustic basis of the perception of intonations by linguists. *Word*, 1965, *21*, 1, 40–54.

*Mildred C. Templin*

# THE STUDY OF ARTICULATION AND LANGUAGE DEVELOPMENT DURING THE EARLY SCHOOL YEARS

For nearly five years I have been conducting a project primarily concerned with the development of adequate production of the sounds of English by children and with the relation of this phonological development to other dimensions of language and to related nonverbal behavior. The major emphasis of my project has been the longitudinal study of the same children from prekindergarten through the fourth grade. Thus their language performance has been from the beginning far beyond the level when pivot classes of words are a major consideration. In my work, for the most part, linguistic and other performances of the children have been evaluated in testing or testlike situations. This fact precludes the consideration of these results as descriptions of the language performance of children in everyday life situations.

The project began with the very practical question of whether children who are going to need speech-sound therapy when they are finishing second grade can be identified when they are in kindergarten, but the scope has been enlarged to include a number of different studies. A possible answer to the initial question is basic to decisions that persons in speech pathology must make if they are to select children to be given speech-sound articulation therapy at an age or grade level below that when adequate articulation can be expected from most children.

Cross-sectional, normative studies have quite consistently shown that seven- to eight-year-old children can satisfactorily utter all the phonemes of English. At this age, any omission or gross distortion of a phoneme or the substitution of one phoneme for another (e.g., *sh*ee for *see*) can be considered to be a deviation in articulatory perform-ance. Such a deviation in the eight-year-old identifies an articulation "problem" and a likely cause for the public-school speech therapist. With five-year-old kindergarten children, however, such deviations may or may not signal an articulation problem because adequate ar-ticulation of the phonemes of English is not yet expected in their speech performance.

It is reasonable that some therapy be given to the five-year-old whose speech is unlikely to improve through growth alone. But to give such therapy to children whose articulation of speech sounds will probably become adequate over the next few years is questionable, unless deter-mined by factors other than the expenditure of professional time and of school funds.

The original aim of the project, then, is really to investigate the pos-sibility of separating the child who is potentially a slow developer from the one who is potentially deficient in articulation and to do this at a point in his development before mature articulation performance can reasonably be expected. It requires a differential diagnosis that will predict whether the developmental potential of the child will result in adequate articulation or in deficient articulation when he reaches the age at which cross-sectional studies have found most children to have mature articulation. (Mature articulation refers to utterances that are recognized as the phonemes of English; a broad classification of a phoneme is used, and no consideration is given to variations of utter-ance within a phoneme.)

## DESCRIPTION OF STUDIES

The project includes a number of research efforts that can be sub-divided into an identification study, a longitudinal study, and a series of ancillary studies. To some extent they are all interrelated. Samples for these studies were selected from approximately 2,500 children, of whom 1,500 were first given speech-sound articulation tests in Spring 1960 before they entered kindergarten and 1,000 were first tested in Fall 1960 when they were enrolled in kindergarten. This number rep-resents about a fourth of the children who enrolled in the Minneapolis Public School kindergartens in the Fall of 1960.

The longitudinal study represents the major emphasis of the lan-guage project. It, too, is concerned with the identification in kindergarten of children whose articulation in second grade will be inadequate enough to warrant speech therapy. Because of the repeated evaluation of the articulation of the subjects and the variety of measures obtained, the longitudinal study has the following additional purposes:

1. The description of the development of consonant phonemes in the same children until adequate articulation is achieved, or at least through the fourth grade.
2. The exploration of the interrelations among articulation and other language skills, such as spelling, reading, and grammatical knowledge, during the early elementary-school years.
3. The identification of language, perception, and personality variables that are related to the production of speech-sound articulation in the first, second, third, and fourth grades.

For this longitudinal study a sample of 490 children was selected from 1,500 children first tested in Spring 1960. Of these, about 435 were still available for testing in Spring 1965. The sample for the longitudinal study was selected on the basis of some factors that seemed likely to be important for the identification of an articulation deviation in kindergarten. First, all 490 were selected from those first tested in Spring 1960 with the idea that earlier information on articulation performances might well be important. I was concerned with the question of whether parents had brought to the spring roundups children about whom they were concerned or with whose speech they were very pleased. When the articulation performance in kindergarten was compared with that of youngsters who had not been brought for earlier testing, no statistically significant difference was found in the total articulation scores of the two groups.

Second, the sample was differentiated on the basis of whether the subjects shifted in their articulation scores that were obtained on measures with and without an aural model presented by the examiner. Some 60 youngsters of the 1,500, who differed 4 or more McCall T-Score points on the articulation scores obtained under the 2 test conditions, were identified and made up the "shift" group.

Two groups of children whose scores on the articulation measure with and without an aural model were essentially the same (in all instances no more than a shift of 2 McCall T-Score points) were also selected for the longitudinal study sample. One was selected because of the total number of misarticulations and the other because of the misarticulation of specific phonemes. Five subsamples were selected whose total scores on the articulation tests with an aural model administered in kindergarten clustered about the 7th, 15th, 30th, 50th, and 98th percentiles. According to cross-sectional normative data, the articulation scores of the children at the 7th percentile would be about like those of three-and-one-half-year-olds. The articulation scores of those at the 98th percentile would be like those of second- or third-grade children. The group at the 50th percentile could be considered a built-in normative group with articulation typical of the kindergarten child.

Three subsamples were identified that misarticulated the single phoneme /r/, /s/, or /l/. Children in each single phoneme group had one sound as a major misarticulation: that is, the misarticulation of /r/ without the misarticulation of /l/ and /s/; of /s/ without /r/ and /l/; and of /l/ without /s/ and /r/. These specific phonemes were selected because they constitute the major articulation therapy loads of public-school speech therapists.

The articulation of the children in the sample was initially tested in Spring, and then again in Fall 1960. Beginning in Spring 1961 and continuing through Spring 1965, the children were tested at six-month intervals on a variety of measures of articulation, speech, language, spelling, reading, intelligence, auditory discrimination, attitudes, personality, and family relations.

The eleventh round of testing, the last six-month testing session planned, was completed in June 1965. It is probable that those children whose articulation of speech sounds has not become adequate at this testing will be followed further. It is also likely that certain language performances of all the subjects in the longitudinal study will again be evaluated when those subjects at grade for their age will be in the sixth and the ninth grades.

## RESULTS

Probably the most important observation that I have made up to this time is that those children with many misarticulations in kindergarten continue to have a considerable number of them when they are in second grade. Because of the consistent findings from the cross-sectional studies that mature articulation was achieved by seven- to eight-year-old children, it was originally planned to terminate the identification and the longitudinal studies when the children at grade for their age had finished the second grade. This was not possible, however, because a larger number of children than anticipated had not yet achieved adequate production of the phonemes of English. The children who had poor articulation in kindergarten, while they improved considerably as a group, still had far from adequate articulation scores in second grade. There were about sixty children in each of the five subgroups, selected on the basis of total number of misarticulations on their kindergarten tests. The group of children who constituted the group around the 7th percentile of the total distribution when they were in kindergarten still had the lowest median at the second grade. Only three children in this group had scores in second grade at or above the median score for the 50th percentile group. At the beginning of fourth grade there was still a substantial number of children with inadequate articulation scores. It is interesting to note that teachers were able to identify in kindergarten those children with the lowest articulation scores. They identified 85 per cent of the youngsters in the group below the 10th percentile.

Another interesting observation was that, although /s/, /l/, and /r/ constitute the most common misarticulations in the caseload of public-school speech correctionists, the appearance of these as single phoneme misarticulations is not consistent. Out of the 1,500 kindergarten children from whom the longitudinal sample was selected, only 22 were located who misarticulated the /l/ but not the /r/ or /s/. We were able to obtain samples of approximately 60 subjects, each with no other difficulty than the misarticulation of the /s/ or the /r/. The pattern for boys and girls in this instance was also quite different. We found only 4 girls out of the 1,500, as opposed to 18 boys, who could be placed in the group with /l/ as a single phoneme misarticulation.

I had predicted that the group of youngsters who shifted in articulation scores when the evaluation was made with and without an aural model would show very rapid improvement. The reasoning followed was that children who could produce adequate phonemes but did not do so consistently under the two testing situations would improve more rapidly because they had, in effect, demonstrated that they were able to produce the correct phonemes. This prediction has not been borne out. We have not yet analyzed the data, but an examination of the descriptive statistics of the articulation measure shows that this group of children performed more like the group selected around the 30th percentile; i.e., the children as a group are below the median and have not shown any rapid increments as yet.

Of particular interest to this conference, I believe, is a preliminary analysis of the data on the relation between production of the phonemes of English and knowledge of English morphological change. The measure developed by Berko (1958) to study morphological change in preschool and first-grade schoolchildren was administered to the subjects in the longitudinal study when they were in kindergarten and in first and second grades.

As you know, this measure samples the child's ability to form plurals, possessives, the third-person singular of the verb, the progressive and the past tense, and the comparative and superlative of the adjective, through the use of nonsense words applied to pictures. A quantitative score was determined, allowing one point for each correct morphological change. The maximum score a child could obtain was 33.

From kindergarten to first to second grade, the mean morphology scores increased for all subsamples of the longitudinal study. The performance of the separate subsamples, however, differed substantially. The mean scores of the /r/ and /s/ single phoneme misarticulation groups (the /l/ group was omitted) were similar to each other and to those of the 50th percentile subsample. The mean scores of the group that in kindergarten had shifted in articulation scores, obtained with and without an aural model, most closely resembled those of the 15th and 30th percentile subsample.

At each grade, mean English morphology scores increased progressively as we moved through the subsamples from the 7th to the 98th percentiles. At the kindergarten level the mean score for the lowest percentile subsample was about 7 and that of the highest percentile about 14. An analysis of variance at the kindergarten level indicates that the differences were statistically significant. While mean scores increased to about 15 for the lowest and to about 27 for the highest percentile subsamples, the morphology scores in second grade still show the same progression for the separate subsamples. Performance on the English morphology test in second grade by youngsters with the poorest articulation in kindergarten is quite similar to that of children selected in kindergarten as having the best articulation. Although the analysis is not complete, the relation seems to persist through the three grades tested. Socioeconomic or intellectual factors may be influencing the tentative results, but the factors of age and experience are controlled. These children are all within about fourteen months in age of each other, and all have had the same number of years of school experience.

The application of rules of morphological change seems to follow a pattern similar to that reported by Berko. Appropriate changes are most frequently correct when achieved by the addition of a sound, next most frequent by the addition of a syllable, and then by a vowel shift. Among the incorrect responses, the most common error by far (80 per cent at kindergarten) is an uninflected response, that is, the repetition of the stimulus word.

The suggestion of the relation of adequacy of articulation of phonemes to morphological change raised the question of whether children exhibit a sensitivity to their language environment that is reflected in more adequate performance in a number of dimensions of language. Two additional and very preliminary looks at the longitudinal data in the light of this question should be reported at this time. In one, I considered the child's ability to provide a meaning for a nonsense word in a sentence. In the other, I considered the child's word-association responses.

At the beginning of the second grade, the children were given the instrument developed by Brown and Berko (1960) for the study of knowledge of word usage. In each of twelve sentences a nonsense word was used as a mass noun, a count noun, a transitive verb, an intransitive verb, or an adverb. A child's response was scored correct if the nonsense word was interpreted as any relevant meaningful word of the same part of speech. Thus in the sentence, "Here is a picture of a little girl thinking about some *huft*," any mass noun was given credit in answering the question, "Can you make up what that might mean?" Although the children's exact responses were taken down and classified, as yet nothing has been done to analyze them. However, no relation has been found in the preliminary analysis between scores on this word usage measure and either the number of misarticulations (subsamples selected around percentiles of total distribution) or type of misarticulations (single phoneme misarticulation subsamples).

Word associations were obtained from the children in the longitudinal sample in the second and fourth grades for the 100 words used by Palermo and Jenkins (1964) in their normative study of word association of children. We, of course, are interested in a number of characteristics of the responses that at this time have not been classified. At present the only score available is a commonality one obtained by summing each subject's associations that are the most common ones for his peers. (The second-grade associations had not been published but were made available by the authors.)

As children get older, they tend to give responses that are the same as those given by their own age-grade groups. It was hypothesized that children would give fewer common associations if they had had more misarticulations in kindergarten than children who had had fewer such utterances. The data are not yet ready to be analyzed to test this hypothesis. However, inspection of the mean scores for the subsamples indicates that at the second grade the mean number of common associations varies from 19 to 32 for children with the most to the least misarticulations. The relation is consistent from group to group selected in kindergarten, except that the 30th and 50th percentile groups have the same commonality score. The mean scores of the single phoneme misarticulation subsamples differ by only one point and are only slightly above that of the 50th percentile subsample.

Inspection of the mean scores for associations obtained from the children in fourth grade does not show any differences that are likely to be statistically significant in mean scores among any of the longitudinal study subsamples.

It is obvious that the relation between the ability to produce the sounds of English and other aspects of language is not a simple one. The very preliminary analyses and inspections suggest that the relation is substantial for morphology, higher at the earlier grade, and does not exist on our measure of word usage. All the relations looked at up to the present time attempt to relate the production of the sounds of English to performance from six months up to four-and-one-half years later on other aspects of language. It is of interest that any relation is found over a span of several years. There is no doubt that, in the future, analyses of the relation of performance on articulation and other language dimensions will be made.

## REFERENCES

BERKO, JEAN. The child's learning of English morphology. *Word*, 1958, *14*, 150–177.

BROWN, R., and BERKO, JEAN. Word association and the acquisition of grammar. *Child Development*, 1960, *31*, 1–14.

PALERMO, D., and JENKINS, J. *Word Association Norms*. Minneapolis: University of Minnesota Press, 1964.

# GENERAL DISCUSSION

## Templin presentation

1. In answer to questions, Templin said that about 85 per cent of the 1,500 children tested in Spring 1960 before they entered kindergarten had at least one misarticulation (exclusive of /hw/) and the same applied to about 75 per cent of those first tested in Fall 1960 when they had just begun kindergarten. The /hw/ was omitted because it was very commonly produced as /w/ and in cross-sectional studies was not found more accurately with increasing age, although all other phonemes improved. Templin stressed that on the tests that they used the error distribution was very skewed: some children at five-and-a-half years got only 10 or 12 items correct on a 47-item test, but the median for that age was 43. The asymmetry continued through second grade. Children below the 35th percentile in kindergarten were the only ones not crowding the top of the scale at second grade.

2. Miller asked whether boys tended to have more reading blocks than girls; there was some reason to think that this might be associated with the fact that most schoolteachers were women and that boys were socially motivated to regard clear pronunciation as effeminate and unappealing. Templin said there were articulation differences that tended to persist over time, but the sex difference was not reflected to the same extent in English morphology. Berko had recorded no sex differences, and it seemed to Templin that many recent studies of the amount of verbal output and of various grammatical characteristics showed much less sex differentiation than studies in the 1930's. Slobin knew of no sex differences in grammatical studies. Lenneberg

thought the question of social attitude was relevant. There was a large incidence of family histories associated with youngsters with gross developmental speech problems, coming from the paternal side twice as often as from the maternal. The incidence of right- and left-handedness was less dramatic, though slightly more boys than girls were left-handed or ambidextrous. There had been interpretation of these data as indicating a genetic influence, and with considerable hesitation Lenneberg thought the fact that the patterns ran through families and were paternal made it doubtful that they could be attributable solely to attitudes. With animals there would be no hesitation at all in making such an interpretation. Kalmus corrected a suggestion that this would be analogous to color blindness, pointing out that this did not pass from father to son. Templin could offer no information about siblings (her study contains none of different ages) or twins (only two pairs). Lenneberg said that something like eighteen or twenty studies, some of them quite sophisticated and careful, comparing fraternal and identical twins had indicated that the identicals tended to have similar histories and abnormalities while the fraternals did not. Slobin referred to a Bulgarian study of 850 stutterers, three-quarters of whom were males. A third of the cases came from families with stuttering, and in 60 per cent of these families the father had the defect. The age range was from two to fifty-five years, and the sex difference was greatest in the stutterers up to five years of age. The author had made comparisons with English, French, and German studies and concluded that the sex bias was universal between the ages of two and five, but he also pointed to other critical periods for the onset of stuttering, such as the beginning of school and puberty, that varied from culture to culture and appeared to be social in origin. In Russia, for example, there was a marked increase in stuttering at seven years, the age of entering school, although in America it was more typically found at five or six years. Slobin said the Bulgarian study favored a physiological explanation for the greater incidence of stuttering among males, i.e., the slower process of myelinization of the cortical motor and speech structures. Lenneberg said the myelinization problem was highly debated and not something to which he would like to attribute stuttering.

3. The common and persistent misarticulation of /r/ and /l/ was queried further; was there something wrong with the pronunciation of either /r/ or /l/, did two phonemes exist or was there only one,

and, if it was the case that two phonemes were being pronounced badly, did any contrast remain? Templin thought what her study really reported was what reasonably well-trained observers heard rather than what the children said, but this probably indicated at least that there was a meaningful contrast. The issue provoked a lengthy discussion.

Liberman found it interesting that children had more difficulty with /s/, /r/, and /l/ rather than with the stop consonants /b, d, g; p, t, k, m, n, ng/ because this was the opposite of what might have been expected from their acoustic characteristics. With stop consonants the acoustic cue was not invariant with respect to the phoneme perceived but varied widely according to the phonetic context. For the class that includes /s, sh, r, l/ the acoustic signal was more nearly invariant with the phoneme perceived. Templin and Fry had both indicated that even the youngest child had least difficulty with phonemes that were acoustically the least stable and the most difficulty with the most stable. It might be relevant that the phones with which the child had least difficulty (stop consonants) were very rapidly articulated, had acoustic standpoints in steady state, and did not go all the way to the locus of the sound spectrum in transitions. The phones with which the child had the greatest difficulty either had a long steady state (/s, sh/), or else they went all the way to the locus and remained there for 20 or 30 msec. An engineer asked to build a voice-operated typewriter would probably expect least difficulty with /s, sh/, and perhaps not very much more with /r, l/, but a good deal with the stops.

Cooper thought the feedback problem might be different for the child and the engineer. The very rapid, ballistically produced stops had to be done well if they were to be done at all. The feedback question there was simply whether the articulation had been right or wrong, and quite possibly all the child had to do was flip the right muscle and he had got it. If he did not get it, he was all wrong. The slower phones allowed time for a continuous adjustment to feedback which the engineer could cope with but possibly the child could not.

Denes drew a distinction between /s, sh/ on the one hand and /r, l/ on the other because the former would be easy both to produce and recognize artificially and the latter would be difficult. He thought /r, l/ were in the small group of sounds where it was still not known what the human being did with his articulation. Liberman agreed that not much was known about the acoustic cues for /r, l/, but on the basis of what was known it would seem that the acoustic distinction was a very simple, stable, and gross one. The engineer would probably not have very much difficulty in detecting it.

Hirsh wanted to stress the significance of the mistaken pronunciation. It was as valuable to know what this was, and whether it could be categorized, as it was to know the sound missed or intended. He also pointed out that there was a continuum of confusion involving not simply /s/ and /sh/ but also /th/, with which they could both be confused, and /f/, with which /th/ was confused. He thought that /r/ and /l/ stood apart as a separate pair. Since these acoustic cues were stable in time and more independent of the phonetic environment than other sounds that did not cause so much pronunciation trouble, he supposed the difficulty could be attributed to place of articulation rather than to those consonant groups where manner of articulation was more important. Transitional cues were available for the stop consonants, for which frequency information was in a sense more redundant because it was controlled by the phonetic environment, and direction of change as well as locus provided cues. Liberman noted that the direction and extent of the transition varied tremendously. The second formant of /d/, for example, before /o/ was a rising transition high in the frequency range, while before /oo/ it was a falling transition low in the frequency range. This seemed to bother the child not at all.

Miller wanted to know whether the difficulty of articulating a phoneme could be discussed without reference to the entire phonemic system of which it was a member. Was there, for example, an absolute difficulty for [r] that would hold in any language regardless of what it was in contrast with? A case in point might be Japanese, where there was no distinction between [l] and [r]. Would Japanese children still have a relatively late acquisition of accurate enunciation of this one phoneme? Hirsh said it depended on who made the judgment; a Japanese phonetician would accept a rather wider spectrum than an American. Liberman referred to Greenberg (1963) who had found that there were some phonemes that occurred in a large number of languages and seemed to carry a very large information load wherever they were used. Other phonemes or phonemic distinctions occurred more rarely in languages, and when they did they tended to be less often used and to carry a lighter information load. He thought, therefore, that there was probably something about the efficiency or utility of certain phonemes which was to some extent independent of the total phonemic system in which they occurred. Fodor thought the right question ought not to be whether there was an /l/ in the language to distinguish from /r/ but whether there was a class of distinctive features characteristic of the /r/. If it was assumed that distinctive features rather than phonemes were discriminated in the first instance, it might be expected that the background of contrast for each distinctive feature in each language would be very similar. In that case, sounds difficult in one language would be difficult in another.

Fry thought there was clearly something special about the class of sounds that were called [r] sounds, for example, in the way it colored speech for practically everyone and its significance in different national accents. It was probably true that this class of sound had an intrinsic difficulty. The articulation of [r] was found difficult in English and also (said Kalmus) in German. Denes pointed out that [r] was articulated in very different ways in European languages. In English it was a fricative consonant, in French it was mostly a uvula fricative sometimes but not always rolled, and in Hungarian and Italian it was rolled. It was dangerous to talk about the difficulty of [r] in different languages.

Ferguson recommended looking at some Caucasian or Northwest Coast Indian languages before jumping to tempting conclusions. Some of these had large numbers of laterals and trills, but the children doubtless learned them at an appropriate age. He was not saying there were many of these languages, but he could probably find a couple of dozen. House wondered whether untrilled laterals developed late in such languages, and Liberman mused on the information load particular laterals and trills might carry.

Ferguson noted that the reasons considered for the order of the acquisition of sounds had been different from those related to the order of acquisition of grammar. One could, he supposed, follow a similar speculative procedure, look for universals in phonology, and ask to what extent phonological machinery was innately built in. House speculated even further and suggested that whoever designed the phonological system had obviously run out of simple acoustic contrast and had added some frills which we now thought of as laterals and liquids and trills and which did not fit into any simple acoustic system. We did not know how to evaluate them, and so we said we did not understand their production. They also turned out to be behaviorally late in developing in children and to be hard to hear. Jenkins added that they were also historically unstable.

Reverting to specific points, Denes observed that hissing was not very difficult for children to produce; why then should they find [s] so hard to use linguistically? Adults understood it very well, and it would seem fairly easy to distinguish either by ear or machine. Hirsh said the particular cluster of /sh, s, th/ was one of the most difficult and often confused sets in the early speech of the deaf child, who had no acoustic reference. If the tongue was gradually moved forward, starting with [sh], a variety of sounds was created, only some of which became categorized as phonemes.

House thought the important articulatory point was that the stop consonants did in fact stop. The place at which they stopped could easily be identified rather grossly because the position differed considerably. Fricatives involved adjusting the tongue and holding it for a short time without anything to rest on. Liberman hastened to end the discussion by agreeing. His original point, he reiterated, was that puzzlement was likely to be the result if these difficulties were looked at from an acoustic point of view; the question should be looked at from the aspect of ease of articulation.

## REFERENCE

GREENBERG, J. H. Some universals of grammar with reference to the order of meaningful elements. In *Universals of Language*, J. H. Greenberg (Ed.), Cambridge, Mass.: M.I.T. Press, 1963; 2nd ed., 1966.

## D. B. Fry

# THE DEVELOPMENT OF THE PHONOLOGICAL SYSTEM IN THE NORMAL AND THE DEAF CHILD

When a child is learning his native language, a very special place is reserved in the total process for the development of the phonemic system because it provides the basis for the whole vocabulary of words that he will acquire during the rest of his life. By the time the normal child is five to seven years old, he has the phonemic repertory of his language complete and thereafter does not add to it, although he will go on learning new words for many years. In order to understand the child's acquisition of language, therefore, we need to have at least some idea of how this vital part of the structure develops.

In the language-learning process, the production of speech is inseparably connected with the reception of speech, and the learning of both go forward together in the young child. There are in fact three aspects to the development of speech in the child: the learning of the motor skills, the mastery of the cues for recognition, and the building up of the store of linguistic knowledge that eventually forms the basis for both the production and reception of speech.

From his very earliest days the normal child gives utterance to sounds as a reaction to his own state; discomfort will cause him to cry out, and the rest of the time he will tend to be silent. At a slightly later stage he will produce sounds of a different character to accompany a feeling of well-being. The only relation of such sounds to speech lies in the fact that the child is using physiological mechanisms of respiration, phonation, and to a certain extent articulation, which will be used later in the acquiring of speech.

Within the first month or so the child will begin to associate the sound of the human voice with pleasant situations, such as that of feeding, but at this stage he probably does not differentiate the voice from other sounds that occur at the same time. Very soon, however, the child responds more specifically to speech and is influenced first of all by the features that convey the emotional attitude of the speaker — the intonation patterns and the voice quality. His reactions are still nonspeech reactions, smiling or crying, and the speech is still for him a part of the total situation, which will also include the facial expression of the speaker and so on, but he is already listening to some aspects of speech and making a differential response to them.

Already at this stage the amount of speech the child hears is important for the future development of his speech. The normal child in the usual home environment is talked to all the time by his mother and by other people, and his ability to listen is continually exercised and extended by the variety of situations and the variety of speech associated with them. It is the link between the mother's speech and situations that are important for the child that brings about this development of the capacity for listening. The child will pay no attention to speech that does not occur in such situations, and hence the mother's talking to her baby during feeding, bathing, and dressing plays a vital role in the acquiring of speech. Even normally hearing children brought up in an abnormal environment, for example in a residential nursery, may well be backward in speech because they are deprived of the constant speech accompaniment to things that interest them.

## THE BABBLING STAGE

During his first year nearly every child, whether normally hearing or not, will produce quite a variety of sounds. These develop out of the comfort and discomfort sounds that have already been mentioned, and therefore the beginning of babbling is not a well-marked stage. When babbling is well established, the utterances are characterized by frequent repetitions of the same syllable or sound, and the significant feature of this stage is that the child is now uttering sounds for the pleasure they give him and not as an expression of his reactions to some particular situation.

At this period two very important developments are taking place. First, the child is discovering the possibilities inherent in the phonatory and articulatory muscle systems. He learns to combine articulation with phonation in a variety of ways. Although he certainly does not acquire all the articulations that he will later need, he does produce some classes of sound that will not be required by the phonemic system of his language. Certain sounds, for example, arise from the combining of sucking motions with phonation, and for the English child these implosive consonant articulations are outside the phonetic scheme of his native language. Similarly, the strongly nasalized vowels that the child utters during babbling will not later be needed for English.

The learning that takes place on the motor side at this stage is therefore of a rather general nature and is absolutely basic to the acquisition of speech. The child is "getting the idea" of combining the action of the larynx with the movements of the articulators, of controlling to some extent the larynx frequency, of using the outgoing airstream to produce different kinds of articulation, and also the idea, which is quite important, of producing the same sound again by repeating the movements.

The second important development at this time is the establishment of the auditory feedback loop. As sound-producing movements are repeated and repeated, a strong link is forged between tactual and kinesthetic impressions and the auditory sensations that the child receives from his own utterances. The pleasure gained from babbling, which comes in the first instance from the sense of movement, is soon enhanced by the child's hearing of his own sounds. While babbling begins as the outcome of the expressive sounds that have preceded it, its continued development depends upon the use of the auditory feedback loop. This explains the observation, which has so frequently been made, that the baby's babbling can be elicited by sounds made to him by an adult; in this situation the baby will respond with his own babbling sounds, although they may be very different from the adult's sound. The auditory stimulus from outside starts up the complex of motor and auditory activity in the child.

Further evidence of this connection between the motor and the auditory side of babbling is found in what very often happens in the child who is born deaf. In such children, babbling usually develops at about the normal age and continues for some time. But at a later stage, when in the normal child the auditory feedback would begin to assume some importance, babbling fades in the deaf child because he lacks the external auditory stimulus from an adult as well as the auditory stimulus from his own babbling. It is found with such children that babbling may continue for a time but will become dependent upon the child's being able to see the adult who is speaking to him. It seems clear, therefore, that in babbling auditory sensations play an important part, and in the deaf child the development of something approaching normal speech requires the continuous provision of auditory stimulation so that babbling will not cease and the all-important links between the motor activity of speech and auditory feedback will be established at the right time.

During the babbling stage, therefore, the child is doing two important things: he is trying out mechanisms that will be needed for speech, combining phonation with articulation and no doubt gaining a certain control of the respiratory system, and he is establishing the circuits by which motor activity and auditory impressions are firmly linked together. He is learning the acoustic effect of making certain movements and finding out how to repeat a movement, how to do it again and again to get more or less the same acoustic result. In one sense he is learning a trick, and the experience lasts him, so to speak, for the rest of his life.

## THE DEVELOPMENT OF ARTICULATION

We have already said that in the babbling stage the child produces a considerable variety of sounds, including some that he will discard later on. He probably does not, on the other hand, make all the sounds that will be needed in his native language or at least does not articulate them quite as he will at a later stage. Changes in articulation as well as new sounds now come about as a result of imitation.

It has been suggested in previous papers and discussions at this meeting that imitation plays very little part in the development of grammar in the child's language. Some of us hesitate to accept this assertion about grammar and feel at least that there is much still to be found out about the way in which grammar develops. When it comes to articulation and the development of the phonological system, however, it seems that imitation does play a very important role. Imitation is here taken to mean simply that the child tries to produce a sound that strikes him as similar to the sound that he hears coming in from outside. Doubts about the part played by imitation must, I believe, be dispelled by the fact that similarities in pronunciation do exist and are very strong, for instance, between the mother and the child, and it is hard to see what mechanism other than imitation could produce this result. The effect is most noticeable, perhaps, in cases where a mother and child have a common dialect that is different from that of everyone else in the environment; in London, for example, it is not unknown for the child of a mother who has a marked Scottish accent to develop the same dialectal pronunciation even though others around him speak southern English or some form of Cockney.

Toward the end of the babbling stage, then, the child begins to copy specifically the sounds made to him by adults and especially, of course, by his mother. Since the control of motor speech activity through auditory feedback is already established in principle, he has at his disposal the means of making his own utterance match more nearly the pattern that is given to him. He hears a word from an adult, and he makes movements that will produce from his own speech mechanism sounds that are as like the word as he can manage at the moment. With repeated imitation and continuous practice he modifies his own movements and so brings the sounds that he utters closer to those he receives from outside. One of the aspects of speech that the child learns to reproduce successfully quite early is the intonation of what is said to him. This is not because rises and falls in pitch are particularly easy to imitate but rather because intonation is closely linked with the affective side of speech; its use grows naturally out of the expressive sounds the child has been making, and the emotional tie between mother and baby ensures that the baby will readily imitate the mood and tone of the mother.

All the changes in speech that take place at this time, and particularly the learning of new articulations, depend upon the continual reinforcement provided by the situations in which the child finds himself. The social and conventional use of speech is already beginning. The mother speaks to the child, using a word or expression appropriate to the situation; the child responds by imitating the word, and his own utterance thus begins to be associated with the situation. The sounds he makes will not be a very close copy at first, but the mother in her turn responds by repeating the word and thus repeatedly gives the pattern and usually shows her approval as the baby in the course of time gets closer to the pattern. In this way articulations that are not very close approximations to begin with are modified progressively until they at last become normal articulations for a given language.

Direct reinforcement by repetition and approval from the mother is not the only pressure that bears upon the child's speech. It is agreed by all observers of infant speech that *recognition* of words, that is to say, the associating of a word with a situation, precedes any deliberate attempt on the part of the child to say the word with reference to that situation. But as soon as the child has even a small repertory of words that he can both recognize and make some attempt at saying, he begins to try them out spontaneously. When this happens, his speech is subject to the constraint of the listener's response just as all adult speech is; if his utterance is sufficiently like the pattern he has heard, he will succeed in producing the response that he wants, and so there is a strong incentive for him to practice and to change his articulation in order to be readily understood. Usually he achieves this first with his mother, and there then follows a period during which the mother has to act as interpreter between the baby and the rest of the world. The process of development is, however, continuous, and when the child finds that articulations that evoke the desired response from the mother fail to do so with other people, he has again to modify his speech so that the sounds resemble more closely those used by the people around him.

During this period, then, the child is perfecting the motor skill that is the basis of all speech, and he is doing so by building up memory stores of different kinds which are to last him throughout the rest of his life. Let us look more closely at what is involved in acquiring a particular word. First, the baby hears a group of sounds associated with a given situation; second, he learns to recognize the sounds; third, he makes his own attempt at reproducing the word, at first without associating it with the situation; fourth, he says the word in the situation in order to call forth a response; fifth, he changes his own utterance to make it match the pattern he has heard in order to obtain more certain and more satisfactory responses; sixth, he continues the modification process until the word gains the desired response from all listeners in all appropriate situations.

A word that is recognized means an auditory pattern stored in the child's memory. When the child utters the word, he links this auditory memory with a very complex pattern of activity. The muscles receive their operating instructions from the brain, and the course of their activity is controlled through the kinesthetic and the auditory feedback loops. Learning on the motor side includes the training of the muscle systems as well as the accumulating of memory patterns in the brain. What the child is doing in the process of modifying his speech is to set up habits of movement with the aid of kinesthetic and auditory information. He arrives at a satisfactory movement by using his ears to judge the resulting sounds, and thus the motor learning in speech is very largely dependent on hearing; the child must be able to hear the results of his own speech movements if he is ever to acquire normal speech or something approaching normal speech. When habits are established, they form a memory store of kinesthetic patterns that are the basis of all future speech movements.

After the learning period is over, we are not quite so dependent on auditory feedback. For example, an adult who is severely deafened, even if this happens quite suddenly, does not immediately become incapable of speech, and it is usually some years before small changes in his articulation become apparent. Again, the hearing adult can continue to talk in the face of noise so loud that he can literally not hear himself speak. Both these examples show that once habits are established kinesthetic information can afford a sufficient basis for speech movements, but this is the result of the long learning period during which auditory and kinesthetic impressions become firmly linked.

## THE DEVELOPMENT OF THE PHONOLOGICAL SYSTEM

Practice in listening and recognition and the acquisition of the rudiments of motor skill are both preparatory stages leading to the development of speech in its full sense, that is, to the learning of the language system. Here it must be made very clear that what has been said up to this point and most of what follows represents an attempt to summarize what *usually* happens in the development of speech and language in the normal child; it does not and cannot in the nature of things indicate a path that must inevitably and inflexibly be followed by every child who learns to talk or to understand speech. The immense individual variations to be found in all aspects of child development would in themselves put this out of the question, but there is the added factor that everything that happens in speech can be brought about in many different ways. Thus we could not say, for example, that if a child failed to babble he could never learn to speak, or that if articulation did not progress in a certain way, the child could not possibly develop the phonological system. In the following discussion of the phonological system, therefore, it should be borne in mind that only the normal course of events is in question, and that in special circumstances and in individual cases the rate of development and the sequence may vary a good deal, and that certain steps in the process may be omitted or reversed without rendering the development of the system impossible.

The child's changes of articulation under the pressure of adult responses to his utterances are the first steps toward establishing the phonemic system. The goal of being understood by everyone is not reached until the system is complete. Naturally the forty-odd units of the English phonemic system, for example, do not crystallize simultaneously in the child's speech. In the earliest utterances that are used consistently, that is to say, in specific situations and with specific referents, only two or three phonemes may be involved. The baby who uses /mama/ and /dada/ and no other words in this meaningful way has a system of just three units, for the system must be thought of as being at each stage complete in itself. The English child does not start with a set of forty pigeonholes of which the majority remain to be occupied during the development of his speech; he is actively constructing the framework, and, as each pigeonhole is added, the shape of the whole structure and particularly the interrelations of the units are changing.

The order in which phonemic units are added to the system in the development of a child's speech varies in individual cases but is largely determined by two factors. The first is that some sounds are intrinsically more difficult to produce than others; they require the use of more muscles, closer control of the amount and the timing of movement, and generally finer co-ordination. Such sounds, which for most children include the consonants /s, r, θ, ð/, are added to the phonemic repertory later than simpler sounds like /p, t, m/.

The second factor is the importance of the various phonemes in the system as determined statistically. The young child is at first exposed to a very restricted language containing comparatively few words, and it is the occurrence of phonemes in this language that will help to determine the order in which phonemes will be added to his system. More exactly, it is the frequency with which the distinction between a given pair of phonemes is employed to mark off one word from another, that is, the occurrence of minimal pairs with respect to phoneme differences or the informational loading of the phonemes.

The order in which phonemes are added to the child's repertory depends, therefore, on the difficulty with which the sound is articulated and the informational loading of the phonemes in the restricted language which he is using and to which he is exposed. Both of these factors will vary from one individual to another. Vowels and consonants develop together to some extent because the syllabic structure of speech demands the use of both. The vowels correspond with the higher intensity stretches in speech, which are more easily heard; but on the other hand the informational loading of vowels is lower than that of consonants, and there is thus less pressure on the child to learn vowel distinctions. In the second half of the first year the child begins with syllables containing only one vowel, phonetically in the region [æ] to [a], and by the age of about eighteen months he will probably have a vowel system containing perhaps eight to ten vowels, including one or two diphthongs. The whole system of about twenty vowels is unlikely to be complete until about the age of three years.

Among the first consonant phonemes to be established in the speech of English children are the /m/ of /mama/ and the /d/ of /dada/, and to these are soon added /p, b, t, n/. Usually a little later appear the velar sounds /k, g/ and the semivowel /w/. At the other end of the scale are several phonemes whose sounds are difficult for the child to articulate, such as /r, θ, s, h, f/, and these are often among the last units to be added to the system. Abnormal articulation of one or other of these sounds may persist for a long time and even be carried on into adult life. This does not mean that the speaker's phonemic system is necessarily abnormal. An adult with a "defective" [r], for example, will make a difference between the two words *wed* and *red* and in fact has both /w/ and /r/ in his phonemic system, although his articulation of [r] is very different from that of most people. When the child is acquiring speech, however, his use of phonemic categories is closely bound up with his ability to articulate sounds, and while his pronunciation is changing rapidly, his phoneme classes will be less well defined; he will tend to make more errors in producing sounds and will more frequently misinterpret what he hears than he is likely to do later on when the complete system is established.

Certain consonant phonemes appear late, not because they present difficulties of articulation but because they occur rarely. The child may acquire /ʃ/ fairly early; the voiced counterpart /ʒ/ occurs mainly in words like *measure, leisure,* which are not likely to occur in the child's restricted language until much later.

The development of the phonological system includes not only the learning of the necessary articulations but also learning the distribution of phonemes. Part of this process is dependent upon the child's recognition and imitation of sequences that he hears, but it is also greatly helped by the occurrence of minimal pairs. If the difference between two phonemes is critical for words he is hearing and using all the time, he will soon learn to use each of the two. In the absence of such pairs, he may take some time to get the distribution of the phoneme right. Two examples may help to illustrate this effect. One child for some time used the pronunciation /distəːv/ for the word *disturb,* although she used /b/ in words like *baby* and *rub,* etc. Since there is no minimal pair /distəːv—distəːb/ in English, there was no strong reason from the point of view of the language why this should not be done, and it was only when she eventually noticed (with the aid of some teasing from a brother and sister) that other people said /distəːb/ that she changed her pronunciation. A similar example was found in the speech of another child who pronounced the word *satchel* as /satrəl/, although she could say both /tʃein/ and /trein/ and would never confuse the two. Here again, had there been a minimal pair /satʃəl—satrəl/, the child would have corrected her pronunciation much earlier than she in fact did.

The learning that takes place about this time also involves one further aspect of phoneme distribution, i.e., the restrictions and prohibitions that the language imposes with respect to phoneme selection. Just as frequently occurring contrasts build up the child's knowledge of permitted sequences, so the nonappearance of other successions of phonemes enables him to learn what is prohibited by the language system. To take some obvious examples in English, it is in this way that the child learns the impossibility of word-initial /ŋ/ and word-final /h/ and learns that word-initial /pl/ is a permitted cluster whereas word-initial /pf/ is a prohibited one in that language. There is here some evidence of an interesting contrast between the acquiring of grammar and the learning of the phonology. While the child will often use analogy in forming grammatical sequences that are not permitted in the adult language, he will not form phoneme sequences that go against the prohibitions of the system and then later have to discard them; he simply does not utter such sequences. This is a further indication of the great role played by imitation in the acquiring of the phonological system.

The rate of speech development varies greatly among individual children, but in the normally hearing child one can expect that by five to seven years of age the phonemic system will be complete and fairly well established. This means that the child is familiar with the forty-odd units in the system, can articulate the sounds appropriate to them, can recognize these sounds when they are produced by other speakers (though not of course by each and every speaker), and does not usually make errors in selecting phonemes to make up the words he is in the habit of using himself. This is the true basis of his native language; his knowledge will be extended in a number of ways, but he will not have to add to his phoneme repertory or to learn any new sounds for the rest of his life.

## ACOUSTIC CUES AND THE PHONEMIC SYSTEM

It is clear that a very important part of this development of the phonemic system is bound up with the use of acoustic cues, both for the monitoring of the child's own speech and for the reception of other people's. We now have a considerable body of information about the operation of these cues in adult speech, although we are still far from understanding fully how they function, but we have no knowledge of the ways in which the use of the cues develops as speech is acquired. Studies of the perception and recognition of speech sounds have however established certain fundamental facts which are relevant to speech development. A listener makes use of acoustic cues only for the purpose of sorting incoming sounds into the right phonemic categories; and he does the sorting not so much by an act of absolute identification, that is, by saying "this sound is /p/," as by determining that "this sound is /p/ not /t/, /p/ not /k/, /p/ not /b/, /p/ not /m/." He has available acoustic cues that are relevant to all these oppositions, so that any one identification will depend on a complex of cues. It is in fact the phonemic system that, as it were, evokes the cue system and not the acoustic cues that "produce" the phonemic categories. When the child has only a very restricted repertory of phonemes, therefore, he will make use of a relatively small number of acoustic cues, and as the number of phonemic units increases so too will the number of acoustic cues that he learns to use. The baby who distinguishes only between /mama/ and /dada/ can deal with the two-consonant system simply on the basis of the continuant nature of /m/ and the interrupted nature of /d/; but these cues will no longer be enough if he adds a third word /baba/ as he will now need a further cue for differentiating between /d/ and /b/, perhaps second formant transition. As the phonological system develops, more and more acoustic differentiations have to be made, and sounds that begin by being indistinguishable to the child are eventually sorted into separate categories.

It has been suggested that the whole process of using acoustic cues to differentiate among sounds and so assign them to phonemic categories is based on the acquired distinctiveness of sounds; that is to say that sounds which begin by being indistinguishable one from another acquire distinctiveness in the course of the language-learning process. Such experimental evidence as is at present available tends to support this view. What has been said here about the development of the phonological system in the child is also very much in keeping with this idea. It is suggested that the child begins by being insensible to differences among speech sounds and that a vital part of language-learning in the early stages is the process by which he becomes sensitive to more and more differences among sounds; that is to say, sounds become distinct from each other and so form the basis for additional phonemic categories.

A further important fact that emerges from work on acoustic cues is that there is considerable individual variation in the way the cues are used in identifying sounds. If two people are to communicate easily with each other by speech, they must have a common phonemic system or one that is to a large extent common; but this does not mean that both will be using exactly the same acoustic cues in exactly the same way. There is not, in other words, a standard set of acoustic cues or a standard arrangement of cues for arriving at given phonemic solutions. For one thing, sensitivity to change in a particular acoustic dimension is found to vary appreciably among individual listeners, and this cannot fail to have an effect upon the way in which cues are combined in carrying out a phonemic identification. When a message is decoded by two listeners, what is required for the success of the communication is that they should reach the same phonemic solution: the fact that they may use acoustic cues in a somewhat different way in order to do so is not important. In experimental work on acoustic cues in speech, we naturally look for some ways of operating that are common to a number of listeners in a language group, but we do not expect to find, and indeed do not find, that every group of subjects will be homogeneous for the purposes of a particular experiment.

## THE DEVELOPMENT OF THE PHONOLOGICAL SYSTEM IN THE DEAF CHILD

From the point of view of the relations between acoustic cues and the phonemic system, a crucial test and a demonstration may be provided by the case of the child who is either born deaf or becomes severely deaf before speech has been acquired. Much of what has been said so far can be summed up by saying that in the reception of speech all the learning is done by the brain; the peripheral hearing mechanism relays information to the brain in the form of nerve impulses, but the organization of this information is solely the work of the central mechanism. If this were not the case or if phonemic sorting at the center depended on a standard and immutable set of items of acoustic information, then we should expect it to prove impossible for the severely deaf child ever to develop the phonological system of a language and consequently to produce or receive speech in a manner at all comparable with that of the hearing child. On the other hand, if the crucial part of the speech-learning process lies in the brain's organization of such auditory information as it receives (and there is no *a priori* reason for believing that the deaf child's brain is less capable of learning than the hearing child's), there would be solid grounds for supposing that the deaf child could develop the phonological system and could therefore go far toward acquiring normal speech.

It has been believed for many centuries, and is still believed by far too many people actually working in this field, that the first of the situations just outlined reflects the position of the deaf child. It is believed that an appreciable number of children are born without the capacity for the sensation of hearing at all and that, in any case, unless the child "hears" exactly what the normally hearing child hears, he can never develop normal speech. During the last ten or fifteen years a great deal of evidence has been accumulating in London and a few other places in the world that flatly contradicts this view. It is obvious that if no auditory information is relayed to the brain, then the whole complex process of acquiring speech cannot go forward. In the Nuffield Centre[1] in London, however, no child has been found in whom it was impossible to develop responses to sound. The impression that a child cannot hear at all is often the result of unsuitable methods of testing and of faulty observation. It has been found, further, that no matter how small the amount of hearing the child has initially, this hearing can be used in the development of speech and will in fact show every evidence of increasing in amount with teaching. As a result, the

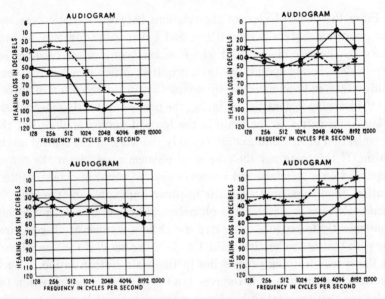

Fig. 1. Audiograms of four children found in schools for the deaf who had very little comprehension of speech.

clinic has produced many instances of children with very severe hearing losses (70, 80, and 90 dB over the whole audible range in the better ear) who have developed excellent speech, sometimes indistinguishable from normal, and who have consequently been educated successfully among normally hearing children in an ordinary school.

Surprising as this result may at first appear, it is much less so if we adopt the premises outlined in the first part of this paper: the para-

[1] The Nuffield Hearing and Speech Centre is a unit of the Royal National Throat, Nose, and Ear Hospital, London. It was founded and directed for many years by the late Miss Edith Whetnall, who was responsible for the most important pioneer work in this field.

mount importance of the development of the phonemic system and the dependence of this development on the complex interactions of auditory and kinesthetic feedback without which the motor skills of speech cannot be satisfactorily acquired. To put this in another way, we may say that the amount of speech a child develops depends not so much on the amount of hearing *per se* as upon the use he is able to make of his hearing for language-learning.

This point is clearly illustrated by Figures 1 and 2. Figure 1 shows

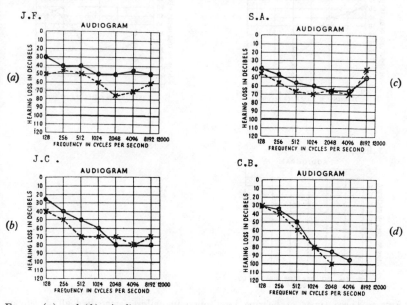

FIG. 2 (*a*) and (*b*): Audiograms of two children in schools for the deaf who had practically no speech. (*c*) and (*d*): Similar audiograms of two children who had used their hearing from an early age, had developed excellent speech, and were being educated in ordinary schools.

the audiograms of four children who have quite a fair degree of hearing, yet who can understand very little speech and can produce little speech that is intelligible to the average listener. These children were all found in schools for the deaf. Figure 2 gives the audiograms of four more children, all of whom were born deaf; cases (*a*) and (*b*) are again those of two children who have practically no speech, can just distinguish between vowels, and recognize a few familiar words only; cases (*c*) and (*d*), however, whose hearing losses are comparable with those of the other two children, have learned to talk, to understand speech, and are being educated in hearing schools. Nor is the type of hearing loss much more significant for language-learning than the degree of loss; the three children whose audiograms are shown in Figure 3 all acquired excellent speech and were able to take their place in hearing schools.

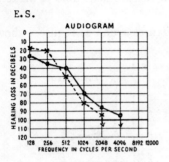

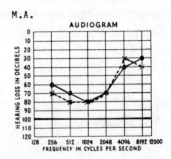

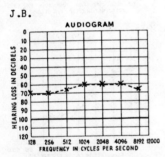

FIG. 3. Three types of hearing loss found in children who had all developed excellent speech and were in ordinary schools.

Here then are examples both of children who have developed the phonological system and of those who have failed to do so, and it is evident that we cannot distinguish between them on the grounds of hearing loss. If there were a certain amount of auditory information that must be received in order to develop the phonological system and if the reception of that information were in itself enough to develop it, then either all the cases shown in the figures should have acquired speech or else none of them should have done so.

The reason why these deaf children have failed to develop the phonological system is simply that they have not been exposed to enough speech. Had steps been taken to ensure that they heard speech continuously from an early age, their development of speech and language would have followed much the same course as that of a normally hearing child. This statement, again a surprising one to some people, can be substantiated from many examples of children who, although born deaf, have been given the chance to hear speech all the time and have developed speech of their own that is completely intelligible to the ordinary listener and sounds astonishingly natural.

There can be little doubt that all these children have the English phonological system fully developed, and in nearly all cases the grammar is also complete. While one would not say that their speech is at all times indistinguishable from that of hearing children, one can certainly say that it is very different from what many of us recognize so immediately as "deaf" speech, and it is, above all, highly intelligible.

One conclusion to be reached from the study of such children is inescapable and confirms what was said earlier in this paper: there cannot be, so to speak, a set of standard acoustic cues that everyone has to use in forming the phonological system of English. Though we cannot be sure exactly what acoustic information is being relayed to the brain in such cases, we are at least sure that it differs from that which reaches the brain of the normally hearing person. This suggests that these children must, as it were, forge their own sets of cues, which enables them to develop the phonological system.

How are such results achieved? The first essential is early diagnosis, preferably before the age of nine months or one year, and the possibility of such diagnosis depends of course largely on the spread of information among parents and the medical profession about the problem of the deaf child and the need for early discovery of deafness. Once a severe degree of deafness is found or even suspected in a child, the whole aim of subsequent treatment and training is to enable the child to progress through the stages of acquiring speech in the same way as the hearing child.

It is obviously necessary to get the maximum of acoustic information to the brain, and the child is therefore fitted with a hearing aid as soon as possible. Many of the children in the Nuffield Centre have been using aids since the age of nine or ten months. There is now a good deal of evidence in favor of fitting each child with two aids so that both ears may be working continuously. The normal child makes good use of two ears, and it may well be that in the speech-learning process this factor has considerable importance, although the evidence on this point is at present rather hard to systematize.

It has been said already that all babies, whether normal or deaf, begin to babble at a certain stage. In the deaf child provided with hearing aids, the babbling continues its normal course instead of fading out and so performs the all-important function of establishing the links between the auditory and kinesthetic feedback loops and the motor speech mechanism. In many cases where diagnosis of deafness has taken place later than the normal babbling stage, it has been found that the child begins to babble spontaneously some time after the hearing aid has been fitted. This will not of course happen immediately after the aid is provided, and in some children there may be a delay of some months, but when the babbling comes it performs its proper function as a preparation for speech.

Apart from the question of providing suitable hearing aids, the whole success or failure of treatment depends upon the mother. It is she who has to understand the problem and realize what is required, that is, that the child should hear as much speech and hear it as continuously as possible. The mother has to talk to the child even more than she would do to a hearing child and to make sure that her speech can be heard. This is particularly difficult at the stage when the baby becomes mobile and is able to crawl away from its mother. When the hearing child does this, he is still able to hear the mother's speech and so the learning process continues; in the case of the deaf child, even though he is wearing a hearing aid, it is generally necessary for the mother to take special measures to keep close to the baby.

If this method is adopted, then there is every chance that the child will progress through the normal stages of the development of speech, even though he may be slower in doing so than the hearing child. He will develop the knowledge of the phonemic system of the language and with it the ability to make use of the redundancy of the language. In doing so he will, of course, form his own set of acoustic cues based on whatever information his peripheral hearing mechanism is able to relay to his brain, but this fact is not particularly important. What matters is that as the child learns more and more of the language system, the constraints of the system become stronger and stronger and ensure that he is able eventually to reach the right solution in all problems of phonemic sorting.

There remains a somewhat intriguing question with regard to the production of speech. If a severely deaf child learns to produce speech that sounds normal, he is clearly nonetheless controlling his movements on the basis of fed-back auditory signals that are far from normal. He is in fact producing a proportion of acoustic output that has no effect on his own auditory system. Why is he able to do this? We are far from knowing the full answer to this question, but part of the answer must lie in the point that has been made several times, that an essential part of the speech-learning process is the linking of the auditory and kinesthetic feedback systems. When the child imitates a particular sound sequence, he makes movements that will produce sounds matching as nearly as possible the pattern he receives. The deaf child, because he receives a distorted pattern, will try to reproduce this distorted pattern and in doing so will in some degree come close to making the "right" movements. Some of the acoustic output is therefore a by-product, as it were, of these right movements. There is undoubtedly much that is unknown and unexplained about this whole process. It would seem most likely that once the habits of movement are established in the deaf child, he may lean rather more heavily on kinesthetic feedback as a control system than the hearing person does, but there is no doubt at all that during the learning period the linking of auditory and kinesthetic impressions is the key. Only if we give the deaf child the opportunity to form this link, and hence to build up the phonological system and all the necessary store of auditory and kinesthetic memories, can we enable him to acquire speech that is really serviceable as a means of communicating with his fellow men.

## GENERAL REFERENCES

FRY, D. B. Coding and decoding in speech. In *Signs, Signals and Symbols*, Stella E. Mason (Ed.), London: Methuen, 1963, pp. 65–82.

———— and WHETNALL, EDITH. The auditory approach in the training of deaf children. *Lancet*, 1954, *1*, 583–587.

HARDY, W. G., PAULS, MIRIAM D., and HASKINS, HARRIET L. An analysis of language development in children with impaired hearing. *Acta otolaryngol.*, Suppl. 141, 1958.

JOHN, J. E. J., and HOWARTH, JEAN N. The effect of time distortions on the intelligibility of deaf children's speech. *Language and Speech*, 1965, *8*, 127–134.

KELLMER PRINGLE, M. L. and TANNER, M. The effects of early deprivation on speech development. *Language and Speech*, 1958, *1*, 269–287.

LEWIS, M. M. *Infant Speech*. London: Kegan Paul, 1936.
MORLEY, M. E. *The Development and Disorders of Speech in Childhood*. London: Livingstone, 1957.
WHETNALL, EDITH, and FRY, D. B. *The Deaf Child*. London: Heinemann, 1964.

## Ira J. Hirsh

# TEACHING THE DEAF CHILD TO SPEAK

### A discussion of Fry's presentation

I shall discuss deaf children in a general way to provide a focus for our consideration of language development in the normal child because I think deaf children are important in this regard. However, they will cease to be important if the kind of teaching program Fry discusses continues throughout the world, for then we will not have any contrasts to which to point. For those of you not familiar with the speech of the deaf, I must point out that the speech that we have heard (on recordings presented by Fry) is remarkably good.

A proper perspective for considering the results of teaching that we have just heard is the kind of categorization found in the schools for deaf children in several countries of Western Europe, especially the Netherlands and Belgium. Like the Tracks I and II of some of our larger school systems, two categories and separation into two kinds of classes are based on hearing for higher frequencies. In general "deaf children" have hearing losses of at least 80 or 90 dB in the better ear, but Track I children also show some sensitivity for frequencies higher than 500 or 1,000 cps, while Track II children do not. All of Fry's cases are Track I; that is, their audiograms show responses throughout a fairly wide range of frequencies. Such a child in a school for the deaf is a very good bet for speech production.

In our own school, the Central Institute for the Deaf in St. Louis, such a child is in the minority. I think in a way that Miss Whetnall and Dr. Fry would like that to be the exception in any school for the deaf. A 90-dB threshold is not very good, but if the child can demonstrate sensitivity into the high frequencies, then he should gain speech early and might be educated in a regular school.

More specifically, the children left in the special school will show some thresholds at 70 or 80 or 90 dB in frequencies up to 500 cps and then no observable response above, in either ear. I think there were none of these in Fry's collection. I have no idea about what proportion of deaf children show some sensitivity in the high frequencies; it is an important point only because the discrimination of speech patterns is considerably aided by sensitivity to high frequencies and because a high-frequency response indicates that its basis is probably auditory. There has already been some discussion about the possible confusion of tactile and auditory responses. It is in cases where only low-frequency responses occur that confusion becomes apparent. The skin does not respond very well at 1,000 cps and above.

In talking about the implications of deafness and the learning of speech in deaf children for general development theory, I must further separate out two kinds of children — one group presently in schools for the deaf in this country or elsewhere, or who have been in schools for the deaf, and another group who are now coming into these schools. The first and older group are children whose exposure to language begins at about six years. These are usually children who have been quite isolated by their extreme sensory deficit and who come to formal schooling without having passed through any of the phonemic stages that Fry has discussed. Communication within the family is mostly established by gesture. The child can make his wants and demands known by tugging on coat sleeves and going to objects that are desired, and so on, but there is no vocal communication. The school preparation of these children brings them to a formal classroom situation with no verbal habits established, not even appropriate motor patterns, with little or no vocabulary, no concept of syntax, and certainly no setting of linguistic forms through practice and self-speaking and play with sounds.

I can characterize the language instruction of these children very simply by pointing out that whereas for the normal child language is learned, for these deaf children language is taught. Language instruction in schools for the deaf is more like second-language-learning in normal schools. The child does not acquire a grammar, nor does he acquire a phonemic vocabulary from ordinary experience. Syntax and a phonemic vocabulary are, so to speak, taught to him by the teacher. She knows the grammar of the language and tells him about it in very formal ways, much earlier in this curriculum than you would find in the elementary school curriculum of children with normal hearing. The information that is provided to the child for speech production on his part varies from school to school.

I should have prefaced these remarks by pointing out that I am talking about schools whose aim it is to get children to talk as opposed to an alternative school system where they learn to use a conventional language of signs. Here, the aim is to get these children to talk. It is also the aim to get them to understand spoken speech in some way, but there is a sharp dispute as to how to do this. Some would emphasize visual information alone or visual information coupled with tactile information. Others would favor the so-called multisensory approach, using all available channels. And still others, particularly those associated with what I may call the audiological school, would say that you should suppress visual information in order to sharpen up discriminations for what little auditory possibility there is.

I should call attention to the tremendous amount of information available in the face of a talker when sound is excluded completely. It was an interesting experience for me to converse with a man as totally deaf as I think we can find, and also blind. We kept up a rather good, sustained conversation for about a half hour. His speech was very deaf in quality but reasonably intelligible, and he had very little difficulty understanding mine with his fingers placed along my jawbone and his thumb pressed against my lower lip. He knew something about phonation from his little fingers hanging down on my throat, about the height of the jaw from fingers lined up on the jawbone, and a little bit about lip articulation from his thumb. And I did not restrict my vocabulary particularly.

I only mention this in order to point out that there is a considerable amount of information even without the acoustic cues, and it is this kind of information that the teacher with the new deaf child trades on for a number of months. She will try to get sound out of the child, using very simple syllables like *baba, mama,* and so on. And at least in our school, which I suppose is a multichannel school, they will use any modality that is available. If the child, on being instructed to say *papa* or *baba* says *mama,* then the teacher will simply take his hand and put his fingers in front of her face in order to point out that for the *pa* there is a breath of air, and for the *ba* less so, and for the *ma* there is none at all. He will combine this kind of cue with other cues in order to make this stop-continuant distinction. Auditory cues are also utilized when they are available, but with sensitivity restricted to low frequencies there are only certain kinds of auditory cues available.

I am assuming now that no precise information can be gained from the inaudible high frequencies, even with amplification, but only a crude rhythmic signal. Of course, we have to ask the phonetic experts what exactly this information might be. I have a notion that there is considerable information in the time envelope, if I may use that expression, for continuous speech. Plosives and continuants can certainly be distinguished on the basis of a gross change in the sound form with time. Distinctions can also be made among certain vowels that differ from each other with respect to the first formant alone. And although the teachers may not be able to spout acoustic theory, they seem to have developed some contrived vocabularies that emphasize these contrasts in early use of the auditory system.

Language instruction that may be of more general interest in the present context is characterized by writing and reading earlier than might be expected in the normal child. Our kindergarten children are already being taught with syllables in written form on the blackboard, and this becomes part of the chain of instruction. The object is signified by the written representation and then by the spoken representation as well. The elementary school curriculum, if our school is typical, is much like an ordinary elementary school curriculum except that there are constant speech-correction and auditory-discrimination exercises superimposed on the ordinary subject matter, reading and arithmetic and so on.

## THE LANGUAGE OF THE DEAF SPEAKER

I want to say a few things about the new look in deaf education. But before I do, I would like to talk a little about what happens with these youngsters later on. Remember that these are children whose speech is far from normal and who have learned their language with considerable difficulty. Fry's children in a sense learned their language as a first language by responding to the sounds around them in appropriate ways. Those sounds became sounds of exposure for them by virtue of considerable amplification. The ones that I am talking about have not learned their language in that way. They weren't exposed to sound, by and large, even through amplification, until about the age of five or six years.

Miss Helen Woodward, Supervisor of Education at our school, did a series of pencil-and-paper Berko-type tests,[1] studying the acquisition of rules for morphological changes by adolescent and just preadolescent deaf children (Woodward, 1963). The differences between these children and children in a control group taken from an ordinary public school were in summary simply not remarkable. There were only two that were significant, and I can't even remember which two features those were.

In still another study (Simmons, 1963), carried out by Dr. Audrey Simmons, Head of Aural Rehabilitation, she presented sequences of four pictures that are supposed to suggest a story, at least when seen in order (Figure 1). The children were required to tell or write a

Fig. 1. Example of test material.

story. Figure 2 indicates the total number of words used in these productions by children aged from nine to thirteen years. There were twenty deaf and twenty hearing children in each group at each age level. Note that both the hearing children (triangles) and the deaf (circles) in general spoke fewer words in responding to these picture

[1] See p. 178.

tasks than they wrote. I cannot even speculate about the bump at age ten in the written compositions.

Figure 3 indicates the average number of sentences produced by children in the eight- to fifteen-year-old range. I shall not go through all

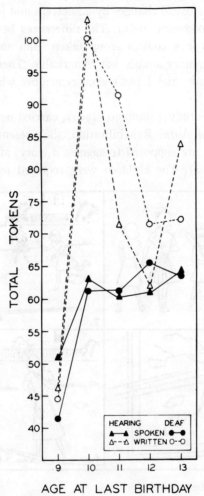

FIG. 2. Average totals of word tokens produced.

the business about how we determined what a sentence was; all the compositions were judged by four graduate students from our English department, and there were a lot of trial runs in order to establish some agreement about the use of a word, what part of speech it was, and so on. This was a particular difficulty with the spoken compositions, of course. The thing to note is that, on the average, the deaf seemed to speak more sentences than the hearing. This is because they are using shorter ones; they generate the same number of words by producing more sentences. There is again the difference at age ten between the speech and the writing.

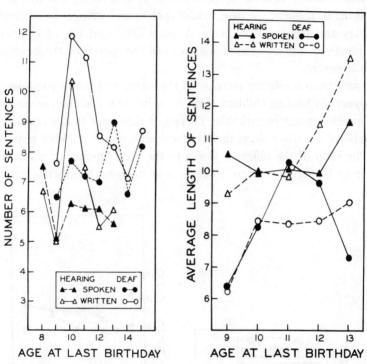

FIG. 3. Number of sentences produced.    FIG. 4. Average length of sentence.

Of more direct interest, I think, is the average length of sentence (Figure 4). In the speech of the normally hearing child, the average is about ten words up to age twelve, when it starts to increase. The length of the spoken sentence of the deaf child increases up to age eleven and then, I think, stays put. The apparent drop for the thirteen-year-olds is explicable. By this age only the most difficult cases are still in our school, so they form a kind of selected group. The aim, in general, is to try to get these youngsters out into public schools as soon as the teachers think they can go, and by thirteen we are left only with the ones who still have not made it.

The "subordination ratio" (Figure 5) is perhaps the most straightforward measure of sentence complexity. It represents the ratio of subordinate-clause verb to main-clause verb and does not seem to change drastically with age for the deaf, although an increase occurs in both the speech and writing of hearing children.

Other analyses have shown that the emergence of elaborated complex sentences in the written compositions of older hearing children is not reflected in those of the deaf, whose spoken and written forms tend to display the same constructions. A more developed use of compound conjunctions and compound sentences in the speech of the hearing is also apparent.

Apart from a relative increase in the number of nouns employed by ten-year-old hearing children, differences in the use of the various parts of speech are not remarkable. There is a difference in the use of conjunctions, but this reflects the relative complexity of sentence structure.

The ratio of the different words to the total number of words used is given in Figure 6. Here there does seem to be a rather systematic

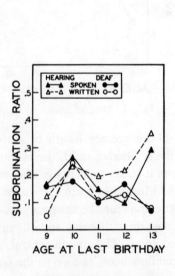

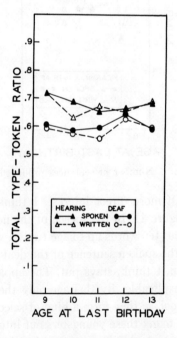

FIG. 5. The subordination ratio: a measure of sentence complexity.

FIG. 6. Total type-token ratio.

difference between hearing and deaf children over at least the first three years for both the written and the spoken forms, indicating greater variety of vocabulary.

I have been describing some of the differences between deaf and hearing children, but I should emphasize that the language output, at least with respect to these formal quantitative measures, does not show the drastic big differences that might be predicted considering that the deaf children came late to language-learning without the kind of preparation we have discussed.


## THE NEW LOOK IN EDUCATING THE DEAF

The new look in the education of deaf children is quite new in this country and a little less new in England and the Low Countries of Europe. It involves a great emphasis on some of the features that Denis Fry and Edith Whetnall have demonstrated very convincingly, starting with the early application of some form of amplification to a deaf child, particularly when he can be detected early, say within the first year. There is then a division into two camps, both of which emphasize the important role of the auditory loop in the feedback mechanism involved in the control of speech production. One group emphasizes drill, practice, and contrasting phonetic dimensions, and the other emphasizes more the enriched immediate environment of the child.

These approaches are not necessarily incompatible with each other. They represent, however, the differing emphases of people who have sponsored one or the other kind of education. Both camps can point to successes, and I suppose both camps equally often hide their failures. Some compromise is probably the best solution.

It is obvious that without amplification and early acoustic stimulation the deaf child has a rather dull existence. The fact that he is not in remote communication with people outside of his visual environment means that he experiences less of whatever normal children experience in these first years. And so you will find in some preschool programs lots of emphasis on a classroom — if it must be a classroom — equipped like a home, with bathtubs and all sorts of features that synthesize a rich home environment. In small European countries, like Belgium and the Netherlands, there is much more emphasis on doing this training in the home and getting the mother to be the assistant teacher. However, there is even some dispute on whether the mother should be conceived of as an assistant teacher or whether she should rather just maintain her mother role.

The effect of home training, even on severely deaf children, is already being seen in schools for the deaf; these children seem to be able to get along much faster than those who have had no special training. So now we are really talking about a quite new group of children so far as schools for the deaf are concerned. It might be that if enough pretraining is done, all the schools for the deaf could be put out of business. This would delight no group more than ours.

## REFERENCES

SIMMONS, A. A. Comparison of written and spoken language from deaf and hearing children at five age levels. Ed.D. Dissertation, Washington University, St. Louis, 1963.

WOODWARD, H. M. E. The structural component of linguistic meaning and the reading of normally hearing and deaf children. M.A. Thesis, Washington University, St. Louis, 1963.

# GENERAL DISCUSSION

## Fry and Hirsh presentations

1. Reference to a "new look" in education of the deaf child raised the question of what the "old look" looked like. Templin characterized it as deprivation of exposure to language until the child was of school age, followed by formal instruction focusing on the role of isolated words rather than an experience of language as a continuous medium for the expression of ideas. With such children, at sixth-grade level there was an additional emphasis on manual language, which further deprived them of the experience of syntax and of the functions of language.

Lenneberg outlined studies made in schools for the deaf in the eastern United States, where the method of instruction again involved formal attempts to teach rules of language. The rules were based on traditional grammatical theory, which might well be a handicap because it could not generate proper sentences. Lenneberg agreed with a suggestion that it was fortunate the teachers were constrained to speak English while teaching this grammar and that complete and correct sentences were occasionally written on the board. Tests had been made to determine the competence of these children in aspects of language that did not figure in the traditional grammar, such as the use of the article. In general it was found that the formal instruction had little effect; the children's sentences were very different from those normally found and similar to those discussed by Templin and by Hirsh.

2. There were comments about how well Hirsh's subjects appeared to perform despite their old-look experiences, contrary to the implications

of Fry's argument. Fry proposed that differences would have occurred if the St. Louis studies had been extended down to age five, and Hirsh concurred. Hirsh also pointed out that the children in the studies he reported had to a large extent been selected for training on the basis of intellectual competence, and their performance should be regarded as above average. Their language production in fact varied considerably in intelligibility, and the analysis had been made not of the raw productions but of transcripts by teachers experienced in understanding distorted deaf speech. Templin said that her own work in state schools involved old-look children with many difficulties in language. For example, a thirteen-year-old boy, given words from which nine-year-old hearing children were able to construct sentences, would produce strings like *the man has a strong*. The deaf children were not without ability, but they had been handicapped by long periods without productive experience of the use of language.

3. Lenneberg referred to a California study (Woodward and Barber, 1960) of how much information could be transmitted by visual cues alone. Performance by both untrained hearing subjects and trained deaf subjects were uniformly poor, and hearing subjects in fact did better than the deaf on identification tasks. The apparent skill of the deaf in using visual cues was probably due to their excellent guesses; the California study eliminated all contextual cues, and the deaf were unable to make use of what syntax they commanded to make predictions about what was being said. Lenneberg suggested that acquired linguistic information helped considerably in enabling the deaf to utilize sensory cues and communicate by lip reading.

4. It was suggested that the peak in the number of words produced in written compositions by Hirsh's ten-year-old subjects (Figure 2) might be attributed to an emphasis on written composition at this grade level. However, Hirsh pointed out that the effect was present in both hearing and deaf ten-year-olds, and the hearing children were probably a grade or two in advance of the deaf.

## REFERENCE

WOODWARD, MARY F., and BARBER, CARROLL G. Education of the aurally handicapped; a psycholinguistic analysis of visual communication. *University of Southern California, School of Education, Cooperative Research Project No. 502*, 1960.

Eric H. Lenneberg

# THE NATURAL HISTORY OF LANGUAGE

## CHARACTERISTICS OF MATURATION OF BEHAVIOR

Why do children regularly begin to speak between their eighteenth and twenty-eighth month of life? Surely it is not because all mothers on earth initiate language training at that time. There is, in fact, no evidence whatever that any conscious and systematic teaching of language takes place, just as there is no special training for stance or gait. Superficially it is tempting to assume that a child begins to speak as soon as he has a "need" for it. However, there is no way of testing this assumption because of the subjectivity of the notion "need." We have here the same logical difficulties as in testing the universality of the pleasure principle as the prime motivation. To escape the inevitable circularity of the argument, we might ask, "Do the child's needs change at a year-and-a-half because his environment regularly changes at that time or because he himself undergoes important and relevant changes?" Society and parents do behave somewhat differently to an older child, and thus there are some environmental innovations introduced around the time of the onset of speech; yet the changes of the social environment are to a great extent in response to changes in the child's abilities and behavior. Quite clearly the most important differences between the prelanguage and postlanguage phases of development originate in the growing individual and not in the external world or in changes in the availability of stimuli. Therefore, any hypothesis that pivots on an assumption of need may be restated: the needs that arise by eighteen months and cause language to develop are primarily due to maturational processes within the individual. Since needs *per se* can be defined only in a subjective and logically circular manner, it is futile to begin an inquiry into the relevant factors of speech development by the adoption of a need hypothesis. Instead, one must try to understand the nature of the maturational processes. The central and most interesting problem here is whether the emergence of language is due to very general capabilities that mature to a critical minimum at about eighteen months to make language and many other skills possible, or whether there might be some factors specific to speech and language that come to maturation and are somewhat independent from other, more general processes.

Unfortunately, the importance and role of maturation in the development of language readiness cannot be explored systematically by direct experiment, and we are reduced to making inferences from a variety of observations and by extrapolation. The difficulty is that we cannot be certain what kind of experiments or observations to extrapolate from. Behavior is far from the monolithic, clear-cut, self-evident phenomenon postulated by psychologists a generation ago. Different aspects of behavior make their emergence at different periods in the life cycle of an individual and for a variety of causes. Further, the spectrum of causes changes with species.

The hallmarks for maturationally controlled emergence of behavior are four: (1) regularity in the sequence of appearance of given milestones, all correlated with age and other concomitant developmental facts; (2) evidence that the opportunity for environmental stimulation remains relatively constant throughout development but that the infant makes different use of such opportunities as he grows up; (3) emergence of the behavior either in part or entirely, before it has any immediate use to the individual; (4) evidence that the clumsy beginnings of the behavior are not signs of goal-directed practice.

Points (1) and (2) are obvious and need no elaboration. Point (3) is a commonplace in the embryology of behavior. A vast array of motor patterns may be observed to occur spontaneously or upon stimulation in embryos long before the animal is ready to make use of such behavior. The so-called *Leerlaufreaktion,* or vacuum activity, observed by ethologists is another example of emergence of behavior at given developmental stages and in the absence of any use or need fulfillment (for details see Hess, 1962; Lorenz, 1958).

Point (4), the relatively unimportant role of practice for the emergence of certain types of behavior with maturation, has been amply demonstrated in animals by Carmichael (1926, 1927), Grohmann (1938), and by Thomas and Schaller (1954). Similarly, children whose lower extremities have been immobilized by casts (for the correction of congenital hip deformations) at the time that gait normally develops can keep perfect equilibrium and essentially appear "to know" how to walk when released from the mechanical handicap, even though their muscles may be too weak during the first weeks to sustain weight over many steps.

Generally there is evidence that species-specific motor coordination patterns (*Erbkoordination*) emerge according to a maturational schedule in every individual raised in an adequate environment. The emergence of such patterns is independent of training procedures and extrinsic response-shaping. Once the animal has matured to the point at which these patterns are present, the actual occurrence of a specific pattern movement may depend on external stimuli or internal ones (for instance certain hormone levels in the blood) or a combination of the two (Lehrman, 1958a,b).

The aim of these comments is to direct attention to *potentialities* of behavior — the underlying matrix for behaving — instead of to a specific *act*. If we find that emergence of a certain behavior may be partially or wholly attributed to changes within the organism rather than causative changes in the environment, we must at once endeavor to discover what organic changes there are. Unless we can demonstrate a somatic basis, all of our speculations are useless.

The four characteristics of maturationally controlled emergence of behavior will now be employed as touchstones, so to speak, in a discussion of whether the onset of language may reasonably be attributed to a maturational process.

## EMERGENCE OF SPEECH AND LANGUAGE

### The Regularity of Onset

The onset of speech consists of a gradual unfolding of capacities; it is a series of more or less well-circumscribed events that take place between the second and third year of life. Certain important speech milestones are reached in a fixed sequence and at a relatively constant chronological age. Just as impressive as the age constancy is the remark-

*TABLE 1    Simultaneous Development of Language and Coordination*

| Age in Months | Vocalization and Language | Motor Development |
|---|---|---|
| 4 | Coos and chuckles. | Head self-supported; tonic neck reflex subsiding; can sit with pillow props on three sides. |
| 6 to 9 | Babbles; produces sounds such as "ma" or "da"; reduplication of sounds common. | Sits alone; pulls himself to standing; prompt unilateral reaching; first thumb opposition of grasp. |
| 12 to 18 | A small number of "words"; follows simple commands and responds to "no." | Stands momentarily alone; creeps; walks sideways when holding on to a railing; takes a few steps when held by hands; grasp, prehension, and release fully developed. |
| 18 to 21 | From about 20 words at 18 months to about 200 words at 21; points to many more objects; comprehends simple questions; forms two-word phrases. | Stance fully developed; gait stiff, propulsive, and precipitated; seats himself on child's chair with only fair aim; creeps downstairs backward; has difficulty building tower of three cubes; can throw a ball, but clumsily. |
| 24 to 27 | Vocabulary of 300 to 400 words; has two- to three-word phrases; uses prepositions and pronouns. | Runs but falls when making a sudden turn; can quickly alternate between stance, kneeling or sitting positions; walks stairs up and down, one foot forward only. |
| 30 to 33 | Fastest increase in vocabulary; three- to four-word sentences are common; word order, phrase structure, grammatical agreement approximate language of surroundings, but many utterances are unlike anything an adult would say. | Good hand and finger coordination; can move digits independently; manipulation of objects much improved; builds tower of six cubes. |
| 36 to 39 | Vocabulary of 1,000 words or more; well-formed sentences using complex grammatical rules, although certain rules have not yet been fully mastered; grammatical mistakes are much less frequent; about 90 per cent comprehensibility. | Runs smoothly with acceleration and deceleration; negotiates sharp and fast curves without difficulty; walks stairs by alternating feet; jumps 12"; can operate tricycle; stands on one foot for a few seconds. |

able synchronization of speech milestones with motor-development milestones, both of which are summarized in Table 1.

The temporal interlocking of speech milestones and motor milestones is not a logical necessity. There are reasons to believe that the onset of language is not simply the consequence of motor control. The development of language is quite independent of articulatory skills (Lenneberg, 1962), and the perfection of articulation cannot be predicted entirely on the basis of general motor development. There are certain indications for the existence of a peculiar, language-specific maturational schedule. Many children have a word or two before they toddle and thus must be assumed to possess a sufficient degree of motor skill to articulate, however primitively; yet the expansion of their vocabulary is still an extremely slow process. Why could they not rapidly increase their lexicon with "sloppy" sound symbols, much the way a child with a cleft palate does at age three? Similarly, parents' inability to train their children at this stage to join the words *Daddy* and *byebye* into a single utterance cannot be explained on the grounds of motor incompetence because at the same age children babble for periods as long as the duration of eight or ten syllables. In fact, babbled "sentences" may be produced, complete with intonation patterns. The retarding factor for language acquisition here must be a psychological one or perhaps better a cognitive one, and not mechanical skill. Around age three manual skills show improved coordination over earlier periods, but dexterity is still very immature on an absolute scale. Speech, which requires infinitely precise and swift movements of tongue and lips, all well-coordinated with laryngeal and respiratory motor systems, is all but fully developed when most other mechanical skills are far below their levels of future accomplishment. The evolvement of various motor skills and motor coordinations also has specific maturational histories, but the specific history for speech control stands apart dramatically from histories of finger and hand control.

The independence of language development from motor coordination is also underscored by the priority of language comprehension over language production. Ordinarily the former precedes the latter by a matter of a few months, especially between the ages of eighteen and thirty-six months. In certain cases this gap may be magnified by many years (Lenneberg, 1964). Careful and detailed investigations of the development of understanding by itself have only been undertaken in more recent years (Brown and Bellugi, 1964; Ervin, 1964; Ervin and

Miller, 1963). The evidence collected so far leaves little doubt that there is also an orderly and constant progression in this aspect of language development.

The development of children with various abnormalities affords the most convincing demonstration that the onset of language is regulated by a maturational process, much in the way the onset of gait is dependent upon such a process, but that at the same time the language-maturation process is independent of motor-skeletal maturation. In hypotonic children, for instance, the musculature in general is weak, and tendon reflexes are less active than normal. Hypotonia may be an isolated phenomenon that is quickly outgrown or it may be a sign of disease, such as muscular atrophy, carrying a bad omen for the child's future motor development. Whatever the cause, muscular development alone may be lagging behind other developmental processes and thus disarrange the normal intercalation of these various processes. Here, then, speech and language emerge at their usual time, while motor development lags behind.

On the other hand, there are some children with normal intelligence and normal skeletal and motor development whose speech development alone is markedly delayed. We are not referring here to children who never learn to speak adequately because of acquired or congenital abnormalities in the brain, but of those who are simply late speakers, who do not begin to speak in phrases until after age four, who have no neurological or psychiatric symptoms that can explain the delay, and whose environment appears to be adequate. The incidence of such cases is small (less than one in a hundred), but their very existence emphasizes the independence of language-maturation processes from other processes.

There are also conditions that affect all developmental processes simultaneously. These are diseases in which growth and maturation are retarded or stunted through a variety of factors, for instance, of an endocrine nature as in hypothyroidism; or retardation may be due to an intracellular abnormality, such as the chromosomal disorder causing mongolism. In these cases all processes suffer alike, resulting in general "stretching" of the developmental time scale but leaving the intercalation of motor and speech milestones intact (Lenneberg, Nichols, and Rosenberger, 1964). The preservation of synchrony between motor and speech or language milestones in cases of general retardation is, I believe, the most cogent evidence that language acquisition is regulated by maturational phenomena.

The evidence presented here rules out the possibility of a direct causal relationship between motor and speech development. Normally, growth and maturation proceed at characteristic rates for each developmental aspect. In the absence of specific retardations affecting skills or organs differentially, a picture of consistency evolves, such as represented in Table 1 or in the many accounts of normal human development (McGraw, 1963; Gesell and Amatruda, 1947).

The use of the word "skill" brings out another interesting aspect of the emergence of speech. With proper training probably everybody could attain some proficiency in such diverse skills as roller-skating, sketching, or piano-playing. However, there are also vast individual differences in native endowment and considerable variation with respect to the age at which training is most effective. Perfection can rarely be expected before the teens. The establishment of speech and language is quite different; a much larger number of individuals shows equal aptitude, absence of the skill is rare, and onset and fluency occur much earlier, with no particular training required.

Nevertheless, individual differences in time of onset and reaching of various milestones exist and need to be accounted for. The rate of development is not constant during the formative years, and there may be transient slowing in the rate of maturation, with subsequent hastening. This is hardly surprising in view of the complex interrelation of intrinsic and extrinsic factors that affect development. Nevertheless, there is a remarkable degree of regularity in the emergence of language. Figure 1 illustrates the regularity in the attainment of three major language-development levels and Figure 2 the sudden increase in vocabulary size, particularly around the third birthday.

In a survey of 500 middle- and lower-class children in the Boston area, examined in connection with an epidemiological study, I found that nine out of ten children had acquired all of the following verbal skills by the time they reached their thirty-ninth month: ability to name any object in the home, fair intelligibility, ability to comprehend spoken instructions, spontaneous utterance of syntactically complex sentences, and spontaneity in oral communication. The field observations were made in the child's home by specially trained social workers who worked with a screening test and a schedule of questions. Any

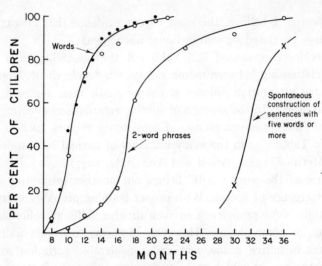

- • 49 Austrian children *(Bühler, 1931)*
- ○ 114 British children *(Morley, 1957)*
- ✕ 500 American children *(Boston, author's observation)*

FIG. I. Emergence of various developmental milestones in the acquisition of language.

child who was found or suspected to fall short of these standards was referred by the social worker to my office where he was examined by a speech therapist, an audiologist, and by myself. Fifty-four children were thus referred and found to fall into the following classifications:

## TABLE 2 Distribution of Causes for Failing Language-Screening Test (*given to 500 children at about the third birthday*)

| | |
|---|---|
| 1. Uncooperative child but, upon more intense examination, apparently normal speech development (health good, environment adequate). | 7 |
| 2. Poor articulation but otherwise normal onset of language milestones (health good, environment adequate). | 29 |
| 3. Various types of speech defects associated with psychiatric conditions. | 9 |
| 4. Speech defects associated with other behavioral disorders due to gross environmental abnormalities. | 2 |
| 5. Speech defects associated with nervous system disease. | 3 |
| 6. Delayed onset of speech, unexplained (health good, environment adequate). | 4 |

Differences in age of onset become much less dramatic if we scrutinize these statistics. Of 486 children who were free from nervous or mental disease and were raised in an adequate environment — all chil-

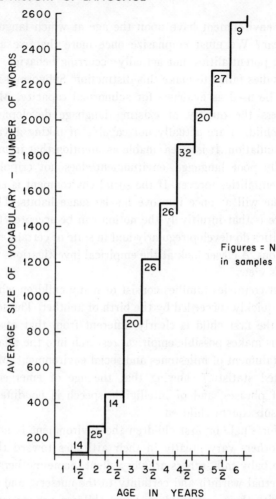

FIG. 2. Average vocabulary size of ten samples of children at various ages.

dren in the sample except those of Groups (3), (4), and (5) — only 33 (less than 7 per cent) were below the norm of attainment.

## The Relation of the Environment to the Age of Onset

It is obvious that a child cannot acquire language unless he is exposed to it. Apart from this trivial point the role of the environment is not immediately clear. There are two major problems: How are the infant's eventual capabilities for language acquisition affected by environmental variations during his prelanguage life, and what influence does the environment have upon the age at which language capabilities appear? We must emphasize once more that we are concerned here with potentialities, not actually occurring behavior. Many of the earlier studies failed to make this distinction. Subnormal speech habits may not be used as evidence for subnormal capacity. Most language tests assess the quality of existing language development but not whether children are actually not capable of taking advantage of existing stimulation. It is a reasonable assumption that in most instances in initially poor language, environment does not cripple the child's basic potentialities forever. If the social environment is enriched early enough, he will at once improve his language habits. The important point here is that intuitively the notion can be accepted that language potentialities do develop regularly and in spite of certain environmental deprivations. A closer look at the empirical investigations supports precisely this view.

In most countries families consist of many children where the birth of one is quickly succeeded by the birth of another. The social environment of the first child is clearly different from that of a subsequent child. This makes possible empirical research into the relation between age at attainment of milestones and social environment. Morley (1957) contributed statistics showing that the age of emergence of single words, of phrases, and of intelligible speech is no different for first than for subsequent children.

Even for single or first children the environment is not always the same. Mothers vary greatly in their attitudes toward their children. Some use baby talk, others are very silent. Some mothers bring a natural maternal warmth and certainty to the nursery, and others are ill at ease with their first children. Some children are welcome additions, but others are not. Further statistics compiled by Morley indicate that variables such as "mother's ability to cope," loss or temporary absence of either parent, or socioeconomic class are not predictive of the age of emergence of various milestones in speech development.

Morley's findings are not contradicted by studies that report differences in speech habits of children of the upper, middle, and lower class (Bühler, 1931; Irwin, 1948; and many others). These are usually cross-sectional studies in which the nature and quality of speech is compared with a norm, but the age of onset of certain speech phenomena is not determined. Morley found that the language habits that emerged at the common time soon showed signs of impoverishment in the underprivileged, and unintelligibility occurred more commonly in second and subsequent children than in first. Thus the influence of the environment upon speech habit is undeniable, even though the onset of speech habits is relatively unaffected.

The differences observed in the speech habits of upper- and lower-class children are, actually, difficult to evaluate because of the many covarying factors. For example, the influence of malnutrition and of diseases that delay development is higher among poorer children, who may also be emotionally less amenable to testing situations than those from more carefree homes. In attempts to estimate the child's vocabulary by means of flash cards, an assumption is made that the relative frequency of occurrence of words in the vocabularies of upper and lower class is identical. This is not necessarily valid.

The role of environment is documented most drastically by the studies on the development of children in orphanages (Brodbeck and Irwin, 1946; Dennis and Dennis, 1951; Fisichelli, 1950; Goldfarb, 1943; McCarthy, 1954). Leaving aside the old question of the possible differences in biological stock between this and the general population, there is no denying that the institutional life leaves its mark on speech and language habits. On the other hand Goldfarb (1945) and Dennis and Najarian (1957) have given an illustration of covert processes in the unfolding of potentialities. Children reared in orphanages are frequently below average in speech and motor development when tested at three, but when retested at six or seven they are found to have caught up with the control population. As soon as their environment is enriched, perhaps through greater freedom to move around, they are able to make use of the greater stimulus availability.

Lenneberg, Rebelsky, and Nichols (1965) have studied emergence of vocalization during the first three months of life as it relates to the parents' speech and hearing. Children of congenitally deaf parents (deaf father and mother) were compared with children born to hearing and normally speaking parents. Among the six deaf families studied, five of the babies had normal hearing, but in one case the baby was born deaf. Twenty-four-hour tape recordings were made biweekly in the child's home and compared qualitatively and quantitatively. The environment of the two groups of children differed in two ways: (1) the amount, nature, and occasion of adult vocalization heard by the babies differed significantly, and (2) the baby's own vocalizations could never be responded to by a deaf mother who, we discovered, could not even tell whether her child's facial expressions and gestures were accompanied by silence or noise. While babies born to hearing parents appeared to vocalize on the occasions of adult vocalization, the babies born to deaf parents did not. Nevertheless, they made as much noise and went through the same sequence of vocalization development with identical ages of onset (for cooing noises) as the control group.

I have also been able to observe older hearing children born to deaf couples, though I have not undertaken a statistical study. These observations, on a dozen children in five families, leave no doubt that language onset is never delayed by this dramatically abnormal environment, even though the quality of vocalization of the preschool children tends to be different; children very soon became "bilingual" in the sense that they use normal voice and speech for hearing adults and abnormal voice and "deafisms" for their parents.

How universal in human society is the onset of speech? Do cultural attitudes toward child-rearing influence its emergence, or are there languages so complicated that no one can master oral communication until puberty or so primitive that the entire system is learned by every child before he begins to toddle? There are many studies on child development in primitive cultures, and most authors have described every minute deviation from the norm of western society. Strangely enough the onset of speech has rarely been a subject of a detailed study in the anthropological literature (but see Austerlitz, 1956; Kroeber, 1916). Apparently no field worker has even been struck by any discrepancies between the vocalizations or communicative behavior among the children of "primitive" and "western" man. Lenneberg, Putnam, Whelan, and Crocker (in preparation) have investigated this problem further by direct field observations among the Dani of Dutch New Guinea, the Zuñi of the American Southwest, and the Bororo and some Gê tribes of Central Brazil. In these investigations children were given tests of sensorimotor development, such as coordination for reaching, nature of the grasp, and the ability to walk, stand on one leg, or throw a ball. Tape recordings were made of the vocalizations of the babies before they appeared to be in possession of the common language, as well as of their utterances throughout their physical development to age three. In addition, information was obtained from native informants about the linguistic competence of the various children studied, their fluency, types of mistakes in articulation, syntax, and choice of words, and on the parents' attitude toward their children's speech development. In some instances the chronological age of the child studied was not known, and therefore neither the motor nor the language achievements could be compared directly with the age of emergence in American children. But the chronological age was not as important as the question whether developmental progress, gauged upon the emergence of definite motor skills, marked also the beginning and major milestones of the child's speech development and whether the concordances between speech and motor development observed in western children were also found in children of these cultures. As far as we can judge from the analysis of the material so far, the answer is clearly yes. The first words appear at about the time that walking is accomplished, and by the time a child is able to jump down from a chair (or its equivalent), tiptoe, or walk backward three yards, he is reported by the informants to be communicating fluently, even though certain inaccuracies and childlike usages seem always to persist for a longer period. Anthropologists have pointed out that the label "primitive language" is misleading when applied to any natural living language. The developmental studies here support this view in that they indicate that no natural language is inherently more complicated or simpler to learn by a growing child than any other language.[1] There seems to be no relation between progress in language acquisition and culturally determined aspects of language.

In summary, it cannot be proved that the language environment of the growing child remains constant throughout infancy, but it can be shown that an enormous variety of environmental conditions leaves at least one aspect of language acquisition relatively unaffected: the age of onset of certain speech and language habits. Thus, the emergence of speech and language habits is more easily accounted for by assuming maturational changes within the growing child than by postulating special training procedures in the child's surroundings.

## The Role of Utility in the Onset of Speech

There is evidence, though only of a circumstantial nature, that language does not emerge as a response to an experienced need, as a

---

[1] Slobin, at this conference, reported that several aspects of Russian morphology and syntax are not learned by the Russian child until after entering school. However, he informed me in personal conversation that the forms acquired later are rarely used (or ever used correctly) in colloquial discourse.

result of discovery of its practical utility, or as a product of purposive striving toward facilitated verbal communication. I have made tape recordings of the spontaneous noises made during play by congenitally deaf children. In two instances periodic sample recordings were made of deaf children of deaf parents from the first month of life. Sixteen other deaf children were recorded between their second and fifth years. In most instances follow-up recordings are available throughout an eighteen-month period. All eighteen children vocalized often during concentrated play; the quality of their voices was quite similar to that of hearing children, and in certain respects the development of their vocalizations was parallel to that observed in hearing children, though the deaf did not develop words. Nevertheless, cooing appeared at about three months, babbling sounds were heard at six months and later, and laughter and sounds of discontent were virtually identical with those of the hearing population. It was particularly interesting to note that many of the deaf children, during their spontaneous babbling, would produce sounds that were well-articulated speech sounds such as /pakapakapaka/. This is not to say that there was no difference between the deaf and hearing children over six months. The deaf had a tendency to engage in certain types of noise more persistently, while the hearing would tend to go frequently through a wide range of different types of babbling sounds, as if to run through their repertoire for the sheer pleasure of it. No precise quantitative measures of amount of vocalization could be made on the children after the first three months, but subjectively the hearing children were much more vocal in the presence of others than the deaf.

A healthy deaf child two years of age or older gets along famously despite his total inability to communicate verbally. These children become very clever in their pantomime and develop techniques for communicating their desires, needs, and even opinions, that leave little to be desired. There is no indication that congenital peripheral deafness causes significant adjustment problems within the family during preschool years. This observation has an important bearing on the problem of motivation for language acquisition. Language is extremely complex behavior, the acquisition of which, one might have thought, requires considerable attention and endeavor. Why do hearing children bother to learn this system if it is possible for a child to get along without it? Probably because the acquisition of language is not, in fact, hard labor — it comes naturally — and also because the child does not strive toward a state of perfect verbal intercourse, normally attained only two years after the first beginnings.


## The Importance of Practice for the Onset of Speech

Closely related to the question of utility is the problem of practice. Do cooing and babbling represent practice stages for future verbal behavior? We have every indication that this is not so. Occasionally the natural airways above the voice box become narrowed because of swelling in connection with disease, and an opening must be made into the trachea below the larynx for insertion of a tube through which the patient can breathe. This prevents the patient from making sounds because most of the expired air escapes before it can excite the vocal cords. I have examined a fourteen-month-old child who had been tracheotomized for six months. A day after the tube had been removed and the opening closed, the child produced the babbling sounds typical of the age. No practice or experience with hearing his own vocalizations was required.

Comparable observations may be made on children not older than twenty-four months who are admitted to pediatric hospitals because of severe physical neglect by the parents. Characteristically, they are on admission apathetic, unresponsive babies who seem to be grossly retarded in their motor, social, and sound development. After a few weeks of hospital care they blossom out, begin to relate to the nursing staff, and make all the noises that are heard in infants of comparable age. If the neglected child is over three or four years of age, environmental deprivation will have contributed to severe emotional disturbance often more typical of psychotic conditions (Davis, 1947). However, some children with psychoses, regardless of whether parental neglect was a contributing factor, give excellent demonstrations of "subclinical" language development. There are children who fail to communicate with the world around them, including their own parents, and who give an impression of muteness and incomprehension from their second year of life on. Yet in response to treatment, or even spontaneously, some will often snap out of their state of isolation and almost miraculously begin to talk fluently and up to age level (Luchsinger and Arnold, 1959, and my own experience). Practice is, of course, not the same as learning. In these children it is fair to say that they have not practiced speech and language in the same manner

as normal children might, but we cannot say that they have not undergone years of learning. They simply had not chosen to respond.


### *"Wolf Children"*

It is difficult to refrain from referring to the stories of children
supposedly reared by wolves and other cases of extreme neglect. Yet
a careful analysis of this literature has convinced me that even the
most fundamental information is usually missing in the descriptions
or omitted altogether from the case reports. The children are invariably
discovered by well-meaning but untrained observers, and the urgency
for getting help to the victims is so overwhelming that the scientifically
most important first months are least well documented. The nature
of the social and physical environment is never clear, and the possibility of genetic deficiencies or congenital abnormalities can never be
ruled out. One child reported by Davis (1947) was discovered at age
six without speech but was said to have made very rapid progress,
going through all the usual baby language stages, and within a period
of nine months attained complete mastery of speech and language.
In the same article a comparable case is described, also discovered at
age six, but this child only began to speak at age nine. At the time of
her death at ten-and-one-half, she could name people and communicate
her needs by a few sentences. The behavioral descriptions of this
child point to severe psychosis and feeblemindedness. Descriptions of
children supposedly reared by wolves or growing up in forests by themselves are plentiful, but none is trustworthy (Koehler, 1952). Singh
and Zingg (1942) have collected the entire material, and an excellent
commentary may be found in Brown (1957). The only safe conclusions
to be drawn from the multitude of reports is that life in dark closets,
wolves' dens, forests, or sadistic parents' backyards is not conducive to
good health and normal development. It is impossible to say why
some of these children are capable of overcoming the insults inflicted
upon their early health while others succumb to them. The degree
and duration of neglect, the initial state of health, the care provided
for them after discovery, and many other factors are bound to influence the outcome; in the absence of information on these points,
virtually no generalizations may be made with regard to human development.

We started by developing criteria for the distinction of behavioral emergence due to changes of capacity within the growing individual (regularity in onset, differential use of environmental stimulation with growth, independence from use, and superfluousness of practice). Applying these criteria to language we have found strong suggestions that the appearance of language is primarily dependent upon the maturational development of states of readiness within the child, assuming the existence of an adequate environment.

## AGE LIMITATION TO LANGUAGE ACQUISITION

Complementary to the question of how old a child must be before he can use the environment for language acquisition is that of how young he must be before it is too late to acquire speech and language. There is evidence that the primary acquisition of language is dependent upon a certain developmental stage which is quickly outgrown at puberty. I have presented detailed evidence for this elsewhere (Lenneberg, in press) and shall confine myself to a few summary statements. The evidence is largely based on clinical experience with acquired aphasia.

### The Relation of Age to Recovery from Acquired Aphasia

The outlook for recovery from aphasia varies with age. The recovery chance has, so to speak, a natural history that is the same as the natural history of cerebral lateralization of function. Aphasia is the result of direct, structural, and local interference with the neurophysiological processes of language. In childhood such interference cannot be permanent because the two sides are not yet sufficiently specialized for function, even though the left hemisphere may already show signs of speech dominance. Damage to it will interfere with language, but the right hemisphere is still involved to some extent with language and so there is a potential for language function that may be strengthened again. In the absence of pathology, a polarization of function between right and left takes place during childhood, displacing language entirely to the left and certain other functions predominantly to the right (Ajuriaguerra, 1957; Hécaen and Ajuriaguerra, 1963; Teuber, 1962). If, however, a lesion is placed in either hemisphere, this polarization cannot take place, and language function together with other functions persist in the unharmed hemisphere.

Notice that the earlier the lesion is incurred, the less grave is the outlook for language. Hence we infer that language-learning can take place, at least in the right hemisphere, only between the ages of two to about thirteen. That this is probably also true of the left hemisphere follows from observations on language development in the retarded and in the congenitally deaf, discussed later.

A unique pathological study of congenital aphasia was reported by Landau, Goldstein, and Kleffner (1960). This was a child who died of heart disease at age ten. This patient, in contrast to the cases discussed so far, had not begun to develop speech until age six or seven. At that time he was enrolled in a class for congenitally aphasic children at the Central Institute for the Deaf. By age ten, the authors report, "he had acquired considerable useful language." A postmortem examination of the brain revealed bilateral areas of cortical destruction around the Sylvian fissure in the area of the central sulcus, together with severe retrograde degeneration in the medial geniculate nuclei of the midbrain. The authors conclude that "Language function therefore appears to have been subserved by pathways other than the primary auditory thalamocortical projection system." I am citing this case here to illustrate the far-reaching plasticity of the human brain (or lack of cortical specialization) with respect to language during the early years of life. There is clinical evidence that similar lesions in a mature individual would have produced severe and irreversible defects in reception and production of speech and language. The implication is that the brain at birth and during the subsequent maturation process may be influenced in its normal course of organization, which usually results in the specialization of areas.

Postnatal cerebral organization and reorganization have been demonstrated by several workers for a variety of mammals (Benjamin and Thompson, 1959; Brooks and Peck, 1940; Doty, 1953; Harlow, Akert and Schiltz, 1964; Scharlock, Tucker, and Strominger, 1963; and others). Various kinds of postnatal cortical ablations leave no or very minor deficit, whereas comparable ablations in later stages of development result in irreversible symptoms.

## Arrest of Language Development in the Retarded

The material reviewed might give the impression that the age limitation is primarily due to better recovery from disease in childhood and that the language limitations are only a secondary effect. This is probably not so. In a study by Lenneberg, Nichols, and Rosenberger (1964), fifty-four mongoloids (all raised at home) were seen two to three times per year over a three-year period. The age range was from six months to twenty-two years. The appearance of motor milestones and the onset of speech differed considerably from individual to individual, but all made some progress — even though very slow in many cases — before they reached their early teens. This was true of motor development as well as of speech. In all children seen in this study, stance, gait, and fine coordination of hands and fingers were acquired before the end of the first decade. At the close of the study 75 per cent had reached at least the first stage of language development; they had a small vocabulary and could execute simple spoken commands. But interestingly enough, progress in language development was recorded only in children younger than fourteen. Cases in their later teens were the same in terms of their language development at the beginning as at the end of the study. The observation seems to indicate that even in the absence of structural brain lesions, progress in language-learning comes to a standstill after maturity. Figure 3 is a graphic illustration of the empirical findings.

## The Effect of Deafness on Language at Various Ages

The study of acquired deafness during childhood and later life gives further insight into the importance of age in language acquisition. The most common cause of sudden and total loss of hearing is meningitis. The virulence of the disease is such that many a child falls ill and is left without hearing practically overnight. Throughout childhood sudden acquisition of deafness has an immediate effect upon voice and speech, and, before the age of six, also on language habits. Within a year or less the small child, say up to about four years of age, will have lost the ability to control his voice and articulatory mechanisms for ordinary speech sounds and will develop noises and habits very similar or even indistinguishable from those heard and seen in the congenitally deaf. His education has to be relegated to special teachers in the schools for the deaf. Both these populations, those who become deaf before and those after the onset of speech, sound and behave like the congenitally deaf children. But those who lose hearing after having been exposed to the experience of speech, even

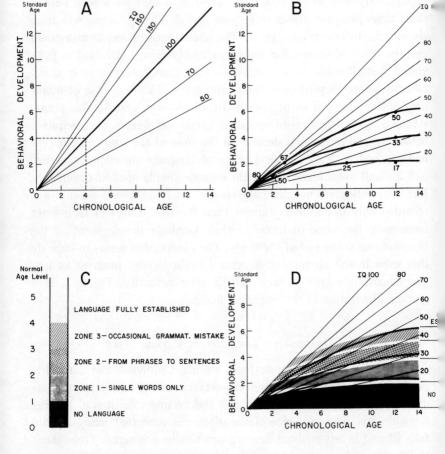

FIG. 3. The triple relationship between chronological age, IQ as measured by the M
Palmer Test, and the attainment of stages in language development. A. The
representation of constant IQ's; B. predictable tendency of IQ to decay in
forms of mental retardation; C. traversal of certain language stages at
ages in normal development; D. empirical determination of the relationship b
the three parameters in the mentally retarded.

for as short a period as one year, can be trained much more easily in all language arts, even if formal training begins some years after they have become deaf. On the other hand, children deafened before completion of the second year do not have any facilitation in comparison with the congenitally deaf (based on work in progress). It seems as if even a short exposure to language, a brief moment during which the curtain has been lifted and oral communication established, is sufficient to give a child some foundation on which much later language training may be based. The effect of deafness thus complements our knowledge obtained from the effects of acquired aphasia. While the prognosis for recovery from aphasia gets worse and worse with advancing age after about ten, the prognosis for speech habilitation in the deaf improves directly with the advance of age at onset of the disorder.

Fry presents material at this conference that stresses the paramount importance of age in the establishment of optimal speech habits. He has recorded utterances of children whose audiograms would indicate profound hearing loss, but whose quality of voice, intonation patterns, and articulation are far superior to anything that is achieved either in America or the European continent. Fry's explanation is that these children were provided with hearing aids during earliest infancy and were given intensive "sound training" long before school started. In America children are also given hearing aids and sound training, but the latter does not begin seriously until age four or even later, and the hearing aids are often given little attention until school begins. If these findings can be verified on a larger scale, it would indicate an even shorter span of the critical age for optimal language acquisition than advocated in this paper.

## CONCOMITANTS OF PHYSICAL MATURATION

Language cannot begin to develop until a certain level of physical maturation and growth has been attained. Between the ages of two and three years, language emerges by an interaction of maturation and self-programmed learning. Between the ages of three and the early teens, the possibility for primary language acquisition continues to be good; the individual appears to be most sensitive to stimuli at this time and to preserve some innate flexibility for the "organization of brain functions" to carry out the complex integration of subprocesses necessary for the smooth elaboration of speech and language. After puberty the ability for self-organization and adjustment to the physiological demands of verbal behavior quickly declines. The brain behaves as if it had become set in its ways, and primary, basic language skills not acquired by that time, except for articulation, usually remain deficient for life. (New words may be acquired throughout life because the basic skill of naming has been learned at the very beginning of language development.)

I shall now make a few comments on the state of the brain during the initial period for language acquisition. I must stress, however, that this is not an attempt to discover the specific anatomical or biochemical basis of language development *per se*. The specific neurophysiology of language is unknown, and therefore it would be futile to look for any specific growth process that would explain language acquisition. Nevertheless it may be interesting to know in what way the brain, particularly the cerebral cortex, is different before the onset of language and after primary language acquisition is inhibited. The answer to such a question does not point to the cause of language development but tells us something about its substrate and its limiting or prerequisite conditions.

In a separate paper (Lenneberg, in press) I have collected anatomical, histological, biochemical, and electrophysiological data on the maturation of the human brain. I have presented the material there in the form of a series of maturation curves, one example of which is shown in Figure 4. While the curves differ one from the other, they are all intercorrelated, as might be expected. Their significance for a study of language acquisition is simply this: the curves define what is meant by maturation of the brain. All of the parameters of brain maturation studied show that the first year of life is characterized by a very rapid maturation rate. By the time language begins to make its appearance, about 60 per cent of the adult values of maturation are reached. Then maturation rate slows down and reaches an asymptote at just about the same time that trauma to the left hemisphere begins to have permanent consequences. Thus, by the time primary language acquisition comes to be inhibited, the brain can also be shown to have reached its mature state, and cerebral lateralization is irreversibly established.

The question remains of what the significance is of the coincidence between these brain-maturation phases and the onset and gradual decline of the capacity for language-learning. Could they be entirely spurious? The infant's obvious incapacity to learn all but the most primitive beginnings of language during his first fifteen months is, at least intuitively, attributable to a general state of cerebral immaturity. The maturational data for the end of the critical period is more difficult to interpret. If it were not for the consequence of different types of evidence that language acquisition is indeed inhibited at this time, the maturational data alone would lack all interest. As it is,

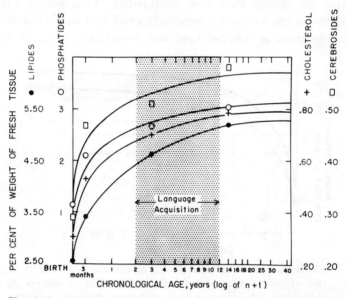

FIG. 4. Chemical composition of the human cerebral cortex plotted as a function of chronological age (based on data by Brante, 1949, and Folch-Pi, 1955). This is one of a family of similar curves published in Lenneberg (in press).

however, we may think of these data as contributing to the diverse circumstantial evidence that puberty marks a milestone for both the facility in language acquisition and a number of directly and indirectly related processes in the brain. I am, therefore, suggesting as a working hypothesis that the general, nonspecific states of maturation of the brain constitute prerequisites and limiting factors for language development. They are not its specific cause.

This hypothesis leads to a rather revealing generalization. Because the various aspects of cerebral maturation are so highly correlated, we may think of maturation of the brain as a single variable (perhaps as a shorthand sign for the sake of the following demonstration). As the brain matures, the growing infant successively attains various developmental milestones, such as sitting, walking, and joining words into phrases. In Figure 5, we see these milestones as "developmental horizons," signifying thereby the breadth of the maturational accomplishments; that is to say, sitting or walking are not the only developmental achievements of these various periods; at the same time there is a whole spectrum of sensory and motor development, and sitting or walking are merely their most outstanding characteristic. Figure 5 shows that if the normal maturation function is slowed down, developmental horizons are reached later and, most importantly, the spacing

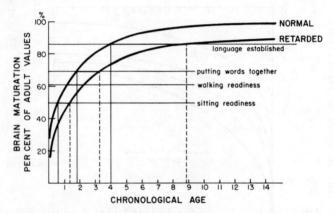

FIG. 5. Relationship between general rate of maturation of the brain, in per cent of mature values, to chronological age. The parameters are normal individuals and a typical case of a mentally defective individual. In the defective, developmental milestones fall farther and farther behind.

between the milestones becomes more prolonged without altering the order of sequence. Normally twelve to fourteen months elapse between sitting and putting words together, and language is fully established within another twenty months. But in the retarded the lapse between sitting and putting words together may be twenty-four months, and language may not be established fully for as long a period as another sixty months. This is precisely what is found in generally retarded children. Their earliest milestones seem delayed by just a few months, but the delay is increased with advancing age, and the lag behind the norm becomes worse and worse even though the retarding disease may be completely stationary and maturation is progressing steadily but slowly. The autopsy findings of brain weight of retarded individuals conforms fairly well to this picture, though retardation may be caused by so many different factors that it is not surprising that the correlation is not perfect.

The working hypothesis expounded here does not postulate cerebral "rubicons" or any absolute values of brain weight or composition as the *sine qua non* for language. It is not so much one or the other specific aspect of the brain that must be held responsible for the capacity of language acquisition but the way the many parts of the brain interact. Thus it is mode of function rather than specific structure that must be regarded as the proper neurological correlate of language.

## GROWTH CHARACTERISTICS OF THE HUMAN BRAIN

The irrelevance of absolute values, such as brain weight, for the capacity of language is discussed in Lenneberg (1964). The example is cited of nanocephalic dwarfism where brain weight and brain-body weight ratio may temporarily be identical with the corresponding values of a three-year-old chimpanzee. It is only when we look at some aspect of the ontogenetic histories of the two organisms that differences appear and the nanocephalic dwarf follows the developmental history of man, whereas the chimpanzee has a curve of its own. Any parameter of maturation must be studied in relation to the natural history of the organism's life cycle.

Species differ in their embryological and postnatal developmental courses. Much more important for an understanding of speciation are the ubiquitous failures of ontogeny to repeat phylogeny in specific detail, the species-characteristic deviations from the hypothetical course of a "general" history of evolvement. Consider the ratio of the weight of the brain to the weight of the entire body; let us call this the *brain-weight index,* a number that does not change appreciably after maturity, although it cannot remain completely constant because the body weight of a young adult slowly increases with advancing age. At birth, however, the index is about six to seven times the value of adulthood, and it decreases gradually throughout infancy and childhood.

Man's brain-maturation history is unique among primates. All lower forms approach the adult condition at a relatively quicker pace than man (Schultz, 1940, 1956). On the other hand, except for man's first six months, there is no brain-weight index value that is unique to him, as shown in Figure 6. His adult index value is about 2.2; in chimpanzee that value is attained shortly before midinfancy. At the end of the first childhood quarter the chimpanzee's index is 3.5, which is the same as man's at the close of the third quarter. It is not the measurements themselves that are different but the developmental stage at which these values are attained. When we discussed the nanocephalic dwarf, we were comparing a form near puberty with a form shortly before midinfancy, and hence the values for both brain and body could be matched. But the present material points to a fundamental difference between dwarf and chimpanzee, namely, their

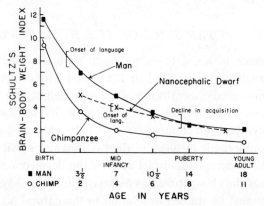

FIG. 6. Brain-body weight ratio as a function of age. The developmental curve of the nanocephalic dwarf resembles that of a normally growing human, whereas that of the chimpanzee always remains different.

developmental history. The dwarf quickly approaches the human curve and merges with it by puberty.

In comparison with lower primates, man's brain remains large throughout life. Yet we obtain a different view if we compare the growth rate of the brain *per se*. Man's body increases at a slightly faster rate than chimpanzee's, but the difference is not very startling. The growth curves of the brains are very different, however. During the first quarter of childhood man's brain gains about 800 grams as against 110 in the chimpanzee. In terms of relative increase man's brain weight at birth is only 24 per cent of the adult weight, while chimpanzee starts life with a brain that already weighs 60 per cent of its final value. During the first quarter of childhood the chimpanzee's brain gains only 30 per cent, whereas man's gains 60 per cent.

What conclusions may be drawn from these differences? We do not have the maturational data for chimpanzee brains that we have for human brains, but it is interesting to note that in man growth characteristics of the brain weight are closely paralleled in time by growth of microscopic structures, by growth in chemical compounds, and by growth in electrophysiological parameters. There is always rapid acceleration in the first quarter and attainment of the adult condition by puberty. By extrapolation we may assume that the maturational events of the chimpanzee brain during childhood differ from those in man in that at birth his brain is probably much more mature and all parameters are probably more stabilized than in man. This would indicate that the facilitation for language-learning is not only tied to "a state of flux" but to a maturational history that is characteristic for man alone.

We should not suppose that one might be able to train a chimpanzee to use a natural language, such as English, simply by delaying the animal's physiological development. When physiological delay occurs in man (as in mongolism), it also protracts his speech development. The onset of speech is regulated by maturational development of certain physiological and perceptual capacities that are probably lacking or take on different forms in lower primates. Maturational retardation cannot induce growth of the basic biological matrix for cerebral language organization.

Pertinent to man's prolonged maturational history is the hypothesis that man constitutes a "fetalized" version of a more generalized primate developmental course. Kummer (1953) presents much evidence to show that man's development is not simply a slowed-down version of ape development but has a history all of its own. The cross-species comparison shows that man's brain has a peculiar and species-specific maturational curve. Add to this our earlier observation that man is unique among vertebrates in the functional asymmetry of neurophysiological process within the adult brain. Only man has hemispheric dominance with lateralization of function and marked preference with respect to side in the use of limbs and sensory organs. Notice that cerebral dominance and dexterity are not present at birth but regularly emerge in the course of early development and are thus clearly tied to maturational processes. I have, indeed, cited evidence that laterality is a process of innate organization and polarization that is inevitable in the normal course of development but may be blocked, so to speak, within certain age limits by destruction of tissue in either hemisphere. I would like to propose that lateralization is a phenomenon of growth and development in man.

The development of language, also a species-specific phenomenon, is related physiologically, structurally, and developmentally to the other two typically human characteristics, cerebral dominance and maturational history. Language is not an arbitrarily adopted behavior, facilitated by accidentally fortunate anatomical arrangements in the oral cavity and larynx, but an activity that develops harmoniously by necessary integration of neuronal and skeletal structures and by reciprocal adaptation of various physiological processes.

## SUMMARY OF THE ARGUMENT

The notion "need" explains nothing because (*a*) of its subjective nature and (*b*) if the infant's needs change in the course of the first two years of life, they do so because of his own growth and maturation and not because of arbitrary extrinsic factors.

We must assume that the child's capacity to learn language is a consequence of maturation because (*a*) the milestones of language acquisition are normally interlocked with other milestones that are clearly attributable to physical maturation, particularly stance, gait, and motor coordination; (*b*) this synchrony is frequently preserved even if the whole maturational schedule is dramatically slowed down, as in several forms of mental retardation; (*c*) there is no evidence that intensive training procedures can produce higher stages of language development, i.e., advance language in a child who is maturationally still, say, a toddling infant. However, the development of language is not caused by maturation of motor processes because it can, in certain rare conditions, evolve faster or slower than motor development.

Primary language cannot be acquired with equal facility within the period from childhood to senescence. At the same time that cerebral lateralization becomes firmly established (about puberty), the symptoms of acquired aphasia tend to become irreversible within about three to six months after their onset. Prognosis for complete recovery rapidly deteriorates with advancing age after the early teens. Limitation to the acquisition of primary language around puberty is further demonstrated by the mentally retarded who can frequently make slow and modest beginnings in the acquisition of language until their early teens, at which time their speech and language status becomes permanently consolidated. Further, according to Fry, the profoundly deaf must receive sound training and prosthetic aid as close to age two as possible to develop good speech habits. The reverse is seen in acquired deafness where even short exposure to language before the onset of the disease improves prognosis for speech and language, the outlook becoming better in proportion to the length of time during which the patient had been in command of verbal skills.

Thus we may speak of a critical period for language acquisition. At the beginning it is limited by lack of maturation. Its close seems to be related to a loss of adaptability and inability for reorganization in the brain, particularly with respect to the topographical extent of neurophysiological processes. (Similar infantile plasticity with eventual irreversible topographical representation in the brain has been demonstrated for many higher mammals.) The limitations in man may well be connected with the peculiar phenomenon of cerebral lateralization of function, which only becomes irreversible after cerebral growth phenomena have come to a conclusion.

The specific neurophysiological correlates of speech and language are completely unknown. Therefore emergence of the capacity for language acquisition cannot be attributed directly to any one maturational process studied so far. But it is important to know what the physical states of the brain are before, during, and after the critical period for language acquisition. This is the prerequisite for the eventual discovery of more specific neural phenomena underlying language behavior. One finds that in almost all aspects of cerebral growth investigated, about 60 per cent of the mature values are attained before the onset of speech (roughly at two years of age, when speech and language become rapidly perfected), while the critical period comes to a close at a time when 100 per cent of the values are reached. This statement must not be mistaken for a demonstration of causal relationship between the variables involved. It merely suggests what structural and physiological substrates there might be that limit the capacity for cerebral organization and reorganization.

Species differ in their embryological and ontogenetic histories. Brain-maturation curves of *Homo sapiens* are different from those of other primates. Man's brain matures much more slowly, and there is evidence that the difference is not merely one of a stretched time scale but that there are intrinsic differences. Thus man is not born as a fetalized version of other primates; the developmental events in his natural

*TABLE 3  Summary Survey*

| Age | Usual Language Development | Effects of Acquired, Lateralized Lesions | Physical Maturation of CNS | Lateralization of Function | Equipotentiality of Hemispheres | Explanation |
|---|---|---|---|---|---|---|
| Months 0 to 3 | Emergence of cooing. | No effect on onset of language in half of all cases; other half has delayed onset but normal development. | About 60 to 70 per cent of developmental course accomplished. | None: symptoms and prognosis identical for either hemisphere. | Perfect equipotentiality. | Neuroanatomical and physiological prerequisites become established. |
| 4 to 20 | From babbling to words. | | | | | |
| 21 to 36 | Acquisition of language. | All language accomplishments disappear; language is reacquired with repetition of all stages. | Rate of maturation slowed down. | Hand preference emerges. | Right hemisphere can easily adopt sole responsibility for language. | Language appears to involve entire brain; little cortical specialization with regard to language though left hemisphere beginning to become dominant toward end of this period. |
| Years 3 to 10 | Some grammatical refinement; expansion of vocabulary. | Emergence of aphasic symptoms; all disorders recover without residual language deficits (except in reading or writing). During recovery period two processes active: diminishing aphasic interference and further acquisition of language. | Very slow completion of maturational processes. | Cerebral dominance established between 3 to 5 years, but evidence that right hemisphere may often still be involved in speech and language functions. About one quarter of early childhood aphasias due to right hemisphere lesions. | In cases where language is already predominantly localized in left hemisphere and aphasia ensues with left lesion, it is possible to re-establish language presumably by reactivating language functions in right hemisphere. | A process of physiological organization takes place in which functional lateralization of language to left is prominent. "Physiological redundancy" is gradually reduced and polarization of activities between right and left hemisphere is established. As long as maturational processes have not stopped, reorganization is still possible. |
| 11 to 14 | Foreign accents emerge. | Some aphasic symptoms become irreversible (particularly when acquired lesion was traumatic). | An asymptote is reached on almost all parameters. Exceptions are myelinization and EEG spectrum. | Apparently firmly established, but definitive statistics not available. | Marked signs of reduction in equipotentiality. | Language markedly lateralized and internal organization established irreversibly for life. Language-free parts of brain cannot take over except where lateralization had been blocked by pathology during childhood. |
| Mid-teens to senium | Acquisition of second language becomes increasingly diffi-cult | Symptoms present after 3 to 5 months post insult are irreversible. | None. | In about 97 per cent of the entire population language is definitely lateral- | None for language. | |

history are *sui generis*. The hypothesis is advanced that the capacity for language acquisition is intimately related to man's peculiar maturational history and the unique degree of lateralization of function. Table 3 presents the argument in tabular form.

## REFERENCES

AHRENS, R. Beiträge zur Entwicklung des Physiognomie- und Mimikerkennens. *Z. Exp. Angew. Psychol.*, 1954, *2*, 412–454 and 599–633.

AJURIAGUERRA, J. DE. Langage et dominance cerebrale. *J. Francais d'Oto-Rino-Laringol.*, 1957, *6*, 489–499.

ALTMAN, P. L., and DITTMER, D. S. (Eds.). *Growth including reproduction and morphological development*. Federation of American Societies for Experimental Biology, Washington, 1962.

ANDRÉ-THOMAS, ST. ANNE-DARGASSIES. *Études neurologiques*. Paris, 1952.

AUSTERLITZ, ROBERT. Gilyak nursery words. *Word*, 1956, *12*, 260–279.

BENJAMIN, R. M., and THOMPSON, R. F. Differential effects of cortical lesions in infant and adult cats on roughness discrimination. *Exp. Neurol.*, 1959, *1*, 305–321.

BRANTE, G. Studies on lipids in the nervous system; with special reference to quantitative chemical determination and topical distribution. *Acta Physiol. Scand.*, 1949, *18*, Suppl. 63.

BRODBECK, A. J., and IRWIN, O. C. The speech behavior of infants without families. *Child Development*, 1946, *17*, 145–156.

BROOKS, C., and PECK, M. E. Effect of various cortical lesions on development of placing and hopping reactions in rats. *J. Neurophysiol.*, 1940, *3*, 66–73.

BROWN, R. W. *Words and Things*. Glencoe, Ill.: Free Press, 1957.

—— and BELLUGI, U. Three processes in the child's acquisition of syntax. In *New Directions in the Study of Language*, E. H. Lenneberg (Ed.), Cambridge, Mass.: M.I.T. Press, 1964.

BÜHLER, C. *Kindheit und Jugend* (3rd ed.). Leipzig: Hirzel, 1931.

CARMICHAEL, L. The development of behavior in vertebrates experimentally removed from the influence of external stimulation. *Psychol. Rev.*, 1926, *33*, 51–58.

—— A further study of the development of behavior in vertebrates experimentally removed from the influence of external stimulation. *Psychol. Rev.*, 1927, *34*, 34–47.

—— The onset and early development of behavior. In *Manual of Child Psychology*, L. Carmichael (Ed.), New York: Wiley, 1954.

DAVIS, K. Final note on a case of extreme isolation. *Am. J. Sociol.*, 1947, *52*, 432–37.

DENNIS, W., and DENNIS, M. C. Development under controlled environmental conditions. In *Readings in Child Psychology*, W. Dennis (Ed.), New York: Prentice-Hall, 1951.

—— and NAJARIAN, P. Infant development under environmental handicap. *Psychol. Monogr.*, 1957, *71*, 7, Whole No. 436.F.

DOTY, R. W. Effects of ablation of visual cortex in neonatal and adult cats. *Abstracts, Comm. XIX Int. Physiol. Congr.*, 1953, 316.

ERVIN, S. M. Imitation and structural change in children's language. In *New Directions in the Study of Language*, E. H. Lenneberg (Ed.), Cambridge, Mass.: M.I.T. Press, 1964.

—— and MILLER, W. R. Language development. *Child Psychology*, 62nd Yearbook, National Society for the Study of Education, 1963.

FISICHELLI, R. M. *A study of prelinguistic speech development of institutionalized infants.* 1950, quoted by McCarthy, 1954.

FOLCH-PI, J. Composition of the brain in relation to maturation. *Biochemistry of the developing nervous system: Proceedings of the First International Neurochemical Symposium*, H. Waelsch (Ed.), New York: Academic Press, 1955.

FONTANA, V. J., DONOVAN, D., and WONG, R. J. The "maltreatment syndrome" in children. *New England J. Medicine*, 1963, *269*, No. 26, 1389–1394.

GESELL, A., and AMATRUDA, C. S. Developmental diagnosis: normal and abnormal child development. In *Clinical Methods and Pediatric Applications*, 2nd ed., New York: Hoeber, 1947.

GOLDFARB, W. The effects of early institutional care on adolescent personality. *J. exp. Educ.*, 1943, *12*, 106–129.

—— Effects of psychological deprivation in infancy and subsequent stimulation. *Am. J. Psychiat.*, 1945, *102*, 18–33.

GROHMANN, J. Modifikation oder Funktionsregung? Ein Beitrag zur Klärung der wechselseitigen Beziehungen zwischen Instinkthandlung und Erfahrung. *Z. Tierpsychol.*, 1938, *2*, 132–144.

HARLOW, H. F., AKERT, K., and SCHILTZ, K. A. The effects of bilateral prefrontal lesions on learned behavior of neo-natal infant, and pre-adolescent monkeys. In *The Frontal Granular Cortex and Behavior*, T. M. Warren and K. Akert (Eds.), New York: McGraw-Hill, 1964.

HÉCAEN, H., and AJURIAGUERRA, J. DE. *Les gauchers, prévalence manuelle et dominance cérébrale.* Paris: Presses Universitaires de France, 1963.

HESS, E. H. Ethology: an approach towards the complete analysis of behavior. In *New Directions in Psychology*, R. W. Brown, E. Galanter, E. H. Hess, G. Mandler, New York: Holt, Rinehart & Winston, 1962.

HOOKER, D. Evidence of prenatal function of the central nervous system in man. *James Arthur Lecture*, New York, 1958 (quoted by Peiper, 1961).

IRWIN, O. C. Infant speech. *J. Speech and Hearing Disorders*, 1948, *13*, 224–225, 320–326.

KOEHLER, O. "Wolfskinder," Affen im Haus und vergleichenda Verhaltensforschung. *Folia Phoniatrica*, 1952, *4*, 29–53.

KROEBER, A. L. The speech of a Zuñi child. *Amer. Anthrop.* 1916, *18*, 529–534.

KUMMER, B. Untersuchungen über die Entwicklung der Schädelform des Menschen und einiger Anthropoiden. *Abhandlungen zur exakten Biologie*, fasc. 3rd ed., Borntraeger, Berlin: L. v. Bertalanffy, 1953.

LANDAU, W. M., GOLDSTEIN, R., KLEFFNER, F. K. Congenital aphasia; a clinico-pathological study. *Neurology*, 1960, *10*, 915–921.

LEHRMAN, D. S. Induction of broodiness by participation in courting and nest-building in the Ring Dove (*Streptopelia risoria*). *J. comp. Physiol.*, 1958(*a*), *51*, 32–36.

―――― Effect of female sex hormones on incubation behavior in the Ring Dove (*Streptopelia risoria*). *J. comp. Physiol.*, 1958(*b*), *51*, 142–145.

LENNEBERG, E. H. Understanding language without ability to speak: a case report. *J. abnormal soc. Psychol.*, 1962, *65*, 419–425.

―――― Speech as a motor skill with special reference to nonaphasic disorders. *Monogr. Soc. Res. Child Developm.*, 1964.

―――― A biological perspective of language. In *New Directions in the Study of Language*, E. H. Lenneberg (Ed.), Cambridge, Mass.: M.I.T. Press, 1964.

―――― Speech development: its anatomical and physiological concomitants. In *Speech, Language, and Communication. Brain and Behavior*, V. E. Hall (Ed.), (in press).

―――― NICHOLS, I. A., and ROSENBERGER, E. F. Primitive stages of language development in Mongolism. In *Proceedings of the Assoc. for Res. in Nervous and Mental Disease*, 42nd Annual Meeting, New York, 1964.

―――― REBELSKY, F. G., and NICHOLS, I. A. The vocalizations of infants born to deaf and to hearing parents. *Vita Humana* (Human Development), 1965, *8*, 23–37.

LINDSLEY, D. B. Brain potentials in children and adults. *Science*, 1936, *84*, 354.

LORENZ, K. Z. The evolution of behavior. *Sci. Amer.*, 1958, *199*, No. 6, 67–78.

LUCHSINGER, R., and ARNOLD, C. E. *Lehrbuch der Stimm- und Sprachheilkunde*, 2nd ed., Wien: Springer, 1959.

MC CARTHY, D. Language development in children. In *Manual of Child Psychology*, L. Carmichael (Ed.), 1954.

MC GRAW, M. B. *The Neuromuscular Maturation of the Human Infant*. New York: Hafner, 1963.

MORLEY, M. *The Development and Disorders of Speech in Childhood*. London: Livingstone, 1957.

PEIPER, A. Die Schreit- und Steigbewegungen der Neugeborenen. *Arch. Kinderhk.*, 1953, *147*, 135ff.

―――― *Die Eigenart der kindlichen Hirntätigkeit* (3rd ed.). Leipzig: G. Thieme, 1961.

SCHARLOCK, D. P., TUCKER, T. J., and STROMINGER, N. L. Auditory discrimination by the cat after neonatal ablation of temporal cortex. *Science*, 20 Sept. 1963, 1197–1198.

SCHULTZ, A. H. Growth and development of the chimpanzee. *Carnegie Inst. Wash. Pub. 518, Contrib. to Embryol.* 1940, *28*, 1–63.

―――― Postembryonic age changes. In *Primatalogia: Handbook of Primatology*, H. Hofer, A. H. Schultz, D. Starck (Eds.), Basel: Karger, 1956.

SINGH, T. A. L., and ZINGG, R. M. *Wolf Children and Feral Man*. New York: Harper, 1942.

SMITH, M. E. An investigation of the development of the sentence and the extent of vocabulary in young children. *University of Iowa Stud. Child Welfare*, 1926, *3*, No. 5.

STIRNIMANN, F. *Schweiz. med. Wschr.* 1938, p. 1374ff.

TEUBER, H.-L. Effects of brain wounds implicating right or left hemisphere in man: hemisphere differences and hemisphere interaction on vision, audition, and somesthesis. In *Interhemispheric Relations and Cerebral Dominance*, V. B. Mountcastle (Ed.), Baltimore: The Johns Hopkins Press, 1962.

THOMAS, E., and SCHALLER, FR. Das Spiel der optisch isolierten, jungen Kasper-Hauser-Katze, *Naturwiss.* 1954, *41*, 557–558.

*Richard Allen Chase*

# EVOLUTIONARY ASPECTS OF LANGUAGE DEVELOPMENT AND FUNCTION

*A discussion of Lenneberg's presentation*

Lenneberg's paper has directed attention to some important and neglected issues concerning the development and function of language. It is my purpose to share the ideas that I have formulated in consideration of his arguments.

## LANGUAGE AND EVOLUTION

### Biological Origin of Language

One fundamental property of human language that is shared by all biological communication systems is that of information exchange. Biological systems demonstrate the ability to exchange information between parts of the system as well as between the system as a whole and its physical and social environment. In the case of the human, it is quite as necessary that respiratory center neurones be informed about the carbon dioxide concentration of the blood as it is that ideas be transmitted from one person to another. This spectrum of information-exchange capabilities can be vastly expanded at both ends, for at one extreme we appreciate that subcomponents of single cells transfer information (Quastler, 1953) and at the other extreme we appreciate that man possesses communicative capabilities that permit the construction of cosmologies (Durkheim, 1926). I am suggesting that language function be considered as part of a broad continuum of information-exchange operations that function to regulate and integrate

biological activity, that the key to understanding the biological origin
of communication systems resides in appreciating that all categories
of biological activity generate specific information requirements, and
that communication systems provide specialized capabilities for receiving, processing, and transmitting biologically essential information
(Etkin, 1964; Marler, 1959; Tinbergen, 1964). This point of view
suggests that communication systems evolve in specific forms in order
optimally to meet specific needs for information transfer necessary for
the preservation, growth, and development of an organism (Blair,
1963; Busnel, 1963; Moulton, 1963; Tembrock, 1963).

### The Nonlinear Phylogeny of Biological Communication Systems

*Critique of continuity theories of language.* Most efforts to trace the
evolution of language or of the systems for the exchange of information
between animals have focused on the formal properties of the productive
aspects of language function. Efforts to document linear evolution of
the form of communicative behavior have been generally unsuccessful (Critchley, 1960; Lenneberg, in preparation). When we consider
communicative behavior in the context of information exchange, these
nonlinearities in evolution become more readily understandable. When
communicative behavior is considered in the context of information
exchange, we are compelled to survey the receptive features of these
systems as well as their productive features. The sensory receptor
systems provide absolute limits on the kind and amount of information
that can be received by an animal. A survey of receptor-system neurophysiology reveals so much variation in functional properties that we
are forced to conclude that different species of animals literally
function in different experiential worlds (Cohen, 1964; Marler, 1959;
Tinbergen, 1957; Uexküll, 1957; Vallancien, 1963).

The image of a visual stimulus on the retina of an octopus eye is
smaller and less perfectly resolved than the image of the same object
on the retina of a human eye. This is a function of the smaller size
of the octopus eye and the presence of fewer receptor cells in the
octopus retina. The structure of the compound eye of insects generates
a completely different representation of the same visual stimulus
(Tinbergen, 1965). When we consider the additional differences in
neural mechanisms for the processing of visual information in these
three species, it becomes additionally apparent that the information

entering the visual system of each, although generated by the same visual stimulus, is so different that it would be surprising indeed if the related response behaviors of the three species were formally comparable.

Similar noncomparabilities of sensory transduction and processing functions apply to all interspecies comparisons of sensory mechanisms. However, when we conduct this survey of sensory mechanisms in parallel with behavioral observations, it becomes readily apparent that the sensory systems of each species have evolved capabilities for selectively admitting information of special biological importance. One finds, in addition, that there is a close conformity between the information-reception and information-generation capabilities of animals. Both the receptive and productive aspects of communication are readily related to specific categories of information exchange of unique importance to the animal in question (Marler, 1959, 1961; Tinbergen, 1964). Specific communication systems mediate information transfer associated with relationships between parents and young, the acquisition of food, the identification of mates, the identification of predators, and other comparably urgent categories of behavior. Different species of animals have very different biological needs, dictated by extreme differences in the physical environment in which they must survive. This heterogeneity of circumstance generates heterogeneous needs, and it is to be expected that these heterogeneous needs will be met by the utilization of heterogeneous communication strategies.

*Comparison of animal and human communication systems.* When we survey the communication systems of animals, we find that they represent the capabilities necessary for transferring information essential to preservation and development (Marler, 1959). Animal communication systems demonstrate capabilities that can be related to both quantitative and qualitative aspects of information exchange, as well as to the environment in which the animal must exchange this information. Some species live in environments in which visual and auditory communication would be extremely difficult. We find among such species highly structured systems of tactile and chemical communication (Marler, 1959; Wilson, 1963). In the ant we find that specific chemical substances activate and guide foraging workers in search of food and new nest sites, induce acts of grooming, food exchange, the care of immature ants, and behavioral sequences involving the disposition of the dead (Wilson, 1963).

As another example, the flash patterns of fireflies convey information about sex identification essential for mating. For the species *Photinus pyralis*, the male flashes at a regular time interval of about 5.8 seconds. The female flashes back just 2 seconds after the termination of the male flash. The male does not respond to the flash patterns of other males, but he will approach a wide variety of lights, differing in color and flash duration, as long as they flash 2 seconds after the termination of the male flash. In a crucial experiment, males were made to flash 2 seconds after other males, by mechanical stimulation, and under these circumstances they were tracked down just as though they were females (Marler, 1959).

Species in which behavior is mediated by complex social interrelationships generate, by virtue of this fact, needs for the transmission of more complex messages. As the information content of a message increases, a correspondingly more complex message-generating system must evolve. We find a corresponding evolution of communication systems that can meet these requirements (Darwin, 1873; Marler, 1959). Posture and facial expressions become used as a means of communicating social position and emotional states. Primates demonstrate the capability of sending messages that affect the way in which other messages are interpreted (Altmann, 1965). This sort of "communication about communication" has been designated as "metacommunication" (Ruesch, 1951). Primates frequently direct social messages to specific individuals by posture and facial expression (Altmann, 1965).

These examples serve to demonstrate that the productive features of animal communication systems are specifically suited to quantitative and qualitative, species-specific requirements for information exchange. In addition, these communication capabilities respect unique features of the physical environment in which information must be exchanged. In view of the broad variability in information-exchange requirements generated by physical differences among animals and differences in their physical and social environments, one would not expect an evolutionary survey of the form of communication systems to demonstrate significant linearities. One would expect such a survey to reveal progressive efficiency and pertinence of communicative transactions that sensitively respect species-specific biological needs and environment-specific contingencies.

*The correspondence between information-exchange requirements and communication-system capabilities.* An effective biological communication system is one that allows the transfer of information essential for the performance of vital biological functions. Efficiency of such information transfer depends upon the development of a high degree of specificity in signal production and reception operations (Marler, 1959; Murray, 1964; Tinbergen, 1964). This specificity is characterized by the generation of stimuli that are uniquely suited in their form to the sensory-reception and sensory-processing capabilities of the species. A considerable economy is effected by the generation of *categories* of signals and the definition of specific signal criteria that determine membership in one category or another. These features allow a receiving organism to limit its sensory processing to a determination of a circumscribed subset of signal characteristics rather than a detailed processing of the entire fine structure of a stimulus.

A high degree of specificity in communication systems can be achieved by genetically determined limitations in the response characteristics of transducers that allow them to respond only to biologically significant stimuli. The female silkworm moth produces a volatile chemical substance that attracts the male over considerable distances. This response of the male is specific to the female secretion and certain closely related unsaturated alcohols. Electrophysiological studies on the response characteristics of isolated male antennae demonstrated minimal responsiveness to a wide range of chemical substances, with the exception of the female secretion and closely related chemical substances, all of which evoked strong responses (Marler, 1961).

In other instances, the specificity of behaviorally active stimuli probably depends upon central processing operations. This is probably the case for visual stimuli that are effective in releasing the gaping response of young thrushes (Tinbergen, 1964). Tinbergen and Kuenen determined the essential visual information necessary to release the gaping response of the young thrush. The use of cardboard dummies, designed to represent some of the features of the parent bird, demonstrated that an effective stimulus must (1) move, (2) be larger than 3 mm in diameter, and (3) be above the horizontal plane passing through the nestling's eyes. If the gaping response was to be directed, the stimulus would in addition have to have an external protrusion from the body. This protrusion must have a diameter about one-third that of the body and be closer to the nestling than the body. The simple, rigidly defined criteria of visual stimuli that trigger a specific behavioral response probably depend upon a genetically determined recognition system, involving determination of whether a visual stimulus meets certain criteria without the processing of information in the visual stimulus that would be irrelevant to this decision.

Evidence for genetically determined preferential fixation by human infants on visual stimuli that have some of the formal features of the human face has been provided by the work of Fantz (1961, 1965). His studies demonstrate that human infants under five days of age preferentially fixate upon patterned visual stimuli that have formal correspondences to human faces. Less fixation is accorded brighter and colored stimuli.

The speech communication system emerges in the context of active exchange of acoustic information that ultimately results in the development of a system of speech-motor gestures that conforms to the system of speech-motor gestures utilized by the adult culture. A great deal of the information that allows for the correspondence of the child's speech and language system with the speech and language system of the adult culture arrives through the auditory pathways. A congenitally deaf child does not acquire normal speech, and his language capabilities are also diminished (Fry, this volume; also Myklebust, 1960; Stokoe, 1964; Whetnall and Fry, 1964).[1] This does not represent a problem in learning but a problem in information exchange. When the developing nervous system programs its categories of speech-motor gestures, it draws heavily upon acoustic representations of the speech-motor gestures of the adult culture and the acoustic correlates of the child's efforts to reproduce the adult speech-motor gesture. As Fry has pointed out, the phonological system of the deaf child represents the product of normal learning operations, but learning that is referenced to distorted acoustic models. A comparable failure of speech and language development is demonstrated by the child with normal hearing developing in an environment in which he is deprived of the opportunity of hearing adequate samples of adult speech (Spitz, 1947). The development of the speech communication system as a function of active exchange of acoustic information between infants and adults guarantees that the speech system a child learns will bear an appropriate conformity to the speech system of those individuals with whom he must exchange information. McNeill has noted that the parents of

---

[1] See also: *Studies in the psychology of the deaf* (by the Psychological Division, Clarence W. Baron Research Department, The Clarke School for the Deaf, Northampton, Massachusetts), *Psychological Monographs*, 1940, *52*.

lower-class children are less likely to expand children's sentences into the nearest well-formed adult equivalents and thereby make the discovery of linguistic universals more difficult for their children. In contrast, the parents of middle-class children engage in such expansions very frequently. Retardation of language development in lower-class children is considered to be related to this phenomenon, at least in part. It may be, however, that the language development of the lower-class child is retarded only when measured by middle-class standards of normal language development. It is possible that the behavior of the lower-class parent is not simply a function of diminished motivation and interest in the child's communication but might reflect important differences in systems of information exchange characteristic of this group. Linguistic competence, in the usual sense, may not be as useful to the lower-class child as other communication operations.

Plasticity in the acquisition of vocal communication is observed in animals with much simpler vocalization systems, under circumstances in which the sharing of specific signal features is essential to the communicative function. Recognition of an infant by its mother is a pertinent example. In the case of the elephant seal, Bartholomew (1962) observes that shortly after birth the pup calls to the mother who in turn replies, directing her barks directly to the pup, frequently from a very short distance. Barking from the mother is noted to occur even when the pup is silent. When pups are removed from their mother, they immediately start to vocalize and the mother immediately begins to respond. The two call back and forth while moving toward each other. It seems reasonable to suppose that the exchange of vocalization between mother and infant, immediately after birth, results in the generation of a vocal communication system subserving the specific function of mutual identification.

It should be noted that plasticity in the learning of communicative function does not compromise the development of specificity of communicative function. Rather, plasticity increases the probability that the particular form specificities assume will be compatible with local communication requirements.

## Behavioral and Structural Evolution

*Structural evolution and physics.* Lenneberg has noted that the evolution of anatomic structure shows far less species variability than the evolution of behavior. The relative constancy of a good deal of the anatomical componentry of biological systems is probably explicable in terms of constant features of the physical universe that constitute, in a sense, the shared experience of all biological systems. When we survey the evolution of the human ear, we find that some of its basic building blocks can be traced back to the lateral line organ of the fish (Vallancien, 1963; Van Bergeijk, Pierce, and David, 1960). This organ contains sensory cells that have a very fine filament embedded in a gelatinous space. These hair cells transduce pressure changes into corresponding electrochemical codes in nerve fibers. Morphologically comparable components are found in the basilar papilla of the frog and in the mammalian organ of Corti. The hair cell is undoubtedly an extremely effective mechanism for the transduction of pressure changes into electrochemical codes. The morphological comparability of hair-cell components in transducer systems responsible for providing information about pressure changes in the environment is undoubtedly explicable in terms of relatively constant features of the physical universe. However, the response characteristics of the lateral line organ of the fish and the mammalian organ of Corti are so vastly different that it is meaningless to speak of comparabilities of function at the organ level paralleling comparabilities of form at the cellular level (Vallancien, 1963).

*Behavioral evolution: relations to structural evolution and the rationale for variability.* It is to be expected that behavior, or the function of a biological system, will demonstrate more change in the course of evolution than will the formal properties of the anatomical components underlying these functional capabilities. This generalization follows from the fact that behavior, or function, is invariably the result of a system of interacting components. If a single component is changed, it may radically alter the over-all system performance.

For example, Geschwind (1965) has argued that the evolution of a new association structure in the human brain, allowing for the mixing of information from each of the primary sensory projection systems, underlies the human ability to attach names to objects. This structure is the inferior parietal lobule, which includes the angular and supramarginal gyri, a region that receives few afferent fibers from the thalamus. It stands geographically at the point of juncture of cortical projection areas for vision, hearing, and somesthesis and may well receive most of its afferents from adjacent association areas. Geschwind argues that such an "association area of association areas" permits the intermodal associations necessary for object-naming, which is of course a fundamental requirement for the language function. In this sense, the evolution of this new parietal association region results in a change in language capability far out of proportion to the morphological change in the primate brain that it represents physically. This is the case because such an association area permits interactions of sensory information-processing systems that are already highly developed.

The sound emission systems of the Arthropoda are simple and highly constrained. The stereotyped acoustic signals generated by Arthropoda subserve identification and orientation functions essential for mating. These acoustic messages demonstrate no modification as a function of learning, and their simple and stereotyped morphology may even be used for taxonomic purposes (Dumortier, 1963). In contradistinction, some bird species demonstrate marked modification in their song patterns as a function of acoustic experience, provided that this experience is made available at an early stage in development (Bremond, 1963; Marler, 1961). In man, we not only find far greater plasticity with respect to the effect of acoustic experience on the evolution of vocal communication systems, but this plasticity survives in some measure throughout life.

We observe in the course of evolution the development of greater plasticity with respect to the organization of communication systems. The advantage of such an evolutionary development is clear, as it allows communication systems to develop specificities of function that are particularly suitable to the environmental circumstances in which the organism must live. The ontogeny of communication capabilities that respect the fine structure of the environment in which the animal must live guarantees that the animal will not only be able to communicate information efficiently but in a manner that is pertinent to local features of the physical and social environment. This capability also permits modification of communicative function in a manner appropriate to changes that occur in the physical and social environment. In some sense I think that the history of our studies of structural evolution have misguided our studies of behavioral evolution. Significant constancies in the form of the anatomic componentry of biological systems is readily referable to constancies in the physical universe. On the other hand, functional capabilities have evolved as a result of the efficiency and pertinence with which they mediate the requirements of biological growth and survival. These requirements reflect great variability, generated by variabilities in the basic structure of biological systems and the structure of their physical and social environments. We have already noted that the disproportion between the invariability demonstrated in structural evolution relative to the variability demonstrated in behavioral evolution does not pose a paradox, insofar as behavioral functions are generated by systems, and very small changes in components of a biological system may have profound effects on the range and character of its functional operations.

A survey of the ontogeny of vocalization in the human demonstrates the manner in which vocalization capabilities meet specific and very different needs for information transfer at different stages of development. The cry of the human infant is an efficient system for informing adults about categories of affective experience, such as hunger, pain, and pleasure. The early exercise of naming behavior may be more closely related to the important psychological functions of exploring the surrounding physical universe and realization of the differentiation of self from this physical universe than it is to the acquisition of language *per se*. Fry has indicated that the early acquisition of ability to reproduce patterns of adult speech reflects imitation of intonation patterns out of proportion to other formal properties of the speech of the adult. Intonation patterns are closely associated with the affective aspects of speech communication, and these observations support the position that vocalization behavior of the infant and young child assumes a disproportionate capability for communicating information about affective states (Spitz, 1957), to be supplemented at a later stage in development by proportional capability for the communication of more objective categories of experience, such as the operations of logical thought.

Communication is regulative of behavior, and successful communication systems are characterized not simply by their capability of transmitting more information, but more importantly by their capability of transmitting the right kinds of information. It is probable that the capacity for language in the human builds upon many already developed capacities for the processing of information from the environment and the generation of messages pertinent to specific biological functions.

Before we can understand the genetic substrate of language capabilities and language disorders (Witkop and Henry, 1963), we must attain a more perfect understanding of the subfunctions upon which language function builds. Are the classification and relational operations essential to the attainment of linguistic competence in the human the same at some level of neurophysiological function as the classification and relational operations underlying logical thought (Inhelder, 1960)? Are the temporal processing operations required for the decoding of acoustic messages the same as the temporal processing operations that impose temporal organization on other categories of subjective experience (Efron, 1963; Milner, 1962; Neff, 1961)? Is the capability of storing acoustical information, essential to the decoding of phonological, syntactic, and semantic structure of spoken language, the same as the storage capability that underlies all memory functions (Brain, 1951)? Greater illumination of issues such as these must precede adequate understanding of the genetic substrate of language ability and disability.

The development of language capabilities is often correlated with physical and chemical parameters, such as brain weight, brain size, and regional concentrations of chemical substances in the brain (Lilly, 1963). Such correlations can be misleading, insofar as they encourage the inference that the physical and chemical constitution of the brain at the time when language capability first appears represents the essential substrate of language capability. The fact that the human brain is of a particular size and weight and contains specific concentrations of certain chemicals at the time that language capability achieves a certain level of competence does not mean that the same degree of competence might not have been evidenced at an earlier stage of physical maturation if environmental contingencies had been other than they were. Nor do such observations permit us to decide which features of physical growth and maturation are related to language capability and which are not. The fact that a functional capability has not appeared at a particular stage in development does not mean that it could not have appeared. The correlation of physical and chemical parameters of maturation with functional capability gives a very imperfect understanding of the essential features of physical growth and maturation underlying language capability.

Genetically transmitted structure determines the organization and integration of all biological activity. It is a commonplace to consider the metabolic operations that underlie physiological function, including the constant renewal of the physical structure of biological systems, as a direct product of genetically imposed constraints. It is less common to consider the organization of relations between organisms in specific social and physical environments as under genetic regulation. However, the analogy becomes compelling when we consider that these relations are regulated by the communication functions of organisms and that these communication functions are, in turn, regulated by their genetically determined physiological substrates.

At several points in this discussion we have noted the way in which the isolation of subsets of information related to the understanding of language function, and concentration upon formal description of these subsets of information, can grossly mislead our efforts to understand the biological nature and development of language behavior. Correlations between the physical and chemical constitution of the brain at critical periods in language development (with respect to phylogenetic and ontogenetic development) encourage misleading inferences about the essential features of physical growth and maturation underlying language capability. In a similar manner, analysis of the structural evolution of receptor, effector, and central nervous system structures suggests linearities in structural evolution that can mislead efforts to reconstruct the history of functional or behavioral evolution. As we have stressed, behavioral evolution shows far greater nonlinearity than structural evolution. When comparable strategies of formal analysis of development are applied to the study of language behavior in the human, and in addition the evolution of the phonological system and the evolution of the syntactic system are studied separately and in isolation from considerations about the environment in which the infant lives and grows, comparable errors in inference are bound to arise. That one can survey the formal characteristics of human language development through infancy and early childhood and construct rules that explain the formal transitions that ultimately result in linguistic performance closely corresponding to that of the adult culture does not allow the inference that all of the language performance of the child represents a linear unfolding of adult language capabilities. It seems far more likely that stages in the development of phonological organization, syntactic organization, and interactions between the two, are at specific junctures in development complete and effective systems for meeting the requirements for information exchange characteristic of that developmental stage. Formal characterization of the linear approximations of phonological and syntactic organization of child language to the phonological and syntactic organization of adult language, in isolation from parallel analysis of the specific information-exchange requirements characteristic of different stages in development, is more likely to generate logical order than biological sense.

## SUMMARY AND CONCLUSIONS

We have considered the biological origin of language to reside in the compelling needs for the transfer of information between biological systems essential for their preservation, growth, and development. When we survey the evolution of communication systems, we observe progressive refinements referable to the following issues: (1) the ability to formulate messages involving categories of information that subserve vital biological functions; (2) the formulation of messages in a manner optimally suited to the transduction and processing capabilities of the intended receiver, respecting the specific features of the physical environment in which messages must be exchanged; and (3) plasticity of capabilities for learning specific communicative operations, resulting in a greater degree of adaptability of communicative capabilities suitable to local, and sometimes changing, communication needs.

The needs of different biological systems vary greatly as a function of significant differences in their physical organization and their physical and social environments. Communication systems evolve in a fashion that optimally meets these specific and variable needs for information transfer. In this context, we do not expect to observe linear progression of the form of communication functions through the course of evolution. On the contrary, we expect to find increasing variability in the form of communication functions as these functions become progressively more efficient and pertinent to the specific problems of information transfer that characterize a particular species in a particular environment. The physical substrate of behavior would not be expected to show the variability in its evolution that the evolution of behavior shows. This follows from the fact that behavior is the result of systems of functional operations, and relatively small changes in the physical componentry of a single subsystem can radically alter the output of a system as a whole.

# REFERENCES

ALTMANN, S. A. Social behavior of anthropoid primates: analysis of recent concepts. In *Roots of Behavior: Genetics, Instincts, and Socialization in Animal Behavior,* E. L. Bliss (Ed.), Ch. 20, New York: Harper, 1965.

BARTHOLOMEW, G. A., and COLLIAS, N. E. The role of vocalization in the social behavior of the northern elephant seal. *Animal Behavior,* 1962, *10,* 7–14.

BLAIR, W. F. Acoustic behavior of amphibia. In *Acoustic Behavior of Animals,* R. G. Busnel (Ed.), Ch. 23, Amsterdam: Elsevier Publishing Company, 1963.

BRAIN, R. *Speech Disorders.* Washington: Butterworth, 1951, pp. 69–91.

BREMOND, J. C. Acoustic behavior of birds. In *Acoustic Behavior of Animals.* R. G. Busnel (Ed.), Ch. 24, Amsterdam: Elsevier Publishing Company, 1963.

BUSNEL, R. G. On certain aspects of animal acoustic signals. In *Acoustic Behavior of Animals,* R. G. Busnel (Ed.), Ch. 5, Amsterdam: Elsevier Publishing Company, 1963.

COHEN, M. J. The peripheral organization of sensory systems. In *Neural Theory and Modeling,* R. F. Reiss (Ed.), Ch. 13, Stanford, Calif.: Stanford University Press, 1964.

CRITCHLEY, M. The evolution of man's capacity for language. In *The Evolution of Man; Mind, Culture and Society,* S. Tax (Ed.), Vol. 2 of *Evolution After Darwin,* Chicago: The University of Chicago Press, 1960, pp. 289–308.

DARWIN, C. *The Expression of the Emotions in Man and Animals.* New York: D. Appleton and Company, 1873.

DUMORTIER, B. Morphology of sound emission apparatus in arthropoda (Ch. 11); The physical characteristics of sound emissions in arthropoda (Ch. 12); Ethological and physiological study of sound emissions in arthropoda (Ch. 21). In *Acoustic Behavior of Animals,* R. G. Busnel (Ed.), Amsterdam: Elsevier Publishing Company, 1963.

DURKHEIM, E. *The Elementary Forms of the Religious Life: A Study in Religious Sociology.* Illinois: The Free Press, 1926.

EFRON, R. Temporal perception, aphasia and déjà vu. *Brain,* 1963, *86,* 403–424.

ETKIN, W. Theories of socialization and communication. In *Social Behavior and Organization Among Vertebrates,* W. Etkin (Ed.), Ch. 7, Chicago: The University of Chicago Press, 1964.

FANTZ, R. L. The origin of form perception. *Sci. Amer.,* 1961, *204,* 2–8.

—— Pattern discrimination and selective attention as determinants of perceptual development from birth. In *Perceptual Development in Children,* Aline H. Kidd and Jeanne L. Rivoire (Eds.), New York: International Universities Press, 1965.

GESCHWIND, N. Disconnection syndromes in animals and man. *Brain,* 1965, *88,* No. 2, 237–294; No. 3, 585–644.

INHELDER, BARBEL, and MATALON, B. The study of problem solving and thinking. In *Handbook of Research Methods in Child Development,* P. H. Mussen (Ed.), New York: Wiley, 1960.

LENNEBERG, E. H. *The Biological Bases of Language.* New York: Wiley, 1967.

LILLY, J. C. Critical brain size and language. *Perspectives in Biology and Medicine*, 1963, *6*, 246–255.

MARLER, P. Developments in the study of animal communication. In *Darwin's Biological Works: Some Aspects Reconsidered*, P. R. Bell (Ed.), Ch. 4, Cambridge: Cambridge University Press, 1959.

—— The filtering of external stimuli during instinctive behavior. In *Current Problems in Animal Behavior*, W. H. Thorpe and O. L. Zangwill (Eds.), Ch. 6, Cambridge: Cambridge University Press, 1961, p. 158.

—— Inheritance and learning in the development of animal vocalizations. In *Acoustic Behavior of Animals*, R. G. Busnel (Ed.), Ch. 9, Amsterdam: Elsevier Publishing Company, 1963.

MILNER, BRENDA. Laterality effects in audition. In *Interhemispheric Relations and Cerebral Dominance*, V. B. Mountcastle (Ed.), Baltimore, Maryland: The Johns Hopkins Press, 1962, pp. 177–195.

MOULTON, J. N. Acoustic behavior of fishes. In *Acoustic Behavior of Animals*, R. G. Busnel (Ed.), Amsterdam: Elsevier Publishing Company, 1963.

MURRAY, M. J., and CAPRANICA, R. R. Recent studies of the auditory and vocal behavior of the bullfrog. *Quart. Prog. Rep.* M.I.T. Research Laboratory of Electronics, 1964, No. 74.

MYKLEBUST, H. R. *The Psychology of Deafness: Sensory Deprivation, Learning, and Adjustments.* New York: Grune & Stratton, 1960.

NEFF, W. D. Neural mechanisms of auditory discrimination. In *Sensory Communication*, W. A. Rosenblith (Ed.), Cambridge, Mass.: M.I.T. Press, 1961, pp. 259–278.

QUASTLER, H. The specificity of elementary biological functions. In *Information Theory in Biology*, H. Quastler (Ed.), Urbana: University of Illinois Press, 1953, pp. 170–188.

RUESCH, J., and BATESON, G. *Communication: The Social Matrix of Psychiatry.* New York: W. W. Norton & Co., 1951.

SPITZ, R. A. Hospitalism. In *The Psychoanalytic Study of the Child.* Vol. 2, New York: International Universities Press, Inc., 1947, pp. 113–117.

—— *No and Yes: On the Genesis of Human Communication.* New York: International Universities Press, Inc., 1957.

STOKOE, W. C., JR. Language structure and the deaf child. *Report of the Proceedings of the International Congress on Education of the Deaf,* Gallaudet College, June, 1963. Washington: U.S. Government Printing Office, 1964, 967–971.

TEMBROCK, G. Acoustic behavior of mammals. In *Acoustic Behavior of Animals*, R. G. Busnel (Ed.), Ch. 25, Amsterdam: Elsevier Publishing Company, 1963.

TINBERGEN, N. The evolution of signaling devices. In *Social Behavior and Organization Among Vertebrates*, W. Etkin (Ed.), Ch. 8, Chicago: The University of Chicago Press, 1964.

—— and KUENEN, D. J. Feeding behavior in young thrushes. In *Instinctive Behavior*, Claire H. Schiller (Ed.), Ch. 4, London: Methuen & Co., Ltd., 1957.

—— and THE EDITORS OF LIFE. *Animal Behavior,* New York: Time, Inc., 1965.

UEXKÜLL, J. VON. A stroll through the worlds of animals and men; a picture book of invisible worlds. In *Instinctive Behavior: The Development of a Modern Concept,* Claire H. Schiller (Ed.), London: Methuen & Co., Ltd., 1957.

VALLANCIEN, B. Comparative anatomy and physiology of the auditory organ in vertebrates. In *Acoustic Behavior of Animals,* R. G. Busnel (Ed.), Ch. 19, Amsterdam: Elsevier Publishing Company, 1963.

VAN BERGEIJK, W. A., PIERCE, J. R., and DAVID, E. E. *Waves and the Ear.* New York: Doubleday & Co., 1960.

WHETNALL, EDITH, and FRY, D. B. *The Deaf Child.* London: Heinemann. 1964.

WILSON, E. O. Pheromones. *Sci. Amer.,* 1963, *208,* 100–112.

WITKOP, C. J., and HENRY, F. V. Sjögren-Larsson syndrome and histidinemia: hereditary biochemical diseases with defects of speech and oral function. *J. Speech and Hearing Disorders,* 1963, *28,* 109–123.

# GENERAL DISCUSSION
## Lenneberg and Chase presentations

1. Chase had commented that he regarded Geschwind's model for the evolution of naming behavior (see p. 260) as the kind of clear-cut hypothesis that was badly needed. Other participants thought the idea — that nominalization required the ability to mix information processed in the auditory system with information processed in the visual system and that this was not possible before the phylogenetic development of the parietal association areas — was limited and even unintelligible. Lenneberg expressed doubts about the accuracy of the observations. Geschwind's argument was based on an assumption about specific structure in the brain, which Lenneberg thought was difficult to maintain in the face of the small effect of childhood lesions that he had discussed. Premack felt the hypothesis was neither relevant nor irrelevant but based upon egregious error. From the data and theory that Geschwind propounded, it could be demonstrated logically that blind children should be unable to speak. Chase asserted that a good deal of this part of the discussion was based on confusion of Geschwind's position.

2. Chase referred to potential dangers of plotting measures of language performance and measures of physical maturation of the nervous system on the same time axis, inviting the inference that the level of physical maturation at each point in time is necessary for the level of performance observed at the same point in time. He suggested that the specific communicative needs that characterize different stages of development are significant determinants of patterns of language per-

formance. Fodor and Lenneberg raised objections to this position. Fodor's argument was that any attempt to show that each linguistic structure corresponded to a need would rapidly generate the conclusion that human language was the worst possible system for communication. Logicians who had investigated language had started by throwing out almost all its syntactic baggage, essentially because it was enormously complex, mathematically absurd, and uneconomical. Nobody in his right mind would attempt to build an artificial language based on phrase structure plus transformations, yet such a system was of necessity brought from one language to another and acquired by every child in learning his first language. Fodor did not think it worth while even to try to devise an argument that such syntactic complexities facilitated communication — unless one happened to be an infant human being learning a first language.

When Chase objected that this was a question for field biology, to be studied in a behavioral context, Lenneberg asserted that this was exactly what he was trying to do. His studies with deaf and retarded children had shown that the stages of language development could not be changed by any variation in need or environmental circumstances. As Hirsh had indicated, the peripherally deaf child could develop perfectly adequately without language. Why should a child bother to learn a language when he could get everything he needed, more or less, simply by tugging on a sleeve? The opposite also applied — language did not occur simply because need existed. Many therapists would say to a mother, "Go home and withhold the cookie until the child says 'cookie'" — but there was no indication that this induced language. Biological evidence was available in many field observations of this type, even though it was not possible to conduct controlled experiments; it offered a wealth of information militating against the notion of the salience of need. The definition of need would have to undergo so much contortion to account for the development of language under varied circumstances that he was just not willing to use the notion as explanatory.

3. Lenneberg agreed with Chase that a genetic approach to language would probably not be fruitful because language did not happen to be a matter of single traits. There were however some studies involving specific language deficits which seemed to have some of the earmarks of genetic interference; twin studies and family pedigree studies came particularly to mind. Fodor asked whether Lenneberg had seen any

connection between the role of genetic structure in growth rate and the kinds of highly specific information transmission that he (Fodor) and McNeill had proposed. Was there any analogue or genetic mechanism that was known to be capable of transmitting information of this nature? Lenneberg said he certainly knew of nothing like it.

*H. Kalmus*

# ONTOGENETIC, GENETICAL, AND PHYLOGENETIC PARALLELS BETWEEN ANIMAL COMMUNICATION AND PRELINGUISTIC CHILD BEHAVIOR

The task originally allotted to me in this symposium was to discuss aspects of animal and infant behavior that either serve communication or are in other ways comparable with language. To this I shall add some more general comments on the ontogeny, genetics, and phylogeny of behavior, prompted by contributions of other participants.

A general discussion of the various kinds of arguments, from animals to man, and their validity (Haldane, 1956) would far exceed the scope of my contribution. Such arguments are obviously useful, but linguists may more specifically want to know what help they might get from the findings of the ethologists in their study of animal behavior. How far are these findings relevant to human language and its development? To this question two opposite and extreme answers have been given. If human language is studied as a *competence,* characterized mainly by a formal syntactic structure and as a logical system, then existing studies of animal behavior and communication, which deal almost entirely with *performance,* have as yet very little to contribute to the study of linguistics.[1] If, on the other hand, one takes a more biological point of view and considers human language only as one of the many

[1] Fodor has pointed out to me that it might be rewarding to apply theory of grammar and syntax to certain forms of sequential animal behavior, not necessarily of a communicatory nature. Highly ritualized animal behavior would offer the best prospects (Huxley, 1965). A syntactic structure has been discovered in the eating habits of man (Halliday, 1960). Our daily menu may be considered as a succession of meals, each consisting of successive courses, helpings, and mouthfuls. These various units have a descending rank, and in each of them a great variety of substitutions is possible.

forms that animal communication has taken, then the whole force of the success of the comparative method can be invoked to justify a language student's interest in animal behavior.

There remain however two aspects of infant behavior that are independent of this dichotomy of approaches, the facts that many elements of prelinguistic child behavior are perfectly comparable with those of primate behavior and that these elements are present during the emergence of speech, interacting with it. A child is not simply a "larva" or a learner preparing for adulthood; at any moment he is also an integrated social personality.

Before describing a few features of prelinguistic and in fact non-acoustic infant-mother communication, it might be useful to give some indication of what I mean by such words as "communication" and "vocalization." It could be argued that the earth and the moon communicate because there is definite interaction between these two bodies, but that seems to me to go perhaps a little too far. I would rather confine myself to the two most powerful kinds of communicatory systems in biology. One is the sensory-neuro-muscular system, operative in language and behavior and the one this conference is dealing with, and the other is the genetical system. Genetics, like language and other forms of communication between individual animals, can be understood in terms of interactions between individual, highly organized entities, such as gametes or neural systems.

When the interaction between two nervous systems is compared with that between separate parts within one such system, language and other forms of communication appear in some ways to be substitutes for the synapses between neurons. The connection between two nervous systems is neither organic nor chemical but is mediated by signals that pass through the outside world.

These signals may be very complex, being produced by elaborate effector machinery. Another equally complex system may exist for receiving and analyzing the signals. Signals may be specific and discrete and elicit specified classifiable reactions. If signals in the form of ritualized behavior or of language are mutually exchanged, then we speak of communication. Sometimes rather similar packet exchanges may occur within our nervous system, underlying what the classical philosopher so charmingly called the dialogue of the soul with itself.

I think it is a poetical but also very profound thought that there are different parts of one's self that argue with each other. In any group of scientists one expects considerable argument within people in addition to the more obvious argument between them. But this is by the way.

## INFANT COMMUNICATION

It was my original intention to describe several of the very diverse communication systems in the animal kingdom, especially those utilizing modalities other than sound, such as odor, color, pattern, or touch, but instead I shall refer to a recent short review article by Sebeok (1965). Some insight into the complexity of the analysis of information transfer by animals may also be gained from a paper by Kalmus (1964), which should dispel the notion, still prevalent among non-zoologists, that animals are incapable of abstraction or symbolic transformation.

There is however one special case of "animal behavior" of particular interest in the present context, namely, that of infants at the prelinguistic stage. In comparison with the communication systems of many anthropoids, including the signs used by adult man, the sign language of small children is not very richly developed, probably because a baby is such an immature creature, lacking the motor skills of adult organisms. Its sensory functions are probably also not fully developed. Ethologically most rewarding during infancy are the interactions between mother and child. Touching the mouth of a newborn baby with the mother's nipple or some object of similar quality normally elicits sucking immediately. In turn the cry of the baby usually brings the mother along. This acoustic releaser is very specific, and mothers who will not wake from a loud noise, like that of a telephone bell, will be alerted by the soft whimpering of a child. The mutual release between mother and infant is analogous to the interactions between gaping fledglings and their food-carrying parents.

After a few weeks the child produces a more pleasing releaser than its crying: it starts to smile. This has the powerful function of endearing the baby to its mother, and thousands of unwanted children have probably suddenly made themselves desirable in this manner. The smile of an infant is itself a released reaction, which at first may be elicited by a variety of objects. Later on, only a face will provoke it and, still later, only the mother's face. The exact time of these changes varies in individual children but not their sequence.

This narrowing of the releasing response can be followed experimentally to an ever more specific stimulus. I remember a very eccentric German pediatrician who explored this maturation in the following manner. He put the most horrific things on his head and face in order to get young babies to cry, but they just smiled. However, at a certain age, they ceased to smile and became frightened. This change in many children can be easily demonstrated simply by adding dark glasses to a familiar face. At a later age crying and other negative reactions may be elicited by any face except that of the mother (Ambrose, 1961).

Some linguists are prone to underestimate the complexities and the power of nonlinguistic communication in both animals and people. The recognition of the mother by the child, and in fact the recognition by any particular individual by another of the same or a different species, is a most intriguing performance (Keiter, 1965). I am not very good at this myself; having traveled for almost a month over the United States and lectured to many groups of people, I certainly would not recognize them all. But I would recognize many. Now this largely mysterious faculty is an instantaneous, complex, analytical response to a very complex stimulus, and it is nonverbal. It is also obvious that mutual recognition is of great biological importance and a prerequisite for many other forms of communication. It is perhaps less obvious that the sophistication and complexity of the processes involved in recognition are in some ways comparable with the sophistication and structure of speech reception, except of course that the recognition processes seem to operate simultaneously and not as time sequences as in speech. Whether this distinction is important or not, I don't know.

## ANIMAL VOCALIZATION

I do not think the vocalization of animals can as yet contribute very much to our knowledge or the understanding of grammar and syntax, possibly because the interest of the ethologist has quite naturally been first focused on the semantic and functional aspects of the sounds animals produce. But there is no doubt in my mind that animals can do very many complex things of which we have not the faintest inkling, and I think even the study of vocalization is still promising for the linguist.

By studying the acoustic behavior of animals (Busnel and Busnel, 1964), be they insects, frogs, birds, or mammals, we can often infer that they do convey messages to each other. I shall mention only the simplest form, which is called anaphony. If two individuals of a species regularly alternate in their vocalizations, one may conclude that they are interacting with each other, an impression often reinforced by observing also nonvocal interactions. If one animal can be shown to "reply" to tape recordings of the sounds produced by another — or for that matter by itself — communication appears quite convincing, and statistical analysis of the process can begin.

Vocalization usually occurs at special occasions. At the primate laboratories at Orange Park, for instance, feeding time is a great occasion for the very bored anthropoids. A colossal hue and cry goes up among the chimpanzees, and within five seconds the whole colony of chimps, orangs, gorillas, and monkeys have changed their behavior in a chain reaction starting from a single first acoustic signal.

Occurrences of this kind are so vivid that the persistence of certain naïve conjectures is perhaps understandable. There exist for instance at least two chimpanzee vocabularies. The more serious one is by Hayes (1952), who tried very hard to teach some English words to his home-reared "Vicky" and thought that she learned a few. However, at the age of five years the chimpanzee had given up the use of the word "mama" and said only "tsk" when begging for a puff from a cigarette; in addition she clicked her teeth together when she wanted a car ride. Less credible is an English-monkey, monkey-English dictionary of some thirty words by Schwidetsky, a well-known zoologist and former assistant director of Washington Zoo; it was reported in a popular television journal. This contains a chimpanzee word for food spelled "ngahk," which was alleged to be related to the German for nutcracking, which is "knacken." Arguments of this nature only show how divorced linguistics and zoology can get.

A few words can be said concerning the development of chimpanzee vocalizations under different environmental conditions. In Orange Park I saw a number of chimpanzees, now mostly adolescent, who had been brought up in situations of severe social deprivation, prevented even from seeing the person who handled them (Davenport and Menzel, 1964). When they were very young, they "swam" on their bellies on the floor in a helpless fashion, though they were perfectly able to walk. Later they developed mannerisms similar to those of neurotics or psychotics or of people in solitary confinement, sometimes resembling the effects of neurological lesions. They still showed vacuum activities like gyrations, tics, shaking, fidgeting, and preoccupations with their own bodies two years after having rejoined the colony.

The vocalization of these animals, I was told, hardly developed while they remained isolated. They produced the normal kind of respiratory pleasure sounds, something like "ha ha ha," when fed or when their diapers were changed, and in distress they produced a faint whimper. However, I was told that they have now more or less a full repertoire of chimpanzee utterances, some of which I heard myself, and that they also produce them on the "right" occasions. They have thus to a certain extent recouped the acoustic signal system of their species. The fact that their vocalization seems more normal than their other motor behavior may simply indicate that voice is not much implicated in their stereotyped actions or in their fantasies but is used only in situations of more or less stark reality. It may on the other hand also indicate the innate and inflexible character of these utterances.

## ASPECTS OF GENETICS

Having to some extent dealt with my assignment, I want now to comment on certain statements, mostly of a genetical kind, that have been made during this conference. My first point is terminological; it concerns the words "genetic," "genic," and "genetical." These three adjectives have been repeatedly used as if they were interchangeable, which they are not (Kalmus, 1955). The word "genetic" had been used by psychologists before the advent of modern genetics; it then meant ontogenetic and should still be used in this way. Determination by genes should be called "genetical" or "genic," and the use of "genetic" for "phylogenetic" is altogether bad.

My second point is perhaps more serious. I feel compelled to make a most elementary statement concerning genetics, namely, that it is a science of *differences* and nothing else. It is misleading to speak of a particular gene for any normal character, such as intelligence or grammatical speech; such traits are dependent on the correct interactions of a multitude of genes. Only if we can show that related individuals can be classified into two or more natural classes, and that by the rules of Mendelism the particular classes segregate, may we speak of a genetical difference and look for a code difference in the DNA — in a particular place in a particular chromosome. That is all that genetical methodology can do legitimately. It will be easily realized that the kind of genetics most likely to be done in language research will be quite illegitimate; nevertheless it may be moderately productive, as in the studies based on similarities in idiosyncratic behavioral characteristics of monozygotic twins reared apart. These characteristics must to a considerable degree be genetically determined, but they are difficult to interpret in detail.

A fundamental difficulty for studies in linguistic genetics derives from the noncongruity of genetical entities and behavioral elements, such as speech characteristics. In his book *The Sounds of Language* (1961), Brosnahan has expounded an idea of Darlington (1947, 1955) that certain European regional preferences for specific articulations of sounds — in particular the /th/ sounds — are caused by demonstrable differences in the speech organs of the inhabitants of the particular regions and that these differences are genetical in nature. There seems to be very little evidence for this idea and a great deal against it. But apart from that, the whole construct rests on a misconception concerning the relation of behavioral characters and gene differences. As an illustration of an appropriate relation I shall briefly describe a special form of mental deficiency caused by inborn metabolic error, where a small percentage of mental defect is a consequence of the homozygosity of a recessive autosomal gene, resulting in phenylketonuria (Figure 1).

This condition, besides causing mental retardation, diminishes the pigment of the skin, hair, and possibly the eyes of the affected children and is diagnosed by a simple chemical test of the urine or blood. These various criteria for separating phenylketonurics from their normal siblings are of very different efficiency. The chemical tests result in complete separation, whereas the morphological and mental characters of normal and affected children overlap to a considerable degree. It would be impossible to distinguish by psychological tests alone between phenylketonurics and the vast majority of mentally defective children with an unknown etiology. There has been some success in keeping phenylketonuric children on a diet free of phenylalanine and thus preventing damage to their brains, but such a treatment would

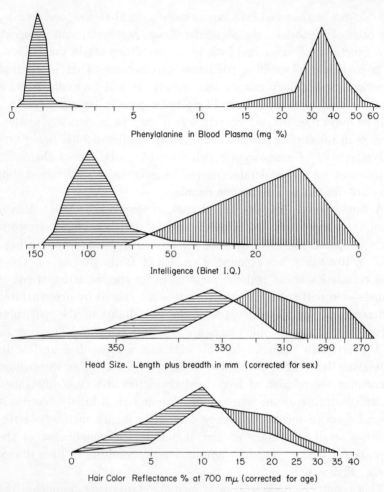

FIG. 1. Discrimination between normal people and phenylketonurics by means of different characters (after Penrose, 1951).

be quite useless in any other oligophrenic child. Lenneberg (this symposium) has mentioned another rare metabolic defect, histidinemia, which affects language development more specifically than phenylketonuria. But for this condition, too, chemical tests should prove more reliable than psychological procedures.

This raises the question of the validity of inferences drawn from abnormal structures or functions for the understanding of normal structures and functions and their evolution. When I was young, I thought this was a fairly foolproof procedure. But it now appears to me that although nature's experiments may occasionally tell one something about its ways, this is rarely anything very decisive. In particular, one hardly gets an insight into the phylogeny of the complicated systems that underlie communication and, specifically, language. These we must assume to have resulted from subtle coadaptive changes over many generations, involving many minor shifts in gene frequencies and environmental factors. In contrast, pathological deviation may be etiologically much simpler and, if hereditary, may be caused by a defect in one gene locus only.

Alternatively, genetical defect may derive from grosser deviations, such as the loss of parts or even of a whole chromosome or the presence of a supernumerary, one as in mongolism. From these basic geneti-

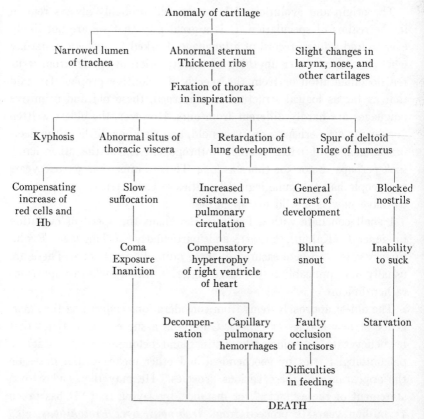

Fig. 2. Relation of the multiple effects of a lethal gene on the developing rat. The earliest detectable disturbance is in the cartilage (after Grüneberg, 1947).

cal defects one can derive what Grüneberg (1947) has called a pedigree of causes (Figure 2). The ramification of symptoms in hereditary and other clinical syndromes may proceed in a multiple way and may thus result in death from a variety of causes. From the varied courses of such diseases alone it would be hard to guess that they are manifestations of the same original defect; this only emerges from family studies or breeding experiments. It is obvious that none of these gross pathological manifestations bears any resemblance to any previous stage in the evolution of the affected organisms. There is no sign of coadaptation and very little functional compensation.

## RATES OF EVOLUTION

The origin and evolution of language will probably always remain in the realms of speculation. It is a great pity that we are not likely ever to find a fossil record of a language. I asked Lenneberg yesterday whether one can infer anything of the evolution of speech from written documentation or from the speech of primitive peoples. He said that as far as logical structure is concerned, these old and primitive languages are hardly different from ours. However, the oldest written documents are perhaps 5,000 years old, and we know little of the fleeting languages of tribal people. Anthropogenesis, on the other hand, took perhaps 100 or 500 times as long. Thus to infer that 500,000 years ago people had the same logical faculties or competences for speech as we have now is a wild extrapolation.

I shall conclude with a few remarks about the speed of evolution in general (Kalmus, 1965a), and particularly of language. Evolutionary rates can be measured in three quite different ways. These are usually not applicable to the same material, which makes comparisons rather difficult.

The oldest approach stems from considerations concerning the emergence of new species or genera. Observing a succession of types that he believes to be sufficiently distinct and belonging to a lineage, a paleontologist tries by geochemical and other means to put dates on the appearance of these various "species." He may then end with a statement of these "facts," for instance, by saying that "It has taken 17 million years to proceed from *Archippus*, over *Protohippus*, etc., to our modern horse." It is obvious that such a statement must be based on many subjective and even arbitrary impressions.

The second and more respectable method of estimating evolutionary rates is based on measurement. Fossils of vertebrate structures, like teeth or bones, or gastropod shells or hard fruit, are arranged in what one considers to be lineages of descent, and suitable features of these objects are then measured to assess their changes. In this way the necessity of deciding what constitutes a new species or genus is avoided, and more objective statements are arrived at, such as saying that "During several million years the paracone of the third molar of these horses has about doubled in height — or grown by several millimeters." This corresponds to an average increase of 3 to 10 per cent of the original value per million years or, in Haldane's (1949) units, to 30 to 100 "microDarwins." While dimensional changes of this kind form a reasonable basis for estimating and comparing the evolutionary rates of similar structures in similar organisms, it is unfortunately true that owing to the phenomenon of allometry various parts of the anatomy of the same lineage can change at very different rates. Thus no unitary rate for "species evolution" can emerge from these measurements.

The third kind of measurement of evolutionary rates is based on numerical changes in gene frequencies and can as a rule only be applied to living material. Very exceptionally, as with certain fossil snail shells and possibly with the blood groups of mummies, one may assume to be dealing with the same genes that exist today and follow such frequency changes into the past. Changes that lasted only a hundred years or slightly more have been reported, notably a darkening in the appearance of several moth species (industrial melanism, Kettlewell, 1956) and the depletion of silver foxes in East Canada (Haldane, 1942).

Complete changes of alleles in one or several genetical loci have been observed in bacterial colonies in the course of one or a few days. On the other hand no apparent change in 600 million years has been noticed in some marine (*Lingula*) lamp shells, so it seems not very useful to talk about evolutionary rates in general.

One may however speculate about the evolutionary speed of various elements in language and other means of animal communication. Phonetic, syntactic, and grammatical changes have been rather frequent in the European languages in the last 2,000 years. Their vocabulary has also changed considerably. Even less stable are some tribal languages that lack the conservative influence of writing. It is very unlikely that these changes in language are in any way connected with changes in gene frequencies. Rather are they comparable with the spread of certain animal habits, like the opening of milk bottles by tits of several species in England (Fisher and Hinde, 1949) or the recently developed depredation of the green, unripe fruit of the early flowering shrub *Daphne mezereum* by green finches (Petterson, 1956). The evolution of the sensory-neuro-motor faculties on which language capacity depends was of a coadaptive nature and, as such, must have depended on much slower changes in gene frequencies.

Nevertheless there are two bases for assuming that these changes may have been not too slow in terms of generations. The first is that many of the structural and functional "elements" of the speech apparatus exist in mammal species other than man and must have existed in our ancestors before they could speak. The further adaptation of these pre-existent features and their incorporation into the service of speaking must have greatly reduced the number of required genetical changes. Second, it is conceivable that the acquisition of the rudiments of language through concomitant changes in social organization (Kalmus, 1965*b*) may have effected a profound change in the selective forces operating on man. If this conjecture should be correct, the evolution of the language faculty from a certain point in time could be visualized as an "explosive" and self-accelerating process, perhaps coming to an end after several hundred generations. Something of this sort may have occurred in the evolution of another social animal, the honeybee; Zeuner (unpublished) believes that among the ancestors of *Apis mellifica*, speciation that had been reduced for millions of years "suddenly" accelerated during the eocene, giving rise to the social insect as we know it today (Kalmus, 1965*b*). The complex communication system that we know to exist in this species (von Frisch, 1946) must have had a similar history.

## REFERENCES

AMBROSE, J. A. Factors affecting the development of the smiling response as a social releaser in human infancy. *Animal Behav.* 1961, *9*, 116.

BROSNAHAN, L. F. *The Sounds of Language*. Cambridge, England: Heffer and Sons, 1961.

BUSNEL, R. G., and BUSNEL, M. C. *Acoustic Behavior of Animals*. Amsterdam, London, New York: Elsevier Publishing Company, 1964.

DARLINGTON, C. D. The genetic component of language. *Heredity*, 1947, 269–286; *Nature*, 1955, 175–178.

DAVENPORT, R. K., and MENZEL, E. W. Stereotyped behavior of the infant chimpanzee. *Arch. gen. Psychiat.*, 1964.

FISHER, J., and HINDE, R. A. The opening of milk bottles by birds. *Brit. Birds*, 1949, *42*, 347–352.

FRISCH, K. VON. Die Tänze der Bienen. *Öst. Zool. Z*, 1946, *1*, 1–48.

GRÜNEBERG, H. *Animal Genetics and Medicine*. London: Hamish Hamilton, 1947.

HALDANE, J. B. S. Selective elimination of silver foxes in Eastern Canada. *J. Genet.*, 1942, *44*, 296–304.

——— Suggestions as to quantitative measurement of rates of evolution. *Evolution*, 1949, *3*, 51–56.

——— The argument from animals to man: an examination of its validity for anthropology. *J. Roy. Anthrop. Inst. Gt. Brit.*, 1956, *86*, 1–14.

HALLIDAY, M. A. K. Categories of the theory of grammar. *Word*, 1960, *17*, 241–282.

HAYES, K. J. Analysis of chimpanzee intelligence; how is it enhanced by experience, and how is it limited by genetic factors? *Yearbook Amer. Philos. Soc.*, 1952, 179–180.

HUXLEY, SIR JULIAN (Ed.). Ritualization of behavior in animals and man. *Discussion, Meeting, Roy. Soc.*, London, 1965 (in press).

KALMUS, H. The genetic and the genetical aspects of behavior. *Br. J. Animal Behav.*, 1955, *3*, 38.

——— Animals as mathematicians. *Nature*, 1964, *202*, 456–60.

——— Evolution and time. In *The Voices of Time*, New York: George Brazillier, 1965(*a*), pp. 330–352.

——— The social organization of animal communities; origins and general features. *Symp. Zool. Soc. London*, 1965(*b*), *14*, 1–12.

KEITER, F. The behavioral consequences of morphological diversity. *Wenner-Gren Symposium No. 27*, New York, 1966.

KETTLEWELL, H. B. D. A résumé of investigations on the evolution of melanism in lepidoptera. *Proc. Roy. Soc.*, 1956, *145*, 296–303.

PENROSE, L. S. Measurement of pleiotropic effects in phenylketonuria. *Ann. hum. Genet.*, 1951, *16*, 134–141.

PETTERSON, M. Diffusion of a new habit among greenfinches. *Nature*, London, 1956, *177*, 705–710.

SEBEOK, T. A. Animal communication. *Science*, 1965, *147*, 1006–1014.

# GENERAL DISCUSSION
## Kalmus presentation

1. The observation by Kalmus that the evolution of language must have been explosive led to an inquiry about evidence. Kalmus replied that obviously none existed because nothing was known about the chronology. Nevertheless language evolution must have been explosive, and he could imagine several possibilities. Assuming that the elaboration of language coincided with group existence, for example, it was known that most anthropoids existed in groups. It was also known that social coherence profoundly affected selection, which operated then on the group rather than on individuals. There would be inbreeding as well, which was the optimal condition for genetical change. Moreover a group with a primitive communication system would probably be very much more likely to survive and multiply than other groups.

Miller remarked on the great many features found common to all human languages. Had convergence occurred, or why had different forms of language not evolved? One explanation might well be that language evolved very suddenly, once only and not so very long ago, so that there had been no time for evolution from the universal pattern. People who knew anything about the fossil record, however, tended to reject this, regarding sudden developments as unthinkable. Several participants noted disagreements or inconsistencies among biologists and geneticists about the rate at which the brain grew and the development of language, although suggestions had been made (notably by Haldane) that both were rapid. Cooper questioned how language, if it developed very suddenly, could have reached comparatively isolated regions like Australia, which was often pointed to for its deviant forms of animal and plant life.

To avoid forced choices between analogies and homologies and the postulation of convergence or coincidence, which were uninteresting in any comparative analysis, Kalmus recommended the consideration of "parallelologies," or parallel sequences of development.

2. Kalmus was interested in a comment by Fodor concerning the possibility of syntactic analysis of nonverbal behavior and asked for more information. Fodor provided it as follows:

The question whether there exist homologies between human languages and nonverbal behavior in humans and infrahumans is, of course, very complicated, and much of the interest of the question lies in the discovery of concrete examples of such homologies. I shall not try to present many such examples here but only to make a few general remarks about their character.

In the first place, it seems to me a mistake to suppose that the relevant homologies obtain between human languages and the behavior systems ethologists and psychologists study under the title of "animal communication." For it is obvious that all sorts of inter- and intraspecific information exchanges are continuously taking place between animals and that, in very many cases, the decision to call one but not another of the behaviors that mediate these exchanges "communication behavior" is quite arbitrary. Indeed, one would suppose that very often the appropriate analogy for animal communication is not human language but human "paralinguistic" communication. Animals, like humans, must often communicate information about their goals, intentions, emotional states, motivation, etc., as an incidental consequence of their on-going behavior. If the zigzag flight of a sparrow communicates "danger" to other birds in its neighborhood, the best human analogy is perhaps someone acting panicky rather than someone saying "look out."

Even in cases where we feel strongly that the communicatory function of animal behavior is primary rather than incidental (as, for example, in the classic case of the bee dance), it often enough turns out that the behavior is a ritualization of some performance whose primary function has nothing in particular to do with communication. Ritualized pecking sometimes signals aggression in chickens. Here there is perhaps a functional correspondence between the behavior of the animal and certain human communication behaviors, but one would hardly expect structural homologies between the behaviors that mediate that function. In general, to suppose that because behaviors function as communication devices in animals and humans they ought to exhibit structural homologies is like supposing that because swimming in fish subserves the function that walking does in humans the structure of the motions in the two cases ought to be similar.

The first point, then, is not that it is senseless to ask questions about the general structure of behavior in animals and men. Nor is it denied that human language may importantly illustrate those structures. But it does seem unreasonable to suppose that the relevant place to look for structural similarities must be in cases where we find functional convergence. I do not, for this reason, find it surprising that most comparative analyses of human and animal languages lead to the conclusion that the two have very little in common.

Let us start again, looking first at the linguistic end. A syntax could be thought of as nothing more than a system that has the property of specifying a certain infinite set of objects (i.e., of "structural descriptions") which, in turn, have the property of being in one-to-one correspondence with the sentences of a language. On this view, the theoretical relations in terms of which this mapping is effected correspond simply to formal relations among sentences or parts of sentences, and no claim is made for their role in such psychological processes as using or learning language.

As insight into language structure has accumulated, however, it has begun to seem increasingly unlikely that the elaborate organization natural languages persist in displaying plays no role whatever in the data-processing that underlies the use of language. It has thus seemed necessary to ask what, if any, psychological interpretation can be placed upon the theoretical constructs in terms of which a syntax describes the structure of sentences in a natural language. As soon as this question is asked, it becomes immediately evident that there are very natural ways of providing psychological interpretations for certain of the theoretical constructs employed in the linguistic formalism.

For example, one of the things that a syntax automatically does in the process of enumerating the sentences of a language is to impose a parsing. Thus, any syntactic theory of English would have to say, at some point, that

(i) John plays chess better than Jim

has something like the parsing

(ii) (John) ((plays) (chess)) ((better) (than) (Jim))

From a purely linguistic point of view — and quite independent of any psychological claims one feels inclined to make on behalf of the syntax — this bracketing is necessitated by such facts as the following:

(iii) There is a sentence *John plays chess* but no sentence \*John plays chess better than; i.e., *better than Jim* must be marked as a unit.

(iv) There is a sentence *that boy plays chess better than Jim*; i.e., *John* must be marked as a unit, presumably of the same general kind as *that boy*.

(v) There is a sentence *John eats*; i.e., *plays chess better than Jim* must be marked as a unit, presumably of the same general kind as *eats*, and so on.

In short, there are formal relations within and between the sentences of a language such that certain sequences longer than one element operate in a more or less unitary fashion and such that n-tuples of such longer-than-elementary units may operate in recognizably similar fashion. The bracketing a syntax supplies provides for a partial characterization of this fact and is therefore motivated in ways that have nothing directly to do with considerations of the psychological processing of language.

If, however, any claim at all is to be made for the psychological reality of the bracketing employed in a syntax, it seems to me that there is only one reasonable hypothesis as to what function that bracketing could subserve. That is that the bracketing provides an answer to the question of what the segments are into which sentences are perceptually analyzed and in terms of which utterances of sentences are integrated. In short, the bracketing must be interpreted as providing an analysis of complex linguistic percepts if it is to be thought of as making any psychological claim at all.

There now exists, in fact, a reasonably substantial body of evidence in favor of the view that the bracketing does correspond to an analysis of a sentence into perceptual segments; i.e., that at some point in the decoding of a sentence it is analyzed into units that correspond directly to the units articulated by a syntactic parsing. It thus looks as though there is both a linguistic and a psychological basis for treating a sentence not as a string of phonemes deployed left to right, like beads on a string, but rather as a structure in which the phonemic elements are simply the shortest units in a nest of bracketed sequences of various length.

We have said that from the point of view of the linguistic analysis the bracketing captures certain formal relations among sentences and parts of sentences. It does so by marking the fact that sentences that consist of different sequences of phonemes may nevertheless have the same articulation into longer-than-elementary units. But the bracketing aids in marking intersentential relations in a still more profound way; namely, by articulating the domains to which certain later (transformational) syntactic rules apply. For example, suppose we want the syntax to represent the fact that the order of noun phrases in the English passive sentence is a permutation of the order in the corresponding active. Thus (vi) corresponds to (vii), etc.

(vi) *the wolves* ate *the serfs*
(vii) *the serfs* were eaten by *the wolves*

We can formulate the appropriate rule for performing this permutation only insofar as we have some mechanism that permits us to represent the noun phrases as units upon which syntactic operations can be effected. This is, once again, precisely the role of the bracketing. In particular, the bracketing permits one to represent the active sentence as composed of three longer-than-elementary units; e.g., *the wolves, ate,* and *the serfs* in the case of (vi). Over such abstract units, transformational operations of permutation, deletion, adjunction, etc., can be defined.

In short, the view of the sentences of a natural language that emerges in linguistics is that of a set of strings, each exhibiting complicated internal structure, over which structures various syntactic operations are defined. Presumably, the psychological counterpart of these remarks is that the integration and decoding of linguistic behavior involves both the resolution of sentences into units corresponding to those articulated by the bracketing and the performance of the relevant transformational operations upon those bracketed sequences.

Now, what I want to suggest, without trying to prove it, is that this situation is found very generally in animal behavior: i.e., it is very often the case that the behavior of animals, and the nonverbal behavior of man, exhibits a bracketing into units of longer-than-one element and that the units yielded by this bracketing are available for various further operations of extinction, adjunction, reordering, etc. This is to say that, stochastic models to the contrary notwithstanding, animal behavior does not typically consist of a chain of gestures deployed in time but exhibiting no internal structure beyond articulation into elements. Rather the observable, temporally arranged behavior the animal produces corresponds to the bottom level of a "tree." The reality of the higher nodes of the tree (or, equivalently, of the longer-than-elementary units in the behavior chain) is demonstrated by the fact that operations of extinction-relearning, generalization, and the rest of the paraphernalia of behavior change can operate not only on the elements but also on the units into which the elements are bracketed.

This is not entirely a new idea. For example, the notion that tree notation is appropiate for the representation of behavior is widely held by ethologists. Tinbergen, in particular, has used trees in graphing the mating behavior of sticklebacks. Nor do all the examples of bracketing in nonverbal behavior derive from innate performances. To consider just one case from learned behavior, it has been recognized since Lashley that it is physiologically impossible that the performance of highly skilled, overlearned actions, like the typing of "the" by a proficient typist, can be viewed as the production of a behavior chain. In particular we cannot think of typing "the" as a matter of producing "h" as a response to proprioception from the production of "t" and producing "e" as a response to proprioception from the production of "h" (or "th"), if only because the speed with which such performances are typically executed does not allow for the conduction of the relevant proprioceptive stimuli. In some sense then, the choice of "the" must be represented as one choice, not three. That is, in the habit structure of the typist, "the" is bracketed as a unit.

What has not been noticed as widely as the need for bracketing in the description of nonverbal behavior is that the bracketing a piece of behavior receives tends to be preserved under all sorts of operations that can be performed upon that behavior. Thus, if you have a string of gestures *aabbcc* which, for one reason or another, you suppose must have the bracketed representation (viii) (e.g., because of inherent similarities between the gestures bracketed together or for any of indefinitely many other reasons), then it is a good bet that you will

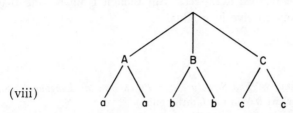

(viii)

find it easier to extinguish *aa* alone than to extinguish *ab* alone (i.e., the behavior *abcc* will be less easy to "shape" than the behavior *bbcc*); it is a good bet that the animal will be less likely to pause between units of the same type than between units of different types (e.g., pauses will be observed more frequently between *a* and *b* than between $a_1$ and $a_2$); it is a good bet that either retraining or, in the case of innate behavior, crossbreeding will produce *bbccaa* more readily than *aabbcc;* it is a good bet that if any of the behavior turns up as a displaced response elsewhere in the animal's repertoire, it will be *aa* or *a* or *bb* or *b* or *cc* or *c* but not *ab* or *bc* or *ac*. (For examples, see Bever and Weksel, forthcoming.)

But notice that the remarks in the preceding paragraph simply amount to saying that bracketing of behavior is preserved under psychological operations that satisfy such formal descriptions as deletion, adjunction, permutation, etc.; and saying this is equivalent to saying that the grammar that underlies the behavior is transformational.

In short, then, one way to think about the problem of homologies of behavior is to represent the behavioral repertoire of an animal as a language, of which the gestures the animal may be observed to make correspond to terminal elements. One can then ask whether the grammar that generates that language is formally similar in one or another respect to the grammar that generates a human language. It used to be assumed, in both psychology and linguistics, that such formal similarities do in fact obtain; for it was assumed that both behavior sequences in infrahumans and human languages could be described by Markov sources. We now know for sure that this is wrong for natural languages. The question arises whether it may not be wrong for nonverbal behaviors as well. I am betting that it will turn out, in the next decade or so, that in general the grammar that underlies behavior in animals will be transformational; i.e., that the case in which animal behavior really does consist of chains will prove rather exceptional and that normally, when we deal with operations on behavior, we are deal-ing with operations defined over trees. But though I am betting that way, I am not about to give long odds.

## REFERENCE

BEVER, T., and WEKSEL, W. *The Structure and Psychology of Language.* New York: Holt, Rinehart & Winston (forthcoming).

*David Premack and Arthur Schwartz*

# PREPARATIONS FOR DISCUSSING
# BEHAVIORISM WITH CHIMPANZEE

We find ourselves in the regrettable position of having undertaken a highly improbable experiment that we now have to justify. As everyone knows, the only competent way to justify such experiments is by the method of last laughs. Unfortunately, however, we are very far from succeeding or, for that matter, failing; in fact, we have only begun. Additionally distressing is the fact that we could easily provide a closely woven argument against the experiment, unlike the loose speculation we must now engage in in order to defend our position. All this suggests that we are irrational. While this is difficult to deny altogether, some assurance may be found in the knowledge that we arrived at this untenable position by an entirely respectable path, by a prior set of experiments nearly all of which are rational.

The principal reason for trying to teach apes to talk is to be able to do certain experiments that could not be done otherwise. Suppose there were no white rat — would not psychology have had to invent one? Analogously, the gauntlet of linguistic experiments we have in mind demands a language-competent species other than man; whether or not the species will have to be invented is what we propose to study.

We were not seduced by experimental prospects alone, however. An additional condition is the assumption that there are degrees of language competence. Thus, we do not propose to study whether infrahuman species can acquire human grammar. Instead, we contemplate the possibility of a continuum of linguistic competence, of psychologically weaker and stronger grammars, as it were. Between the lowly call system and human grammar, nature appears to have provided little or nothing. We hope to be able to synthesize intermediate cases in the laboratory.

## WEAKER GRAMMARS: CHILDREN AND FEEBLEMINDED

Two obvious places to seek grammars weaker than that of the human adult are aments and normal children. Frankly we were surprised by the amount of speech shown by feebleminded children (70 to 80 IQ range), not so surprised, however, as to accept unqualifiedly the conclusion that, down to IQ 50, the grammar of normals and aments do not differ (Lenneberg, forthcoming). For IQ's below 50, a group at which we have not yet looked, Lenneberg concedes differences. Normals and aments may yet prove to differ in such a way as to exemplify a scale of grammar-acquiring devices (GAD's). It would be surprising if they did not, to some degree at least, for the standard picture of feeblemindedness is that of an over-all deficit not merely one of intelligence, and it is difficult to see why the GAD should escape the deficiency.

The grammar of the normal child is a more certain topic than that of the ament, though it too is in the early stages of investigation. Enough has been done to establish that the child acquires adult grammar in stages, some of which have been tentatively characterized. The early stages are apparently nontransformational; phrase-structure rules alone will give an adequate account of the output (see McNeill, this volume, for a critical summary of this literature). It is less clear how many phrase-structure grammars the child is to be credited with, one comprehensive grammar whose parts are variously active at different times or one that is acquired piecemeal, e.g., the NP component preceding the VP, etc.; but there is development of one kind or another in any case. Then, too, the acquisition of the optional transformations is apparently piecemeal rather than wholesale. If each stage of child development was frozen, together the stages would form a crude scale of increasing grammatical complexity. A range of grammatical power might be pictured by a series of species, each of which had as its adult grammar the grammar of the human child at one of its stages of development.

## INTERMEDIATE LANGUAGES

For what must an organism show understanding before it can be considered language-competent? Is it sufficient if the organism responds appropriately to one kind of simple sentence, with the proviso that responding is not disrupted by new words or even combinations of new words? A monosyllabic language is unknown among natural cases, also apparently a language that is nontransformational, while a system limited to one sentence type may easily represent so severe a departure as to no longer qualify as language. But what exactly are the boundaries?

Intermediate possibilities are apparently unrepresented in nature. To appreciate how lacking they are, consider the (nonedible) accomplishments of the bee. Envision chimpanzees, for example, communicating bee information with ape machinery. The chimp is seen giving directions by pointing, indicating distance by the ancient handspan of the fisherman, and perhaps conveying amount and/or kind by some intensive property of stomping or screeching. These few gestures could handle the bee's message, if not improve upon it, for distance, quantity, and quality are evidently confounded by the bee. The bee's devices are remarkable, but once information is divorced from these devices, we may see how relatively meager the former is. The intermediate cases would be most interesting if they observed certain minimal requirements, one of which is kind and diversity of information communicated.

Rather than attempt to describe formally what we would accept as an absolutely minimal case of language, we will list some properties in the order of their centrality. We will list the properties without prejudice as to the underlying behavior mechanisms. It is distinctly possible that neither classical nor operant conditioning will provide an adequate account of the dispositions found in language behavior, but it is much less clear what kinds of dispositions will be required. Our list contains four properties, each of which can be easily subdivided, so there is nothing sacrosanct about the number. Nor are the properties intended to be exhaustive; that they assume a number of other properties will be self-evident.

We would require a concatenation of open classes as the weakest of the four properties. The more central properties could not be instanced by less than a sequence of responses. Also, the concatenation must be of classes, not responses, and classes must be defined functionally rather than physically. This is the weakest or most descriptive of the criteria: from the outside, language looks like a concatenation of open classes with fairly complex class definitions. Given behavior that fulfilled these properties, we would suspect language but would require further evidence.

Second, it should be possible to generate the behavior from a set of rules, though the ability to do so would not itself establish the validity of the rules (confirmation would require the usual fulfillment of predictions from the model). But this property alone is not sufficient. For example, there is some evidence that chimps can be taught to play ticktacktoe — behavior that can be generated by rules. But we would be disinclined to accept ticktacktoe, checkers, or any other such game as language; they would seem more nearly analogous to an uninterpreted system, a syntax without semantic content.

With the property of displacement we would close unqualifiedly on language. We must assert reference without simple stimulus control, reference to an outside world that is not at the same time the cause of the behavior of the reference. If every concatenation of classes, though in principle derivable from rules, were nonetheless subject to traditional stimulus control, there would seem little ground for setting language aside as other than a complex case. But it seems inexcusably promissory to insist that language is merely an instance of unusually complex conditioning when attempts to handle the facts of displacement with conditioning models are unacceptable in a number of ways. There is no suggestion, however, that displacement is dependent upon a particular kind of rule. Thus we can find nothing that links displacement to a transformational as opposed to a phrase-structure grammar.

A final property we would add is instruction. Organisms without language can be trained, but those with language can be instructed. We see instruction as presently resisting completely all attempts at stimulus-response explication. Several possible applications of instruction, of a theoretically interesting variety, have never been tried. These would include instructing an organism in a powerful language with the use of a weak (and more easily acquired) language that was in fact acquired in the usual inductive manner. The subject, having acquired the weak language, is then instructed: "These several sounds you have been using are phonemes; we will now add these additional phonemes, these transformational rules, etc." A question of interest is what the strength of the weak language must be in order to permit instruction in a stronger language.

If we can produce these properties in laboratory cases, we will have no hesitation in accepting the behavior as language. The weak criteria of a concatenation of open classes and description by rules would arouse our suspicion that language was present. But they are not sufficient. Displacement and instruction are, we believe, the indubitable symptoms; though it is no simple task to provide operational definitions for either, we assume that both are highly recognizable. Distressing is the distance between the weak and strong criteria, between the first two and last two properties. It would give strength to the notion of a continuum of language competence to be able to find some intermediate criteria. Perhaps they will be generated by the experiment, by the behaviors that arise.

## CONVENTIONALIZED CALL SYSTEM

The major alternatives we considered among intermediate laboratory cases ranged from what might be called an arbitrary call system to a reduced human grammar. A call system not natural to the species but acquired on the basis of learning would at least duplicate the conventional character of human language; the system would be operant rather than reflexive as in the natural call system. Such a system might duplicate the essential properties of the child's holophrastic (McCarthy, 1954) phase, i.e., use of individual words as sentences. If the animal went about as the child does, labeling the items in its environment that incite its curiosity as well as calling out for certain of them, and this with acquired rather than reflexive sounds, it would be a hopeful first step. But the approach would have a low ceiling, and then limited versions of such essentially holophrastic systems have already been reported (Hayes, 1951). That is, nonconcatenative (single response) labeling and requesting of items in the environment have been reported in infrahumans.

Of greater interest are the possibilities of concatenation. The child of course advances from a holophrastic or single-word stage to the concatenation of words and therewith to syntax. Is concatenation found in natural call systems? If there is a tendency to say no, it is not warranted by the data. Furthermore, the question of concatenation is not properly limited to the call system. Since the call system is but a part of animal social or communicative behavior, a small part in the chimpanzee (Nissen, 1951), we do better first to define social behavior and then look for concatenation in that broader domain.

Unfortunately, field studies rarely provide sequential data, and only recently has such data begun to appear in even limited form (Altmann, 1965). Even without the data, however, it seems all but certain that substantial sequential dependencies will be found throughout primate social behavior. Consider the rather weak properties to which concatenation can be reduced: (1) responses of the same kind are not evenly or randomly distributed in time but occur in groups or bursts, and/or (2) occurrence of responses of one kind are not independent of occurrence of responses of a different kind. With this operational definition, concatenation is certain to be found throughout mammalian or even vertebrate behavior. In caged rats, we find third- and fourth-order dependencies between different response classes, not in social behavior where it might be considered less striking but even in *ad libitum* eating, drinking, and running (Kintsch and Premack, 1965). Thus the establishment of concatenation in natural social behavior or even in an acquired call system could do little more than bring these behaviors into line with nonsocial behaviors, indicating that both are subject to similar controls.

More interesting of course would be the finding that dependencies could not be accounted for by a finite state device. But this seems quite improbable, for the output of even the child can probably be accounted for by such a device. That is, we could hardly expect an infrahuman subject, advancing from a single-word holophrastic stage to the possible emission of short strings, to exhibit dependencies of a kind found only in the adult human (or child with adult grammar). Quite probably, a simple concatenative stage may represent the terminal possibility for the infrahuman.

In addition, the artificial call system we envisioned would have built from a "morphemic" base — each sound was to have been a "word" — a unit not subject to further subdivision. We decided instead to attempt a phonemic language. All questions concerning holophrastic stage, development of concatenation, nature of sequential dependencies are thus retained, but added to them are questions contingent upon the attempt to give the language a phonemic base.

It is of interest to speculate briefly as to factors that could lead from a call system to phonemic language. Hockett and Ascher (1964) have proposed one possible course of development. They envision a protohominoid with a call system including the usual undifferentiated cries, among others one for food and another for danger. A situation arises presenting equally potent stimuli for both cries, with the result a composite cry combining, say, the initial portion of the food cry with the terminal portion of the danger cry. Should such blends, as Hockett and Ascher call them, occur in number, cries could no longer be discriminated as wholes, i.e., recognized by attending indiscriminately to any part of the cry. Rather, it would become necessary to process a cry, part by part; given cries with like initial parts, it would be necessary to consider that fact and thus suspend judgment until a match could be made with the terminal portion of the cry. The necessity to process cries segment by segment, brought on by overlap between the different cries, would open the way for the development of a phonemic system. This much of the Hockett-Ascher development is plausible, but they overlook the fact that cries in a call system are reflexive, elicited by events in the external world. Phonemes, in contrast, are not subject to such stimulus control, and indeed not even the lowly babbling, let alone the subsequent speech sounds, are subject to unconditional environmental elicitation as in the reflex. Hockett and Ascher must therefore additionally devise a means whereby reflexive behavior becomes nonreflexive. A neurological problem confronts their argument, too, probably the counterpart of their behavioral difficulty; viz., the brain part mediating the call system — vestiges of which are said to be found in man — is considered to be functionally and structurally independent of the cortical speech centers (Magoun, 1958). Thus, the assumption that speech did not evolve out of the call system is apparently more compatible with the psychological and neurological evidence than the opposite assumption made by Hockett and Ascher. This of course contributes little to the question of how the phoneme did evolve.[1]

What are the advantages of a phonemic approach? In a "small" world, one with few items, limited relations, and a low rate of change, advantages might be slight. But in a "large" world, demanding many different sounds, the advantages would be great. It is doubtful, to begin with, whether any organism could produce a sufficient number of non-overlapping gestures, vocal or otherwise, to cope with a "large" world. The phoneme circumvents this first-order problem by the large number of combinations that even a small set of elements affords. Second, there

---

[1] The notion of a "call system" is itself suspect; the concept of a set of indivisible cries elicited by configurations such as food, mate, danger is a construction upon inadequate evidence and, we think, unlikely to survive. That the cries are indivisible rather than combinations of more elemental units is not a conclusion based on extensive attempts to discover elemental units. Further, the cries that our caged animals make appear to depend upon intensity of stimulus no less than upon kind; different stimuli of equal intensity may prove to produce the same cry.

is an advantage to reception. Phonemes permit a more economical decoding system than that of a simple list (which undifferentiated cries would necessitate). Items that fail to match the template on the first phoneme could be eliminated, and only the remainder, items that do match on at least the first phoneme, need be retained and searched for a match on the second phoneme, etc. Where phonemes consist of binary properties, recognition could proceed by a series of binary decisions. The average number of steps required to locate an item in a hierarchical structure is always less than for an equal number of items in a nonhierarchical structure. Phonemes permit a hierarchical structure.

## CHIMPANZEE EXPERIMENT

We chose infant chimpanzees as subjects, far less for their cognitive riches than for their temperamental resemblance to man. In emotion and curiosity they recall human children. In the extreme degree to which they adopt a human as a mother surrogate, we see these similarities as being most deeply confirmed. Nevertheless, it will surely not be possible to persuade anyone who has not had direct experience of both child and chimp of how much one organism recalls the other; we will therefore simply recommend the experience and spare the rhapsodics. However, it should not be considered that we count the temperamental factor lightly with regard to language. On the contrary, those characteristics of speech that are frequently cited as confounding an S-R learning account seem to arise as much from temperamental as from cognitive factors. Consider displacement, the characteristic that distinguishes human speech from any call system; it would seem to be a property of play no less than of speech where, too, there is minimal local control, a relative independence of external events and deprivation states. Lacking a theory of play, we can do no more than recommend that speech may have its roots in play. In any case, we felt vindicated in the choice of the chimpanzee by recent field studies emphasizing chimp curiosity (Goodall, 1963) in contrast to the relative absence of this disposition in the gorilla (Schaller, 1963). Extreme degrees of play and curiosity may be more characteristic of man and chimp than of primates in general.

Though qualified for speech by temperament, the chimp is apparently lacking in a suitable speech apparatus (e.g., Keleman, 1948).

Moreover, it is a poor imitator of human sounds. Previous attempts to train the chimp to imitate speech sounds have failed resoundingly, and we have not meanwhile devised a superior method. But our concern is neither imitation nor even phonology. We would accept any device that would open the question of language competence in the chimp, without regard for its similarity to man's speech apparatus. If only devices sufficiently parallel to that of man will work, we would have ample reason for attempting to arrange a parallel, but we are not interested in isomorphism as such.

Given that the chimp is unable to produce human sounds, ought we not to accommodate him by producing his sounds? A spectographic analysis of the chimp's call system might reveal features that would be useful in selecting distinctive features for an artificial system. The chimp might have special propensities for the auditory properties of its call system (though if there is any distinctiveness here it may be quite as acquired as are man's for the phonemes of his language). (Liberman *et al.*, 1962.) However, inasmuch as the call system is presumably nonphonemic, it will not provide a set of elemental differences. The only differences for which augmented discriminability would be likely are those between one call and another; and it is hardly clear how to use differences of this kind in an artificial system. Moreover, it needs to be kept in mind that the cries themselves could not be used. They are already unconditionally attached to events in the environment — food, mate, danger, etc. — and thus could not be reassigned according to convention. The human imitation of chimp calls could be used for one purpose — to determine whether humans can participate in chimp social behavior, whether the chimp will accept the human as a member of its social system. Many chimp sounds are not difficult to produce, consisting of clicks, grunts, lip smacks, and buzzes, and we have several times informally checked the infant chimp's response to our imitations. The results generally confirm that the chimp will admit man into its social organization, but they illuminate the question of language so little we have not seen much point in making the experiments formal.

We might circumvent altogether the chimp's production of sounds by restricting our inquiry to comprehension. It has been suggested that production is not necessary for comprehension (Lenneberg, 1962), and comprehension has been shown to precede production in normal development (Brown and Bellugi, 1964). Moreover, there is already work of this kind in the Hayes experiment; the chimp was shown to be further advanced in comprehension than production, though the magnitude of the disparity — greater than that found in the child — was almost certainly due to the animal's difficulties in producing human speech sounds. Unfortunately the Hayes work, having been done some time ago, does not examine comprehension for grammatical distinctions in the degree we would prefer today.

Aside from wishing to study production, we have two further reasons for not restricting the study to comprehension (though of course it would be studied along with any study of production). First, though overt production may not be a necessary condition for comprehension, it may be conducive to it. Furthermore, in the case reported by Lenneberg (1962), we do not know at what point "up the line" production was blocked. If the failure was relatively peripheral, it may be that all the events in the productive sequence prior to the emission of the actual sounds are in fact necessary conditions for language-learning. Second, should comprehension be studied with respect to a natural language with its unlimited and unknown demands upon learning capacity or to an artificial language with its more nearly modifiable demands? The use of natural language would of course benefit the experimenter: he would not have to learn a new artificial language to perform the comprehension experiment but could expose the infrahuman infant to the same verbal environment as the child; he might even attempt to introduce didactic contrasts in the training sample. But it is difficult to believe that natural language would provide the simplest rule-instancing environment to which the infrahuman could be exposed and for which comprehension could be tested. Worlds far simpler than that which underlies natural language can be envisioned, and it would be for the artificial languages of such simplified worlds that comprehension (no less than production) should first be tested.

## ARTIFICIAL LANGUAGE

Because we rule out both a natural language on the grounds of its nonoptimizing complexity and the chimp's natural sounds for the reasons given, we have no alternative but to devise an artificial system. Are there deep reasons for insisting upon an auditory language? Not enough is known about auditory as opposed to visual information-processing to recommend sound unqualifiedly as the physical basis of the language. Certain properties of human language, e.g., syllabification, clearly reflect and exploit its auditory composition, but it is not clear that a language could not be designed for the visual case that would equally exploit the unique features of vision. Fusion, which is discussed later on, seems to be uniquely realizable with acoustic as opposed to visual events, but this impression may simply reflect training. Fusion needs to be considered on the productive side, too, and here perhaps the coarticulation of the vocal apparatus may offer possibilities superior to any that the hands might afford which, as may be seen, would be the productive system in the case of visual representation. That is, it is necessary to consider not only how written language might undergo a fusion comparable to the spoken syllable but also how our natural system for producing visual events would produce the fusion (or perhaps more important, what the salience of the neural feedback would be from synchronous manual events). It has been suggested that vision and audition have separate memory stores (Penfield and Roberts, 1959) and also that short-term auditory storage is longer than visual (Sperling, 1963), though perhaps only because of the unique possibilities of rehearsal with auditory material (provided it is pronounceable). Still if the visual events were suitably simplified, they too might be made "pronounceable," i.e., rehearsable, e.g., by being "drawn" in the air (A. Premack, personal communication). Perhaps there are not overriding reasons for insisting that language be auditory, but the one we have devised is, though for quite simple reasons.

First, it is easier to catch the animal's attention with acoustic rather than visual signals, and second, to the extent that the characteristics of human phonology are understood, we may benefit by attempting to simulate them (though given the controversy concerning the perceptual basis of human speech, we have several times wished we had tried stone-rolling where, no matter what we had done, it could not have been judged improper by one theory or another). In brief, we have provided the infant chimps with an artificial motor and auditory system, as a means of surmounting the production problem while still keeping the language auditory. The motor system has the advantage of engaging the animal's interest; the spontaneous manipulation in the infant chimp, upon which the system is based, might even be likened to babbling in the human infant. The behavior is free of local control, develops by maturation rather than reinforcement, and in both species is the subsequent basis of important adult behaviors.

## ATTEMPTED SIMULATION OF DISTINCTIVE FEATURES

The chimp's own vocal system is unsuitable on two grounds: the sounds it does produce are linked to the outside world by evolution rather than training, and the human sounds that we would like it to produce it cannot produce, or only most inadequately. Figure 1 pre-

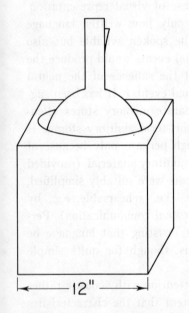

FIG. 1. The "joystick." The lever is easily displaced from its central rest position to tilt up to 40° from the vertical in any direction.

sents a picture of the apparatus that we have offered the chimp as a substitute for its own vocal apparatus. The large size of the apparatus represents an attempt to attract the young chimp's attention; if and when learning proceeds sufficiently, the apparatus will be changed from a (very sturdy) toy to a miniaturized device that will have advantages in both portability and speed of operation. Plans call for the adult chimp to wear the miniaturized device attached to either its waist or wrist.

The apparatus is essentially a joystick. The stick, shown in the vertical position in the illustration, can be swiveled in all directions and tilted to a maximum of 40 degrees. Attached to the side of the stick is a small pressure gauge that registers the strength of the grip on the stick. Actually the stick does not swivel independently of its base, like the standard joystick, but rather stick and plastic hemisphere in which the stick is mounted swivel together as a single unit. Building the stick and base in a solid unit and swiveling them together prevent the chimp from reaching into the space that would otherwise develop between the stick and base as the stick is moved.

An auditory circuit is connected to the stick, so that different positions of the stick result in different sounds. Both the stick as a motor system and the associated auditory system are an attempt to instance Jakobson's (1961) distinctive features model. (After building the device we found a geometric representation of Jakobson's model by Cherry [1956], of which our apparatus is a nearly perfect mechanical translation.) Any displacement of the stick can be described in terms of five different motor dimensions. These are *pressure* on the stick, *tilt* (the angle the stick makes with the horizontal), *displacement* in the east-west plane, *displacement* in the north-south plane, and the *duration* the stick is displaced from resting position. The advantages of this system may be appreciated by comparing it with any of a number of possible "button" or successive devices. If there were one or more buttons per dimension and an output required a value from each dimension, the buttons would have to be operated successively, a sequence of choices at the risk of memory. This apparatus registers simultaneously on all dimensions, overcoming the memory problem of successive choices.[2]

With each of the five motor dimensions is associated an auditory dimension, in one case according to the correlations shown in Table 1 (how best to correlate the motor and auditory features is at present an experimental question). The motor dimensions are continuous in principle, while some of the auditory dimensions are continuous (duration) and others are discrete (noise). The auditory outputs associated with the motor dimensions are of varying degrees of discreteness, but these differences are nonessential (in the present apparatus), having been dictated more by funds than theory. To appreciate how the system operates, consider the motor-sound correlations depicted in Table 1.

The 40 degrees of tilt of which the stick is capable is divided into four equal bands with each of which is associated one of four *tones*,

[2] We are indebted to Anne Premack for originally suggesting the joystick application and to J. Snell and M. Hulse (University of Missouri, Science Instrument Shops) for design and construction.

*TABLE 1    Motor-Sound Correlations*

| Auditory | Motor |
|---|---|
| 1. frequency | tilt |
| 2. amplitude | pressure |
| 3. friction | east vs. west |
| 4. steadiness (vibrato) | north vs. south |
| 5. duration | hold in position |

the highest being produced by the first 10 degrees of tilt (from resting position) and the lowest by the last 10 degrees. *Friction* (a white noise overlaying the tone) is present in only 2 degrees, either present or absent, and is correlated with displacement in the north-south plane. *Vibrato* (a pulsing of the tone), like friction, is either present or absent and is correlated with displacement in the east-west plane. *Amplitude* is correlated with the squeeze button on the stick; loudness of any sound increases, in three steps, the harder the stick is gripped. Finally, *duration* of the sound is correlated with duration the stick is displaced from resting position.

With the present pilot equipment, any grip sufficient to operate the pressure gauge for a minimum of .025 sec will result in a sound, the particular nature of which is determined by the position of the stick. In Figure 2, the motor and auditory space has been depicted in terms

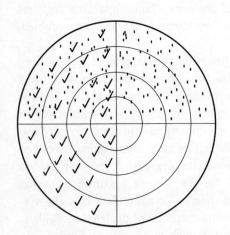

Fig. 2. The "auditory space." Three dimensions are shown: specks represent noise, checks represent vibrato, and each concentric band represents a tone.

of four concentric circles. Each band represents 10 degrees of tilt; when the stick is held anywhere within the innermost band, it will produce the highest of the four tones; anywhere within the next band, the same note an octave lower; and so on to the fourth band, where the tone produced is the lowest of the four. Now picture the entire circle to be bisected both vertically and horizontally. From the point of view of the user, all stick positions in the upper half of the circle will be noisy; i.e., tones will be accompanied by friction or white noise, while all those in the lower half of the circle will be clear. In a like manner, from a user's point of view all stick positions to left of center will be vibrato (i.e., tones will pulse), while all those to right of center will be steady. Furthermore, now combining vertical and horizontal sections, the user will find the upper left quadrant noisy and pulsing, the lower right quadrant clear and steady, etc. Not represented in the figure are the last two features — amplitude and duration. But they may be easily included by the kinds of instructions that would have to be given to the stick in order to select a sound.

For example, to produce a low-loud-pulsing-noisy sound, grip the stick hard and push it to the upper left quadrant about as far as it will go. In contrast, to produce a high-soft-steady-pure sound, grip the stick lightly and move it slightly to the lower right quadrant. "Lightly," "hard," "about as far as it will go" — this kind of approximation is quite sufficient for the operating commands and is, as such, an encouraging evaluation of the system as opposed to one that required more precise commands. The present system will accept crude commands because, first, the phonemic code recognizes only two relativistic degrees of any dimension, and second, the motor and auditory systems are related by sectors not by points. For example, holding the stick anywhere within zero to 10 degrees of tilt will produce the lowest tone, while merely holding it above center will add noise to the output, etc. Thus the stick need not be maintained at a point for the minimum .025 duration in order to obtain an output, but anywhere within broadly defined zones.

The tones are produced by Baldwin electronic organ tone generators, which deliver a square wave to the speaker made up of the fundamental frequency and many odd harmonics. Friction is produced by a Zener diode and is nearly white noise. Vibrato is produced by shifting the fundamental frequency of the tone up and back to base at a rate that is adjustable for discriminability. Amplitude is adjusted for discriminability from a maximum possible output of 10 watts to a minimum of approximately 8 milliwatts. Schmidtt triggers are used to key the different values of each dimension.

As there are five dimensions — frequency, amplitude, noise, vibrato, duration — if each is dealt with in terms of two values, the system will permit thirty-two phonemes. Of these we plan to use only fourteen in the simplified language; we have overprovided deliberately, for a reason that will be made clear when we discuss the training procedure. As much for the experimenter's benefit — who after all must learn the language so as to be able to model it — as for the subject's, we have arrived at the fourteen phonemes by reducing the English system as follows (where our ranking of sounds tends to agree with that of French, Carter, and Koenig [1929] and more recently Denes [1963], even after the reduction):

| p, b, | → "p" | | l, r | → "r" |
|---|---|---|---|---|
| t, d, č, ǰ | → "t" | | u, w | → "u" |
| k, g, | → "k" | | i, j | → "i" |
| f, v | → "f" | | æ, a | → "a" |
| s, š, z, ž | → "s" | | ε | → "ε" |
| θ, ð | → "θ" | | ə | → "ə" |
| n, ŋ, m | → "n" | | ɔ | → "ɔ" |

Our matrix (including redundancies) is thus:

|  | p | t | k | f | θ | s | n | r | u | i | ε | a | ə | ɔ |
|---|---|---|---|---|---|---|---|---|---|---|---|---|---|---|
| Frequency | − | − | − | − | − | − | − | + | + | + | + | + | + | + |
| Friction | + | + | + | + | + | + | + | + | − | − | − | − | − | − |
| Amplitude | + | − | + | + | − | − | − | − | − | − | + | − | + | − |
| Steadiness | + | + | + | − | − | − | + | − | − | − | + | + | − | + |
| Duration | + | − | − | + | + | − | + | − | + | − | + | + | − | − |

## EVALUATION OF SYSTEM

We should emphasize that the entire system is exploratory, a first model, and just beginning to undergo evaluation. That is, prior to using the device as a would-be phonological instrument, there are a number of properties that require evaluation; in this section we will mention some of them and the points of interest to which they give rise.

Although the present choice of auditory dimensions was guided largely by practical considerations, they are not an unrealistic starting point. Their discriminability for a chimp will be evaluated by appropriately modified psychophysical techniques. Two points of interest arise in this otherwise routine evaluation. First, an attempt will be made to predict the confusion matrix for paired comparisons of the intended fourteen phonemes on the basis of their distinctive features (see Miller and Nicely, 1955). The simplest application of the distinctive feature model to perception would require an additivity assumption: discrimination should be proportional to the number of different features that obtain between pairs of phonemes. We will be interested to see how well the data are predicted by this simple assumption. Second, natural language data strongly suggest that phonemic differences acquire exceptional distinctiveness (Liberman et al., 1957). The course of this development cannot be easily studied in man, however, for to separate maturation from learning would require rearing infants without exposure to language. But this control is an easy one with infrahumans, and thus we intend to compare the discriminability of the fourteen to-be phonemic sounds when they are simply sounds and after they have been introduced as the basis of language.

Are human language sounds uniquely discriminable as some suggest (e.g., House, Stevens, et al., 1962), not to be approached psychophysically, or can their function be approximated or even improved upon by artificial sounds? Whatever the answer to this question, we suggest that the evidence so far offered does not justify the uniqueness judgment. For example, House et al. discount the possibility of a "speechiness" dimension on the grounds that machine-generated sounds were not discriminated in proportion to their resemblance to speech sounds. Rather, while the sounds most resembling speech were best discriminated, those least resembling speech were next best discriminated. But does this support the interpretation offered? An experiment of the same kind but more revealing for interpretation was recently reported by Suppes et al. (1962). Working with native American speakers, they found Russian phonemes that most resembled English phonemes to be best discriminated but those that least resembled English to be next best discriminated.

Rather than necessarily establishing anything about the uniqueness of natural language sounds, both experiments suggest that a new code can be learned best when most like an already learned one but that intermediate degrees of similarity lead to confusion, so much so that the new code is learned better if it does not resemble the old one at all. This same conclusion may possibly be reached without any recourse to natural language sounds. Suppose we use artificial codes, one well learned, the others resembling the established one in varying degrees;

will the results differ? Gratuitously attributing special properties to speech sounds will, of course, block experimentation of the present kind even before it properly begins.

It has been suggested that our assumption of spatial "dimensions" is unwarranted (I. Hirsh, personal communication). The fourteen intended phonemes may simply represent for the animal fourteen points on a nearly homogeneous surface, i.e., fourteen values of one dimension rather than combinations of the five binary motor dimensions we have in mind. Because we have no evidence that chimps use our geometry — up/down, left/right, tilt, etc. — and worse, cannot readily show experiments that would either elucidate their geometry or assure that they had acquired ours, we are now following the suggestion and attempting to arrange more direct motor correlates of the auditory features by associating different qualities of movement with different sounds. For example, the stick, on being moved to left of center (and thereby producing vibrato), pulsates with the vibrato but moves unpulsingly to right of center, where the accompanying tones are steady. This only partly solved problem raises two others, where evaluation has only begun and changes are certain.

Our redundancy is too low, as may be seen by counting the number of features by which our phonemes differ (an average of three features per phoneme pair), and we intend to add further auditory dimensions without increasing phonemes. Next, we have no evidence concerning the ability of our system to withstand distortion; in a laboratory we need not anticipate the extreme conditions that natural language has been shown to tolerate (Miller, 1956), but we will need some resistance to distortion. Finally, we have no idea as to possible isomorphisms between motor and auditory correlations. To us pitch "feels better" with tilt than with squeeze, but even on a matter as relatively simple as this one we have no evidence. Even more important, the chimp has not yet indicated to us his "natural" pairings. It may been seen that the apparatus is dogged by more than a few low-level questions.

## FUSED SPEECH

We have placed the present problem in a category of its own for, although it is merely technical, we think it bears rather basically upon the success of the project. The problem is this: in the form just described, the joystick is capable of what amounts to spelling but not of fused speech. The stick will emit one phoneme after the other rather than fuse phonemes to produce syllables (and syllables to produce words) as in normal speech. How much of a disadvantage this represents is worth studying in its own right, but to do so we must first solve the fusion problem. Not until we can produce fused "speech" can we compare it with the spelled variety.

Fusion in natural language depends upon coarticulation, upon synchronization of several articulatory mechanisms. Thus the fused character of a CV syllable is achieved through the influence of the vowel-producing articulators upon the articulators determining the consonant. The details of the fusion, worked out by the Haskins group (Liberman *et al.*, 1962), show the consonant to affect perception of the vowel in a specific manner, viz., by changing the transition frequency of the second formant. Of interest is the fact that, although in the written representation of CV, V follows C, in the spoken syllable V affects the initial part of the syllable, making it clear that the spoken order is not left to right but that, as it were, V has been decided upon either before or simultaneous with the emission of C. The fusion is therefore at the level of the "instructions" to the articulatory mechanism and simply reflected on both the motor and auditory sides.

The details of syllabic fusion in the natural case suggest two possible means of introducing fusion into the present system. To begin with it is clear why fusion does not exist in our system; there is only one articulator, the stick itself. One solution therefore might consist of adding an articulator (Liberman, personal communication). If there were one stick for vowel sounds and another for consonants, it seems likely that synchronizations between them could be worked out that would tend to fuse their sounds in the manner of a syllable. Perhaps the substance of this proposal could be incorporated in a device that would minimize the additional problems raised by two sticks; certainly the use of two sticks would deepen the appreciation for the simultaneous-stick system as opposed to the successive-button approach. Nevertheless, the synchronous operation of two sticks is clearly more demanding than anything posed by one stick, though by what factor is unknown; the animal's capacity for such tasks is yet another research problem.

One stratagem, whose fascination we do not allow to be degraded by uncertainty, is to train a naïve animal on a "weak" language with a single articulator and spelled output, and then transfer it by instruction in the weak language to the more complex motor case, two articulators and fused output. We are attracted by this alternative because the motor complexity of coarticulation would then descend upon a sophisticated animal, not a naïve one. Admittedly, man does not proceed in this fashion; the child coarticulates before he opens his mouth grammatically. But we are not trying to simulate man so much as devise a training program for nonman; for this creature, the training program might be advised to begin with single articulation and spelled output and withhold coarticulation and fusion for a later stage.

A second alternative would bring fusion into our system without adding articulators, though necessarily at some cost, this time in delay of feedback rather than motor complexity. In a word, syllabic fusion is normally produced by synchronous movements of two articulators; it could also be produced by successive movements of one articulator. That is, we could require two movements of the stick to produce one sound, a sound that would be a fusion of the two individual sounds associated with the two movements of the stick. The disadvantage is a delay in feedback between the sound and all motor gestures other than the last gesture in the series. Though the delay is inescapable, we do not think that it need be critical, particularly not for an animal that is trained with delay of feedback from the outset. Moreover, the disruptive effect of delay, which is initially so marked for the human, is overcome with sufficient training in most cases (Goldiamond *et al.*, 1962). There is even evidence that the initial disruption may be a transient; King and Wolf (1965) found that human subjects, given delay of feedback in free recall, fail on immediate recall but show surprisingly little deficit when tested later for retention.

To see how fusion might be arranged in our system without co-articulation, consider the fourteen intended phonemes to be divided into, say, six vowels and eight consonants. Picture the stick positions for the six vowels and eight consonants to be distributed over the motor hemisphere as shown in Figure 3. The eight consonants are located along the periphery of the motor space with duplicate sets on both sides, and the six vowels are aligned vertically along the center. This motor distribution is designed to accommodate the restriction of all words in the language to a CVC form. Now all words will have essentially the same motor shape: the stick will describe an arc starting with the selection of a consonant, pausing in the middle for the vowel, and ending with selection of the terminal consonant.

Each word will consist of two separate though closely spaced sounds, viz., CV and VC. CV will be produced by first selecting from the periphery of the motor space one of the eight consonants and then directing the stick toward the center for selection of the vowel. VC,

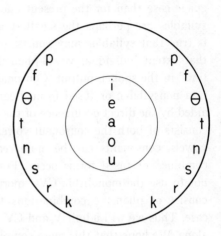

Fig. 3. Redistribution of phonemes. This possible re-
arrangement of the sound
units is intended to ac-
commodate the "fused
syllable" of CVC struc-
ture.

which will complete the word, will be produced in a comparable though simpler manner: the vowel will carry over from CV, so that the production of VC will require only one move, selection of the terminal C. For a right-handed ape, the motor pattern of all words could thus consist of a movement of the stick from left to right, with the angle from side to center determined by the anticipated choice of vowel.

Fusion will take place as follows: selection of the initial C will not be accompanied by sound, rather sound will not occur until V is also chosen, and at that time the sound that occurs will be a fusion of C and V. The fused or syllabic sound can be simultaneous with the choice of V, but there will be an inevitable delay between the choice of C and the occurrence of sound. In the production of VC and the completion of the word, fusion will take place comparably, except without delay of feedback. Because the vowel will carry over from the first syllable, only one gesture will be needed to complete the word, and sound can be concurrent with this gesture.

It is interesting to observe that with this system the individual phonemes will never occur but will exist as elements in the memory of a tape or computer, which will cause them to be combined syllabically and thus emitted as a fused sound upon the proper selection of C and

V or V and C. The phonemes can be easily stored on tape — that is merely a technical problem. The question of interest is: Will the individual phonemes get stored in the chimp's head? It should be observed that this intriguing question is no less germane for the natural language case than for the present one where, too, so far as we can see, syllables are perhaps the smallest acoustic units that are spoken. It is true that syllables may consist of individual vowels alone, and to that extent individual vowel-phonemes may have "direct representation" in the spoken output. Consonants, however, typically occur only in a nonsyllabic or fused form. Learning of the consonants should be aided by the direct occurrence of the vowels. Presumably, where output consists of both the consonant-vowel combinations and the individual vowels, consonants can be more readily abstracted than if only the combined or fused forms occur. For this reason and others, we plan not to use the monolithic CVC morpheme rule but to allow words to consist of phoneme combinations that are syllables in the natural case. Thus we will admit V and CV sequences as words, and not CVC alone. We hope that this more complex segmentation rule will be compensated by the greater number of words for which it provides as well as the increased access to individual phonemes. Indeed we might accept individual consonants, too, as free forms, and thus give the animal direct access to all individual phonemes and to all their fused combinations. Although this extension may complicate segmentation-learning, it has not been ruled out as a possibility, and we are planning to research the topic along with the general evaluation of the auditory system.

Although phonemes will have no simple acoustic reality, syllables can be decoded back to phonemic constituents on the basis of common elements of both an acoustic and motor nature. Thus all syllables containing the same initial consonant but varying in the vowel will share acoustic and motor properties, even as will all syllables consisting of the same vowel but differing in the consonant. An overt syllabary based however upon phonemic constituents need not lead to the storage of syllables — as the ultimate unit of memory — any more than the fact that man talks in words has led to the storage of words as the ultimate unit of memory. The animal will have to arrive at the phonemes by the same process of abstraction as does man presumably, although it is our point that his opportunities for abstraction in the present system are no less than those in natural language. But can we not augment the opportunities? Since it is not our intent to simulate the natural case, could we not include in the training program something that would lighten the burden of abstraction? Perhaps the actual taped phonemes could simply be played to the animal at selected intervals, along with pictures of the moving joystick, so as to establish the motor-acoustic correlations. We are not sanguine about the contribution this would make, but then we do not know. Indeed, is there a known method for potentiating abstractions?

## FUSION OF WHAT?

What is to be fused and how? Whether we attempt to produce syllables with successive movements of one stick or synchronous movements of two, there are likely to be important constraints on the kinds of acoustic events that will fuse as well as critical temporal parameters. Because in the natural CV case the syllabic effect involves a formant change, one may ask whether fusion and formant are intimately related in the sense that no other acoustic properties will subserve the effect equally well. On the other hand, the formant change may be perceptually irrelevant, a fortuitous by-product of the coarticulation that underlies the fusion. Recent emphasis on motor theories of speech perception (Liberman *et al.*, 1962) might lead one in this direction, suggesting that we may do better to direct the question to the motor properties of the stick rather than to the acoustic correlates.

A similar question can be directed at the vowel-consonant distinction, apparently a universal distinction (Greenberg, 1962), and one that evidently plays a basic role in syllable formation. How shall we incorporate this distinction? We have made all consonants noisy, all vowels clear; but this obviously weak parallel could be strengthened. At present we are resisting wholesale changes in the auditory system until we have settled the matter of fusion. How and what we decide to fuse will force decisions on lesser issues. In the meantime we cannot but be encouraged by the recent demonstration that the acquired distinctiveness of cues, which is so potent in speech sounds, can be produced experimentally in a nonlanguage context (Cross *et al.*, 1965). Claims for the uniqueness of discriminative processes for speech continua may increasingly prove to be gratuitous, though we will be most relieved when fusion is achieved with artificial sounds.

Our high interest in fusion arises from the fact that the efficiency of a system apparently depends critically on how integrated and integratable are the stimuli of the system. There appear to be optimal rates of stimulus presentation, so that confusion can result when signals are either too slow or too fast. The kind of chunking (Miller, 1956) that the word and syllable represent, involving actual physical change of individual phonemes as we have seen, would appear to be of a higher order than the grouping that might occur by the temporal proximity of items alone. A contrast of this kind is found in written and spoken language. Graphemes do not fuse, i.e., written letters may vary depending upon their context, so that we may speak of allographs (e.g., the terminal r or t, etc.), but there is no written counterpart to the spoken syllable. Still, chunking is known to occur in the visual case; e.g., perception is retarded by presenting the word as too slow a succession of letters (Gibson, 1965). But since integration in the visual case is not subserved by any syllabic device, it must arise either by (1) simple temporal succession and/or (2) leaning heavily upon the underlying auditory code (see Conrad, 1964). The latter is also supported by the fact that the integration of visual letters is apparently best for nonsense material that is pronounceable. How much integration would arise in a visual system that did not have a typical auditory code to lean upon, or in a nonsyllabic auditory system, is difficult to estimate. Not only are questions of chunking or integration of high interest, but an artificial language would seem to be ideal for their investigation provided, that is, that we can manage to produce both fused and spelled output.

## Comparison with Reading Machines

Inevitably, comparisons will arise between the present system and the several versions of reading machines for the blind (see Nye, 1964). Because these devices have so far proved to be less than heartening successes, their failings would seem to reflect adversely on our system. Their slow rate of reception, approximately 60 words per minute compared to 150 to 200 wpm for natural speech, has been their great deficiency. One basic difference between our system and these prosthetics needs to be observed, however. In our language-user, we have the natural condition of a speaker-hearer. The language has thus a motor base, with the advantage to perception this is likely to provide (cf. Liberman *et al.*, 1962). In contrast, a typical reading machine is a scanner-converter device: visual input to auditory output. In this respect our system is fundamentally closer to the natural arrangement. (We make no claim that reading machines for the blind could be improved by making greater motor demands on the user, but it would certainly seem strategic in the light of the Haskins work to so engage the reader.) In another respect we turn away from the natural case by not insisting that our sounds be speechlike. But here we feel that recent work (e.g., House *et al.*, 1962; Suppes *et al.*, 1962) counsels switching into a different auditory system entirely. That is, either the sounds should be completely speechlike or should not resemble speech at all; intermediate cases apparently lead to confusion rather than positive transfer. Thus on two counts, as a motor base providing the neural mediation of a new auditory system, we consider our system to be more promising than cursory comparison with reading devices would suggest.[3]

## TRAINING PROCEDURE

We defer to the last the great problem of what language to teach the chimp and here delay briefly to say a few words about how the animal should be trained, in the course of which we describe an experiment that may shed some light on babbling. Children today acquire language in a manner that is unlikely to have changed since Moses induced Hebrew (from those speech sounds that commingled with the lapping of the waves). Is tutelage necessary or helpful, and if so, what kind? No one knows. Nor do we see much sense in accepting the fictional reconstruction that attributes the entire process to differential reinforcement. Indeed, as things stand we see no recourse but to simulate the natural case, the mother-child relation. Though it is not known what in this relationship is critical, the relationship nonetheless now comprehends the only known "method" for language acquisition.

In attempting to simulate the natural case, we will simply aim at three gross factors: (1) development of affectional relation between infant and mother surrogate, (2) provision of a curiosity-inducing world sufficient to provoke labeling, and (3) massive exposure to

---

[3] The history of reading devices for the blind suggests a leap from poor artificial codes to simulation of natural sounds. Our system may be seen as the neglected middle: an improved artificial code.

samples of the language (though here we are prepared to try a major departure from the natural case and in one instance make the massive exposure nonsemantic; see next section for "Britannica experiment"). Needless to say, there is no serious assurance that any of these factors are vital. For example, the child might be so "programmed" that exposure to a language sample 1/1000th of the present average sample (whatever that may be) would do the trick. Because there is no concrete information, we are obliged to simulate rather slavishly. Besides, it should be admitted, we like infant chimps.

The chimps are bottle fed, diapered, and generally attended by two compassionate graduate students. Ultimately, the parent surrogates will be taught the language, though not until we have mastered it ourselves, after which they will model it for the chimps. Equipped with joysticks like those of the chimp, one producing a soprano range and the other a baritone, mother and father surrogate will speak exclusively in stick language to one another when in the animal's presence and of course to the animals themselves. For not less than four hours daily the animals will be cut off from all sounds except those of the stick language and of course their own cries, which are infrequent however, the chimp infant being startlingly silent compared to the human. For example, when the "mother" holds the animal, giving it its bottle with one hand, her other hand will be engaged with the stick, feeding in appropriate verbal inputs along with the milk. Taped recordings of stick language will be substituted for the missing radio and TV and will be played throughout the day, some of them in coordination with visual displays of the objects being named. So in one way or another the animal will be bombarded throughout the day with samples of the language whose rules it is to learn.

## *"BABBLING"*

But we cannot wait until the chimp is making speeches before deciding that we are on the right track. The study will necessarily be long-term; children do not manifest grammar before about eighteen months, and we could not reasonably ask an earlier starting date of the chimp. For this reason we need periodic assessments of progress and, in particular, early indicators. In the child these might consist of babbling, of the emergence of phonemes and prosodics (though the actual course of this development in man appears to be but poorly known). Can we obtain a similar assessment in the present case despite the sharp differences between a joystick and a maturing vocal system.

Perhaps the earliest experiment we could perform, which would ultimately be informative on several scores, concerns the animal's acquisition of the fourteen phonemes from the infinitely many positions the stick can take. The experiment that could contribute to this question requires departing from the typical verbal environment; but it seems well worth doing, for the departure would not seem harmful to the ultimate language objectives and the information could be obtained only with the departure.

We would depart from the natural case mainly in the first of the three steps of which the experiment would consist. Since in the last step the stick and accompanying sounds will form the basis of a language, the two earlier steps are aimed at providing base data by which to analyze the effect of participation in language upon the motor and acoustic events. Thus in the first step only the chimp will have a joystick (there will be no language, as it were), and the stick will be silent, i.e., unaccompanied by sound. This might be likened to a vocal system that was not yet wired for sound and was being exercised without influence from outside language sounds. The chimp will simply be given access to the stick at an intersession interval sufficient to prevent permanent habituation (Premack and Bahwell, 1959; Premack and Collier, 1962), which could be harmful to the long-range intentions of the experiment. The high manipulativeness of the species, for which we already have evidence, will be relied upon to produce an impressive operant level.

Step two differs from step one only in that, after the records stabilize at one, the auditory system will be connected, and now each stick position will yield its associated sound. The parent surrogates will not yet be talking to the chimps, so the sounds that now accompany the motor gestures will be simply sounds, not the embodiment of a language. Step two will thus provide a base for evaluating such changes in both motor and auditory discrimination as may be brought about by participation in language. Relying upon step two as base data to evaluate any unique changes that language experience may produce will be both of the studies mentioned earlier, viz., prediction of confusion matrix from distinctive features and development of acquired distinctiveness of cues. In addition, step-two data will provide the base for evaluating the emergence of phonemes, our immediate interest.

Only at step three will simulation of the natural case begin. Parent surrogates equipped with joysticks will now provide language samples, so that the joystick sounds will begin to acquire a linguistic history. The chimp by now has had ample experience in producing all possible sounds of the system, but now, of these total possible sounds, only combinations of a particular fourteen will occur in the "parental" input. Will these fourteen increase in frequency in the chimp's output?

In talking to and within earshot of the animals while at the same time attending them, the parent surrogates will thus associate the language sounds with activities and the possibility of reinforcement. According to standard hypotheses, the phonemic sounds may thereby acquire reinforcement value and as a consequence come to be increasingly produced by the chimps in contrast to the nonphonemic sounds that, being only weakly reinforced if at all, should fall off in frequency. In brief, the free manipulation ("babbling") of the chimps should now drift toward those sounds that are functional in the language. "Phonemic drift" may be a critical indicator — whether or not reinforcement plays any role in its development — for it is hard to envision the further development of language without it. That is, if a nondeaf child were to fail to show phonemic drift, the subsequent course of his speech development would seem gravely in doubt; in the same manner, if the animal's stick-babbling does not in some ways reflect the addition of the "parentally" modified environment, we would think further developments to be no less in doubt. Thus a failure of development of phonemic drift could forestall months of futile effort, even as its occurrence could be an enormously heartening sign.

Will reinforcement play the role here that tradition has assigned to it, or will it be as irrelevant as dissenters claim? Obviously one point of an experiment like the present one is to avoid both claims. Direct tests of the reinforcement hypothesis can be easily arranged. An association between activities prorated as to reinforcement value and the frequency of occurrences of selected phonemes is precisely the kind of thing for which such experiments are suited. These tests must be instructive, for to our knowledge there is not one case where reinforcement has actually been shown to affect any property of infant babbling, either its form or frequency. Even the tests purporting to show reinforcement of infant smiling (Rheingold *et al.*, 1959), a far weaker effect than would be involved in development of a phonemic repertoire, are equivocal for failing to control for increased frequency by nonreinforcement variables, e.g., stimulus elicitation and/or arousal. Though to be sure, chimp evidence could not prove that the process was the same in man, but it could at least establish the possibility.

Moreover, either confirmation or refutation of the reinforcement hypothesis in the present case would be of unusual interest. Disconfirmation would infirm the standard extrapolations from simple animal examples and urge caution in further extrapolations. On the other hand, if the phonemic drift should show an appreciable sensitivity to reinforcement contingencies, it would constitute a reinforcement outcome of unusual complexity, one rather far removed from the direct and simple effects of most animal examples.

Consider that the sounds associated with reinforcement in the parents' speech hardly consist of the individual phonemes. Indeed we have already seen that if fusion is produced by successive gestures, the individual phonemes will never occur; even if synchronous gestures are used, though individual phonemes could then occur, they are extremely unlikely to, inasmuch as speech will consist of words not phonemes. Thus it will be words or sentences or sentence fragments, in any case not phonemes, that will be associated with potentially reinforcing situations. The phoneme is thus at least two abstractions removed from the actual acoustic events that will be associated with the possibility of reinforcement: it is only a constituent of a combination of sounds and, as we have seen in the case of the syllable, a somewhat modified constituent at that. These facts received little attention from standard extrapolations of animal reinforcement, which make the matter seem very simple indeed: the parents' sounds become reinforcing, and the child, in attempting to imitate them, develops a phonemic repertoire. It should already be clear that a proreinforcement outcome would call for substantial further explication. As a first step it would be quite interesting to determine what the so-called phonemic repertoire actually consisted of, phonemes or, as even the present slight analysis would suggest, some other "units."

## WEAKER WORLDS AND LANGUAGES FOR WEAKER GAD'S

Consider that man is not the only grammar-acquiring device (GAD). The chimpanzee and perhaps many other species, but especially playful and bright species, are GAD's. These devices come in varying strengths, however, so that no infrahuman GAD can acquire human grammar. But they can acquire grammars that have been proportionately attenuated to suit the weaker theory-constructing capacities of the species. These are our basic assumptions, and we reiterate them here prior to taking up the main question to which they lead; viz., what would constitute a set of inputs for which it would be easy to devise a theory, and what factors account for the difficulty? To do justice to the proposed experiment, we need some answers to this question, though unfortunately we cannot do more than provide suggestions here.

A first difficulty we have in dealing with this question is synthesizing semantic and syntactic criteria. We tend to evaluate the demands a grammar would make on the theory-constructing capacities of a species by semantic criteria in one moment and syntactic the next and have difficulty bringing them together. We will begin with the syntactic side, which will lead rather directly to what we will call the Britannica experiment.

## BRITANNICA EXPERIMENT

The child's acquisition of language is often held to be the more remarkable in view of the apparently haphazard nature of the language samples to which he is exposed. Structures that might be contrasted, e.g., singular-plural, present-past, affirmative-negative, apparently are not, nor does there appear to be any methodical progression from simple to complex constructions. Although no detailed accounts of training samples are available, the impression is nonetheless that there may be virtually no constraints on what would constitute an effective training sample. To the surprise that this may occasion, the reply is apt to be that the child, in devising a theory of the language inputs, is guided by strong genetic constraints; he thus neither needs nor receives more from the outside than an opportunity to test his hypotheses.

What remains puzzling in the light of this view is the frailty of the child's comprehension, how easily it can be undermined. Constructions beyond a certain complexity, though employing familiar lexicon, will readily thwart his comprehension; in fact, a body of literature exists to solve this problem, viz., children's books. There would appear to be this paradox. In reading material one must choose narrowly to be assured of the child's comprehension, whereas for material from which the child is to invent a theory of language, there is the greatest latitude.

This paradox can be resolved by holding that comprehension is not a necessary condition for the acquisition of language — despite the fact that it would appear to be a part of the normal course of events. During the period in which utterances consist of single words or often bursts of the same word, the utterance is frequently accompanied by a gesture in one degree or another. For instance, a child may say "clah!" over and over, meanwhile pointing up at a clock. The gesture raises the question of correspondence between utterance and world and thus permits a judgment on comprehension. Additionally, when the child is not commenting with heightened arousal on provocative features of his world but demanding parts of it, the correspondence between his demand and what will placate him permits some judgment on comprehension. These can only be weak judgments to be sure, there being no syntactic component, though the examples suggest that there is a nascent semantic component and that it alone will permit some judgment as to comprehension.

The examples also suggest a straightforward way of testing the necessity of comprehension for the development of language. Suppose the semantic factor were removed altogether; if this were done, the notion of comprehension would become inapplicable. Consider that the infant is exposed to a semantically uninterpreted input and that arrangements are made to test for the possible acquisition of syntax as such. This experiment could be done by restricting the child's verbal input to material read to it. Such material would be strictly nonreferential for the child and would have the effect of restricting its input to a semantically empty grammar. Though any material would do, the experiment would seem to have an ideal form: we picture a parent swathed in a bathrobe sitting alongside a crib reading aloud from Britannica.

Is this proposal utterly absurd, in the sense that there are no grounds for imagining that "training" of this kind may have a facilitating effect? On the contrary, if the grammatical classes are defined within the syntax, though semantics may normally figure in the hypothesis-testing surrounding these classes, in principle the classes should be acquirable without benefit of semantics. Indeed, in order to use semantic information as a source of hypothesis-testing, the child would first have to learn semantic-syntactic associations. But if the syntactic definitions, the substantive components such as VP, NP, etc., are genetic, it would almost seem unnecessary if not gratuitous for the child to bother with such associations. That is, when the genetic constraints are concentrated in the syntactic component, it seems a little strange that the child in the normal case learns a semantic component at all.

We are setting one chimp aside for a Britannica-type experiment on the assumption that if the experiment fails it may not jeopardize a more conventional second try. This kind of experiment would have one enormous advantage: it would circumvent the requirement that we learn the artificial language. The language could be modeled by a computer. The program would not have to include a psychological model — there would be no semantic responsibilities — but would have only to instruct the stick according to the rules of the syntax. A tape recorder could do the job even more simply. We would not actually have to know the language in order to produce a preselected set of sentences in the language or, if we simulate the natural case, preselected set of sentence fragments. (Presumably, the relation between fragment types and sentence types is universal over human languages, being determined largely by memory and processing limitations: thus our spontaneous efforts at sentences in stick language are almost certain to produce fragments of the usual variety; once produced, they could be rehearsed as needed.) To avoid the possible fortuitous development of a semantic component, the sounds would be introduced more or less at random with respect to on-going activities. The question of what language to model we leave unsettled here and will discuss it at the end of the paper. At this point we wanted to establish the possibility of a syntactic experiment, of an approach that discounted the semantic component altogether. In the following section, we reverse this trend and attempt to give semantic considerations their due.

## THE SIMPLE GRAMMARS OF SIMPLE WORLDS

A procedure for generating grammars of varying complexity, as opposed to evaluating the complexity of existing grammars, would be to operate upon the world where the grammar is to be used. For example, consider a world that is divisible into relatively few classes, where the number of relations that can be instanced by members of the classes is few and nearly identical for all classes, and finally, where the actual number of relations instanced by any class is few; i.e., the rate of change is low. The grammatical devices that would be demanded by such a world would seem to be far simpler than those required by the natural world.

The apparent counterargument to this suggestion is the absence of a functional relation between cultural and grammatical complexity. For example (disregarding one's persuasion in linguistic theory), much work has been done on non-Indo-European languages to reveal recurrence of certain syntactic-logical mechanisms, suggesting that certain grammatical properties are culture-independent. But while the differences between, say, Mohawk and current American culture are undeniable, it is questionable whether these differences are of a kind that could be arranged experimentally, that would operate upon the "constancies" of the world, and thus would be expected to influence grammar. That is, the standard interpretation of the independence between cultural and grammatical complexity may be premature. A functional relation may be proved when the proper experiment is done, when significant differences are first established in the independent variable.

Consider the apparent universality of the agent-action-object sentence form. Although it is so deeply ingrained that imagining other organizations is difficult, nonetheless any one of three changes would seem almost certain to eliminate the concept of agent and thus change the sentence paradigm. If all organisms were identical, the concept of agent would be irrelevant; similarly, if all lived briefly enough, personal identity would be obviated. But a less drastic kind of change, which would more nearly preserve our basic world but alter some of its basic parameters, might well produce the same changes. Picture a world in which object constancies are reduced. Simply reducing the length of time for which, in Berkeley's sense, the aggregates of attributes remain correlated might dispel not only the concept of agent but that of continuant, thus getting rid of "object" as well. Cultures, however, do not operate upon object constancies, upon basic parameters of the world; if they did and still failed to affect grammatical complexity, the independence would be striking; but the present independence is trivial with regard to the question of the effect of the world upon grammar.

McNeill (this volume) asks why the child abandons the holophrastic approach, where words are used as sentences, for what may be a dictionary of sentences, to move ultimately to syntax. His answer that the holophrastic is abandoned because of intolerable ambiguity and the sentence dictionary because of intolerable storage, suggests at the same time that worlds could be arranged that would preclude these intolerabilities and that these changes from one modality to another would not take place. Foss and Jenkins (personal communication) have found that humans in miniature language tasks store rather than compute until the "load" reaches a certain level. One can imagine worlds so restricted that a dictionary of sentences would do nicely for communication.

Similarly, the creativity for which a grammar provides so handsomely, in contrast to a dictionary of sentences, would seem to be a "response" to a world that makes grammatical creativity a necessity. Though we have never seen any actual figures, the rate at which new sentences are produced and encountered is apparently extremely high, repetition of the old sentence being the rare event rather than production of the new sentence. Yet one can imagine a world so restricted and stabilized that grammatical creativity would be a superfluity if not a source of error.

Consider agent identification as one of the many cases that are involved in grammatical creativity but one that is seemingly representative. We encounter such sentences as *the woman who sold buttermilk on the east side of town and whose daughter was expelled from Vassar in the middle of the year. . . .* The relativization here is obviously a powerful device, enabling unlimited creativity, needed for purposes of identification in a world where agents are too numerous to be labeled, where the number of relations an agent can assume is indeterminately large, and where the rate of change in the relations assumed is exceedingly high. However, in a world whose agents consisted of Tom, Dick, and Harriet, identification could always be by labeling, and there would be no need for a grammatical device of the complexity of relativization.

A first step in the experimental construction of intermediate languages may thus be a simplification of the environment; the grammar and speech on which the infant is trained could then be commensurately simplified. Reduce the number of types; limit the kind and number of relations, e.g., allow only two-term relations, all of them symmetrical, etc.; control strictly the rate of change, i.e., allow items to enter no more than $x$ relations per unit time. A world so constrained would reduce substantially the occasion for grammatical creativity — the new sentence might become the rarity — and reduce commensurately the complexity of the grammar needed for communication. Perhaps care must be taken not to overstep the boundaries of simplification and devise a world that would give no occasion for grammar. But there would seem little danger; though worlds where communication would be "nicely served by a dictionary of sentences" can be imagined, they are much less easily constructed. Nothing is known of the chimp's tendency to store rather than compute, though its short-term memory in the one test that is available (Hayes, 1953) looks surprisingly like that of man (Kintsch, 1965). One possibility would be to increase the environmental load and complexity progressively, but this may be superfluous in that the infant appears to grade environmental complexity by its own devices, by responding to only so much of the world at a time. It is always possible to add to a simple world those features that would invite more complex grammatical devices. For example, the class of agents could be increased beyond Tom, Dick, and Harriet, to the point where identification could no longer take place by labeling. The present problem is to find the simplest starting point; pressures for computation could always be added.

Aside from the fact that it should obviously be short, what is the most suitable sentence paradigm for a chimp? Is agent-action-object, or some shorter version thereof, appropriate? The species too must be considered along with the world in attempting to modify and assess grammatical complexity, but we have said little about the species factor because there is so little that can be said. It is not unreasonable to assign the chimpanzee a set of hypotheses, to assume that the chimp would approach the decoding of language as it would any other discrimination problem. This does not avail us much, however, because we cannot enumerate the hypotheses; even if we could, it is not clear how much farther this would carry us. In a discrimination problem this information could be exploited by making certain that the "correct" hypothesis was salient to the animal. But in the case of language this would do little more than lead the animal to correct class definitions, while making no direct contribution to syntactic mechanisms. Perhaps the mechanisms that underlie phrase structure and transformational constructions are general, operating not only in the context of language but throughout sequential behavior.[4] But if this is so, it is still not clear how to structure the language input for the chimp so as to activate or potentiate these possible mechanisms. Further, there is the suggestion that the organism may impose its own structure initially rather independently of the structure of the input. Slobin reports that the early grammar of the Russian child is apparently no less positional (cf. Braine, 1963) than that of the American child, though in Russian word order is not the prime syntactic device it is in English; moreover, the order of the child's sentence is said to be nonsentential with respect to the most typical adult order. Knowledge of the chimpanzee that would suggest semantic markers or constructional mechanisms and thus guide the makeup of the grammar is not at hand. The most that we can say here is that an agent-action sentence paradigm may be suitable in that the chimp fulfills at least a necessary condition for such a paradigm: viz., it recognizes individual members of the species. This is seen clearly throughout its social behavior.

We can always fall back on formal criteria to measure simplicity of grammar. If we measure simplicity in terms of number of rules and number of terms per rule, the appeal is nonetheless in part to common sense, for it is difficult to find data showing the acquisition of rules — more specifically, the acquisition or recall for strings generated by rules — as a function of the number of rules and number of their terms. There is at best the indication that strings generated by rules are learned more rapidly than comparable strings that are not the output of any structure (e.g., Esper, 1925; Miller, 1958; Smith,

[4] Having recorded the vocalization of our animals under several fixed conditions, such as the arrival of a keeper or food preparation, we are now testing for sequential dependencies between components of the cries. We intend to incorporate into the grammar of the artificial language whatever sequential dependencies we find in the natural vocalization rather than to devise the grammar solely on grounds of simplicity as we have so far.

1964); but these data encourage the use of a grammar without indicating what kind of grammar.

Perhaps one way to arrive at simple grammar is partly to duplicate the task of the language learner: (1) Describe the world according to its main parameters, e.g., classes, relations, rate of change. (2) Enumerate the kinds of sentences this simplified world is apt to occasion. (3) Devise a theory that will generate these kinds of sentences and no other. This carries out the assumption that grammatical complexity bears some relation to the complexity of the world and at the same time manages to get from the world to the grammar.

## THE GRAMMAR (SYNTAX)

Two considerations, then, guide the kind of grammar we should first attempt: first, the world so restricted as to render superfluous some of the apparent complexities of natural language; and second, the model of language structure afforded by current linguistic theory. These considerations suggest the use of a phrase-structure grammar of a highly restricted type: e.g., context-free rules, minimal nesting, no self-embedding, no recursiveness.[5] A provisional sample is given in Table 2. Sentences described by this grammar would be short (averaging perhaps three to five words), with a typical structure that is coordinate (the agent-action-object or simply agent-action types) except for modification of a very limited sort with respect to nouns and verbs. Because the output of such a grammatical model is unobscured by deletions, inversions, and the like, and the structure of the typical utterance is relatively "shallow," the semantic content should be more readily accessible from the phonetic signal than otherwise.

A further reason for keeping the syntax comparatively "unstructured" is to avoid conflicting with whatever "natural" principles of structuring the chimpanzee may have. For example, we intentionally neglect conjunction (of any sort — morpheme, phrase, and sentence) so as to invite it from our subject who may have his own semantic interpretation, e.g., emphasis or substitutability or whatever, rather than ad-

---

[5] A nonrecursive grammar need not lead the animal to store rather than compute. The number of possible sentences can be quite "large" and increased indefinitely by the addition of new words.

dition. Or, to illustrate another kind of openness, we offer as input only one sort of question utterance, signaled by a sentence-initial particle Q: this prefixing to the entire string permits the broadest scope to the Q, and allows situational context to delimit the questioned item in the string. Will the subject impose his own italics in some way

TABLE 2 *Sample Phrase-Structure Grammar*

| (1) | S | — | $\left(\left\{\begin{matrix} Q \\ I \\ N \end{matrix}\right\}\right)$ NP + Pred |
| (2) | Pred | — | $\left\{\begin{matrix} \text{(Quant)} \quad \text{Adj} \\ \text{VB} \end{matrix}\right\}$ (Loc) (Tm) (Reason) |
| (3) | VE | — | Tense + V (Man) |
| | | | $\left\{\begin{matrix} \text{NP} \\ \text{V} \end{matrix}\right\}$ |
| (4) | Reason | — | $P_{reas}$ |
| (5) | V | — | $\left\{\begin{matrix} \text{Vintrans} \\ \text{Vtrans + NP} \end{matrix}\right\}$ |
| (6) | Tense | — | future, past |
| (7) | Loc | — | here, there, ... $P_{loc}$ + NP |
| (8) | Tm | — | now, then, ... $P_{tm}$ + NP |
| (9) | Man | — | hard, fast, ... $P_{man}$ + NP |
| (10) | NP | — | Noun (Pl) |
| (11) | Noun | — | (Mod) N |
| (12) | N | — | $N_{pro}$, $N_{com}$ |
| (13) | Mod | — | Det (Quan) (Adj) |
| (14) | Det | — | $\left\{\begin{matrix} N_{pro} \\ \text{the} \end{matrix}\right\}$ |
| (15) | $N_{pro}$ | — | 1, 2, 3 |
| (16) | Quan | — | (Numeral) (Quant) |
| (17) | Quant | — | + enough, − enough |
| (18) | Adj | — | sad, happy, big, hungry, ... |
| (19) | $P_{reas}$ | — | for, to, ... |
| (20) | $P_{tm}$ | — | after, before, ... |
| (21) | Numeral | — | one, two, ... |
| | etc. | | |

(To reduce inflectional lengthening of words, "present," "singular," and "enough" are left unmarked.)

on the spotlighted item? Stress, pause, repetition, repositioning of Q as an attachment to the item, etc. — all are probable modes of underlining, and we would not like to forestall this "expression" from the animal by our own linguistic predilections.

In addition to declarative and interrogative agent + action (object) sentences, the grammar provides for an imperative and a negative. It is difficult (for us) to communicate without these forms, and we have attempted to introduce both in as broad and unstructured a manner as possible to permit the animal to modify them according to its own structuring tendencies. For example, the imperative is a simple affix to a base string, like the Q, while the negative is simply a particle that is optional to all major sentence types.

Smaller details of the syntax include an article — demonstrative on nouns, rather like *this/that,* though neutral with respect to the nearness-remoteness distinction — that serves also as an exclamatory "pointer," something like a maid-of-all-work pronoun. Number in the noun system and tense in the verb are included, partly for the cues that such affixes (pre- for the verb, surf- for the noun) yield toward formation and identification of form classes, but partly also for the possibility that some other time and counting system may reveal itself through a distortion of the input. Obviously, we are not leaving things "open" here, and, to be sure, our decisions about what areas of syntax (and semantics) to leave open are arbitrary. Recursive conjunction we feel to be a probable addition by our subject; affixation for such things as number and time we see as less likely and therefore are willing to supply one arrangement, simply to see what will happen to it — acceptance, rejection, or reinterpretation. In sum, we approach our subjects with a relatively "weak" system, thereby hoping not to overtax the actual capacities of the animal but instead to invite some additional structuring of its own. Necessarily, we start with our own grammatical model (phrase-structure) and concatenations of morphemes that are described in a certain precise way by our model. Next, we collect the linguistic output of the chimp and, relying as we must on the same linguistic theory and its consequent models, write a description for such a corpus. Comparative analysis will then reveal how much of our system has been absorbed and how much has been contributed by the subject. From an animal's production we should be able to derive guidelines by which to extend whatever linguistic competence it may manifest.

## REFERENCES

ALTMANN, S. A. Sociobiology of Rhesus Monkeys. II: Stochastics of social communication. *J. Theor. Biol.,* 1965, *8,* 490–522.

BRAINE, M. The ontogeny of English phrase structure: the first phase. *Language,* 1963, *39,* 1–13.

BROWN, R., and BELLUGI, U. Three processes in the child's acquisition of syntax. *Harvard Educ. Rev.*, 1964, *34*, 133–151.

CHERRY, C. Roman Jakobson's "Distinctive Features" as the Normal Co-ordinates of a Language. In *For Roman Jakobson, Essays on the Occasion of his sixtieth birthday*, compiled by M. Halle and others, The Hague: Mouton & Co., 1956.

CONRAD, R. Acoustic confusions in immediate memory. *Brit J. Psychol.*, 1964, *55*, 75–84.

CROSS, D. V., LANE, H. L., and SHEPPARD, W. C. Identification and discrimination functions for a visual continuum and their relation to the motor theory of speech perception. *J. exp. Psychol.*, 1965, *70*, 63–74.

DENES, P. B. On the statistics of spoken English. *J. acoust. Soc. Amer.*, 1963, *35*, 892–904.

ESPER, E. A. A technique for the experimental investigation of associative interference in artificial linguistic material. *Language Monogr.*, 1925, No. 1.

FRENCH, N. R., CARTER, C. W., and KOENIG, W. The words and sounds of telephone conversations. *Bell System Tech J.*, 1929, *9*, 290–324.

GIBSON, ELEANOR. Learning to Read. *Science*, 1965, *148*, 1066–1072.

GOLDIAMOND, I., ATKINSON, C. J., and BILGER, R. C. Stabilization of behavior and prolonged exposure to delayed auditory feedback. *Science*, 1962, *135*, 437–438.

GOODALL, JANE. Chimpanzees. *Nat. Geographic*, 1963, August, 274–308.

GREENBERG, J. Is the vowel-consonant dichotomy universal? *Word*, 1962, *18*, 73–81.

HAYES, CATHERINE. *The Ape in our House.* New York: Harpers, 1951.

HAYES, K. J., THOMPSON, R., and HAYES, C. Concurrent discrimination learning in chimpanzees. *J. comp. physiol. Psychol.*, 1953, *46*, 105–107.

HOCKETT, C. F., and ASCHER, R. The human revolution. *Current Anthrop.*, 1964, *5*, 135–168.

HOUSE, A. S., STEVENS, K. N., SANDEL, T. T., and ARNOLD, JANE B. On the learning of speechlike vocabularies. *J. verb. Learn. verb. Behav.*, 1962, *1*, 133–143.

JAKOBSON, R., FANT, C. G. M., and HALLE, M. *Preliminaries to Speech Analysis.* Cambridge: M.I.T. Press, 1961.

KELEMAN, G. The anatomical basis of phonation in the chimpanzee. *J. Morphology*, 1948, *82*, 229–256.

KING, D. J., and WOLF, S. The influence of delayed auditory feedback on immediate and delayed memory. *J. Psychol.*, 1965, *59*, 131–139.

KINTSCH, W. The effects of repetition on the short-term memory function. *Psychon. Sci.*, 1965, *2*, 149–150.

———— and PREMACK, D. Stochastic analysis of free responding. Paper read at Psychometric Society, Niagara Falls, 1965.

LENNEBERG, E. H. Understanding language without ability to speak: a case report. *J. abnorm. soc. Psychol.*, 1962, *65*, 419–425.

———— The capacity for language acquisition. In *The Structure of Language*, J. Fodor and J. Katz (Eds.), Englewood Cliffs, N.J., 1964(*a*), pp. 579–603.

———— Language disorders in childhood. *Harv. Ed. Rev.*, 1964(*b*), *34*, 152–177.

——— *The Biological Bases of Behavior.* New York: Wiley (forthcoming).

LIBERMAN, A. M., HARRIS, K. S., HOFFMAN, H. S., and GRIFFITH, B. C. The discrimination of speech sounds within and across phoneme boundaries. *J. exp. Psychol.*, 1957, *54*, 358–368.

——— COOPER, F. S., HARRIS, K.S., and MAC NEILAGE, P. F. A motor theory of speech perception. Paper read at Speech Comm. Seminar, Stockholm, Sept., 1962.

MAGOUN, H. W. *The Waking Brain.* Springfield, Ill., 1958.

MC CARTHY, D. Language development in children. In *Manual of Child Psychology* (2nd ed.), L. Marmichael (Ed.), New York: Wiley, 1954, pp. 492–630.

MILLER, C. A. The magical number seven, plus or minus two: some limits on our capacity for processing information. *Psychol. Rev.*, 1956, *63*, 81–97.

——— Free recall of redundant strings of letters. *J. exp. Psychol.*, 1958, *56*, 485–491.

——— and NICELY, PATRICIA E. An analysis of perceptual confusions among some English consonants. *J. acoust. Soc. Amer.*, 1955, *27*, 338–352.

NISSEN, H. W. Phylogenetic comparison. In *Handbook of Experimental Psychology*, S. S. Stevens (Ed.), New York: Wiley, 1951.

NYE, P. W. Reading aids for blind people—a survey of progress with the technological and human problems. *Med. Electron. Biol. Engng.*, 1964, *2*, 247–264.

PENFIELD, W., and ROBERTS, L. *Speech and Brain Mechanisms.* Princeton, 1959.

PREMACK, D., and BAHWELL, R. Operant-level lever pressing by a monkey as a function of interest interval. *J. exp. Anal. Behav.*, 1959, *2*, 127–131.

——— and COLLIER, G. Analysis of nonreinforcement variables affecting response probability. *Psychol. Monogr.*, 1962, *76*, No. 5 (Whole No. 524).

RHEINGOLD, HARRIET L., GEWIRTZ, J. L., and ROSS, HELEN W. Social conditioning of vocalizations in the infant. *J. comp. physiol. Psychol.*, 1959, *52*, 68–73.

SCHALLER, G. B. *The Mountain Gorilla: Ecology and Behavior.* Chicago: University of Chicago Press, 1963.

SMITH, K. Grammatical intrusions in the free recall of redundant strings of letters. Paper read at Midwestern Psychol. Assoc., May 1964.

SPERLING, G. A model for visual memory tasks. *Human factors*, 1963, *5*, 19–31.

SUPPES, P., CROTHERS, E., WEIR, RUTH H., and TRAGER, E. Some quantitative studies of Russian consonant phoneme discrimination. *Institute for Math. Studies in Social Sciences*, Stanford University, 1962, Tech. Report No. 49.

P. B. Denes

## COMMENTS ON "PREPARATIONS FOR DISCUSSING BEHAVIORISM WITH CHIMPANZEE"

Speech is a means of communication that is highly efficient from several points of view and resists noise and distortion to a remarkable extent. Despite the great ease with which we communicate by speech, it is by no means easy to understand the nature of this process. The articulatory and acoustic events that accompany the speech act are far from sufficient to explain it fully. We feel sure that language structure plays an important part in the process, yet when we build models of the speech process to facilitate better understanding of its nature, we rarely include linguistic factors. The reason for this omission is probably that we do not have enough hard facts about these linguistic factors, and even what is known is not understood well enough to be applied easily. A better understanding of language is therefore highly desirable. This may perhaps be achieved by looking at very simple forms of language. The early language behavior of children, and animal languages, can provide examples of such simple language forms.

One thing that impressed me in listening to our discussions is that even the first descriptions of the child's or the animal's language are usually made in terms of the language units of adult human speech: phonemes, words, sentences. It may perhaps be interesting to know also whether children really operate with these units in the early stages of their development or, alternatively, how and when they acquire them. Let me illustrate this with two examples, one concerned with the so-called segmentation problem and one with the process of imitation.

337

The adult listener has no difficulty in interpreting the continuous acoustic speech signal as a chain of discrete language units. Yet when we examine this acoustic signal — and process it through what we consider the best possible model of the human speech perception process — we find it next to impossible to divide it into discrete segments, each to correspond to one of the language units we hear so clearly. Given that we find it difficult to postulate a logical process for segmenting speech wave, it would be interesting to find out how a child develops his ability to segment. How does he operate before he has acquired the concept of the word, and how does he experiment to approach what we adults call a word? The descriptions we heard at these meetings were mostly concerned with how children build up the edifice of language from individual words rather than how they acquire the concept of the word.

The second point I wanted to make concerns imitation. Imitation and babbling have been mentioned extensively during our discussions about language development, and it was always assumed that there is something in adult speech that children can imitate directly when they babble. In point of fact it is by no means obvious what it is that children imitate when they babble. The child's vocal mechanism is considerably different in size from that of an adult's, and he can therefore rarely, if ever, produce exactly the same sound as the adult.

When we examine the vocal tract and larynx as acoustic generators, we must come to the inevitable conclusion that the resonances, or formants, of a child's vocal tract are in a higher frequency range than that of the adult's. Also, a child's larynx vibrates in a higher frequency range than that of an adult. For this reason the fundamental frequency, or pitch, range of the child is higher. Because of the higher fundamental frequency, the harmonics are more widely separated, and therefore the spectral envelope of the sound produced is less precisely defined. In other words sounds generated in larger vocal tracts excited by lower fundamental frequencies are both more intelligible and have different formant frequencies than those produced by smaller vocal tracts excited by higher fundamental frequencies.

The essence of this part of my remarks is this: Does the child imitate the sound qualities of the speech of adults, or does he somehow obtain information about the vocal tract movement made by the adult and try to imitate these movements? It would be very interesting to have an answer to this question.

# GENERAL DISCUSSION
## Premack and Denes presentations

1. The comments by Denes provoked a good deal of discussion in their own right, and the line between the end of his formal comments and the beginning of the general discussion has been quite arbitrarily and ungenerously drawn. Part of the following discussion took place as a discursive interpolation while Denes was still metaphorically on his feet, and the tail of his prepared comments became dispersed in the general flow of debate.

The first catalyst was an observation during his remarks on segmentation. He was taken as implying that children first acquired the concept of words and then built up the structure of language from this basis. Kalmus thought children started to distinguish words only later, when language behavior had begun; segmentation into words was not prelinguistic. Denes preferred to say that linguistic behavior began when the behavior could be described in terms of words and sentences, but he did not know whether it began with phrases or single words. Hirsh said that if it was right that children — some children — could imitate intonation long before they began to establish phonemic categories in their own output, the segmented words in adult speech could provide rather gross markers that might be imitated in a prephonemic stage before the child began to distinguish among speech sounds. Denes found this reasonable but questionable.

Lenneberg thought there were very good grounds for debunking the notion that babbling played such a tremendous role in the development of language. Some children babbled very little or perhaps not at all.

There was other evidence that young children who lost language for a short period of time, especially with acquired aphasia, would babble, but that when similar disasters happened in older children, their progress did not include a babbling stage at all. They started at a higher stage. There was other evidence, not good evidence but suggestive, of a period at which children who had been deprived environmentally and not learned language could be exposed to language. The reports seemed to indicate that children at six or seven years of age could learn language faster than was the case in normal development and without the privilege of babbling. The notion that babbling was a practice for later language strained his imagination. Why should children want to practice anything for the future? In animal behavior there were many paradigms that humans interpreted as play or practice, such as kittens "mouse-catching" with paper balls or the fledgling wing movements of birds, but there was quite ample evidence that if this was suppressed a wide variety of behavior still developed rapidly at a later stage.

Slobin pointed out that if a female rat was raised without any opportunity to carry things around, she would not retrieve her young. Young chimps who did not play with other chimps became sexually incompetent. This did not mean they had a goal image of adult behavior while they were playing.

Denes appealed that all he was asking was whether children learned the identity of words because their parents gave them speech in segments that did correspond to words and that they learned to put together into language, or whether they in fact listened to language as adults used it and found some ways of their own of segmenting this into words? Lenneberg thought excellent hunches were available on that question, even in the absence of exact empirical research. It was quite clear that mothers and parents and home environments differ a great deal, and they certainly differ from culture to culture, but there was no evidence that parents had to adopt something like an organized system of baby talk for a child to develop proper speech. In the face of this tremendous variety, all children learned words and language.

Denes persisted that he was seeking a hint as to how this was done, but Lenneberg could not help; he just wanted to object to the idea that the babbling stage was essential and that it was relevant to Premack's experiment or to any other theory.

2. The second major topic was based on the disparity described by

Denes between the acoustic characteristics of adult and child vocal systems and the difficulty this posed for theories depending on imitation. Kalmus said that imitation need not be an exact replica of what was heard; only a unique relationship was required, and if a child had some form of input transformational system, he would feel that what he produced agreed with what he heard. Hirsh thought that even if Denes threw out the entire vowel series a child might for example still have a chance to imitate stops versus continuants, voicing versus non-voicing — a tremendous amount of information that had much less to do with the size of the cavities of the vocal tract. Denes remarked that Kalmus's superimposition of a transformational system did not seem to reduce the number of unknowns and reiterated his basic question: Does the child imitate sounds or movements?

Denes added that it was by no means certain that a child's vocal apparatus could produce formant and fundamental frequency relationships similar to those produced by adults. For example, for a number of speech sounds an adult's first formants had a lower frequency than the fundamental frequency of a child's voice. Only measurements and calculations — which he did not think had yet been made — could show whether a child's formants shifted in proportion to fundamental frequency compared with an adult's voice.

Miller asked whether it would not be possible to make inferences from the pattern in the overtones above what was normally known as the formant. Could an engineer do this? Denes thought it likely that the clues for finding the first formant in cases when the fundamental frequency was higher than the first resonance of the vocal tract were an order of magnitude smaller than the normal case where the fundamental frequency was lower than the first resonance of the vocal tract. Even so, the human being could under certain circumstances make the distinction fairly easily. He remembered a recording, made by the late Meyer-Eppler, of a child singing vowels with fundamental frequencies of, he believed, 800 and 1,000 cps. The vowels were selected so that the recognition of the first formant was important for distinguishing one from the other. These formants were all below the fundamental frequency, yet the vowels could be distinguished perceptually without undue difficulty. He emphasized that he had raised the issue of the imitation of superficially dissimilar sounds from the point of view of motor theory of speech. If it was easier to explain a child's imitation of adult speech by reference to an articulatory shape, then this would be just a further confirmation of the importance of motor feedback on speech perception.

House proposed that the answer to Miller's question was yes. If amplitude-linked formant activities were to be believed in, then there would be amplitude relationships in the upper end of the spectrum, even though ill-defined, to tell something about the low and unperceived end of the spectrum. It should be possible to infer that there was a first formant somewhere, even though it was not well defined in the spectrum. The problem was complicated a little more in the child's speech, however, because general definition was fairly poor, and it was not possible to be sure about amplitude functions even at the high end of the spectrum because of the wide spacing of the harmonics.

Liberman gained the most agreement by observing that the vowel system even in adults tended to be a mess; it was not understood very well, and more research was necessary.

3. Denes also raised the topic of unique child languages. In several different houses he had found small children with a language of their own that was not understandable to adults although it was understandable to other children in the household. The smallest child might say something that was quite incomprehensible to Denes and to the mother. She would then ask the brother, who was perhaps two years older than the speaker, to interpret. The brother obviously had no difficulty in understanding what the smaller child had said and repeated the utterance.

Piaget (1926) had devoted half of his book on speech and thought in the child to exactly this, said Miller. Piaget asked whether children understood children better than adults understood children, and the answer was no.

Fodor could think of at least one clear counterexample. There was just this kind of relation in a family, and the parents thought the younger child was suffering from speech retardation. What had happened was that the younger child had a complete phonology of English plus a few extra rules — a version of pig Latin and two extra dialectic rules. He also had a brother who knew both systems, and the brother would translate. As soon as the extra rules were understood, it was easy to work out what the child was saying. But because the brother translated effectively and the child had no particular desire to talk directly to his parents, he used his own system.

Kalmus thought the difference would be whether the children were of the same family group or not. Denes noted that other participants had suggested that it was difficult to investigate the prelanguage behavior of children because they so very quickly acquired some rudimentary form of adult language. He wondered whether looking at the type of children's speech that only children understood might be a way of finding out more about prelanguage behavior.

4. None of the participants — Premack included — was particularly optimistic that any of his chimpanzees would terminate the project conversing with the experimenters, but there was a broad sympathy with the aim and a lively interest in the methodology. A valuable purpose would be served if the negative result, when (and if) it occurred, was a convincing one, after everything had been done to optimize all conditions in the subjects' favor. It might, for example, be possible to find out whether the chimpanzee was capable of handling a phonemic system at any level. Premack stressed that the first aim of the project was to see if anything analogous to phonemic drift occurred from the chimpanzees' initial response probabilities — whether unreinforced and nonimitative "babbling" on the joystick would converge on the experimenters' restricted "phonology" after exposure to the permissible sounds of the system. This would indicate a particularly complex learning phenomenon because the individual elements of the system would never be differentially reinforced, but only certain combinations.

5. There was doubt whether the joystick would be optimal for the chimpanzee, especially with regard to the attempt to link it with a CVC phonemic system. Premack rejected a suggestion that his device was simply a musical instrument and claimed it was designed to instance the distinctive features aspects of Jakobson's (1963) theory of phonology. House objected that no one had ever been able to distinguish Jakobson's distinctive features in any acoustic sense and argued that Premack's system was in no way analogous to language because it took no account of what happened at the motor level. The speech spectrum was not a consequence of acoustic end products being uniquely associated with complex simultaneously occurring motor events; there would be much less difficulty in constructing machines to produce and analyze speech if it did. Premack responded that Jakob-

son's theory, however imperfect a model of natural language, was nevertheless the best model and guide for the design of his system. There was also evidence from Pollack and others of the advantages of multidimensional codes that would recommend the general approach Premack had taken to phonology. House's task, Premack felt, was not to demonstrate Jakobson's possible inadequacies but to show Premack and Schwartz a better approach. House felt Premack and Schwartz should use natural sounds, and there was support for a suggestion that the chimpanzees should be tested to discover which human speech sounds they could best discriminate. Premack said they had considered analyzing spectograms of chimpanzee vocalizations to see if they could offer a base for a phonetic system. They would not, however, use natural sounds unless they were prepared to abandon production and study only comprehension. Lenneberg's one clinical case notwithstanding, they still considered that comprehension and production might interact, the one facilitating the other. To study production, artificial sounds were necessary. The chimp was a poor imitator of human sounds, and they considered the use of his natural sounds inadvisable because they might well be related to already established events. Moreover, the assumption that the discriminative processes of speech continua were unique was, Premack thought, a gratuitous one. Several participants pointed to the similarities between the human and chimpanzee vocal and articulatory apparatus, despite differences in detail.

There was some unresolved difficulty in comprehending Premack's motivation in pursuing the joystick approach, except perhaps for the facilitating effect it might have at the early, purely manipulative and attention-focusing stages of the project. Cooper, for example, could not see why a "five-dimensional Morse code" that had never been shown to work with humans should be regarded as particularly appropriate for chimpanzees. Nevertheless he supported Premack in rejecting suggestions that the first efforts should be directed toward establishing "naming" behavior, the association of sounds with objects. A favorable outcome here would indicate communication but not language and would be neither particularly surprising nor particularly useful. On the question of codes used for reading machines, Premack thought that none of them had ever utilized distinctive features theory.

6. Cooper predicted difficulty with Premack's proposed feedback

delay (p. 314) in order to achieve a smooth and "coarticulated" syllabic output, pointing to the disruptive effect of delayed or desynchronized auditory feedback on human speech production. Premack acknowledged the risk but hoped to avoid the danger since the delay would be both slight and present from the beginning of the learning situation. Liberman suggested that a twin-joystick system would offer more effective coarticulation and also help the listener, chimpanzee or human, in recovering any heard phoneme. Recovery would be most complicated with the current system because with areal production there would be a very large number of ways of going into any particular phoneme. Premack said the twin-joystick possibility had been considered and rejected because of other considerations. The major objection was that two sticks were more complicated than one.

Liberman also saw production rate as a critical factor with regard to the higher levels of organization that Premack was seeking. If his sounds were generated phoneme by phoneme, the maximum rate would be far slower than the ten to fifteen phonemes per second achieved with natural speech. This slow delivery might perhaps put an intolerable load on the listener in his attempts to analyze and integrate temporal sequences. The problem was analogous to that with reading machines for the blind, no successful system for which had yet been found because their rates all tended to flatten out at about twenty words a minute after long practice. Kalmus saw advantages in miniaturizing the system, as Premack proposed, in order to speed up production rate.

7. Fodor predicted failure on the basis of a study by Ferster (1964) who had attempted to train a chimpanzee to count on the basis of a binary system. The subject had failed to get past eight — argued Fodor — because it had obviously failed to realize the highly systematic recursive structure of the binary system. If the chimpanzee had failed with this task, which could be regarded as involving an extreme simplification of English, he did not see how it could possibly master Premack's system. Premack argued vigorously that the reported experiment was irrelevant; it was conducted in completely different circumstances, was vulnerable to criticism in terms of both theory and method, and was quite unrelated to language, dealing instead with a specific conceptual ability to count. There was a failure to come to terms over whether chimpanzees' conceptual limitations in the count-

ing study could be related to language-learning and whether the subject was actually given the chance to master the idea that the binary system was productive.

8. There was considerable speculation about how well the human participants might be expected to master the phonology and grammar of Premack's experiment. Liberman, for example, thought it would be even money who would have the most difficulty, chimp or man. Premack replied that he had learned to produce the phonemes but that Schwartz had made the most progress and was able to locate the phonemes in the motor space. There was a suggestion that a young child might have more success in learning the system than either the chimp or Schwartz, and the device itself was seen as a possible technique for studying ease of acquisition of various syntactic systems.

## REFERENCES

FERSTER, C. B. Arithmetic behavior in chimpanzees. *Sci. Amer.*, May 1964.
JAKOBSON, R. *Collected Works*. The Hague: Mouton & Co., 1963.
PIAGET, J. *The Language and Thought of the Child*. New York: Harcourt, Brace, 1926.

*James J. Jenkins*

# REFLECTIONS ON THE CONFERENCE

Thomas Kuhn (1962) in his provocative analysis of the history of science stresses the vital role that is played by the current "paradigm" in the conduct of any particular science. He defines a paradigm as a consensus that a particular general conception of the field is "correct." This in turn implies that certain problems are worth while and others are meaningless, that certain procedures are productive and others are not, and that specific kinds of data are relevant and others irrelevant. In short, a paradigm is an agreement to regard the field and the enterprise in a given way, and it structures and interprets the history, the problems, and the evidence that are related to the field. When an old paradigm is challenged by a new conception, difficulties and conflict ensue. The battle is a strange one, for by the very nature of the contest it is foregone that the adversaries will not understand each other. Typically, they cannot even agree on a common ground of comparison, for the definition of what constitutes appropriate ground is itself involved in the contesting points of view.

It is by now a commonplace to observe that linguistics has experienced and is experiencing a revolution of the first magnitude with the new paradigm of the generative grammarian. Its conceptions of tasks, methods, and goals have changed radically, and its history is being rewritten in the light of present views. As a corollary to this (though somewhat less well understood), psycholinguistics is quite naturally undergoing a violent and far-reaching revision. The restructuring of this infant science is further complicated by the fact that not only has the linguistic paradigm changed but the old paradigm in psychology is weakening before a variety of attacks, though a new paradigm has not yet taken its place.

In 1953 at the Summer Seminar on Psycholinguistics (Osgood and Sebeok, 1954), it was easy to conceive of psycholinguistics as a confluence of three compatible fields, linguistics, learning theory, and information theory. All fields paid lip service to a positivistic, operationalist image of science. All agreed in "hard data" and envisioned science as a set of descriptive laws, summarizing (and preferably arising from) analytic treatment of observable language behavior. As Maclay (1964) has pointed out, this was a false consensus that rapidly dissolved with further consideration and further development of the parent disciplines. With the proof that natural languages were not finite state languages, it should have been plain that the supposed paradigm for psycholinguistics was not viable.

While it is hard to give form to the emerging paradigm for psycholinguistics, it is easily seen that the nature of some questions has already been drastically altered. In 1953, it seemed that the task of accounting for the acquisition of language was going to depend on the exploitation of learning theory. It was "surely clear" that language was learned from models and the only questions to be cleared up had to do with the "shaping" of behavior through direct reinforcement or the subtle business of deciding the nature of secondary reinforcement or the difficult problem of deciding what was meant by a "satisfying state of affairs."

With the linguistic revolution, however, the nature of the problem changed. It is by no means clear now that language is "learned" in the old meanings of that term. Further, it does not appear that "what is learned" is what the old model said. And it is by no means evident that the learning of language is dependent on reinforcement, either direct or secondary.

At the same time psychology has been undergoing a disturbing search for a new paradigm. As Hebb (1960) suggests, the fervor of the sweeping revolution of behaviorism has been exhausted. He calls now for a second phase of the movement, urging psychologists to turn again with new tools to problems of basic interest that were swept aside by the behaviorists as being unapproachable. A set of demands for serious analytical study of thought processes and structured behaviors (e.g., Miller, Galanter, and Pribram, 1960; Russell, 1963) attests to the inadequacy of the old psycholinguistic paradigm and the dissatisfaction that contemporary psychologists experience under its constraints.

Given the almost unbelievable rates of change of its parent disciplines, it is small wonder that psycholinguistics is in violent disorder. When one picks up a volume with "psycholinguistics" in its title, it is impossible to predict its point of view, conceptual apparatus, or even the range or types of problems treated. It is clear that in this collection of papers the dominant paradigm, both explicitly and implicitly accepted, is that of the generative grammarian. I think it is fortunate that we have had as much convergence as we have had, for two reasons: first, because it has made communication possible and, second, because I believe that the paradigm of the grammarian will soon be seen to be the most fruitful way for both linguist and psychologist to approach language.

There are problems for the psychologist in fitting his attitudes and biases into this approach. A fundamental distinction, which is of great importance in this paradigm, is that between *competence* and *performance*. It is further held by the linguists that a theory of competence must of necessity precede a theory of performance, but it is a commonly held view in psychology that one ought to begin with performance and work one's way backward. Different research strategies and philosophies of science are involved, and even with a general agreement about the general nature of the final theory, one may attempt to proceed in different ways. Some of the conflict in the choice of a way has been evident in this conference.

Within the subject matter there are difficulties in working out the generality of terms and their interrelations. The words "segmentation," "combination," "pattern," "order," "arbitrariness," etc., occur in the domains of both phonology and grammar. That there are fundamental similarities in the basic process at work in these related systems can scarcely be doubted, yet no one is prepared to give a set of language-acquisition rules that attempts to embrace both areas. Surface resemblances and analogies of relationships cannot yet be shown to reflect the same underlying processes.

The distinctions between competence and performance on the one hand and issues in phonology and syntax on the other are useful in examining the positions of the conference participants and serve as rubrics for an overview of the discussions.

## COMMENTS ON THE CONFERENCE

The conference can be seen as reflecting a polarization of views of language acquisition, one originating on the phonological end of the dimension and the other on the grammatical end. The characteristic differences in these views are most closely related to differences in the phenomena that are most salient in each domain and to specific aspects of the subject matter of phonology and grammar.

One polar position is anchored by McNeill's stimulating paper on the acquisition of syntax. Everyone must be indebted to this paper, both for summarizing the problems and the data and for holding the extreme view on innate ideas that it expresses so forcefully. At the other pole (with some distortion of his position) we can think of Fry's paper, which seems to emphasize the role of certain experiences, the need to move through the development of levels of skill and complexity, the importance of learning to listen, etc. The first view seems to stress emerging competences; the second, the shaping and polishing of performances.

The polarity that can be attributed to these views extends to many areas. For example, it appeared easy for most participants to accept sets of constraints in the phonological domain, largely perhaps because these constraints dealt with the vocal tract and various portions of the "plumbing" as they contributed to and influenced phonological structures. Physical structures and their consequences are familiar friends. In contrast, at the grammatical end one is asked to accept a set of constraints that have to do with "structures" about which we know virtually nothing in the physical sense but which are supposed to have far-reaching impacts on the grammar-making machines in our heads. The final product is to be a device that produces unseen but vital underlying sequences, and it is supposed to match the unseeable machines to whose products the child has been exposed. Small wonder that this has the appearance of black magic and dark mysteries.

The polarization that can be read into these positions may or may not be desirable. It may well be that we will need one theory for the physical-phonological development, so to speak, which stresses physical constraints and does require certain kinds and sequences of experiences, while at the same time we need another theory for the acquisition of syntax, which puts the emphasis on "templates in the speaker's head," relative independence of specific experience, and so forth.

But even if these views of language acquisition could be set far enough apart to be called separate views, it is clear from the conference that they face many of the same perplexing problems. Any theory of any part of language acquisition requires an external model. No one has maintained yet that a child is born speaking a native language; he must at least hear it first. But it is not clear how the hearing of the language effects his acquisition. As both McNeill and Lenneberg have pointed out, we do not know that a child needs tuition nor is it even certain that he profits from tuition when it is given to him.

No theory of language acquisition can work until a child can make some sort of relevant fragmentation of the language he hears. Only when he can find out what some of the relevant aspects are or when he can make some relevant class discriminations does he get a toehold into the language system, and only then can the more general aspects of the theories come into play. Just as this is the point at which McNeill's proposal was extensively criticized, so it is a troublesome issue for all accounts. When one examines the physical stream of speech, it is apparent that the acoustic flow is not firmly and reliably divided into relevant units. Phonemes do not mark themselves, and indeed they may well resist detection by sophisticated means of analysis in the hands of an expert who knows what he is looking for. The same problem, then, is found at both theoretical poles; one must somehow specify "breaking points" in the language environment for the theories to take hold, but at present we do not know how to solve this problem in either place.

Another similarity between the extremes may be identified with respect to the problems posed by production of speech. Both grammar and syntax can be said to be "imitative" in some respect. But the "copy" is physically and grammatically different from the model in the environment. We don't seriously expect children's syntax to match adult syntax, nor do we expect the child's acoustic product to match the adult's. Apparently children haven't the right kind of equipment for either task. But with respect to both phonology and grammar we use "imitation" and "copying" as descriptive terms, meaning of course that some transformation or some conversion of the model is matched. We surely need to find out what it is that is matched. This is simply a new way of asking old questions: What are the important dimensions? What are the units? What are the relevant universals of language that are detected and employed? We seem to recognize instances of matching and copying by sorting out the important cues from the welter of irrelevant cues, but the "sorting out" itself depends on the listener contributing his knowledge of the language system, its apparatus, and a certain amount of knowledge of the world and its saliencies. The ability to see a match or observe a copy thus seems to depend on already knowing the language — an awkward conclusion if one wishes to employ such behaviors in language-learning. It is surely difficult to talk about reinforcing or correcting or illustrating "correct" language behavior if the proper application of the reinforcement, correction, or illustration depends on already knowing what is supposed to be taught. It is difficult to escape the trap here.

The stickiest problem for the psychologist of all those sketched here, however, is the problem Fodor outlines: How can the child *by any set of devices we could imagine* learn what isn't there? One psychological position holds that the corrections, revisions, and shaping of language behavior are all instances of the application of reinforcement to a fluctuating behavior stream. But when we recognize that it is not enough to shape the surface behavior, that it is the underlying and covert processing that must be developed, it seems futile to pursue a program that cannot in any way deal with this particular formulation of the problem.

Some years ago I set myself the task of applying the Skinnerian analysis of language acquisition to a variety of limiting cases, including the case of the deaf child and the case of the mute child. On the Skinner view, as I saw it (though I am not by any means a good practicing Skinnerian), teaching the deaf child is relatively easy. One appropriately applies the reinforcements, and the child speaks. There is little reason to suppose that it should take him much longer to learn to speak than the normal child. The mute child on the other hand appeared to present a much more difficult case because on that analysis he has to learn a different surrogate response of some sort to each aspect of language to be discriminated, and one would expect to have trouble finding such finely differentiated responses if the verbal responses themselves were not available. But obviously these outcomes are contrary to what experience tells us is the case. The psychological analysis is not only irrelevant with respect to underlying structure, it is wrong with respect to actual outcomes.

## SPECIFIC COMMENTS

In addition to the very general problems just cited, a number of interesting specific issues have emerged which should be noted in any overview of the conference.

Persons with the "competence" orientation, chiefly the linguists and linguistically oriented psychologists, pay little attention to the work that language has to do. Others have raised many questions concerning the content, the context, and the role that language must play. I think this concern is both reasonable and important and should be given a place in any complete picture of language performance. Here we need most especially to focus our attention on the interaction of the language system and the semantic system. As Fodor said, the fact that they can be independently described does not at all imply that they are independent in either acquisition or function. Slobin has also put this issue well in pointing out the interaction between categories in language and the categories that are salient in the world. (This point is also one that Roger Brown has made repeatedly in his analyses of language.) There are, of course, a variety of reasons for saliency in both domains. Some features of the world attract attention for simple perceptual reasons of the old-fashioned "figure-ground" sort and some for functional reasons. (The latter must include those that make a difference in the way the child lives, even though they may be hard to perceive.) Some of them are probably suggested to him because of salient features in the language. It seems clear, however, that the systems work back and forth. It is not a question of one system or the other but both systems functioning in this way to produce noticeable categories and conceptualizations of the world.

A second specific issue concerns the importance of the effort Fodor has proposed concerning inference rules. We need clear and precise expressions of the notions of "templates" so that they may become serious candidates for explanations. The importance of this theme is seen throughout the conference. The way this is to be done, however, is in dispute. My preference is for something like a set of inference rules that furnish hypotheses for testing. Language universals, then, would be expressed in terms of the likelihood that infant speakers would arrive at given kinds of hypotheses, given exposure to certain kinds of language inputs. My preference, of course, develops directly from my academic history and from my convictions about the generality of higher mental processes as opposed to a more narrowly specific device that has special rules for language-learning alone. I would prefer a set of rules that are strongly biased toward hypotheses about ordered and dependent şequences. One still has to find a way to break into these sequences, but I am convinced that ordered dependencies will turn out to be very important as specific generators of three or four hypotheses, one of which will turn out to be correct or nearly correct as a solution to a particular family of language constructions.

This suggests, in turn, that we must take seriously the notion of a psychological space in which order has a real meaning. For years psychologists have been putting things that "go together" in psychological spaces. Short distances are ordinarily associated with items that are highly correlated or very "similar" and so on. We locate them adjacently in a psychological space "for convenience," but we don't take the space seriously. The example that Fodor gave of the possible inference rules that might convert *IXJ* sequences (involving *IJ* dependencies) into ordered sets plus permutation rules is an example of a serious suggestion. The resulting psychological space does not simply represent *IJ* as "related." It represents *IJ* as related and ordered *for the purpose of being utilized* in an operation that depends on that relation and that order.

I once engaged in the attempt to show that one inference rule (simple contiguity), properly supplemented with a little machinery, was sufficient to produce an "item and arrangement" linguistic model (Jenkins and Palermo, 1964). While that particular linguistic scheme is now revealed as inadequate, the experience was not wasted. If we again follow this kind of tack, we can build psychological models to achieve the more powerful linguistic schemes and then attempt to discover whether such psychological models behave reasonably and in addition do a lot of work for us in coping with higher mental processes. In the lower stages of the models we can, of course, employ the older contiguity and mediational models for the purposes of developing early categories and provisional groupings that may be needed to provide the raw material for higher-order inferences. No matter how this is handled, clearly it is of great import for both psycholinguistics and psychology to develop inference rules that are capable of producing the kinds of underlying structures that seem to be necessary to the understanding and production of linguistic systems.

Another interesting issue that received attention at the conference is that of "computation" versus "storage." Opinions on this issue tend to split along the already familiar lines of cleavage. In the main, sympathies with generative linguistics incline one to prefer to treat with language as produced by a device applying rules to create an utterance. In contrast, psychological models traditionally tend to emphasize the role of learned, probabilistically sequenced materials, i.e., materials stored in nearly intact form in memory.

No conference participant would deny that the organism has the capacity to do, and in fact does, a lot of computation. On the other hand, that is by no means the entire picture. It is currently fashionable to underestimate the organism's enormous capacity for storage and the uses speakers make of stored materials. The most striking example of storage that occurred to me in reading McNeill's paper is the one that Slobin illustrated so elegantly, the essential storage demanded of the speaker of an arbitrary gender language. Young speakers in such languages are obliged to store specific gender information as part of the raw, root information in the vocabulary item for thousands and thousands of lexical entries. In this case there appears to be no other way for the speaker to accomplish his task. More interesting, perhaps, is the case in which the speaker presumably has the choice between computation and storage; because something *could* be computed does not mean that it *has* been and because something *could* be stored does not mean that it *has* been. Casual observation in English suggests that the speaker stores great amounts of material that he could compute. It would surely be worth while and interesting to know what determines the speaker's decision and his subsequent performance.

In this connection I was grateful for a section in McNeill's paper in which he talked about the choice of strategies by the child. He pointed out that the load on the child's capacities probably pushed him (one would suppose) into more and more elegant formulations of language. We can afford considerable variance in the initial correctness of our inference rules or in the precision with which the "templates" operate if we give up the notion that the child arrives at his system of language by making a series of "correct" discoveries. He may, in fact, have temporarily incorrect and inelegant formulations that the load of listening and speaking may finally require him to store or to compute in more efficient fashion. The "correct" form of the language, then, may finally be represented in the child only after he has been driven successively from one formulation to another, leaving each as the working load becomes too high. It seems also likely that the first formulations may well serve as way stations, giving the child generally and functionally useful categories, though they may lack grammatical precision.

Fry's paper seemed to me to add two specific issues to my list of interesting problems. The first was the notion that the phonological system of the child is complete at each stage, that is, that the phonological system does not just have a couple of pigeonholes that are filled, with everything else remaining empty. The total phonological structure consists of the full range of acoustic stimulation, we presume. It just happens to be sliced up in a simple way at the beginning. I think this is an important contention. It applies equally well on the syntactic side, as may be seen in McNeill's argument. Here, again, amid diversity we find similarities between the phonological and the syntactic positions. There is the same kind of "world filling space with progressive division by hypotheses" postulated at both extremes. The *system* is presumably what the child has to work with, and it is all that he has to work with. It is complete all the time even though it is progressively differentiating.

Another impressive aspect of the paper was Fry's conviction that the presumed innate capacity for language-learning is very strongly related to the fact that language is normally learned acoustically. Language, essentially, is an auditory product. When one takes away the auditory side of language and is forced to present it in the visual domain, the innate processes that make language acquisition such a speedy and impressive performance operate extraordinarily poorly. Language "through the eye" seems to demonstrate little power to activate the language-learning mechanisms and initiate the necessary system-building activities. It is important to note, and a severe brake on my hopes concerning the generality of inference rules, that this critical difference exists. Why this should be so is a question to tax our capacities, both in terms of conceptual notions and in terms of the neurophysiology involved.

While I would still advocate looking for general inference rules, I must agree with Fry's contention that the auditory aspects of language are indeed fundamental. I am sure that everyone who has played language games with children or who has worked with the language pathologies, such as aphasia, has been impressed with the importance of the auditory base of language.

Weir, who is also interested in early auditory manifestations of language, has presented us with a conceptual puzzle. In exploring the data concerning "phonemic drift" in the babbling of children, she appears to be disturbing the set positions of both polar groups. Phonemic drift has frequently been postulated by psychologists as a consequence of presumed primary and secondary reinforcement but has sometimes been considered as being contrary to certain linguistic expectations. To date there is some evidence that this sort of shifting toward the language models in terms of appropriate sound systems does take place. The language sounds that are available in the environment become more frequent in the babbling of the child (whether the children are reinforced for them or not). The fact that there is a drift toward what *will be* "productive" speech noises is an interesting datum for which to account and one which may, in turn, be important in getting at underlying mechanisms that serve to break into the acoustic stream of speech.

Templin in her turn has presented us with another puzzle. In the face of what might be a polarity between events proceeding in the phonology and events proceeding in the development of the grammar, Templin's data suggest a unity. The data begin to reveal that language has an all-of-a-pieceness, that the children who make articulation errors (which we might originally suppose to be relatively trivial, superficial kinds of events with respect to the general development of language) are also the children who fail to keep up with the norms on the Berko Morphology Test, who give word associations that look more like those of younger children than like those of older children, and so on. Here in the midst of what appeared to be a polarization, we find that events in both the phonological and syntactic domains are highly correlated in nature. Language, then, persists in being all of a piece, even though our theories may not yet have joined it together. I think these puzzling data are valuable for us to have.

Finally, I think we must agree that Premack's experiment evaluating the degree of language competence in the infrahuman is a matter of appreciable excitement. Everyone who spoke about this experiment did so with feeling and with the strong anticipation of failure. Many investigators would in fact be very upset if the experiment did not fail. The most serious question raised was whether the failure would be elegant enough to justify the conduct of the experiment. There is no point in merely another failure to teach a chimpanzee to talk. The question is whether the experiment and its test conditions are adequate and whether the conclusion of failure can be pronounced unambiguously. At the same time one must ask if the possible partial attainments are sufficient to afford a demonstration of any kinds of language capacities that the chimp may have or any of the compound abilities that presumably assemble in some complex total fashion to determine language competence and performance. While sentiment against the experiment was strong and somewhat emotional, to me it appeared to be thoughtfully and usefully designed.

It is obvious that the first information of some importance will be attained before any chimpanzee is actually introduced to the apparatus. This is the vital question as to whether a human being (who we know, after all, actually possesses language competence) can learn the system. The questions of the resulting competence and correlated degree of skill in performance have many important applications. The deep general question that lies behind such questions as building reading machines for the blind and talking machines for chimpanzees is whether and to what extent nonlanguage noise may be substituted for natural noises, which up to now have proved to have peculiarly privileged status as auditory events.

Furthermore we must not lose sight of the fact that these experiments may shed light on the question as to whether linguistic competence is a more general behavioral competence than that found specifically in language alone. I, for one, will watch the Premack experiments with great interest.

## FINAL REMARKS

The reader will realize that much of the polarity and conflict that I have attributed to this conference has been injected in an attempt to make the issues more salient and the potential differences more clear cut. In point of fact a reading of the conference papers suggests that there is strong agreement on the general outlines of the coming paradigm for psycholinguistics. While vast portions of this paradigm remain to be detailed (particularly with respect to what constitutes evidence and how acceptable experimentation is to be performed), it cannot be denied that the paradigm of the generative grammarian dominates the field and to all appearances will determine the future shape of the field.

Whether one is a psycholinguist or not, there is clearly a challenge in the air that has to do with accounting for higher mental processes, thinking, systems of behavior, conceptualizations, and the host of issues relating "rules" to behavior. The challenge cannot be met by the older psychology, but the time is past when it could be turned aside as not being a legitimate part of the science. I am hopeful that as we struggle with the issues so clearly revealed in psycholinguistics, we will find a paradigm that will carry us far in the general attack on all such higher mental activities.

## REFERENCES

HEBB, D. O. The American revolution. *American Psychologist*, 1960, *15*, 735–745.

JENKINS, J. J., and PALERMO, D. S. Mediation processes and the acquisition of linguistic structure. In *The Acquisition of Language*, Ursula Bellugi and R. W. Brown (Eds.), *Monogr. Soc. Res. Child Developm.*, 1964, *29*, 1, 141–169.

KUHN, T. S. *The Structure of Scientific Revolutions.* Chicago: University of Chicago Press, 1962.

MACLAY, H. Linguistics and language behavior. *Journal of Communication*, 1964, *14*, 66–73.

MILLER, G. A., GALANTER, E., and PRIBRAM, K. *Plans and the Structure of Behavior.* New York: Holt, Rinehart & Winston, 1960.

OSGOOD, C. E., and SEBEOK, T. A. (Eds.) *Psycholinguistics: A Survey of Theory and Research Problems.* Baltimore: Waverly Press, Inc., 1954.

RUSSELL, W. A. Purpose and the problem of associative selectivity. In *Verbal Behavior and Learning*, C. N. Cofer and Barbara Musgrave (Eds.), New York: McGraw-Hill, 1963, pp. 258–271.

# APPENDIX

*Dan I. Slobin*

## SOVIET METHODS OF INVESTIGATING CHILD LANGUAGE
### A Topical Guide to "Abstracts of Soviet Studies of Child Language"

## *PHONOLOGICAL COMPETENCE*

1. *Conditioned response to words:* Fradkina (1955), Shvachkin (1948).
2. *Concept formation experiments:* Zhurova (1963).
3. *Direct questioning of children:* Zhurova (1963).
4. *Controlled imitation:* Lyamina (1958), Lyamina & Gagua (1963).
5. *Object naming:* Lyamina (1958), Lyamina & Gagua (1963).
6. *Recording and noting:* Levina (1940).

## *GRAMMATICAL AND LEXICAL COMPETENCE*

### *Comprehension*

1. *Ability to follow instructions to manipulate objects:* Sokhin (1959).
2. *Ability to follow instructions to identify named objects:* Istomina (1960), Lyamina (1958, 1960), Mallitskaya (1960).
3. *Interpretation of suffixes attached to new words:* Bogoyavlenskiĭ (1957).
4. *Conditioned responses to verbal stimuli:* Detgyar' (1957), El'kin (1957), El'konin (1955).
5. *Direct questioning of children:* Patrina (1959), Zhuĭkov (1955).

*Production*

1. *Ability to name presented objects:* Istomina (1948, 1960), Lyamina (1958).
2. *Content analysis of picture descriptions and written compositions:* Feofanov (1958, 1960), Meerson (1959).
3. *Analysis of answers to questions designed to elicit certain forms:* Babin (1958), Karpova (1955), Popova (1958), Zakharova (1958).
4. *Ability to apply suffixes to new words:* Bogoyavlenskiĭ (1957).
5. *Recording and noting:* Imedadze (1960), Kasatkin (1958).

## PRAGMATIC FUNCTIONS OF LANGUAGE

1. *Effect of naming on memory:* Kezheradze (1960), Mal'tseva (1957).
2. *Effect of naming on stimulus differentiation:* Ruzskaya (1958).
3. *Effect of verbal instructions on motor behavior:* Vykhodov (1959).

Dan I. Slobin

# ABSTRACTS OF SOVIET STUDIES
# OF CHILD LANGUAGE

BABIN, V. N. Ponimanie protivorechiĭ shkol'nikami II-VII klassov (Understanding of contradictions by pupils in grades two to seven). *Voprosy Psikhol.*, 1958, No. 3, 99–105.

This is an investigation of the understanding and use of complex sentences with subordinate clauses introduced by the conjunction *khotya* (though, although) and *ne smotrya na to, chto* (in spite of the fact that). Pupils were given two sentence-fill-in tasks: (1) sentence completion (e.g., "It's warm today, although ———"; "It's dark outside in spite of the fact that ———"); and (2) conjunction-fill-in (e.g., "We are building factories ——— make our country the strongest one"; "——— the sun shone all week, the ground did not dry out").

The author notes that some contradictions are understood as early as age eight, in contradistinction to Piaget's assertion that such constructions are not understood until eleven or twelve. The following results are presented:

| | *Percentage Correct Responses* | |
|---|---|---|
| *Age* | *Sentence Completion* | *Conjunction Insertion* |
| 8 | 77 | 55 |
| 10 | 80 | 67 |
| 13 | 86 | 80 |

Expressions with *although* are mastered better than those with *in spite of the fact that*. The author concludes that although the latter more clearly expresses opposition, the former is used much more frequently in speech.

Children were much more successful in dealing with contradictions related to human actions than those related to other phenomena. This difference was especially pronounced for the youngest subjects.

Several stages of mastery of grammatically expressed contradictions are described. At the earliest stage there is no sensitivity to the fact that the two clauses of such sentences must be in contradiction: e.g., "The boys were afraid to come to school late, although *the weather was nice"*; "We will certainly keep our promise, although *we helped you*." A causal relation between the two clauses predominates at this stage. For example, in inserting conjunctions, *because* is often used (e.g., "The weather cleared up, *because* there were signs of a storm").

At the next stage, the notion of contradiction is present, but it does not always correspond to possible contradictory situations in the real world. For example: "It was dark outside, in spite of the fact that *the sun was shining"*; "It was cloudy on the steppe, in spite of the fact that *the sun was burning hotly*."

The oldest children perform well on these tasks.

BOGOYAVLENSKIĬ, D. N. *Psikhologiya usvoeniya orfografii (The psychology of learning orthography)*. Moscow: Akad. Pedag. Nauk RSFSR, 1957. Pp. 261–266.

Children of five to six years were tested for their understanding of various suffixes (augmentative, diminutive, and agentive). The suffixes were appended to words not familiar to the children (an animal called a *lar*, a sweet kvas drink called *lafit*, and the fabric *kashemir*). The words were used to name pictured referents. Two children were then asked to explain the meanings of these words with suffixes attached. If they found this task difficult, the words with the various suffixes were then embedded into stories. All of the children could correctly identify the relative sizes of the referents on the basis of the augmentative and diminutive suffixes, but the agentive suffix was more difficult for them to interpret. The author points out that the former do not change the "basic lexical meaning" of a word, while the latter (agentive) does change this meaning, and he speculates that morphological principles of "word change" (e.g., diminutive) are achieved at an earlier age than those of "word formation" (e.g., agentive).

When a child's performance was correct, he still could not be brought to explain the formal differences between the words. E.g., the experimenter would ask: "You were right about the difference between the animals — one is little and the other is big; now pay attention to the words themselves as I say them: *lar—larenok;* what's the difference between them?" It was found that "regardless of the repeated oral presentation of these words, not one of the children (who had no difficulty in determining the semantic difference between these words) could give any sort of answer in this case. The children gave confused and embarrassed smiles, or simply remained silent, making no attempt to analyze the sounds of the words."

In another experiment, children were asked to supply diminutive suffixes to words that do not generally receive such suffixes, or at least not in the experience of the child (giraffe, sheep, acorn, oak, lion, ostrich, nose, wolf, nail). All of the children successfully provided diminutive suffixes, and only diminutive suffixes, of many sorts. Their productions were generally correct, though not all of them of course occur in the Russian language (since at least eight different suffixes were used by the children with these nouns). The only clearly incorrect usage, from the standpoint of standard, adult Russian, was the application of suffixes used only to diminish animate objects to inanimate objects as well. The children were generally correct in choosing suffixes following phonological laws of agreement with the final sound of the root word.

DETGYAR', E. N.  Slovo kak uslovnyĭ tormoz u deteĭ pervykh trekh let zhizni (The word as a conditioned inhibitor in infants during the first three years of life). *Trudy Inst. im. I. P. Pavlova*, 1957, *6*, 212–216. (Translation in *Sov. Psychol. & Psychiat.*, 1963, *1*(3), 14–17.)

Conditioned eyeblink responses to the sound of a bell were established in thirty-eight children between the ages of eleven and thirty-four months. An attempt was then made to establish a conditioned inhibition of the eyeblink response to the word "no." This was difficult or impossible to achieve in cases where the child did not understand the meaning of the word (i.e., when it functioned simply as an auditory stimulus) but was quite easy if the child already understood the meaning of the word. Conditioned inhibition to "no" as an inhibitory stimulus was also facilitated by preliminary training (in those cases where the child did not yet understand the word): ". . . a preliminary instruction in the inhibitory meaning of this word was conducted. Toward this end a game was played with the child daily for two to three weeks. He was shown various toys, which were then hidden, with the experimenter saying 'no rabbit,' 'no doll,' 'no ball,' until the child itself began to say 'no' when the toys disappeared."

Also, even if conditioned inhibition *is* established to a nonsemantic "no," it is of a different nature: "When the word 'no' is known to the infant, the reaction is more clearly pronounced and general in nature: not only is the blinking reflex absent, but so are all the other movements; a special mimicry is observed. The eyes are opened wide. There is a strained facial exprssion, the hands are often opened to the sides, etc. In the cases in which we succeeded in elaborating a conditioned inhibitory response to the unknown word 'no' or to the beat of the metronome, we observed only an absence of blinking responses."

EL'KIN, D. G.  Ob uslovnykh refleksakh na slozhnye slovesnye razdrazhiteli u shkol'nikov (On conditioned reflexes to complex verbal stimuli in children of school age). In *Materialy soveshchaniya po psikhologii*. Moscow: Akad. Pedag. Nauk RFSFR, 1957. Pp. 371–379.

Eyeblink responses were conditioned to spoken sentences. This was easily accomplished for all but the youngest subjects (age ten to twelve); for these subjects it was easiest to condition the response to the sentence, "The experiment is now beginning." It was also easy to condition the response to the sentence, "Today is a sunny day," provided it was true, but almost impossible if it was not true at the time. Once conditioning was established, individual words from the sentence were offered as stimuli. "In children of the 10–12 year-old range, the strength of the conditioned response may be determined by the place of a word in a sentence (first or last), or the loudness of its spoken elements . . . For children in the 12 to 14 year-old range, the main producers of the conditioned response are the subject and predicate of the sentence. For the 14 to 16 year-old children, those parts of the sentence which carry the most semantic weight, or content, of the sentence are the ones which produce the most conditioned reflex activity."

In children in the twelve- to fourteen-year-old range, reversing the word order (sentence still grammatical, Russian being an inflected language) in the stimulus sentence had no decremental effect on the conditioned reflex activity. This was not true of the younger children (ten to twelve).

EL'KONIN, D. B.   Osobennosti vzaimodeĭstviya pervoĭ i vtoroĭ signal'nykh sistem u deteĭ doshkol'nogo vozrasta (Peculiarities of the interaction of the first and second signal systems in children of preschool age). *Izvestiya Akad. Pedag. Nauk RSFSR*, 1955, vyp. 64, 27–47.

A game of lotto was played with children of preschool age (three to six years). Children were to respond to either pictures or names of familiar objects and to the simultaneous presentation of the picture of one object and the name of another.

It was found that for children of all ages a response conditioned to a direct stimulus (picture) was also given to its name. Younger children, however, could not establish differentiation of response, i.e., inhibition of response to pictures and positive response to words. Older children could establish both such a differentiation and its reversal, i.e., inhibition of response to words and positive response to pictures of their referents.

The phenomena are explained on the basis of elective irradiation between the two signal systems (Ivanov-Smolenskiĭ). Younger children (three and four years) are said to be unable to limit cortical activity to one of the two systems. Older children (five and six years) are said to be able to keep inhibitory responses to first signals from spreading to the second signal system but to have difficulty in halting the spread of stimulatory processes from the second signal to the first. (I.e., while they do not respond to words in the same way, they respond to pictures of their referents; they tend to respond to such pictures in the same way that they respond to their names.)

It is concluded that close interaction of the two signal systems is established early in life, with the word achieving increasing dominance in this interaction as children grow older.

FEOFANOV, M. P.   Ob uportreblenii predlogov v detskoĭ rechi (On the use of prepositions in child speech). *Voprosy Psikhol.*, 1958, No. 3, 118–124.

Children of ages three to seven were asked to describe pictures and actions, and their use of prepositions was noted. The earliest prepositions used were those occurring most frequently in the language; these are also the prepositions having the greatest number of meanings (e.g., *na* has some forty-four different senses).

The three most common prepositions — *na*, *v*, and *s* (very roughly, *on*, *in*, and *with*) — were examined in detail. (The article presents many examples, but the presentation of data is entirely discursive and qualitative.) In each case the earliest usages expressed "concrete" relations (primarily spatial). As children grow older, each of the prepositions acquired more senses with those related to time, goal direction, and more abstract or extended relations appearing later. In the author's words: "Initially their use is confined to relations with a concrete meaning understood by the child from visual perception (space relations, relations involving mutuality . . .); then it extends to relations without such visual support (relations of purpose, time relations, and space relations used figuratively)."

FEOFANOV, M. P. Oshibki v postroenii predlozheniĭ kak pokazatel' stepeni usvoeniya grammaticheskogo stroya yazyka (Errors in sentence construction as an indicator of the degree of mastery of the grammatical structure of the language). *Doklady Akad. Pedag. Nauk RSFSR*, 1960, No. 1, 37–38.

This short report is interesting in that it reveals that Russian-speaking children have difficulty with prepositions all the way through their eight or nine years of school (i.e., well into adolescence). The errors are of four types: (1) preposition written as part of following word with no break (many Russian prepositions are single consonants that form a consonant cluster with the next word; e.g., *s nimi, v sadu, k drugu*); (2) use of superfluous, extra prepositions (this is said to be especially common among three-year-olds; e.g., *Mama sidit okolo u pechki*, something like "Mama sits close to near the stove"); (3) omission of prepositions; and (4) incorrect use of prepositions (substitution of a correct by an incorrect preposition in a given phrase).

FRADKINA, F. I. Vozniknovenie rechi u rebenka (The beginning of speech in the child). *Uch. zap. LGPI im A. I. Gertsena*, 1955, 12.

At age seven to eight months the child responds only to the rhythmic-melodic nature of words. For example, response conditioned to the word *voz'mi* generalized to the word *gudit;* responses to *ládushki-ládushki* generalized to *kapitán-kapitán*. Shortly after this age it is possible to condition responses to more specific aspects of word sounds.

At age seven to eight months it is no easier to condition a response to a word than to any other sound; but by age ten to eleven months conditioning to a word requires four times fewer reinforcements than conditioning to other sounds.

IMEDADZE, N. V. K psikhologicheskoĭ prirode rannego dvuyazychiya (On the psychological nature of early bilingualism). *Voprosy Psikhol.*, 1960, No. 1, 60–68.

The article discusses the development of the author's Georgian-Russian bilingual child. The girl's parents and grandfather spoke only Georgian to her;

her grandmother and nurse spoke only Russian to her. At every age the child's lexicon was of normal size in comparison with monolingual children, but consisted, naturally, of words from both languages. The first word appeared at 11 months, and the first pair of translation equivalents at 1,2. Until the twentieth month the child would utter translation equivalents together in one sentence (if she knew both words), spoke mixed sentences, and did not adapt her communications to the language of her interlocutor. Her morphology was productive in both languages, making for word creations of mixed origins.

Where the two languages have similar grammatical cases (e.g., the instrumental), the correct use of a case appeared almost simultaneously in both languages (e.g., the first appearance of the instrumental in Russian came three days after its first appearance in Georgian). Where case systems differ in the two languages, the system learned first would generalize to the other language. For example, in subject-verb-object sentences expressing desire (e.g., "Dali wants a dress"), the object is inflected in Russian, while the subject remains uninflected in the nominative base form; the matter is precisely the opposite in Georgian, where the object is uninflected and the subject receives a dative case ending ("ergodic" case). This child learned the Russian form first and generalized the pattern of object inflection to Georgian (e.g., she said *Dali unda kabas* [Dali wants a dress], instead of the correct *Dalis unda kaba*).

By the end of the second year the child began to separate out the two languages for purposes of communication with different people. If she found both her mother and her grandmother in the room at once, she would repeat her utterances in both languages. These translations were generally not word for word but retained the content generally. When speaking with a given individual, however, she would establish a strong set to continue speaking in that language and, if questioned in the other language, would either ignore the question or answer it in the language she had been speaking (the "wrong" language).

At the beginning of the third year the child began to use the expressions "in Russian" and "in Georgian" and would ask for translation equivalents of new words. By the end of the third year these expressions referred not only to single words but to whole communication situations (e.g., "Don't talk Georgian — Irakli doesn't know Georgian"; said in Russian), and the parents considered a "sense of bilingualism" to have developed. The subsequent rapid development of metalinguistic interest at this early age is interpreted by the author in terms of the special linguistic demands placed upon a bilingual child.

ISTOMINA, Z. M.  Razvitie proizvol'noĭ pamyati v doshkol'nom vozraste (The development of voluntary memorization in preschool age). *Izvestiya* APN RSFSR, 1948, vyp. 14.

Children of ages three to seven were required to memorize a list of words in either a laboratory situation or a game situation (in which the child played the role of a customer in a store, purchasing objects named by the experimenter). For each age group, more words were remembered in the play situation than in the laboratory situation.

*Average Number of Words Remembered*

| Age | Laboratory Situation | Play |
|-----|---------------------|------|
| 3 to 4 | 0.6 | 1.0 |
| 4 to 5 | 1.5 | 3.0 |
| 5 to 6 | 2.0 | 3.3 |
| 6 to 7 | 2.3 | 3.8 |

ISTOMINA, Z. M. Vospriatie i nazyvanie tsveta v rannem vozraste (Perception and color naming in early childhood). *Isvestiya Akad. Pedag. Nauk RSFSR*, 1960, vyp. 113, 102–113. (Translation in *Sov. Psychol. & Psychiat.*, 1963, *1*(2), 37–45.)

Forty children with normal color vision were first asked to match and group color samples and then to identify named colors. In the first part of the experiment, the child was given a card with three circles of the same color (various shades) and asked to choose "those that are the same" from a group of twenty-one colors. Performance was good on this task, only adjacent or related colors being grouped together (red, orange, and yellow; blue and violet). Only a small number of subjects knew color names. "They were most familiar with the word red, and then with yellow, green, and dark blue [*sinii*]. None of the little children gave voice, on his own, to the other color names (orange, light blue [*goluboĭ*], and violet)." They were inconsistent in relating the names they knew to color specimens. While much naming seemed random, in 15 per cent of the cases it was found that children gave a single common name to all of the colors on one half of the spectrum and another to all those on the other half.

In the second part of the experiment, subjects were generally not able to pick out appropriate colors when given their names. "Whereas in the experiments with selection and grouping of colors by object [color sample] the child was subject to confusion of adjacent colors, in the problem of selection by name he was likely to choose color specimens completely at random." Thus, although the child has intuitive color groupings, he does not relate color names to these groupings. "Analysis of the material shows that the finding of a color by name is exceedingly difficult for a small child. The number of errors is greater than the number of correct answers."

It was also found that "Such names as dark blue, dark green, etc., are not employed by the children. (An effort on the part of the researcher to teach them these names met with no success.) It was also found that none of the little children possessed a vocabulary of attributive color names such as orange (the words for orange as fruit and as color differ in Russian), straw-colored, brick-colored, sky-blue, etc. This verbal connection of the names of colors and objects is apparently difficult for children. . . . One may cite cases in which children denote colors by the most unexpected words. Thus, Sveta N. (2,1 years of age), when asked to name a color, answered 'small'; Ira M. (age 2) answered 'sour'; Kolya S. (2,2) answered 'round'; Yura P. (2,0) answered 'new.' "

KARPOVA, S. N. Osoznanie slovesnogo sostava rechi rebenkom doshkol'nogo vozrasta (The preschooler's realization of the lexical structure of speech). *Voprosy Psikhol.,* 1955, No. 4, 43–55.

Children between the ages of three and seven, after preliminary training with counting pictures and orally presented words, were asked to repeat sentences and respond to the questions: "How many words are here?" and "Which is the first . . . second . . . third . . . word?" Most children had no difficulty in repeating sentences, but various types of distortion occurred: (1) Sometimes the child would not repeat the sentence but summarize its meaning in one word (e.g., *E:* "Cold weather came. What words did I say?" *S:* "Winter.") (2) Sometimes the child expanded the sentence with an interpretation (e.g., *E:* "Vanya went home." *S:* "Because it was bad weather.") (3) Sometimes the child would repeat a few important nouns from the sentence (e.g., *E:* "They brought up a kitten and two puppies." *S:* "Puppy and kitty.").

Three stages were observed in the task of counting words and identifying their ordinal positions: (1) The youngest children took the sentence as a unified message and did not break it up on the basis of individual words but on the basis of semantic units (e.g., *E:* "Galya and Vova went walking." *S* (age 4,6): "Galya and Vova went walking." *E:* "How many words?" *S:* "Two." *E:* "What's the first?" *S:* "Galya went walking and Vova went walking.") (Another example: "The boy is laughing." A seven-year-old child said that there is one word here because "only one boy is laughing.") (2) Somewhat older children begin in the same way but change, under repeated questioning, to isolation of the main components of the action described. (E.g., a child aged 6,10, in response to the sentence "Galya and Vova went walking," replied, "There are two words. Vova is one, and Galya is the other.") This isolation of nouns is seen as the first step toward formal analysis of sentences into words. Under further questioning, children at this level begin to break sentences into subject and predicate. (E.g., "Misha ran quickly. What is the first word?" *S* (6,1): "Misha." *E:* "And the second?" *S:* "Ran quickly." (3) A few of the older children were able to break sentences into all of their separate words (generally with the exception of prepositions and conjunctions). Some children at this level even occasionally broke individual words into syllables.

*Per Cent of Children in Each Stage*

| Stage | Age | | |
|---|---|---|---|
| | 3,6 to 5 | 5 to 6 | 6 to 7 |
| 1 | 74 | 45 | 20 |
| 2 | 22 | 32 | 60 |
| 3 | 4 | 23 | 20 |

Training, consisting of having the child move a plastic counter for each word in a sentence, was quite successful. Such external support was especially useful for those children who could not perform the task otherwise. These children could work only with the counters and could not transfer the skill to operating on the words alone. However, children who could perform the original task with difficulty did benefit from motor training when returning to the solely verbal task.

KASATKIN, N. V. Gruppovaya rech' kak osobyĭ vid rechi (Group speech as a special form of speech). *Voprosy Psikhol.*, 1958, No. 2, 47–59.

The author studied the group speech (sometimes called collective speech) of small groups of children aged four to ten. He distinguishes three forms of such speech: (1) collective choral responses, (2) collective statements or repetitions, and (3) collective monologue. Collective repetitions tend to be rhythmic. Children engaging in collective monologue generally do not listen to one another. The author also observed a good deal of collective creative ability — chiefly joint poetry-writing by small groups of children. He finds poetry produced by such groups to be more coherent and unified than poetry produced by individual children.

Generally only simple sentences are produced under all three conditions of group speech.

Group speech can probably be found only in homogeneous groups; it is a form of emotive speech which functions to tie a group together. In the evolution of language this form of speech probably preceded both monologue and true dialogue.

KEZHERADZE, E. D. Rol' slova v zapominanii i nekotorye osobennosti pamyati rebenka (The role of the word in memorization, and some features of the memory of the child). *Voprosy Psikhol.*, 1960, No. 1, 78–85.

(The author is Georgian.) Children of ages four to seven were given three tasks with six lotto cards depicting familiar objects: (1) to place the cards on a blank piece of cardboard; (2) to place each card upon its matching picture on a large piece of cardboard; (3) same as (2), but naming each picture aloud while making the placement. After each placement they were asked to recall the six cards. Performance improved with age and with condition $(3 > 2 > 1)$:

*Average Number of Cards Recalled**

| | *Age* | | | |
| Condition | 4 | 5 | 6 | 7 |
|---|---|---|---|---|
| 1. Simple Placement | 3.2 | 3.6 | 4.2 | 4.8 |
| 2. Matching to Picture | 4.2 | 4.6 | 4.8 | 5.6 |
| 3. Same + Naming | 5.0 | 5.2 | 5.8 | 6.0 |

* Total number of cards was 6.

In the second condition (placement without naming), children of four and five carried the card with them to the array, making a visual match, while the older children looked away from the card to the array, carrying the name of the pictured object as a mediator.

In other experiments using depictions of unfamiliar objects (musical instruments, nonsense shapes), performance on recall was worse, but the effects of age and task condition were maintained in the same order.

LEVINA, R. E. *Nedostatki chteniya i pis'ma u detei (Defects of reading and writing in children)*. Moscow: Uchpedgiz, 1940.

The following are listed as the most common pronunciation errors of Russian children:

1. replacement of voiceless by voiced stops (*naka* for *noga, tom* for *dom*)
2. confusion of *r* and *l* (*tli* for *tri*)
3. confusion of *m* and *n* (*nisok* for *meshok*)
4. confusion of voiced and voiceless sibilants (*zhdorovo* for *zdorovo*)
5. double shift, from voiceless to voiced, and from alveopalatal to alveolar (*zlyapka* for *shlyapka*)
6. "splintering of sounds": disturbance of the type of *abiskvo* for *yablochko*
7. confusion of palatalized and unpalatalized consonants (*tul'* for *stul*)
8. replacement of *ĭ* in diphthongs by *l'* (*tal'* for *chaĭ*)
9. replacement of *r* and *l* by a diphthong with *i* (*boino* for *bol'no*)
10. replacement of *z* by *d* (*Danka* for *Zanka*)
11. replacement of *s* by *t* (*tabaka* for *sobaka*)

LYAMINA, G. M. K voprosu o mekkanizme ovladeniya proiznosheniem slov u detei vtorogo i tret'ego goda zhizni (On the mechanism of mastery of pronunciation of words by children in the second and third years of life). *Voprosy Psikhol.*, 1958, No. 6, 119–130.

Thirty-one children were studied longitudinally from ages 1,2 to 2,6. Two abilities were tested: (1) repetition of words in response to the instruction "Say ———," and (2) naming of objects in response to the question "What's this?" Children can give the appropriate verbal responses as early as 1,3 but with much interference from motor responses and expressive verbalizations. Nonverbal responses (pointing, etc.) declined considerably by age 1,9.

Various types of incomplete responses were observed: (1) the child cannot pronounce the required word but moves his lips and tongue, reproduces the intonation pattern without articulating the word, or pronounces the word soundlessly. The author calls this "verbal tuning," and attributes it to immature coordination of the articulatory apparatus and the breathing mechanism. (2) The child does not utter the required word but one more familiar to him. (3) The child repeats the previously presented word. Generally it was possible to get a response by repeating a word three or four times with intervals of three to five seconds (i.e., in the course of fifteen to twenty seconds). (Adults can repeat words with a latency of 0.6 to 0.7 second.) By age two all of the children could respond verbally to the question "What's this," and 89 per cent of the responses were semantically (though not phonologically) adequate. At about this age children become especially adept at quickly imitating words. A novel object will often so distract a one-year-old that he will attend only to the object and not repeat its name when offered by the experimenter. In these cases the object is removed from view, the name offered again, and the child repeats it with ease. Generally, children of this age were more successful in imitating words in the absence of their referents. (These differences disappear by about age two.)

Contrary to previous opinion and report, children were not better at naming familiar, everyday objects than they were at naming objects whose names were taught in the experimental setting without the opportunity to manipulate them (ages 1,8 to 2,1). The author proposes that motor and verbal responses are often in competition for children of this age: (1) it is more difficult to name objects while playing with them; (2) the output of speech is diminished while the child is learning to walk and while he is walking (as opposed to sitting or standing); (3) the form of speech is more primitive while the child is walking. She proposes further that coordination of various motor acts with each other, and with speaking, is followed by a rapid spurt in language development.

All of the children generally repeated both syllables of two-syllable words, though the pronunciation of a given word varied greatly; e.g., the following are pronunciations of the same word by the same subject on various days of the experiment (stimulus word: kuvshín): kuti, koti, koten', zusin, kuin, atin, unin, kaïvin, kutin, pusyn, basin, sisin, vatin. (Note that there is no steady direction of improvement, as previous authors are said to have stated. "This complicates work directed towards phonetic improvement of children at the second and beginning of the third year of life. One cannot tell which sounds are worth correcting if the child pronounces the word differently almost every time.")

It is proposed that these difficulties are based not on problems of hearing but of articulation. Verbal auditory discrimination is well formed even before the child begins to speak. (This has been demonstrated on the basis of the child's ability to point correctly to objects whose names sound similar. Cf. Mallitskaya [1960], who used the same subjects for comprehension studies. She found, for example, that these children could learn to point correctly to objects with such similar names as koza, osa, and kosa; or baran and baraban.)

Children had more difficulty pronouncing words in sentences than individually. Examples: "Misha K. (2,1) repeated the word selyódka as selyódka but repeated the sentence selyodka na taryélkye as telyótka na alyétkya." "Serezha T. (2,0) correctly repeated the word ananás but repeated the sentence ya lyublyú ananás as lyulya anás."

LYAMINA, G. M. Razvitie ponimaniya rechi u deteĭ vtorogo goda zhizni (Development of speech comprehension in children in the second year of life.) Voprosy Psikhol., 1960, No. 3, 106–121.

Subjects were thirty-two children, studied longitudinally from the ages of 1,1 to 2,6. The study is described as a "pedagogic experiment" aimed at teaching new word meanings to the children (operationalized as correct responding to the instructions "Show where there's a ———" and "Give me a ———").

*Tasks:* (1) Pick an object from an array of five to seven objects used in training; (2) pick an object from an array of twelve or thirteen, including unfamiliar objects; (3) recognize a picture or model of an object on first presentation; (4) identify objects with similar-sounding names; (5) identify one of several objects similar in appearance. (The objects are classifiable on the basis of two sorts of criteria: (*a*) familiar or unfamiliar to the child, and (*b*) capable of being acted upon or not.)

*Results:* Variables leading to difficulty for children aged 1,8 to 1,10 were (1) increasing size of the array, (2) similar-sounding names, and (3) pictures of objects, as opposed to the objects themselves.

Looking at, pointing to, and manipulating a referred-to object were seen as three separable components of responding to names. For example, in response to the instruction, "Give me a ———," the child may look at the correct object, and even point to it, and then give *E* the wrong object. (Cf. Soviet experiments on the directive function of speech.) Apparently the child feels constrained to point at some object, even if the name given by *E* does not correspond to any object in the array. The child may point to the same wrong object again and again, even if he can say, "There is no ———."

The subjects were poor at recognizing pictures until twenty-two months, at which time they could also understand the names and name the objects themselves.

It is easiest to teach a child the name of an object if it is the one new object among a collection of familiar ones. Under such conditions, the new object calls forth an orienting response. The orienting response can be so strong that, even if the child knows the names of the other objects, he may point to the new one when asked to point to one of the familiar ones.

Word-learning is aided by many presentations of objects in different aspects; many different kinds of associations must be built up between word and referent.

It is difficult to do any aspect of experiments of this type with children younger than 1,6.

LYAMINA, G. M., and GAGUA, N. I.   O formirovanii pravil'nogo proiznosheniya slov u detei ot polutory do trekh let (On the formation of correct pronunciation of words in children from one-and-a-half to three years of age). *Voprosy Psikhol.,* 1963, No. 6, 93–105. (Translation in *Soviet Psychol. & Psychiat.,* 1964, *2*(4), 15–27.)

The pronunciation of seventy-three children, between the ages of one-and-a-half and three, was examined in experiments requiring the children to name pictures and to imitate the speech of the experimenters. The article deals with the pronunciation of consonants only. The following were found to be easy for children of this age: p, b, t, d, m, n, g, k, v, l; while the following were found to be difficult: z, s, ž, š, šč, č, ts, kh, f, r. In short, except for bilabials and nasals, stops are easier to pronounce than continuants. The authors state that groove fricatives are especially difficult. The findings are interpreted in terms of physiological maturation of abilities to coordinate air flow and articulation. Evidence for this interpretation is considered to be the finding that affricates and fricatives are generally replaced by stops that maintain the same point of articulation as the sounds which they replace. Replacement of stops by other stops seems to be less systematic as far as point of articulation is concerned.

MALLITSKAYA, M. K. K metodike ispol'zovaniya kartinok dlya razv:tiya poni-maniya rechi u deteĭ v kontse pervogo i na vtorom godu zhizni (A method for using pictures to develop speech comprehension in children at the end of the first and in the second year of life). *Voprosy Psikhol.*, 1960, No. 3, 122–126.

By about the age of nine months a normal child can differentiate objects and understand the gesture of pointing. Pictures at this stage can be used to develop speech comprehension. The purpose of this experiment was to determine the best means of presentation to form a connection between a word and a picture of its referent.

The study was carried out in the division of development and child-rearing of the Institute of Pediatrics of the Academy of Medical Sciences of the USSR. Subjects were ten healthy, normal children, between the ages of 0,9 and 1,6.

Pictures of toys, animals, plants, objects of daily use were attached to four sides of a wooden cube. The experimenter would point to a picture and repeat its name two or three times (e.g., *Vot lisa* = "This is a fox"). The experimenter would then turn the cube, removing the designated picture from view, and tell the child to find that picture. Not more than two pictures were used per session. In a later part of the experiment, several pictures were presented simultaneously on cards.

It took several weeks to train the children to sit calmly and attend to the experiment and even longer to train them to perform as required. Once this training was completed, however, the children became very adept at the task and, by eleven to twelve months of age, could generally learn a new word after two or three repetitions and could easily differentiate and find eight different pictures on two cubes.

After this stage the child was presented with three pictures, one of which was new to him. The new picture evokes a strong orienting response, which weakens as soon as the picture is named. The children were generally able to learn such names after one presentation.

By age twelve to thirteen months more difficult tasks could be posed. The children's attention span had increased from three to five minutes to eight to ten minutes, and some children did not want to leave the room after the experimental session had ended. At this point it was possible to teach three new words in one session, using the triad presentation described above. The three new pictures were then presented simultaneously, and the children were generally able to point to the appropriate pictures in response to the experimenter's naming.

The author summarizes: "The present investigation was carried out with ten healthy children aged ten to fifteen months with a view to find out the possibility of forming word image connections at this age. It was found that even at the age of twelve to thirteen months such connections can be formed under some conditionings after a single reinforcement. The most important condition for developing these connections is the presence of an intense orienting reaction to the named image, as is the case when a new image is placed among other images whose names the child already knows."

MAL'TSEVA, K. P. Naglyadnye i slovesnye opory pri zapominanii u shkol'nikov (Visual and verbal aids in memorizing by school children). *Doklady Akad. Pedag. Nauk RSFSR*, 1957, No. 1, 111–115.

Subjects were children aged nine, eleven, thirteen, and fifteen; and adults (ten subjects per group). Memory for a list of fifteen words was tested immediately after training, and one week later. There were three different training procedures, using different sorts of memory aids: (1) subject was given a collection of twenty pictures and had to pick the corresponding picture for each word in the list to be memorized; (2) subject was given a collection of cards with printed words and had to pick the corresponding card for each word in the list to be memorized; (3) in response to each word on the list, subject was to think of a word similar in meaning and write it down. Half of the subjects went through the training procedures in the order 1–2–3 and half in the order 2–1–3. Different materials were used in each procedure.

Visual supports (Procedure 1) were a better aid for both short- and long-term memory for all subjects than written words (Procedure 2); but selection of words as memory aids by subjects (Procedure 3) was as good as Procedure 1 for the younger subjects and somewhat better than Procedure 1 for the older subjects. The relative advantage of visual over verbal aids decreased with age; this is taken as evidence of "the strengthening with age of the role of the second signal system in memory processes. . . ."

MARTSINOVSKAYA, E. N. Vosproizvendenie zvuko-slogovoĭ struktury slova glukhimi det'mi, nachinayushchimi obuchenie yazyku s daktil'noĭ rechi (Reproduction of the sound-syllabic structure of words by deaf children beginning to learn the dactyl alphabet). *Doklady Akad. Pedag. Nauk RSFSR,* 1960, No. 2, 115–118.

Deaf children beginning to learn the dactyl alphabet were asked to name pictures aloud and then to name them aloud while manually spelling out the name. The latter procedure often helped improve pronunciation. Because there is one letter for each sound in a word in Russian, simultaneous speaking and manual spelling had a positive effect on the common problem of leaving out sounds in deaf speech, thus preserving the syllabic nature of Russian words. Deaf children often confuse voiced and voiceless consonants, and palatalized and unpalatalized consonants; because such distinctions are obligatory in the spelling system, simultaneous spelling and speaking aided the articulatory discrimination of these oft-confused distinctive features.

Dactyl spelling had a detrimental effect on the pronunciation of unstressed vowels, however; these are reduced in spoken Russian but were not reduced in the speech of the deaf subjects (there being no orthographical marker for stress in Russian).

MEERSON, YA. YA. Ob osobennostyakh vzaimodeĭstviya signal'nykh sistem u deteĭ s raznym urovnem razvitiya rechi (Features of the interaction of the signal systems in children at various levels of speech development). *Doklady Akad. Pedag. Nauk RSFSR*, 1959, No. 3, 85–88.

Pictures were described by twenty three-year-olds, sixteen five-year-olds and ten seven-year-olds; aspects of their speech were studied.

The author concludes that verbs are the easiest part of speech for children to learn because the three-year-old has all the "common verbs" in his vocabulary, has a shorter latency in naming with verbs than with nouns, and often labels objects with verbs (e.g., calls a gate "to open," using the infinitive of the verb).

The prepositions *v* (in), *na* (on), and *s* (with) are learned earliest; *nad* (on top of, upon, above), *pered* (in front of), and *mezhdu* (between) are learned latest.

Younger children tend to use the more general adjectives "big-small" for several dimensions, even if their vocabulary includes the more specific terms: "wide-narrow" (*shirokiĭ-uzkiĭ*), "long-short" (*dlinnyĭ-korotkiĭ*), and "tall-short" (*vysokiĭ-nizkiĭ*).

While there were many grammatical overregularizations, children also had difficulty in extending known rules to some rarely heard or unfamiliar words. They found it most difficult to extend the use of action-modifying prefixes to verbs (e.g., *polz*, meaning "crawled," can be prefixed by *v*, the preposition "in," to mean "crawled in"; by the particle *vy*, to mean "crawled out"; by the particle *pere*, to mean "crawled over"; and so on). Even the seven-year-olds had difficulty with these prefixes.

Vocabulary size and grammatical development appeared to be independent.

Three-year-olds often could not name pictures of objects but could name such objects when presented with them directly.

PATRINA, D. T. O ponimanii znacheniya slov doshkol'nikami (On the understanding of the meanings of words by preschoolers). *Voprosy Psikhol.*, 1959, No. 4, 59–63.

The study is directed at children's understanding of metaphorical extensions of the meanings of words of physical description (cold, fresh, deep, to fall, etc.). Children were asked to explain the meaning of phrases like "deep secret." The following are typical of the author's findings:

| Phrase | Percentage of Children Understanding Phrase |
|---|---|
| deep river | 79 |
| deep autumn | 35 |
| deep secret | 13 |
| deep sadness | 6 |

Subjects often attempted to apply the common, physical meaning of words to their metaphorical extensions, e.g., "golden rays" because "they're made of gold."

The author goes on to teach extended meanings through texts and speech in real situations and finds that this training improves children's explanations of such meanings.

POPOVA, M. I.  Grammaticheskie elementy yazyka v rechi deteĭ preddoshkol'nogo vozrasta (Grammatical elements of language in the speech of pre-preschool children.) *Voprosy Psikhol.*, 1958, No. 3, 106–117.

This is a study of the development of grammatical gender in child speech — "a category lacking in lexical meaning." Subjects were fifty-five children ranging in age from 1,10 to 3,6.

Russian has three genders — feminine, masculine, and neuter. Commonly, feminine nouns end in -*a*, masculine in consonants, and neuter in -*o*; however, a number of masculine animate nouns end in -*a*. (There is also a variety of less common endings, all of them unique to a given gender except for certain palatalized consonants, which may be masculine or feminine.) The past tense of the verb carries a gender suffix — zero for masculine, -*a* for feminine, and -*o* for neuter (reduced, when unstressed, to be indistinguishable from the feminine).

This experiment studied gender agreement betwen nouns and verbs in the past tense, using only masculine and feminine nouns. There was a small list of verbs — examples given are *prishel(a)* = came, *ubezhal(a)* = ran away, *pel(a)* = sang, *upal(a)* = fell, *el(a)* = ate, and *pil(a)* = drank — and four series of nouns:

1. animate nouns whose gender distinction is based either on a pair of different words (e.g., boy-girl) or on the arbitrary formal cue of the word ending (e.g., *volk* = wolf [masc.], *lisa* = fox [fem.]);
2. names of animals whose gender within a species is morphologically marked (e.g., *ezh-ezhikha* = male and female hedgehog);
3. names of relatives (appearing early in child's vocabulary), all having the feminine endings -*a* or -*ya*, but some being masculine (e.g., *mama, papa, dyadya* = uncle, *teta* = aunt);
4. inanimate nouns, whose gender is based on purely morphological criteria.

Children were told stories using these nouns, with pictures, and were then asked questions about the stories in the past tense plural (e.g., "Which animals ran away to the forest?" or "Which toys fell on the floor?"). Individual experiments were preceded, a day before, by a group session in which the experimenter began with questions such as the preceding, next read the story, and then answered the questions in subject-predicate form (e.g., "The wolf ran away, the fox ran away. . ."). The 8,914 responses were analyzed. Children were classified into four groups on the basis of their responses:

1. 22 children, aged 1,10 to 3,2 (7 boys, 15 girls): feminine verb ending predominated (0 to 34 per cent correct agreements with masculine nouns, 70 to 100 per cent with feminine nouns);

2. 9 children, aged 2,6 to 3,3 (4 boys, 5 girls): masculine verb ending predominated (75 to 100 per cent correct agreements with masculine nouns, 0 to 40 per cent with feminine nouns);

3. 11 children, aged 2,2 to 3,5 (4 boys, 7 girls): both genders used and equally confused (45 to 81 per cent correct agreements with masculine nouns, 40 to 90 per cent with feminine);

4. 13 children, aged 2,3 to 3,6 (8 boys, 5 girls): generally correct use of both genders (75 to 100 per cent correct agreements with both masculine and feminine nouns).

*Distribution of Subjects into Gender-Agreement Groups on the Basis of Age*

| | | Percentage of Subjects in Each Gender-Agreement Group | | | |
| | | 1 | 2 | 3 | 4 |
| *Age* | *N* | *Feminine* | *Masculine* | *Mixed* | *Correct* |
| 1,10 to 2,6 | 25 | 52 | 8 | 16 | 24 |
| 2,7 to 3,0 | 18 | 39 | 17 | 22 | 22 |
| 3,1 to 3,6 | 12 | 17 | 33 | 25 | 25 |

Note that overgeneralization of the feminine drops with age, overgeneralization of the masculine increases with age, and there is no increase in correct usage over the whole age range.

The following explanations are proposed for the initial overgeneralization of the feminine: (1) it is a strongly and consistently marked gender (*-a*, as opposed to a variety of consonants); (2) Russian-speaking little children tend to use open, prolonged syllables, even in uttering masculine nouns (e.g., *tigra* instead of *tigr*); (3) diary materials show that 70 per cent of the words of children of this age end in *-a*. When the masculine (zero) ending of the past tense emerges in a child's speech, it tends to drive out entirely the earlier feminine (*-a*) ending, which re-enters only later in the period of mixed usage.

Other findings: Feminine animal names, having more familiar masculine roots (e.g., *tigritsa* = tigress) were generally treated as masculine. Some subjects, for example, said: "*Slon* (male elephant), *ezh* (male hedgehog) — that's he; *slonikha* (female elephant), *ezhikha* (female hedgehog) — that's he too, but only bigger." Thus these endings were apparently taken as masculine augmentatives (cf. phonetic symbolism findings).

Children in the fourth gender-agreement group, whose usage was generally correct, seemed to rely on the formal morphological ending rather than on the semantic cue. For example, they still had trouble with names of masculine relatives ending in -*a* (e.g., *papa*), often using feminine past-tense verb endings with such nouns. Other evidence of their reliance on the sound of the noun was the use of feminine verb endings in cases of mispronunciation of masculine nouns (e.g., *tigra* for *tigr*).

The remainder of the study consisted of attempts to train the subjects in correct gender agreement. Training was most helpful for the children in the third group (mixed usage). Self-correction also appeared at this stage. Training was least effective for children in the first group (predominance of feminine verb endings). This is taken as additional evidence for a sequence of stages.

Training was carried on four times per week for two months and, when effective, remained effective for at least two weeks, when a posttest was conducted. Of two types of training, metalinguistic and instrumental, the latter was more effective.

In metalinguistic training the child was rerun through the original experiment, with correction of errors and approval given by the experimenter ("right," "good," etc.).

In instrumental training, model animals were hidden in a little tower and the child was asked: "Who went (plural) into the tower?" If his answer was grammatically correct, the tower doors would open and the appropriate animal would be released. If his answer was incorrect, the doors would not open, and the experimenter would point out his error. If he then corrected himself, the animal would be released: if not, the experimenter would give him special training, and then the game would start over again. This training was highly successful and occasionally would enable children to skip stages, moving from 1 (feminine) to 3 (mixed), or from 2 (masculine) to 4 (correct); or to move rapidly through the stages. Special training in this task was especially helpful, e.g., using only masculine nouns for children in the first stage. (As soon as both forms were present in the child's speech, rapid progress could be made using this instrumental training.)

PORSHNEV, B. F. Rechepodrazhanie (ekholaliya) kak stupen' formirovaniya vtoroĭ signal'noĭ sistemy (Echolalia as a stage in the formation of the second signal system). *Voprosy Psikhol.*, 1964, No. 5, 11–18. (Translation in *Sov. Psychol. & Psychiat.*, 1963, *3*(3), 3–9.)

The fastest sort of verbal response is repetition of the stimulus. Echolalia is probably involved in speech perception; it is a peculiarly second signal system phenomenon because it involves the transmission of auditory impulses to the cortical speech-motor centers.

In ontogenesis there is an early stage at which a child carries out verbal commands that serve as first signals, as they do in the case of animal conditioning. At the stage of echolalia, however, repetition of a command can temporarily inhibit response. When repetition is followed by response, it creates in adults the illusion of comprehension by the child.

Echolalia is probably also an earlier phylogenetic stage. Under conditions of stress one often repeats words. Various individual and mass hysterias involve echolalia, one of the most dramatic examples being the Siberian phenomenon of *meryachenie* (measuring), a mass hysteria in which there is an irresistible repetition of the words and movements of others. Echolalia is also prominent in cases of damage to the frontal lobes. Such patients repeat commands but do not carry them out. Perhaps our ancestors developed this sort of "negative" echolalia to escape being dominated via communication by other members of their species. Negative echolalia in children also serves such a defensive function.

When the child moves from imitative to expressive and inner speech, he can use speech in a directive function. This depends on the superior anterior formations of the frontal lobes, which are a very recent evolutionary development.

RUZSKAYA, A. G. Rol' neposredstvennogo opyta i slova v obrazovanii obob-shchenii u detei doshkol'nogo vozrasta (The role of immediate experience and language in the formation of generalizations by preschoolers). *Doklady Akad. Pedag. Nauk RSFSR,* 1958, No. 3, 77–80.

Children of ages three to seven were required to learn to respond to classes of geometric figures. Figures appeared on the door of a toy garage. The child was to press one of two buttons (right and left) on the basis of the form class of the figure. A correct response was reinforced by the opening of the door and the emergence of a toy car.

*First Series:* Differentiation of triangles and quadrilaterals, with no verbal mediation.

*Second Series:* Preliminary verbal teaching of the names of the types of figures and a verbal explanation of their differences; child required to name each figure before responding.

*Per Cent of Incorrect Responses*

| Series | Age | | | |
|---|---|---|---|---|
| | 3 to 4 | 4 to 5 | 5 to 6 | 6 to 7 |
| First (without naming) | 37.2 | 36.9 | 35.3 | 26.7 |
| Second (with naming) | 39.6 | 31.7 | 17.1 | 8.2 |

(It is not clear whether the same subjects were used in both series. Numbers of subjects are not given. At any rate, it is clear that while there is an improvement with age for both series, it is greater in the case of verbal mediation.)

SHVACHKIN, N, KH. Razvitie fonematicheskogo vospriyatiya rechi v rannem detstve (Development of phonemic speech perception in early childhood). *Izvestiya Akad. Pedag. Nauk RSFSR,* 1948, vyp. 13. (As summarized in D. B. El'konin, *Razvitie rechi v doshkol'nom vozraste.* Moscow: Akad. Pedag. Nauk RSFSR, 1958. Pp. 87–91.)

According to El'konin: "Shvachkin . . . studied children's understanding of words differing by only a single given phoneme. To this end he developed a special collection of words embodying all of the phonemes of the Russian language. N. Kh. Shvachkin taught children to understand these words (each word denoted a given object), and then examined (1) the extent to which understanding is based on the phonemic composition of words and (2) the developmental sequence of the distinction of words differing from one another by a single given phoneme. On the basis of very careful experimental investigation, N. Kh. Shvachkin established the sequence of phonemic development in children between the ages of 11 months and one year 11 months, the general course of which is presented in the following scheme, taken from his work." (The first three ontogenetic stages of receptive discrimination deal with vowels; all of the later stages are consonant discriminations. The sequential numbering is taken to represent an ontogenetic sequence. The sounds are represented by transliterations of the corresponding Cyrillic letters in the original; *kh* represents the velar fricative, as in German *ch;* apostrophes indicate palatalization.)

1. Central vs. noncentral or open vs. closed: *a* vs. all other vowels.
2. Front vs. back or velar vs. palatal: *i* vs. *u, e* vs. *o, u* vs. *o, e* vs. *u.*
3. High vs. low: *i* vs. *e, u* vs. *o.*
4. Vowel vs. consonant: *ok* vs. *bok, ek* vs. *vek, ik* vs. *dik.*
5. Sonorant vs. articulated obstruant: *m* vs. *b, r* vs. *d, n* vs. *g, y* vs. *v.*
6. Palatalized vs. unpalatalized consonant: *n'* vs. *n, m'* vs. *m, b'* vs. *b, d'* vs. *d.*
7. Nasal vs. liquid: *m* vs. *l, m* vs. *r, n* vs. *l, n* vs. *r, n* vs. *y, m* vs. *y.*
8. Intranasal distinction: *m* vs. *n.*
9. Intraliquid distinction: *l* vs. *r.*
10. Fricative vs. nonfricative: *z* vs. *m, kh* vs. *l, ž* vs. *n.*
11. Labial vs. nonlabial: *b* vs. *d, v* vs. *z, f* vs. *kh, v* vs. *ž.*
12. Stop vs. fricative: *b* vs. *v, d* vs. *z, k* vs. *kh, d* vs. *z.*
13. Lingual vs. velar: *d* vs. *g, s* vs. *kh, š* vs. *kh.*
14. Voiced vs. voiceless: *b* vs. *p, d* vs. *t, g* vs. *k, v* vs. *f, ž* vs. *š, z* vs. *s.*
15. Blade vs. groove sibilants: *s* vs. *š, z* vs. *ž.*
16. Liquid vs. glide: *r* vs. *y, l* vs. *y.*

(Shvachkin believes the voiced-voiceless distinction is late because of acoustic similarity between contrasting members of a pair and especially because of their articulational identity.)

SOKHIN, F. A.  O formirovanii yazykovykh obobshcheniĭ v protsesse rechevogo razvitiya (On the formation of linguistic generalizations in the course of speech development). *Voprosy Psikhol.,* 1959, No. 5, 112–123.

This is a cross-sectional study of forty-three children between the ages of 1,11 and 3,5. Understanding of prepositions was tested by the ability to follow instructions to place objects (cubes and rings of various sizes) on or under one another.

Three groups of subjects were discerned on the basis of performance: (1) 11 children, ages 1,11 to 2,4, did not understand the instructions and simply played with the objects; (2) 18 children, ages 2,2 to 3,0, correctly placed one object *on* another, but often making reverse placements (especially when both objects were the same shape); (3) 14 children, ages 2,2 to 3,5, performed adequately.

It was easier for children to put a little object on a big one (28 per cent reversals versus 70 per cent reversals when a large object was to be placed on a small one; 55 per cent reversals when both objects were the same size). It was more difficult to understand *under* than *on,* in that the former instruction requires that one object be lifted and the other placed beneath it. Some children held one object under the table, rather than lift up the object lying above it on the surface on the table. Sokhin argues that the beginning meanings of words are tied to actions and that *under,* in most everyday situations, does not require that an object be lifted.

Children who had difficulty performing in the experimental situation could often show correct comprehension of a preposition in an everyday situation (e.g., "Put the ball under the couch"), where the circumstances constrained the number of possible placements.

Many of the children who had difficulty in comprehending prepositions also omitted them in speaking.

VYKHODOV, G. F.  Opposed activity in the first and second signal systems. *Pavlov J. higher nerv. Activity,* 1959, *9,* 463–468.

*Method:* Subjects were forty-four boys and twenty-four girls aged seven to eighteen. A foot-pedal response was conditioned to a loud bell, as differentiated from three quieter bells. After this response had been consolidated, subjects were presented with simultaneous pairings of the loud bell and the verbal statements ("second signals") "There is no bell" or "No."

*Results:* "Complete inhibition of the motor conditioned reaction was seen as a result of the action of a verbal stimulus denying the existence of the direct conditioned stimulus in some cases. In others the verbal stimulus had no effect on the conditioned reaction. Finally, sometimes there was partial inhibition of the motor conditioned reaction as a result of the effect of the verbal stimulus, the length of the latent period being increased and the size of the conditioned reaction reduced."

These patterns of response were closely related to age. "In general, the frequency with which inhibition of the conditioned reaction by the verbal stimulus was observed increased with the age. The proportion of inhibitory reactions was 21.4 percent in children of 7–8 years, 43.5 percent in those aged 9–11, 70.5 percent in children 12, 76.5 percent in children 13–14 and 74 percent in students aged 17–18." This is taken as evidence of ontogenetic strengthening of the second signal system.

Fatigue also weakens the effect of negative verbal stimuli on responding in this situation. Children were tested at the beginning and end of the school day, and with 35 per cent of the subjects it was found that "before lessons the words 'There is no bell' caused inhibition of the motor conditioned reaction, but they had no effect on the conditioned reaction after lessons. This was obviously connected with the development of protective inhibition in the second signal system with simultaneous increase, by virtue of positive induction, in the excitability of the first signal system. The result was that the effect of the direct stimulus was enhanced and the inhibitory effect from the second signal system weakened, and consequently the direct stimulus won when the activities of the signal systems were opposed."

ZAKHAROVA, A. V.  Usvoenie doshkol'nikami padezhnykh form (Mastery by preschoolers of forms of grammatical case). *Doklady Akad. Pedag. Nauk RSFSR*, 1958, No. 3, 81–84.

Subjects were 200 children between the ages of three and seven. They were shown objects named in the nominative (familiar and unfamiliar names) and asked questions whose answers required placing the name in another case form. Size and color of the objects were varied in order to determine agreement between adjective and noun forms.

It was found that the youngest children do not attend to the gender of the noun, revealed by the nominative form, but use stereotyped case endings for each case in their repertoire, regardless of gender. Those endings used (e.g., *-u* as accusative, *-om* as instrumental) are generally frequent in occurrence and clearly phonetically marked in adult speech.

The case system begins to become more complex when the child classifies nouns on the basis of gender; this generally begins with a bipartite division into nouns ending in *-a* (feminine, and the *-o* neuter ending when unstressed) and those having a zero ending (hard consonants). Mastery of inflection of nouns ending in soft consonants — both masculine and feminine — does not come until age six or seven.)

The third gender — neuter — appears first in its most highly marked form: stressed final *-o* (unstressed final *-o* being phonetically indistinguishable from feminine).

Children's ability to deal with unfamiliar words in this task did not differ from their ability to deal with familiar words. They would, however, frequently try out several case endings aloud, in the use of unfamiliar words, before choosing one ending. The author explains "that this is evidently due to the fact that supplementary auditory and kinesthetic signals from the speech organs, acting upon the cerebral cortex in the process of this repetition, facilitate the child's control over his verbal behavior, and, in the case of difficulties, aid the correct choice of grammatical form."

Self-corrections were frequent — in regard to both familiar and unfamiliar words.

ZHUĬKOV, S. F.  Pervonachal'nye obobshcheniya yazykovogo materiala u mladshikh shkol'nikov (Initial generalization of linguistic material in the youngest school pupils). *Voprosy Psikhol.*, 1955, No. 2, 54–64.

The experimenter attempts to counter Luria's contention that very young children are not aware of words as having an existence independent of objects and that they cannot make words themselves the object of attention. Primaryschool children were asked such direct questions as "Is there a difference between a thing and its name?" and "What do you mean when you say a thing has a name?" All of the children could answer these questions correctly — either at first or after some help was given.

A single male subject, of about age eight, was given a word-association task in which he was required to respond with a number of words sharing a common root. He could not respond to conjunctions, prepositions, pronouns, and adverbs; to the other parts of speech he responded with nouns, adjectives, verbs, and occasionally participles, verbal adverbs, and his own invented words. Performance was based on both sound and meaning. The child had difficulty with suffixes that change the sound of the root word (e.g., the plural of *son* is *sny*); he would sometimes include words with homonymous roots in a single series of related words.

The child was then taught that nouns signify things, adjectives qualities, and verbs actions, and was given single words and asked which of the three categories they belonged to. If the stimulus word was an adjective or noun in a case other than the nominative (Russian has six cases), the child would frequently change the form into the nominative before determining its category membership. This is taken as evidence of the psychological centrality of the nominative. Verbs, however, were dealt with in the form given; it is concluded that verb paradigms do not have a psychologically central point in the way that nouns and adjectives do. The child apparently grasped the form-class implications of suffixes, in that he was able to categorize correctly unfamiliar words.

ZHUROVA, L. E. Razvitie zvukovogo analiza slov u deteĭ doshkol'nogo vozrasta (The development of sound analysis of words in preschool children). *Voprosy Psikhol.*, 1963, No. 3, 20–32. (Translation in *Sov. Psychol. & Psychiat.*, 1964, 2(2), 11–17.)

Children aged three to seven years (fifty-five subjects) played individual games with the experimenter, in which they were required to isolate the first sound (Experiment 1) or the last sound (Experiment 2) in the name of a given animal. (In order for a model animal to cross a toy bridge, the child had to tell the "Wise Old Raven" who guarded the bridge the first or last sound of the animal's name.) The child's own first name was used in a training task preceding the experiment in which *E* pronounced the child's name omitting the relevant sound. (E.g., *E:* "What's your name?" *S:* "Igor." *E:* "Is your name Gor?" *S:* "No, I don't say it that way; I say I-gor." *E:* "Then what did I say wrong; what did I forget to say?" *S:* "You say 'Gor,' but you should say 'I-i-igor.'" *E:* "When I say 'Gor,' what do I forget to say?" *S:* "I-i-i.")

In both experiments, there was a major difference in performance of subjects of three to five and subjects of six to seven (in addition to the finding that the task was most difficult for the youngest subjects). The younger subjects found it necessary to pronounce first the entire word, drawing out or repeating the relevant sound (e.g., "m-m-monkey, m-m-m"; "d-d-dog, d-d"); while the older subjects usually uttered only the first syllable of the word. Isolation of the final sound was always harder than isolation of the initial sound, and isolation of stops was generally harder than isolation of continuants.

It was found that children of three to five were interested primarily in the game of getting animals across the bridge and found the verbal aspects rather a nuisance. The older children, however, "are interested in the word game itself — in its formal, rather than its semantic aspect. They take pleasure in continuing the game after the end of the experiment." In other words, metalinguistic interest is evidenced in the older group.

In a third experiment, forty-four other children, aged four to seven, played a game in which they learned the names of identical dolls wearing jackets of different colors, the first sound of the name of the doll corresponding to the first sound of the name of the color of its jacket (e.g., green-jacketed "Gan," red-jacketed "Ran," etc.). The naming principle was not made explicit to the subjects, and they were tested for their generalization of the principle to dolls wearing jackets of colors not included in the learning trials. The proportions of correct generalizations for each age group were: 4 to 5 years — 12 per cent, 5 to 6 years — 39 per cent, 6 to 7 years — 100 per cent.

# INDEX